The Mendelssohns

The Mendelssohns

Their Music in History

Edited by

JOHN MICHAEL COOPER

AND

JULIE D. PRANDI

OXFORD
UNIVERSITY PRESS

OXFORD
UNIVERSITY PRESS

Great Clarendon Street, Oxford OX2 6DP

Oxford University Press is a department of the University of Oxford.
It furthers the University's objective of excellence in research, scholarship,
and education by publishing worldwide in

Oxford New York

Auckland Bangkok Buenos Aires Cape Town Chennai
Dar es Salaam Delhi Hong Kong Istanbul Karachi Kolkata
Kuala Lumpur Madrid Melbourne Mexico City Mumbai Nairobi
São Paulo Shanghai Taipei Tokyo Toronto

Oxford is a registered trade mark of Oxford University Press
in the UK and certain other countries

Published in the United States
by Oxford University Press Inc., New York

British Library Cataloguing in Publication Data
Data available

Library of Congress Cataloging in Publication Data
Data available

ISBN 0-19-816723-7

1 3 5 7 9 10 8 6 4 2

Typeset in 11.75/13.5pt Fournier
by Graphicraft Limited, Hong Kong
Printed in Great Britain
by Biddles Ltd., Guildford & King's Lynn

Preface

1997 marked the sesquicentennial of the deaths of Felix Mendelssohn Bartholdy and Fanny Hensel. As the commemorative year approached, scholars and musicians around the world increasingly looked back on the siblings' works and their brilliant but troubled reception histories. When it arrived, it was celebrated in concerts, recitals, and conferences. And after it had passed, there was a widespread consensus that despite all the progress since the Second World War, much remained to be done.

Given the widely vacillating reception histories and the bewildering array of problems that characterize the composers' respective œuvres, that conclusion seems beyond question. Indeed, considerable steps have been taken towards what Carl Dahlhaus deemed far afield in 1974 and R. Larry Todd spoke of only cautiously in 1991: a 'Mendelssohn renaissance'. After all, the years since the early 1970s have witnessed the revival of the new *Gesamtausgabe* of Felix's works, and the same period has seen a dramatic upswing of editions and performances of the music of Fanny Hensel. Sizeable steps have been taken towards producing the first reliable and complete inventories of both siblings' works. New, scholarly editions and translations of much of both composers' voluminous correspondence have gradually begun to take the place of the extremely unreliable editions published in the late nineteenth century and reprinted in various collections for the first half of the twentieth century. Scholars are increasingly consulting unpublished as well as published letters, and have undertaken new explorations of virtually every facet of both siblings' works, ranging from studies of sources and compositional process to examinations of musical style and historical context. And orchestras, chamber ensembles, and soloists the world over have begun to explore the neglected and previously unknown works with renewed zeal— thus providing the general musical public with a more detailed picture of the life's work of these two extraordinary, and extraordinarily problematical, representatives of nineteenth-century musical life.

But it is only a beginning, a foundation in wait of an edifice. In *The Mendels-sohns: Their Music in History*, we build on this foundation with a collection of essays by the international community of Mendelssohn and Hensel scholars. These essays represent the diversity of topics in current research concerning the siblings, the variety of approaches employed in current scholarship, and the problems and potentials that beckon as we continue to strive for what Eric Werner promised in 1963, but largely failed to deliver: a new image of the composers and their age. (Werner, of course, promises a new view only of 'the composer' (i.e. Felix); we take it as a reason to be optimistic that such a one-sided perspective can now be offered only with a certain awkwardness.)

The first part of the volume focuses on one of the most vexing issues that confronts scholars as they deal with issues of identity and authority in Felix Mendelssohn's works: the numerous manuscript sources and how they should be interpreted. In Chapter 1 Ralf Wehner explores the labyrinth of continually disappearing and reappearing musical autographs and shows how the constantly changing landscape of available and missing sources can fundamentally affect our knowledge and understanding of Mendelssohn's works, individually and collectively. Pietro Zappalà's study of the sources for the preludes from the *Three Preludes and Fugues for Organ*, Op. 37 then provides a case study that focuses on a newly discovered source and its ramifications for our understanding of these preludes and of the composer's creative process. In Chapter 3 John Michael Cooper examines the relationship between the unpublished concert aria *Infelice! / Ah, ritorna, età dell'oro* and its posthumously published counterpart, *Infelice! / Ah, ritorna, età felice*, Op. 94, arguing that the two are autonomous works and exploring the general implications of this perspective for editors of Mendelssohn's works.

Part II tackles some of the most difficult interpretative issues posed by individual works of Felix Mendelssohn. Peter Ward Jones shows in Chapter 4 that the composer's earliest extant independent composition is not the 'Lied zum Geburtstag meines guten Vaters' of 11 December 1819, as has been traditionally suggested, but rather a Sonata for Two Pianos that Felix composed and performed with Fanny as early as October 1819; Ward Jones's examination of evident stylistic influences sheds new light on the young Mendelssohn's tastes and proclivities. In Chapter 5 Wolfgang Dinglinger grapples with the aesthetic problems posed by the work that the composer said he would most like to see burnt of all his works—the 'Reformation' Symphony, Op. 107. Focusing on little-known correspondence, prominent stylistic allusions, and how the original and revised versions relate to Beethoven's Ninth Symphony, Dinglinger formulates a new theory concerning the programmatic significance of the Symphony and the reasons for Mendelssohn's ultimate rejection of it. In Chapter 6, Julie D. Prandi turns to another controversial work, *Die erste Walpurgisnacht*; she discusses the coincidence in world-view and artistic will between Mendelssohn and his intellectual mentor, the cultural icon Johann Wolfgang Goethe. Examining how the confluence of 'classical' and 'romantic' tendencies in both artists' treatments of this poem calls into question the dichotomy between the two styles, Prandi also explores the curious paradox of the thoroughly Lutheran Mendelssohn, who set numerous biblical texts to music, choosing a poem in which the Christians are the villains and the divine service being honoured is a pointedly pagan one. Finally, Thomas Schmidt-Beste questions the extramusical associations of a work that since the 1850s has been considered unquestionably programmatic, the A minor Symphony, Op. 56 ('Scottish'). Carefully tracing the work's genesis and performance history in published and unpublished documents, Schmidt-Beste argues that by the time the work was completed any Scottish association was at best a dim memory, and that the Symphony in fact reflects an entirely different aspect of Mendelssohn's compositional development.

Part III turns to some of the most problematical and widely misunderstood repertoires found in Felix Mendelssohn's œuvre. Christoph Hellmundt raises questions concerning the nature and aesthetic validity of a group of works that, in Mendelssohn's output, is distressingly elusive: 'occasional' or 'complaisance' pieces. After surveying briefly Mendelssohn's works that may be considered part of this group and examining the composer's views on such music and how it was to be treated, Hellmundt turns to a work that remained unknown and unpublished until 1997, the *Festgesang* 'Möge das Siegeszeichen', demonstrating that it strongly influenced a slightly later work of considerable importance, the symphony-cantata *Lobgesang*, Op. 52. Monika Hennemann takes on a group of compositions that is even more elusive: the immense corpus of unrealized plans for operas. Providing an overview of the prospective librettos for these projects, the composer's references to these plans, and his reasons for rejecting them, Hennemann focuses on the issues of genre, national identity, and Mendelssohn's own perhaps unrealistic demands as reasons for his failure in this essential facet of German musical Romanticism. And in Chapter 10 Douglass Seaton turns to a genre in which Mendelssohn has almost entirely escaped substantive scholarly attention, that of the art song. Seaton argues that Mendelssohn's song output is in fact pervaded with phantom cycles of songs, and explores the different ways in which the composer achieved cyclicity in his choral and solo songs—including one curiously operatic set that has remained unpublished.

In Part IV, Hans-Günter Klein, R. Larry Todd, Camilla Cai, and Françoise Tillard interpret the significance of commonalities and similarities in various aspects of Felix's and Fanny's lives and works. Klein (Ch. 11) draws our attention to some of the earliest surviving documents of the formative years in the siblings' musical education. Examining the first few volumes of the original *Mendelssohn Nachlaß*, he shows the encouragement for composition that Fanny and Felix received at this stage, as well as some parallels and differences

that seem to have decisively influenced their later compositional development. Todd explores a number of instances in which brother and sister alluded
musically to each other's works, and describes empirically a characteristic
Mendelssohnian style that was the product of the musical tastes they developed
together, their frequent exchanges on music, and their common experiences in
their family's salon and the Berlin Singakademie. In Chapter 13 Camilla Cai
proceeds from the acclaim accorded Fanny Hensel and undertakes a stylistic
exploration of the role and nature of virtuosity in her keyboard works. And
in Chapter 14 Françoise Tillard raises important questions concerning the
cultural pressures—the Jewish heritage, the parents' perfectionism, the
increasingly prominent divisions between private and public spheres of
activity—that decisively shaped the lives, works, and cultural philosophies of
Fanny and Felix.

The final section turns to issues of reception history. William A. Little
examines nineteenth-century responses to Mendelssohn's considerable abilities as organist and the ways in which his compositions and performance style
influenced contemporary and succeeding generations of organists. Friedhelm
Krummacher deconstructs the reception history of Mendelssohn's string
quartets and the problems of the traditional view of their positive and negative influences; he ultimately shows that conventional views of the history of
the genre in the nineteenth century are the consequence not of any supposed
epigonal or classicizing tendencies on Mendelssohn's part, but of historians'
insistence on creating an artificially selective image of nineteenth-century
music history as one consisting of heroes and epigones. And finally, in a chapter
that compellingly illustrates the densely tangled web of cultural assumptions
that continue to influence biographers' and critics' responses to Felix Mendelssohn's life and works, Marian Wilson Kimber examines the ways in which
a number of cultural developments after 1850—changing constructions
of masculinity; changing assumptions concerning relationships between
gender, class, and race; and newly emergent evolutionary theories and their
pseudo-scientific racial implications—have crucially influenced the composer's posthumous reception.

Obviously, much remains to be done. One hardly need point out that until
the vast corpus of extant incoming and outgoing letters, diaries, and musical
autographs of both siblings is entirely available to the scholarly public, every
critical interpretation and scholarly reassessment of the lives and works of
Felix Mendelssohn and Fanny Hensel will remain provisional—the edifice
will remain a torso. Still, we hope that this volume's efforts to come to grips
with some of the most perplexing issues posed by the lives and works of the
two composers will answer some of the more pressing needs of the present.

More important, we hope that the findings presented here, and the questions they raise, will spur on future scholarly explorations of the remarkable body of evidence left to history by that most remarkable Mendelssohn family.

This volume is a product of one of the commemorative events of 1997: a four-day international festival titled *The Mendelssohns at the Millennium: Felix Mendelssohn Bartholdy and Fanny Hensel after 150 Years*, hosted by Illinois Wesleyan University on 6–9 March and including twenty scholarly papers as well as performances of numerous unpublished and otherwise little-known works by both siblings. Thanks are thus due first and foremost to IWU and especially to its president, Dr Minor Myers, Jr., whose boundless enthusiasm and support contributed immensely to the atmosphere of excitement and discovery that the festival provided for participants and guests alike. In addition, thanks are due to a number of institutions and organizations whose permission made the volume in its present state possible: the Biblioteka Jagiellońska (Kraków), the Bodleian Library (Oxford), and the Staatsbibliothek zu Berlin — Preußischer Kulturbesitz for assistance in using and reproducing a variety of autograph sources; and the Fogg Art Museum at Harvard University for permission to reproduce Beardsley's caricature of Mendelssohn in Chapter 18. A special debt of gratitude is owed to Hee Seung Lee and Kevin Salfen, graduate students at the University of North Texas, for their diligent work in proofreading and indexing the volume. Finally, the editors wish to thank Michael Wood, Sophie Goldsworthy, and the entire team at Oxford University Press for their fine work; in particular, we thank Bonnie Blackburn for the diligence, meticulousness, and patience she offered at every turn in the editing process.

J.M.C.
J.D.P.

Denton, Texas and Bloomington, Illinois
January 2002

Contents

Part V: Reception History

List of Plates

List of Figures

List of Tables

List of Musical Examples

List of Contributors

CAMILLA CAI Kenyon College

JOHN MICHAEL COOPER University of North Texas

WOLFGANG DINGLINGER Hochschule für Musik, Berlin

CHRISTOPH HELLMUNDT Mendelssohn-Forschungsstelle, Leipzig

MONIKA HENNEMANN Universität Mainz

HANS-GÜNTER KLEIN Musikabteilung, Staatsbibliothek zu Berlin —
   Preußischer Kulturbesitz

FRIEDHELM KRUMMACHER Universität Kiel

WM. A. LITTLE University of Virginia

JULIE D. PRANDI Illinois Wesleyan University

THOMAS SCHMIDT-BESTE Forschungsstelle Cappella Sixtina,
   Universität Heidelberg

DOUGLASS SEATON Florida State University

FRANÇOISE TILLARD Paris

R. LARRY TODD Duke University

PETER WARD JONES Bodleian Library, Oxford

RALF WEHNER Mendelssohn-Forschungsstelle, Leipzig

MARIAN WILSON KIMBER University of Southern Mississippi

PIETRO ZAPPALÀ Università di Pavia

Abbreviations

GB   'Green books' collection of the Bodleian Library, Oxford (volume no. indicated in roman numerals; item within volume indicated in arabic numerals)

MDM   Item held in the M. Deneke Mendelssohn collection of the Bodleian Library, Oxford

ABBREVIATIONS

AMZ   *Allgemeine musikalische Zeitung*

Briefe 1830–2   Mendelssohn Bartholdy, Paul (ed.), Felix Mendelssohn Bartholdy, *Reisebriefe von Felix Mendelssohn Bartholdy aus den Jahren 1830 bis 1832* (Leipzig: Hermann Mendelssohn, 1861; 2nd edn., 1862; 9th edn., 1882)

Briefe 1830–47   Mendelssohn-Bartholdy, Paul and Carl (eds.), Felix Mendelssohn Bartholdy, *Briefe aus den Jahren 1830–1847* (2nd edn., Leipzig: Hermann Mendelssohn, 1870; 3rd edn., 1875; 5th edn., 1882)

Briefe 1833–47   Mendelssohn-Bartholdy, Paul and Carl (eds.), Felix Mendelssohn Bartholdy, *Briefe aus den Jahren 1833 bis 1847 von Felix Mendelssohn Bartholdy* (Leipzig: Hermann Mendelssohn, 1863; 2nd edn., 1864; end edn., 1870)

Catalogue II   Margaret Crum, *Catalogue of the Mendelssohn Papers in the Bodleian Library, Oxford*, ii: *Music and Papers* (Tutzing: Hans Schneider, 1983)

Citron, *Letters*   Citron, Marcia J. (ed. and trans.), *The Letters of Fanny Hensel to Felix Mendelssohn* ([Stuyvesant, NY]: Pendragon, 1987)

Companion   Douglass Seaton (ed.), *The Mendelssohn Companion* (Westport, Conn.: Greenwood, 2001)

Devrient, *Erinnerungen*   Eduard Devrient, *Meine Erinnerungen an Felix Mendelssohn-Bartholdy und seine Briefe an mich* (Leipzig: J. J. Weber, 1869)

Elvers, *Briefe*   Elvers, Rudolf (ed.), Felix Mendelssohn Bartholdy, *Briefe* (Frankfurt am Main: Fischer, 1984)

Elvers, *Verleger*   Elvers, Rudolf (ed.), Felix Mendelssohn Bartholdy, *Briefe an deutsche Verleger* (Berlin: de Gruyter, 1968)

Hensel, *Familie*   Sebastian Hensel, *Die Familie Mendelssohn 1729–1847, nach Briefen und Tagebüchern* (Berlin: B. Behr, 1879; 2nd edn., 1880; 15th edn., 1908; 17th edn., Berlin: Walter de

	Gruyter, 1921; most recent edition, ed. Konrad Feilchenfeldt, Frankfurt am Main: Insel, 1995).
Klingemann, *Briefwechsel*	Klingemann, Karl [jun.] (ed.), *Felix Mendelssohn Bartholdys Briefwechsel mit Legationsrat Karl Klingemann in London*, ed. Karl Klingemann [jun.] (Essen: G. D. Baedeker, 1909)
MHW	Todd, R. Larry (ed.), *Mendelssohn and his World* (Princeton: Princeton University Press, 1991)
MGG	*Die Musik in Geschichte und Gegenwart*, ed. Friedrich Blume, 16 vols. (Kassel: Bärenreiter, 1949–79)
Moscheles, *Briefe*	Moscheles, Felix (ed.), *Briefe von Felix Mendelssohn-Bartholdy an Ignaz und Charlotte Moscheles* (Leipzig: Duncker & Humblot, 1888)
New Grove	*The New Grove Dictionary of Music and Musicians*, ed. Stanley Sadie, 20 vols. (London: Macmillan, 1980)
New Grove II	*The New Grove Dictionary of Music and Musicians*, ed. Stanley Sadie and John Tyrrell, 29 vols. (London: Macmillan, 2001)
NZfM	*Neue Zeitschrift für Musik*
Problem Mendelssohn	Dahlhaus, Carl (ed.), *Das Problem Mendelssohn* (Regensburg: Gustav Bosse, 1974)
Schmidt, *Kongreß-Bericht*	Schmidt, Christian Martin (ed.), *Felix Mendelssohn Bartholdy: Kongreß-Bericht Berlin 1994* (Wiesbaden: Breitkopf & Härtel, 1997)
Sutermeister, *Briefe*	Sutermeister, Peter (ed.), Felix Mendelssohn Bartholdy, *Briefe einer Reise durch Deutschland, Italien und die Schweiz, und Lebensbild* (Zürich: Max Niehans, 1958)
Ward Jones, *Honeymoon*	Ward Jones, Peter (ed.), *The Mendelssohns on Honeymoon: The 1837 Diary of Felix and Cécile Mendelssohn Bartholdy, together with Letters to their Families* (Oxford: Clarendon Press, 1997)
Werner, *New Image*	Werner, Eric, *Mendelssohn: A New Image of the Composer and his Age*, trans. Dika Newlin (London: Free Press of Glencoe, 1963)

PART I

Sources and Source Problems

I

⤙⤚

'It seems to have been lost': On Missing and Recovered Mendelssohn Sources

RALF WEHNER

THE British Library holds an important source of Mendelssohn's *Melusine* Overture. This copyist's manuscript, containing some entries in Mendelssohn's hand, is extremely valuable for our understanding of the work.[1] In a letter from Mendelssohn to Karl Klingemann the composer requests that his friend, who lived in London, 'retrieve in my name the score the Philharmonic has of it, and burn it'. And he emphasizes: 'but it is very important to me that the old score be destroyed. I would also be happy if you could burn Horsley's piano score of it, but if you think that they would not like that, then let it be. Attwood has an old score of it, a sort of sketch; you can allow that one to live.'[2] This letter raises three important issues:

1. A score for *Melusine* was supposed to be destroyed. Fortunately for scholars and posterity, Mendelssohn's wish was not fulfilled.

2. There were additional sources that can no longer be traced. We have to ask: What sort of piano score was it that Horsley had? What became of it? (Evidently it was not burned, since it can still be traced in 1872.[3])

---

[1] Score, headed 'Ouvertüre zu Melusina', copied by Mendelssohn's principal Düsseldorf copyist, Johann Gottlieb Schauseil, with autograph corrections (GB-Lbm, shelf mark Loan 4.779, deposit of the Royal Philharmonic Society).

[2] Letter to Karl Klingemann, 14 Dec. 1835: '[D]ie Partitur, welche das Philharmonic davon hat in meinem Namen geben zu lassen und sie zu verbrennen. . . . dass aber das alte vernichtet werde, daran liegt mir viel. Mir wäre es auch lieber, wenn Du Horsleys Klavierauszug verbrennen könntest; wenn Du glaubst, dass sie es nicht gern sehen, so lass es aber lieber. Attwood hat eine alte Partitur davon, eine Art Skizze dazu, die kannst Du leben lassen'; printed in Klingemann, *Briefwechsel*, 195–6.

[3] See Charles Edward Horsley, 'Reminiscences of Mendelssohn by his English Pupil', *Dwight's Journal of Music*, 32 (1872), 345–7, 353–5, 361–3; repr. in *MHW*, 237–49.

3. What was Mendelssohn referring to when he mentioned the score in Attwood's possession that was 'a kind of sketch'? Concerning this source Peter Ward Jones recently stated, 'no trace remains'.[4] This is unfortunate, for it would be interesting to discover why the early version was actually able to survive. This example typifies the difficulties and problems that confront the researcher who undertakes to follow the tracks of Mendelssohn's autographs.

Let us recall another work that for decades was considered lost, the Kyrie in D Minor. Mendelssohn composed this work during his stay in Paris in 1825 and showed it to Luigi Cherubini; after that, he rarely mentioned it. Since it is included in the composer's *Musikalien* inventory of 1844,[5] but not in Schleinitz's 1848 catalogue of the Mendelssohn estate,[6] George Grove had to note in the Mendelssohn article of his *Dictionary of Music and Musicians* in 1880: 'It seems to have been lost'.[7] By this time it had probably made its way into the possession of the publisher C. F. Peters or the Musikbibliothek Peters, where it remained throughout the Second World War. But by 1945 it had again disappeared. As it turned out, Walter Hinrichsen had taken the autograph with him to the United States.[8] Twenty years later, the Kyrie was in Margaret Deneke's possession. In the 1960s a version for chorus and organ was published, and the full score was finally published in 1986.[9] But such mazes do not always turn out so well. In reviewing the scholarly research one continually encounters references to sources that certainly existed at one time but have subsequently disappeared.

---

[4] Peter Ward Jones, 'Mendelssohn Scores in the Library of the Royal Philharmonic Society', in Schmidt, *Kongreß-Bericht*, 74.

[5] GB-Ob, MDM c. 49, fos. 29–30; see also App. A ('Mendelssohn's 1844 List of Music') in Peter Ward Jones, *Catalogue of the Mendelssohn Papers in the Bodleian Library, Oxford*, iii: *Printed Music and Books* (Tutzing: Hans Schneider, 1989), 283–302.

[6] Manuscript catalogue prepared by Conrad Schleinitz and later revised by George Grove, bearing the title 'Thematischer Catalog von Felix Mendelssohn B. Compositionen u. music. Studien, zunächst von denen welche in den grünen Büchern — die er selbst zusammen gestellt hat, enthalten sind; dann aber auch von solchen die nach seinem Tode Ms. vorgefunden wurden bei Schleinitz.' Several copies of this catalogue have survived (D-B, GB-Ob, US-Wc).

[7] George Grove, 'Mendelssohn', in *Grove's Dictionary of Music and Musicians*, ii (London: Macmillan, 1880), 257.

[8] *Autographen, Erstausgaben und Frühdrucke der Werke von Felix Mendelssohn Bartholdy in Leipziger Bibliotheken und Archiven*, ed. Peter Krause (Leipzig: Musikbibliothek der Stadt Leipzig, 1972), 23.

[9] The piano-vocal score was edited by Ralph Leavis (Oxford: Oxford University Press, 1964), and the full score has been edited by R. Larry Todd (Stuttgart: Carus-Verlag, 1986).

I

This chapter deals with lost sources of Mendelssohn's musical compositions; I shall exclude from my discussion other losses such as the composer's letters, drawings, and watercolours, as well as biographical material from his immediate circle.

It seems that the time is ripe for such an investigation. In 1997 one hundred and fifty years had passed since Mendelssohn's death. The memorial year provided the occasion to assess the results of Mendelssohn research of the past several decades, to summarize the findings, and to forge paths for future research. In recent years a number of important sources have reappeared, giving new momentum to Mendelssohn scholarship. Additional impetus for this undertaking is that it is now possible to proceed with the new Leipzig *Gesamtausgabe* of Mendelssohn's compositions and letters.[10]

In principle, one must distinguish between lost works and works whose sources are lost. The latter group is more diverse. In addition, it is necessary to distinguish between lost works—an expression that indicates a certain finality—and missing works, those that have disappeared or cannot be traced at present. Fortunately, the latter are more numerous, for the word 'disappeared' means only not known to scholars. There is always someone—a collector, a family heir, or a staff member of a public archive—who knows the whereabouts of one source or another. Or it may happen, for example, that the owner of a manuscript does not know it is an autograph; such a person might consider it to be simply a random sheet of music. And how is a person untrained in musicology supposed to know the significance of a dusty score that turns up in the attic? Thus it happens that many pieces are lost to scholars but in fact still exist.

In the strict sense of the word, the term 'lost' can be applied only to those works whose destruction can be documented (as, for example, through the burning of a library).[11] The number of these demonstrably lost sources is extremely small. This chapter, therefore, concentrates on missing works and sources; in a number of cases I shall present evidence for their reappearance. Sources that may be traced but currently are 'inaccessible' will not be considered.

---

[10] Concerning the *Gesamtausgabe*, see Christian Martin Schmidt, 'Konzeption und Stand der Mendelssohn-Gesamtausgabe', in *Felix Mendelssohn — Mitwelt und Nachwelt. 1. Leipziger Mendelssohn-Kolloquium am 8. und 9. Juni 1993* (Wiesbaden: Breitkopf & Härtel, 1996), 131–4.

[11] For example, a piano-vocal score of the first chorus from *Antigone*, Op. 55 that Mendelssohn sent to the music director August Ferdinand Geller in Niesky near Görlitz was lost in a fire that destroyed the 'Pädagogium' Library in that city.

II

It is typical of the transmission of Mendelssohn's music that at any given time certain works have been available while others have disappeared, only to resurface decades later. From early on, the main reason for this problem has been the extensive dissemination of Mendelssohn's manuscripts; this situation has worsened in the twentieth century because of wars, emigration, and a flourishing market for composers' autographs.

There are several ways in which manuscripts might be lost. Some works were lost even during the composer's lifetime because the manuscripts were stolen from him,[12] because he left them behind somewhere, or because he gave them away and later could not remember to whom.[13] Mendelssohn himself did not consider the loss of such pieces to be very tragic. We may recall, for example, the following lovely anecdote reported by George Grove: after the first performance in England of the *Midsummer Night's Dream Overture* 'the score of the overture was left in the hackney coach by Attwood, and lost. On Mendelssohn hearing of it, he said: "Never mind, I will make another".'[14] And on many occasions Mendelssohn knowingly gave away works of which he possessed no other copy, or he composed pieces for albums of which he did not keep a record. These compositions were lost to him; sometimes he thought of them later on and arranged to obtain a copy.[15]

Far more numerous are manuscripts that were lost after the composer's death. Here the issue is not the loss of works *per se*, but frequently the loss of individual sources for works that are otherwise known. For instance, although many of his manuscripts remained in the family in the years immediately following his death,[16] these years also witnessed a substantial number of instances in which the composer's manuscripts were given as gifts to friends

---

[12] See Mendelssohn's letter of 11 Apr. 1830 to his Swedish friend Lindblad: 'In meinem letzten Briefe an Dich glaube ich schon von der Meeresstille gesprochen zu haben; . . . Ich hatte es abschreiben lassen um es Dir zu schicken und die Abschrift sammt meinem Manuscript sind mir gestohlen worden.' Quoted from *Bref till Adolf Fredrik Lindblad från Mendelssohn, Dohrn, Almqvist, Atterbom, Geijer, Fredrika Bremer, C. W. Böttiger och andra* (Stockholm: Bonnier, 1913), 30.

[13] This case obtains, for example, with the *Harmoniemusik*, Op. 24; see Mendelssohn's letter to Simrock dated 15 Feb. 1839, in Elvers, *Verleger*, 225.   [14] Grove, 'Mendelssohn', 264.

[15] See his letter to Breitkopf & Härtel of 17 Apr. 1837, quoted in Elvers, *Verleger*, 60–1: 'Fräulein Grabau hat ein Lied ohne Worte und eines mit Worten von mir, von denen ich keine Abschrift habe und eine solche gern haben möchte; wären Sie vielleicht so gütig mir diese zwei Stücke (natürlich für meine Rechnung) copiren zu lassen und sobald als möglich nach Frankfurt unter obiger Adresse zu schicken?'

[16] See Rudolf Elvers, 'Felix Mendelssohn Bartholdys Nachlaß', in *Problem Mendelssohn*, 35–46.

and acquaintances. Cécile Mendelssohn and other members of the family passed along manuscripts from their supply that they did not consider to be very important, and Mendelssohn's friends also gave their manuscripts away.[17] A crass example of this is found in the case of Louis Plaidy, a piano teacher and colleague of Mendelssohn at the Leipzig Conservatory who owned the autograph of the Lied ohne Worte in A Major, Op. 38 No. 4. Plaidy had many students, and he cut his Mendelssohn autograph into pieces and gave one to each of them as a favour. These fragments were widely dispersed, and only a few have survived.[18] Still, even these are valuable to scholars, since they give some idea of the differences that must have existed between the original version and the published one.

The donation of the bound volumes of the *Mendelssohn Nachlaß* to the Royal Library in Berlin beginning in 1878 guaranteed the scholarly world access to most of the sources. Two problems resulted from this donation: some of the volumes contained materials that were not autograph and there were many autographs that were not included in this collection. And those were precisely the autographs that Mendelssohn had not kept in his home.

A further stage occurred during the second half of the nineteenth and the first decades of the twentieth centuries: the estates of Mendelssohn's friends and contemporaries who outlived him were auctioned, and publishers' archives and other large collections were dispersed. The hyperinflation in Europe in the 1920s necessitated many auctions, and this led to an increased scattering of

[17] See GB-Ob, MDM b. 5, section 'Zum Verschenken geeignet'. Later, too, members of the family continued to give away autographs, as is demonstrated by the remark on a page from *St Paul* today preserved in Brussels: 'Dieses Blatt ist einem handschriftlichen musikalischen Skizzenbuch meines Bruders Felix entnommen, Berlin, 13. Februar 1854. Paul Mendelssohn-Bartholdy' (This page was taken from a manuscript volume of musical sketches by my brother Felix, Berlin, 13 February 1854. Paul Mendelssohn-Bartholdy). See *Catalogue de la Bibliothèque du Conservatoire Royal de Musique*, ed. Alfred Wotquenne (Brussels: J.-J. Coosemans, 1898), i, no. 1092, p. 209. Since as a rule sketches and drafts are not registered or are only briefly summarized in the Schleinitz catalogue, we cannot reconstruct a survey of previously extant manuscripts of this kind. Further examples of autographs that were given away include those for the String Quartet in D Major, Op. 44 No. 1, the first movement of which was given by Cécile Mendelssohn Bartholdy to Ludwig Spohr (the manuscript is currently in D-B, N.Mus.ms. 108), and the 'Duett' for piano four hands (now F-Pc, MS 208), which was given to 'Dem Herrn Kapellmeister Taubert zur Erinnerung an den geliebten Componisten, am Heilig Abend 1859 von Paul Mendelssohn'; and part of Sinfonia VIII, which Paul gave to Henry Smith Huntington as a gift. (Paul gave away separate pages of manuscripts on more than one occasion, thereby effectively turning the pieces into fragments.) Fortunately, these pages were preserved; once bars 476–522 on pp. 213–16 of vol. 6 of the former *Mendelssohn Nachlaß*, they are now preserved as D-B, N.Mus.ms. 25.

[18] For instance, four measures which are held in the Watkinson Library of Trinity College in Hartford, Connecticut (shelf mark Quarto / M/ 22/ M 523/ L5/1800), and the last four bars, which were sold at Sotheby's 17–18 Nov. 1988, lot 403, with facsimile on p. 167.

Mendelssohn autographs. But this was also the great hour of American libraries, which were able during these years to lay the foundations for the important collections they own today.

Finally, the so-called 'Third Reich' had a major impact on the dissemination of Mendelssohn sources. First, many individuals who owned sources were forced to emigrate and in some cases were able to preserve their collections, thus scattering the material further around the world. Secondly, the war resulted in the destruction of many locations where sources were stored. And finally, many sources that may have survived were removed from libraries during the war and have not been located since.

This all has led to an enduring uncertainty about the fate of a number of collections. After the war a systematic account of surviving sources was needed, but so far only preliminary steps have been taken in that direction.

When we turn to the question of where to find information about pieces that have disappeared, a vast array of sources provide clues. These may be briefly classified in the following categories: (1) work-lists, notebooks, and calendars; (2) Mendelssohn's letters; (3) letters to Mendelssohn in which the sender thanks the composer for a specific piece; (4) records such as letters, diary entries, memoirs, or inventories left by third parties; and (5) catalogues prepared by auction houses and antiquarians. Additional sources of information include catalogues of private collections and exhibitions; where available, sketches and drafts that answer questions about the fully formed work to which they pertain; and early biographical and scholarly writings.

All this creates an immense and virtually impenetrable labyrinth in which the scholar can easily get lost.

III

Which works must we consider lost today? As stated above, it is not realistic to attempt to trace all autographs and other sources. Here we can present only a preliminary overview, for there are still too many open questions to permit an exhaustive assessment. Many archives, libraries, and collections still have to be consulted; above all, the many letters to Mendelssohn preserved in the 'Green Books' in the Bodleian Library must be completely examined. In other words: sources will continue to turn up in the future, as will references to works and sources.

All in all, knowledge of more than fifty works or smaller pieces is transmitted only through secondary references, and these compositions must be considered lost. These works are listed in Appendix 1 to this chapter.

The largest part of this corpus comprises lieder. For example, in 1862 a completely unknown song turned up at the auction of a Leipzig firm.[19] Entitled 'Das Menschenherz ist ein Schacht', the lied is reportedly set for alto and piano and based on a text by Friedrich Rückert. From another auction catalogue we learn that it was 'written down for Herr Privy Councillor Teichmann at his specific request';[20] the lied seems to be mentioned nowhere else. The 'request' probably was issued orally. In a letter of 30 April 1842, however, Teichmann thanks the composer and enquires whether he may make a copy for an acquaintance to give to his sister-in-law;[21] presumably, the letter refers to the Rückert lied in question. Neither the autograph nor a copy of this lied has ever turned up.

Another lost song is mentioned in an important letter of 1867 that has thus far received little attention. In this letter, Mendelssohn's son Karl turns to an unnamed music director,[22] suggesting some songs without words for the collection that would eventually be published in 1868 as Op. 102. In the same context Karl mentions a collection of six songs with words—an undertaking that never came to fruition. Of the songs proposed for this collection, the sixth to this day has never surfaced: a setting of 'Es war ein König in Thule', reportedly composed for bass and piano in December 1824.[23]

Also considerable is the number of compositions that cannot be precisely identified because of sparse information. When Mendelssohn mentions a 'lied' in a letter, he may refer either to a song or to a song without words—that is, to a vocal or an instrumental piece. Ambiguous references may therefore easily yield false conclusions. We must also consider that Mendelssohn often provided different titles when he wrote out a new copy of his songs. Thus, a familiar song may hide behind an unfamiliar title.[24]

---

[19] T. O. Weigel, *Catalogue d'une belle collection de lettres autographes dont la vente publique aura lieu à Leipzig, 2 June 1862*, lot 490.

[20] Catalogue of List & Franke, 23 Jan. 1872 (Coll. G. M. Clauss, Leipzig), 139, no. 2569: 'Musique et paroles a.s. Berlin, 1842. 1 p. fol. ungedruckt. "Das Menschen Herz ist ein Schacht"; avec dédicace et titre a.s. "Lied von Rückert für eine AltStimme mit Begleit. des Pianoforte; componirt von . . ." Herrn Hofrath Teichmann auf ausdrückl. Bestellung niedergeschrieben von . . . nebst L.a.s. Leipzig, 1842. 1 p. 8. mit nochmaliger Zueignung des Liedes.'

[21] Letter to Mendelssohn, 30 Apr. 1842 (GB-Ob, GB XV/207).

[22] Letter from Karl Mendelssohn Bartholdy, 1 May 1867, to 'Verehrter Herr Musikdirektor', D-B, Handschriftenabteilung, shelf mark: 2 f 1870 (10).

[23] An indication as to the date is provided by a copy of the song 'Rausche leise grünes Dach', GB-Ob, MDM c. 50, 2/20, fo. 97, which bears the notice: 'Ohne Datum. Neben: König in Thule, Dez. 1824'.

[24] For instance, the song 'Auf dem Meere'; see *International Autographs, N. Y., Catalogue No. 25* (1976), lot 46. This is the same as the song 'Im Süden', Op. 120 No. 3; see *J. A. Stargardt, Berlin, Catalogue 659* (16–17 Mar. 1995), lot 771.

Later in his life Mendelssohn often made gifts of printed scores, which he spoke of in the accompanying letter only as 'the lieder' or volumes of lieder. Since there is also documentation of some autograph volumes of lieder (such as the missing volume for Jenny Lind with autograph drawings),[25] the question of what Mendelssohn refers to in these cases must be left open unless the letter and the music are preserved together.

We could give many other examples of such problems. Pieces mentioned with only vague identifications may be works that are already published, and which therefore are not unknown. For example, we cannot know for certain which specific works were contained in an envelope labelled 'Neue Liederchen' and bearing the jocular inscription 'published by the widow Felix'.[26] Indications found in notebooks that a piece is 'complete' do not necessarily relate to one of Mendelssohn's own works; they might just as well refer to a copy he was making of someone else's composition. Thus, references such as 'lied for Catharine' remain ambiguous.[27] In addition, when compositions are attributed to Mendelssohn but are transmitted only through copies, their authenticity remains questionable. This problem pertains especially to the lieder listed at the end of Appendix 2.[28]

Finally, auction catalogues may contain simple typographical errors, faulty transcriptions, and erroneous datings; these can result in a single autograph being mentioned in different catalogues with different dates, suggesting two different sources where only one exists. Or the catalogue may provide so little information that no precise identification is possible.[29]

As a result, in most cases it is impossible to answer questions concerning a work on the basis of a single source; a wide variety of sources must be considered.

[25] Mendelssohn sent the Album to Jenny Lind at Christmas 1845. For a facsimile of the decoration on the cover of this album, made by Mendelssohn himself, see *The Life of Jenny Lind Briefly Told by her Daughter Mrs. Raymond Maude* (London: Cassell, 1926), 57; see also the collection of songs for Madame Ida Lessing: '. . . Beifolgend übersende ich Ihnen ein Heft Lieder ohne Worte das ich für Ihre Frau zusammengeschrieben habe . . .' (letter to C. F. Lessing, 19 Dec. 1844, held in US-Wc). Similar songbooks have survived, such as those for Frau von Lüttichau (US-STu), Klingemann (D-B), and Queen Victoria and Prince Albert (GB-Lbl).

[26] 'Neue Liederchen gedruckt in diesem Jahr, im Verlag bei Wittwe Felix et comp.' (GB-Ob, MDM c. 24, No. 3, fos. 17–18).

[27] A reference to Catharine Pereira, as is evidenced by Mendelssohn's diary entries in GB-Ob, MDM g. 2, fo. 18ᵛ. The name Catharine occurs a number of times in Mendelssohn's diaries during his stay in Vienna.

[28] Based on Thomas Stoner, 'Mendelssohn's Lieder not Included in the *Werke*', *Fontes artis musicae*, 26 (1979), 258–66.

[29] Typical of these items are brief references such as 'Manuscript Music, 18 bars, with words. Mounted' (*The Anderson Galleries No. 1624* [9 Jan. 1923], No. 178), or: 'Morceau de musique aut., 2 p. in 40 obl. Jolie pièce. Fragment d'un de ses ouvrages' (see *Charavay, Revue des Autographes*, 107 [Sept. 1887], No. 263).

Let us now turn away from the works destined to remain unknown for the foreseeable future, and consider instead the sources for familiar works. In these cases the compositions themselves are known. In recent years, however, a new critical perspective concerning the traditional versions of Mendelssohn's compositions has emerged in scholarship and in practice. Today we ask whether the scores that have traditionally been used in performance are true to the intentions of the composer—for example, does the 'Italian' Symphony as we know and love it, as it has traditionally been published and performed, really represent the composer's final version?[30] This new perspective produces the desire to know more about the sources for the work in question, for both listeners and scholars. Therefore we ask which sources existed, which source was chosen as the basis for the published version, and how the work's compositional history produced one version or another. We must also ask what accounts for the differences between the composer's autographs and the editions that were published under his own supervision. These questions in turn necessitate an investigation of the existing and lost sources.

The original autographs still exist for all but a few of the works published during Mendelssohn's lifetime, although most of the engraver's exemplars are missing. A rather different situation obtains for the works (especially smaller works) that Mendelssohn left unpublished. For example, the engraver's proofs (*Stichvorlagen*) for almost all the posthumously published compositions have survived. (In most cases, these are autographs from the *Mendelssohn Nachlaß*.) In addition, for several works that Mendelssohn left unpublished, copies in another hand or printed scores have survived, although the autographs on which these sources were based are missing.

The source situation is generally favourable for Mendelssohn's larger works—the symphonies, concertos, oratorios, and psalm settings—as well as the organ music.[31] The transmission of the chorale cantatas and incidental music is less positive because the autographs for those works are only partly available. Luckily, a number of authorized manuscript copies compensate for this; however, there are still no reliable sources for *Antigone*, Op. 55 and *Oedipus at Colonos*, Op. 93. The situation presented by the smaller works, on

---

[30] On this particular matter see John Michael Cooper, *Mendelssohn's 'Italian' Symphony* (Oxford: Oxford University Press, 2002). The complete surviving autograph sources for the A major Symphony have recently been published in facsimile; see *Felix Mendelssohn Bartholdy, Symphony Nr. 4 A-dur Op. 90, mit Kommentaren von Hans-Günter Klein und John Michael Cooper* (Wiesbaden: Ludwig-Reichert Verlag, 1997), and the 1834 revision of the last three movements has been published by the same press (2001).

[31] For a case study in how this problem relates to the organ works, see Pietro Zappalà's essay in this volume, Ch. 2.

the other hand, is problematic, as new sources are continually turning up for Mendelssohn's songs and his piano and chamber works.

IV

Let us now turn to some problem areas and rediscoveries.

A number of works appear to be lost. The fate of the Mendelssohn portion of the collection of the Berlin Sing-Akademie, lost since the Second World War, still remains unclear.[32] Another substantial problem concerns the publishing process and the various source materials generated in this context that were lost through the dispersion of publishers' archives. Only a few galley proofs have survived,[33] and the plates were already melted down during Mendelssohn's lifetime.[34] The fate of the *Stichvorlagen* for contemporary English and French editions remains largely unexplored, and hardly any of the manuscripts that were removed from the volumes of the *Nachlaß* have been recovered.

Moreover, most contemporary performance materials probably are lost. Owing to their intended purpose, they continued to be reused until they were worn out, whereupon they were replaced and destroyed. This is unfortunate since they might have provided information about many details of the musical text as well as phrasings, dynamics, and other indications that Mendelssohn gave during rehearsals but failed to enter into his scores.

Many questions are posed by the state of works when portions of them are not documented by surviving autographs—that is, works transmitted fragmentarily[35] (see examples in App. 3). For instance, if a full-page paste-over

---

[32] Even for the bicentennial celebrations of the Sing-Akademie in 1991 this matter could not be clarified. See Gottfried Eberle, *200 Jahre Sing-Akademie zu Berlin: 'Ein Kunstverein für die heilige Musik'* (Berlin: Nicolai, 1991). In 2001 these sources returned to D-B.

[33] For example, the proof sheets for the *Meeresstille und glückliche Fahrt* Overture, Op. 27 (D-LEsm), the 'Scottish' Symphony (US-Wc), the vocal score of *Elijah* (US-NYpm, US-Cu), and some engraver's proofs from Breitkopf & Härtel (D-DS).

[34] See e.g. the letter from the publisher Hofmeister to Robert Schumann, 28 Sept. 1839: 'I still have just a couple of exemplars of Mendelssohn's opera *Gamacho* [*sic*]. The plates have been melted down; therefore, if you wish to have it I can lend it to you, but not give it to you.' ('Von Mendelssohns Oper "Gamacho" [*sic*] habe ich nur noch ein paar Exemplare. Die Platten sind eingeschmolzen. Daher kann ich, wenn Sie es wünschen, nur verleihen, nicht schenken') (PL-Kj, Schumann Corr. vol. 9, No. 1358). My thanks to Dr Matthias Wendt of the Schumann *Gesamtausgabe*, Düsseldorf, for this information.

[35] Circumstances are not always as fortunate as in the case of the 'Mailied', Op. 41 No. 5: bars 1–23 are preserved as D-B, N.Mus.ms. 116, and the remainder of piece can be found on fo. 2 of GB-Ob, MDM c. 16. Nor can a piece always be reconstructed from two facsimile editions, as in

has come loose and been lost, the original reading of the passage is visible, but not the final version sanctioned by the composer.[36] These cases pose daunting problems for editorial methods and issues of performance practice, and unless the lost papers re-emerge, we must seek a compromise solution.

Next, in order to demonstrate the significance and diversity of the volumes of the *Mendelssohn Nachlaß*, I should like to return to one of the points and problems mentioned above and examine it more closely. As is well known, the *Nachlaß* did not arrive in Berlin in complete form. Individual volumes were missing, and individual parts were missing from those volumes that were delivered. Schleinitz's catalog of 1848 provides information concerning the original state of the first forty-four volumes.[37] There, for example, we find references to a *Nachspiel* for organ and a manuscript of the chorale cantata *Wir glauben all an einen Gott*; both pieces are reported as being part of Volume 23. Yet they are not to be found in that volume, and from the pagination of Volume 23 we learn that these autographs must already have been missing when the volumes arrived in Berlin. They are still missing today.

Other works are preserved in the *Nachlaß* only through printed scores or copies. In some cases we have information concerning the fate of the autograph—as, for example, in the case of the F minor Violin Sonata, Op. 4, the autograph of which was given to Joseph Joachim by Cécile. For others there is no indication at all; this is the case with 'The Evening Bell', the chorale cantatas, and the cello sonatas.

But there is also a positive story directly tied to the fate of the *Nachlaß* volumes: the legendary seventeen volumes removed for storage during the Second World War, for decades considered lost, are today preserved in the Biblioteka Jagiellońska in Kraków. The reappearance of these volumes has

the case of the song 'Wie kann ich froh und lustig sein'. The first page of this song is reproduced in Maggs Bros. Catalogue 500 (1928), no. 119 on p. 195, and the second page in Catalogue 469 of the same company (autumn 1925), no. 2095 (pl. XI). This manuscript is now preserved in US-NYp, JOB 82–10.

[36] This is true, for example, of the original version of *Die erste Walpurgisnacht*, which was eventually published as Mendelssohn's Op. 60. Because two collettes are missing in the autograph, the original Berlin version of 1833 (PL-Kj, *Mendelssohn Nachlaß* vol. 37) cannot be reconstructed completely. See Christoph Hellmundt, 'Mendelssohns Arbeit an seiner Kantate *Die erste Walpurgisnacht*: Zu einer bisher wenig beachteten Quelle', in Schmidt, *Kongreß-Bericht*, 76–112, esp. 94 and 98. Similar instances obtain concerning the early versions of *St Paul* and other works.

[37] To date little attention has been paid to the circumstance that not all of the forty-four volumes were bound at that time. In Schleinitz's inventory some of the autographs and copies that belonged in the volumes now numbered 43 and 44 were still unbound, and described as 'Manuscripte in einer Mappe'.

given a powerful momentum to Mendelssohn scholarship, and hopefully it will continue to propel us forward.[38]

The fate of the Sonatina in B flat minor of 1823, mentioned by Julius Rietz in his catalogue,[39] is also interesting. For years, only the first few bars of this work copied by Schleinitz in his catalogue were known, and when Volume 4 of the *Nachlaß* was brought to Berlin the work was already in the possession of Benjamin Fillon, whose collection was auctioned in 1879.[40] The last public reference to the work was an auction of Noel Conway of Birmingham in the 1890s.[41] This auction was one of the most important sales of Mendelssohn autographs,[42] greater in scope even than those of the Klingemann collection[43] and those from the Moscheles estate.[44] Nearly a century passed before anyone but insiders learned that parts of the Conway estate were contained in the Brotherton Collection in Leeds.

Scholars were long puzzled by a work that Mendelssohn composed together with Moscheles and premièred in London on 1 May 1833: a fantasy on themes from Weber's *Preziosa*. In an unpublished letter we read: 'Tomorrow I will play together with Moscheles a new Fantasia for two pianos and orchestra that I wrote after I arrived here—so you can well imagine how hard I have had to work.'[45] The work was published later in a version for two pianos among

---

[38]   Over the course of the years this whole complex has attracted a great deal of attention. A basic summary is provided by Nigel Lewis, *Paperchase: Mozart, Beethoven, Bach—The Search for their Lost Music* (London: Hamish Hamilton, 1981). Although we have known at least since the 1970s that the musical sources are in Kraków, the story of the lost Mendelssohn manuscripts runs through Mendelssohn research into the 1990s like a red thread; and so the point still needs to be made here. Information concerning the Kraków manuscripts may be found in John Michael Cooper, 'Mendelssohn's Works: Prolegomenon to a Comprehensive Inventory', in *Companion*, 701–3.

[39]   Julius Rietz, 'Verzeichniß der sämmtlichen musikalischen Compositionen von Felix Mendelssohn Bartholdy', in *Briefe 1833–1847* (1863), 520.

[40]   *Inventaire des autographes et documents historiques réunis par M. Benjamin Fillon décrits par Étienne Charavay* (Paris: Librairie Charavay Frères, 1879), vol. ii, no. 2410.

[41]   Via the Freemantle and Brotherton collections it finally ended up in Leeds (GB-LEbc). Other parts of the Freemantle collection are found in US-Wc.

[42]   *Rare and Interesting Autograph Letters, Original Manuscripts, and Historical Documents, including . . . the Most Complete and Unique Collection of Original Music Manuscripts, Autograph Letters, Rare Books, Pamphlets, Articles, Programmes, Portraits, etc., of Felix Mendelssohn Bartholdy, sold at Noel Conway & Co., New Street, Birmingham* (Birmingham: n.d. [1890s]). The catalogue contains a 'Chronological List of 201 original autographs'.

[43]   Around 170 letters, sold at J. A. Stargardt 560 (28 Nov. 1962), no. 1157.

[44]   Sold at Leo Liepmannssohn 39 (17–18 Nov. 1911). For more than sixty-five letters from Mendelssohn to Moscheles see also the catalogues of Maggs Bros., London (Christmas 1924, lot 2777, and spring 1927, lot 389).

[45]   Letter from Mendelssohn to his family, 26–30 Apr. 1833: 'Morgen spiele ich mit Moscheles eine neue Fantasie für 2 Claviere ud. Orchester, die ich seit meiner Ankunft hier componirt habe, also könnt Ihr denken wie ich habe arbeiten müssen' (US-NYp, Family letters, no. 159).

Moscheles's compositions as his Op. 87b—but what became of the version for two pianos and orchestra? The autograph materials, titled 'Fantasie und Variationen über Preziosa', remained in the possession of the Moscheles family for more than fifty years. But when Moscheles's estate was auctioned in 1911, the work was not mentioned in the catalogue, for in 1889 Moscheles's son, Felix, had already given it as a present to Anton Rubinstein, who in turn donated it to the library of the St Petersburg Conservatory. The seventy-page folder has remained there, unharmed by the passage of time, for more than a century.[46]

Other collections should also be mentioned briefly. The collection of Varnhagen von Ense fortunately remained intact and is today preserved in Kraków; the same applies to the private collection of François Lang, which today is in Paris. Other collections, such as those of Louis Koch and Hugo von Mendelssohn Bartholdy, were dispersed or formed the beginning of larger collections. Even today large private collections are auctioned or otherwise scattered. The most recent example is the splendid collection of Rudolf Kallir —but this would take us into a field of research that cannot be presented here.

Sources and works may be lost, but the courage to look for such lost documents should never be lost. Naturally this search cannot be completed by one person alone; the list of lost sources remains quite large, and Mendelssohn scholarship still has much to do before all paths that may provide new information have been followed. Nevertheless, the fruits of recent research show that there is reason to hope that the number of truly lost sources can be contained. It is the responsibility of all of us to bring the situation closer to this goal.

—translated by John Michael Cooper

---

[46] My colleague Christoph Hellmundt learned of this source while in St Petersburg, during his preparatory work for the new *Gesamtausgabe*.

APPENDIX I

A Preliminary List of Lost or Missing
Mendelssohn Works

This list includes only works that are documented through secondary sources; it does not identify sources for those works. Compositions that are available in facsimile are not named. Some works listed here may correspond to other works that are known and survive under different titles.

ORCHESTRAL MUSIC

Kindersinfonie (1827)
    Reference: Letter from Fanny Mendelssohn Bartholdy to Klingemann, 25 Dec. 1827, Hensel, *Familie* (1879), i. 180

Kindersinfonie (1828)
    Reference: Letter from Lea Mendelssohn Bartholdy to Klingemann, 30 Dec. 1829, Klingemann, *Briefwechsel*, 70

Kindersinfonie (1829/1830)
    Reference: Letter to the family, 20 December 1831, Sutermeister, *Briefe*, 93–8 (GB-Ob, MDM d. 13)

Three Marches for *Harmonie-Musik* (Düsseldorf, 1833/34)
    Reference: Letter to sister Rebecka, 26 Oct. 1833, US-NYp, Family letters, no. 171
    Comment: These may be the same as the marches in GB-Ob, MDM c. 50, fos. 67–75

ORGAN MUSIC

Organ piece in A major for Fanny Mendelssohn Bartholdy's Wedding (Sept. 1829)
    References: Various letters to Fanny Hensel, 1829

Some organ pieces (Engelberg, 1831)
    Reference: Letter to his father, 23 Aug. 1831, Sutermeister, *Briefe*, 223–9 (GB-Ob, MDM d. 13)

Some organ pieces (Berlin, 1832)
    Reference: Letter to Klingemann, 5 Dec. 1832, Klingemann, *Briefe*, 103

PIANO MUSIC

Piece for Begas (1821)
Reference: Letter to the family, 10 Nov. 1821, US-NYp, Family letters, no. 5

Piece (Lied ohne Worte?) for Fanny on her approaching marriage (Sept. 1829)
Reference: Recollections of Sarah Austin (née Taylor), MS copy in D-B, quoted in Thomas Christian Schmidt, *Die ästhetischen Grundlagen der Instrumentalmusik Felix Mendelssohn Bartholdys* (Stuttgart: M & P Verlag für Wissenschaft und Forschung, 1996), 185

Englische Ballade for Miss M. C. (1829)
Reference: *Aus Moscheles' Leben: Nach Briefen und Tagebüchern*, ed. Charlotte Moscheles (Leipzig: Duncker & Humboldt, 1872), i. 207

Three Waltzes (Switzerland 1831)
Reference: Letter to the family, 11 Aug. 1831, Sutermeister, *Briefe*, 205–8 (GB-Ob, MDM d. 13)

2 Capriccios (1834), [the first one using the piece in C minor for Mary Alexander]
Reference: Letter to Klingemann, 14 May 1834, Klingemann, *Briefe*, 131

Lied ohne Worte (1830s) to Johann Peter Lyser
Reference: Johann Peter Lyser, *Zur Biographie Mendelssohn Bartholdys*, repr. in: *Ein unbekanntes Mendelssohn-Bildnis von Johann Peter Lyser* (Basle: Internationale Felix Mendelssohn Gesellschaft, 1958), 53

Impromptu (1838)
Reference: Letter to Auguste Harkort, 1 Apr. 1838, Albert Cohn (Berlin), catalogue 194 (1889), no. 292

SONGS AND CONCERT ARIAS (ALL FOR VOICE AND PIANO)

Oh me infelice, oh troppo verace ellitri (8 Jan. 1823)
Reference: Leo Liepmannssohn, auction of 12 Oct. 1882, lot 29

Es war ein König in Thule (Dec. 1824)
Reference: Letter from Karl Mendelssohn Bartholdy to an anonymous Music Director, 1 May 1867, D-B, Mss. Dept.

Povero cor
Reference: Letter from Fanny to Mendelssohn, 11 Apr. [1825], GB-Ob, MDM b. 4, Green Books I/9

English song 'Hush thee' for the album of 'Miss Marian' Cramer (May 1829)
Reference: Letter to the family, 8 May 1829, US-NYp, Family letters, no. 58

Galoppade airs for Johnston (summer 1829)
Reference: Sotheby, Wilkinson & Hodge 16–19 June 1930, in lot 321; Diary 30 June 1829, GB-Ob, MDM g. 1, fo. 6ʳ

Lied for Devrient, Scotland (summer 1829)
Reference: Letter to Eduard Devrient, 29 Oct. 1829, Devrient, *Erinnerungen*, 87–90, US-Wc

Von schlechtem Lebenswandel for Devrient, Venice (Oct. 1830)
Reference: Letter to the family, 30 Nov. 1830, Felix Mendelssohn, *Letters from Italy and Switzerland*, trans. Lady Wallace (London: O. Ditson, 1862), 67–6

I love the talking of the giddy breeze (before 1836). Text: Charles Cowden Clarke
Reference: *Musical World*, 1 (18 Mar. 1836), 11

Lied for Josephine Lang (Apr. 1841)
Reference: Letter to J. Lang, 26 Apr. 1841, S-Smf

Lied for Hofrath Teichmann 'Das Menschenherz ist ein Schacht' (Apr. 1842). Text: Rückert
Reference: T. O. Weigel, auction 2 June 1862, lot 490; List & Franke, auction 23 Jan. 1872, lot 2569

Lied for Heinrich Beer 'Alles schwelgt in süßen Träumen' (20 Apr. 1842)
Reference: Album leaf; Collection Meyer-Cohn, cf. J. A. Stargardt, auction of 23–8 Oct. 1905, lot 3368; Collection Wilhelm Heyer, see catalogue by Georg Kinsky (Cologne: J. P. Bachem, 1916), no. 637

CHORAL SONGS

Schwimmlieder (summer 1826). Text: Karl Klingemann
Reference: Devrient, *Erinnerungen*, 26

Folksong 'Ich geh mit Lust in diesen grünen Wald'
Reference: Leo Liepmannssohn, catalogue 39 (17–18 Nov. 1911), in lot 70

Three Lieder for the Leipzig *Liedertafel* (22 Jan. 1837)
Reference: Notice in Mendelssohn's calendar for 1837, GB-Ob, MDM f. 4

'Jagdmorgen' for male chorus (2 Feb. 1841). Text: Heinrich Laube
Reference: Karl Ernst Henrici, catalogue LXXXV (28–9 Jan. 1924), lot 55

CANONS

Canon a 4 'Gesegnete Mahlzeit, prost Mahlzeit, wohl bekomms!' (not before 1825)
Reference: Julius Schubring, 'Erinnerungen an Felix Mendelssohn-Bartholdy', *Daheim*, 2 (1865/6), Mar. 1866, No. 26, 373, trans. in *MHW*, 223

Canon 'Kurzgefasste Übersicht des canonischen Rechts' (3 Violins), for Heinrich Romberg (6 Feb. 1827)
Reference: Leo Liepmannssohn, catalogue 48 (20–2 Oct. 1926), lot 1147 and catalogue 50 (10–11 June 1927), lot 697

Canon a 4 'Wohl ihm' (30 May 1832) [on themes from Moscheles, C Major Piano Concerto]

    Reference: Leo Liepmannssohn, catalogue 39 (17–18 Nov. 1911), in lot 70

Canon for Alfred Julius Becher (before Feb. 1834)

    Reference: Letter from Becher to Mendelssohn, 6 Feb. 1834, GB-Ob, MDM d. 29, Green Books III/31

Canone a 4 for H. C. Schleinitz, n.d. (not before 1835) 'Mit Vergnügen werd' ich kommen'

    Reference: Richard Bertling, *Lagerkatalog* 11 (1889), lot 61

Canon a 2, written in Birmingham (25 Sept. 1840)

    Reference: Maggs Bros., catalogue 303 (Jan./Feb. 1913), lot 500

Canon for [Julius Stern (?)] (19 May 1841)

    Reference: Hellmut Meyer & Ernst, *Lagerkatalog* 52 (12 June 1936), lot 451

Canon a 2 (1840s), in: Album of the grandson of the Berlin physician Ernst Ludwig Heim

    Reference: Collection Meyer-Cohn, cf. J. A. Stargardt, auction of 23–8 Oct. 1905, lot 3372

Canon a 2 for Marie Becker (29 Apr. 1846)

    Reference: Leo Liepmannssohn, *Lagerkatalog* 198 (1917), lot 833

MISCELLANEOUS WORKS REFERRED TO IN OTHER SOURCES (SCORING AND CONTENT NOT KNOWN)

Libera me de sanguinibus (1820s) [possibly a copy of a composition not by Mendelssohn]

    Reference: Etienne Charavay, *Cat. d'une importante collection d'autographes, Composant le Cabinet d'un Amateur connu*, 2 May 1883, lot 123

Psalm 21: 'Herr der König freuet sich' (1821)

    Reference: Friedrich Welter, 'Die Musikbibliothek der Singakademie zu Berlin', in *Singakademie zu Berlin: Festschrift zum 175jährigen Bestehen*, ed. Werner Bollert (Berlin, 1966), 41

[Parody on Weber, *Der Freischütz*] (1822)

    Reference: Letter of Doris Zelter to 'Karoline', Dec. 1822, US-Wc

Piece [Fuga?], written in Doberan (before 17 July 1824)

    Reference: Letter to sister Fanny, 17 July 1824, US-NYp, Family letters, no. 13

Zwei Gesänge zum Dürer-Fest am 18. April 1828. Text: F. W. Gubitz

    'Die Mäzene' (Mäzene gabs vor Zeiten)

    'Kehraus' (Lasset nun den Künsten allen)

    Reference: Leo Liepmannssohn, catalogue 1883, lot 172

'Lied an die Tragöden' (before Sept. 1829)
> *Reference*: Letter to the family, 25 Sept. 1829, US-NYp, Family letters, no. 88;
> Letter of the family to Mendelssohn, GB-Ob, MDM b. 4, Green Books I/88

Piece for Dr Kind in London (Nov. 1829)
> *Reference*: Letter to Dr Kind, 26 Nov. 1829, D-B MA Depos. MG 42

The Sun is dancing on the Streams (June 1829). Text: Allan Cummingham

Song in commemoration of the introduction of Trial by Jury, and the abolition of domestic Slavery, in the Island of Ceylon
> *Reference*: *Musical World*, 3 (2 Dec. 1836), 189 (Review); letter to the family, 5 June 1829, US-NYp, Family letters, no. 65; diary entry of 30 June 1829, GB-Ob, MDM g. 1, fo. 6^r

Piece for the King's band (Feb. 1830)
> *Reference*: Letter to Klingemann, 10 Feb. 1830, Klingemann, *Briefe*, 75; letter from Klingemann to Mendelssohn, 30 Apr. 1830, GB-Ob, MDM d. 28, Green Books II/13

Lied (with or without words?) for a Lady in Hungary (Sept. 1830)
> *Reference*: Letter to Klingemann, 2 Apr. 1832, Klingemann, *Briefe*, 92

Lied (with or without words?) for Catharine Pereira (Vienna, Sept. 1830)
> *Reference*: Diary, GB-Ob, MDM g. 2, fo. 18^v

Tantum ergo (Rome, Dec. 1830) [possibly a copy of a composition not by Mendelssohn]
> *Reference*: Diary, GB-Ob, MDM g. 2, fo. 31^v

Lied (with or without words?) for sister Rebecka (Italy, Dec. 1830)
> *Reference*: letter to the sisters, Dec. 1830, D-B, Depos. Berlin, 3, 37

Neue Liederchen gedruckt in diesem Jahr, im Verlag bei Wittwe Felix (before 1832)
> *Reference*: Cover only has survived, GB-Ob, MDM c. 24, No. 3, fos. 17 f.

Album leaf for A. C. G. Vermeulen (Mar. 1837) 360
> *Reference*: Letter to Vermeulen, 30 Mar. 1837, NL-Amsterdam, Gemeentearchief

Psalm for Joanna Alexander (Mar. 1839)
> *Reference*: Letter to the Alexanders, 1 Mar. 1839, quoted in *Mendelssohn Studien*, 1 (1972), 93

Lied (with or without words?) (before 5 Mar. 1841)
> *Reference*: Letter to 'Verehrtes Fräulein', D-B, N. Mus. ep. 437

Lied (with or without words?), for Pauline Hübner (Apr. 1842)
> *Reference*: Letter from P. Hübner to Mendelssohn, 27 Apr. 1842, GB-Ob, MDM d. 41, Green Books XV/206

Messe for Rektor Latzel in Bad Reinerz (destroyed in 1844)
  Reference: Robert Becker, *Felix Mendelssohn-Bartholdy und Reinerz* (Reinerz: n.pub., 1930)

Album leaf for Antonie Speyer (1844–6)
  Reference: Album, mentioned in Edward Speyer, *Wilhelm Speyer, der Liederkomponist* (Munich: Drei Masken, 1925), 254

APPENDIX 2

A Preliminary List of Missing Mendelssohn Autographs

This appendix is limited to works known only through editions or copyist's manuscripts. Works for which autograph sources (except sketches) are known are not listed.

I. WORKS PUBLISHED BY MENDELSSOHN

Op. 4   Violin Sonata in F Minor
Remark: formerly in Vol. 13 of *Mendelssohn Nachlaß*

Op. 7   *Sieben Characterstücke* (Nos. 3, 5, and 7)
Remark: See also Appendix 3

Op. 8   *Zwölf Gesänge*:
No. 1. Holder klingt der Vogelsang
No. 5. Lass dich nur nichts nicht dauern ('Pilgerspruch')
No. 7. Man soll hören süßes Singen ('Maienlied')
No. 8. Die Schwalbe fliegt ('Andres Maienlied')
No. 9. Das Tagewerk ist abgethan ('Abendlied')
No. 10. Einmal aus seinen Blicken ('Romanze')
No. 11. Willkommen im Grünen ('Im Grünen')

Op. 15 Fantasia on 'The Last Rose of Summer'

Op. 45 Cello Sonata No. 1

Op. 47 Sechs Gesänge:
No. 2. Über die Berge steigt ('Morgengruß')

Op. 55 Incidental Music to Sophocles' *Antigone*

Op. 58 Cello Sonata No. 2

Op. 71 *Sechs Lieder*:
No. 3. Diese Rose pflück' ich Dir ('An die Entfernte')
Remark: Formerly in Vol. 44 of *Mendelssohn Nachlaß*
No. 6. Vergangen ist der lichte Tag ('Nachtlied')

II. UNPUBLISHED AND POSTHUMOUSLY PUBLISHED WORKS

Christe Du Lamm Gottes (chorale cantata, 1827)

Wer nur den lieben Gott läßt walten (chorale cantata, 1829)

The Evening Bell (hp, pf) (Nov. 1829)

Wir glauben all an einen Gott (chorale cantata, 1831)
   Remark: Formerly in Vol. 23 of *Mendelssohn Nachlaß*

Nachspiel (Postlude) in D major (org) (8 Mar. 1831)
   Remark: Formerly in Vol. 23 of *Mendelssohn Nachlaß*

Im Nebelgeriesel ('Zigeunerlied'), Op. 120 No. 4 (before 1832)

Was will die einsame Träne ('Erinnerung') (before 17 Apr. 1837)

An den Rhein, zieh nicht an den Rhein, mein Sohn ('Warnung vor dem Rhein') (Feb. 1840)

Schlummernd an des Vaters Brust ('Nachtgesang') (15 Jan. 1842)

Es freut sich Alles ('Seemanns Scheidelied') (1843)

Berg und Thal will ich durchstreifen ('Frühlingslied'), Op. 100 No. 3 (1843/4)

Incidental Music to Sophocles' *Oedipus at Colonos*, Op. 93 (25 Feb. 1845)

Two sacred choruses (Beati mortui, Periti autem), Op. 115 (Feb. 1837)

On Lena's gloomy heath (concert aria) (Mar. 1846)

III. UNDATED SONGS

Three of four songs ed. by Carl Reinecke (Munich: Aibl, 1882):
   1. Vier trübe Monden sind entfloh'n
   2. Bist auf ewig du gegangen
   3. Weinend seh' ich in die Nacht

Still und freundlich ist die Nacht (cavatina for Adele Schopenhauer)

So schlaf in Ruh' (Hoffmann von Fallersleben).

IV. SONGS POSSIBLY NOT BY MENDELSSOHN (COPYIST'S MANUSCRIPTS SURVIVE IN GB-OB, MDM C. 50)

Ein Mädchen wohnt

Ich soll bei Tage und bei Nacht

Ja, wär's nicht aber Frühlingszeit

Catina belina ('Canzonetta Veneziana')

Wie die Blumen

APPENDIX 3

Some Autographs Transmitting
Only Portions of Works

NB. Not a complete listing; sketches not considered.

1. WORKS PUBLISHED BY MENDELSSOHN

Op. 2 Piano Quartet, last page of finale only.
Source: D-B, Ms.mus.autogr. F. Mendelssohn Bartholdy 13

Op. 7 *Sieben Characterstücke*, three bars from No. 6.
Source: D-B, N.Mus.ep. 28

Op. 21 *Midsummer Night's Dream Overture*, full-score leaves for exposition.
Source: GB-Ob, MDM b. 5 no. 2, fos. 7–12ᵛ

Op. 23 No. 3 *Mitten wir im Leben sind*, bars 1–26 and 59–87 (score).
Source: D-B, N.Mus.ms.22

Op. 27 *Calm Sea and Prosperous Voyage Overture*, leaves from the autograph score (summer 1828):
(1) Score leaves, 102 bars. *Source*: GB-Ob, MDM b. 5, No. 3, fos. 13ʳ–16ᵛ. These leaves may have been connected to (2). (See also R. Larry Todd, *Mendelssohn: The Hebrides and Other Overtures* (Cambridge: Cambridge University Press, 1994), 23.)
(2) 24 bars, sold at J. A. Stargardt, catalogue 624 (24–5 Nov. 1981), No. 684, with facsimile on p. 213. May have been connected to (1).

Op. 33 Three Caprices:
No. 2: Four bars, dated Weimar, 17 Apr. 1841, to L. Sachse.
Source: US-Wc (Whittall Coll.)
No. 3: Four bars from Presto, sold at Sotheby's, 21 Nov. 1990, lot 325, and Hans Schneider catalogue 328 (1992), No. 27

Op. 38 No. 4, Lied ohne Worte (formerly owned by Louis Plaidy):
(1) Four bars. *Source*: US-Hw
(2) Four bars. *Source*: Sotheby's, 17–18 Nov. 1988, lot 403, facsimile p. 167

Op. 41 No. 6 Und frische Nahrung, neues Blut ('Auf dem See').
Source: F-Pbn, MS 197

Op. 46 Psalm 95 ('Kommt, laßt uns anbeten').
Sources: Fragments in D-B, US-Wc, GB-Ob, and private collections

Op. 60 *Die erste Walpurgisnacht.*
>
> *Sources*: Fragments of early versions in D-B, F-Pbn, US-NH, private col-
> lections, and elsewhere

II. UNPUBLISHED AND POSTHUMOUSLY PUBLISHED WORKS

Overture to a burlesque '*L'homme automate*' for small orchestra (1821), last page of
score.
>
> *Source*: GB-Ob, MDM b. 5, fo. 210ᵛ [using the melody of the popular German
> song 'O du lieber Augustin']

Tutto è silenzio, concert aria for A. Milder (23 Feb. 1829).
>
> *Source*: US-Wc (Whittall Foundation)

Op. 83a Variations for Piano (4 hands).
>
> *Source*: D-B, N. Mus.ms. 241 (some bars have been cut away)

2

Editorial Problems in Mendelssohn's Organ Preludes, Op. 37

PIETRO ZAPPALÀ

FELIX MENDELSSOHN BARTHOLDY'S Three Preludes and Fugues for Organ, Op. 37 were published either in the last days of 1837 or at the beginning of 1838. As was customary at the time, the collection appeared simultaneously in two editions, by Breitkopf & Härtel in Germany and by Novello in England. A close comparison reveals that the two editions differ in many places, and although most variants are relatively minor and concern matters not particularly essential to the musical text, there are enough of them—more than one hundred in the preludes alone—to raise some important questions: Why are there so many differences between the two editions? How did these differences arise? Which edition offers the more reliable text?

The editorial problems posed by Op. 37 preludes are exemplified in the primary sources.[1] The following is a brief description of those sources:

1. Source *B* (Staatsbibliothek zu Berlin — Preußischer Kulturbesitz, Ms.mus.autogr. F. Mendelssohn Bartholdy 29, pp. 127–34). Autograph manuscript, eight pages of music with sixteen staves per side. First complete draft of the three preludes; each composition headed 'H.d.m.' ('Hilf du mir'). Prelude No. 1 is titled 'Praeludium' and is dated at the end (p. 129) 'Speÿer den 2.ten April 1837'. Prelude No. 2 begins on page 130 and is dated 'Speÿer d. 4.ten April

---

This essay is a modified and abridged translation of Pietro Zappalà, 'I *Preludi* dei "Präludien und Fugen" op. 37 di Felix Mendelssohn Bartholdy', in Maria Caraci Vela (ed.), *La critica del testo musicale: metodi e problemi della filologia musicale* (Studi e testi musicali, Nuova serie, no. 4; Lucca: Libreria Musicale Italiana, 1995), 287–318.

[1] For reasons of space, in this study I shall discuss only the preludes, not the fugues. In addition, some sketches for the first fugue of the set, found in one of Mendelssohn's diaries (GB-Ob, MDM g. 4, fos. 8ᵛ and 15ᵛ), will not be considered here. For a description of the latter, see Crum, *Catalogue II*, 101.

1837' at its conclusion on p. 131. Prelude No. 3 extends from the bottom of p. 131 to p. 134, and is dated at the end: 'Speÿer d. 6.ᵗᵉⁿ Ap. 1837'.

2. Source *R* (Rome, Biblioteca del Conservatorio di Musica, MS A 134). Autograph manuscript, comprising ten pages of music with sixteen staves per side, plus a title page in Mendelssohn's hand. The title page reads: 'Tre Preludj / per l'Organo / <u>al Signor Abbate Fortunato Santini</u> / in segno di sincera amicizia e di vera stima dal suo / divoto / Felix Mendelssohn Bartholdy / Lipsia li 8 Settembre / 1840'; to this, Santini added in his own handwriting: 'Fortunato Santini'. The beginning of the first prelude, on p. 1, is headed 'Praeludium I.'. On p. 4 the end of the first is followed by the indication 'hier folgt die Fuge in C moll 12/8 Tact', and the beginning of the second prelude is headed 'Praeludium II.'. On p. 6 the end of the second prelude is followed by the indication 'hierauf folgt die Fuge in g dur' and the third prelude is headed 'Praeludium III.'. The end of the third prelude (p. 10) is followed by the indication 'hierauf folgt die Fuge in d moll'.

3. Source *O* (Oxford, Bodleian Library, MS M. Deneke Mendelssohn c. 50/5, fos. 16–20). Contemporary copy, not in Mendelssohn's writing, for Prelude No. 2 from Op. 37. Although *O* was evidently prepared on the basis of *B*, it contains numerous errors (some of which have been corrected in pencil to concur with the printed edition). Because *O* played no role in the compositional history of the Op. 37 preludes, it is of little relevance for this study and will not be included in the discussion below.

4. Source *BH*. First German edition of Op. 37, published by Breitkopf & Härtel in late December 1837 or early January 1838. The title page reads: 'Präludien / und / Fugen / Für die Orgel / componirt und / Herrn Thomas Attwood / Organisten der Königlichen Kapelle / zu London / mit Verehrung und Dankbarkeit / gewidmet / von / Felix / Mendelssohn-Bartholdy. / Eigenthum der Verleger. / 37s Werk. — / [Pr. 1 Rthlr. 8 Gr.][2] / Leipzig, bei Breitkopf & Härtel. / London bei Alfred Novello. / Eingetragen in das Vereins-Archiv.' The edition bears the plate number 5823.[3]

---

[2] See Peter Krause, *Autographen, Erstausgaben und Frühdrucke der Werke von Felix Mendelssohn Bartholdy in Leipziger Bibliotheken und Archiven* (Leipzig: Musikbibliothek der Stadt Leipzig, 1972), 83.

[3] Two exemplars of *BH* were examined for this study. The first is held in the Leipzig Stadtarchiv under the shelf mark 'Gewandhaus Nr. 47'. The title page bears an autograph dedication from Mendelssohn to his friend Conrad Schleinitz: 'An H. C. Schleinitz zum Andenken und Durchsuchen, Leipzig, 27 Jan. 1838 F. Mendelssohn Bartholdy'; the early date of this dedication reveals that it belonged to the first printing of Op. 37, and the absence of a price suggests that it was a presentation copy from the press to the composer. The second exemplar is found in Rome, Biblioteca del Conservatorio di Musica, and its musical text differs in some details from that given in the Leipzig exemplar. The different price on the Rome exemplar ('1 Rthlr. 10 Ngr.') suggests that it represents the 1869 reprint of the 1838 edition.

FIG. 2.1. Provisional *stemma codicum* for sources of Preludes to Mendelssohn's Op. 37

5. Source *N*. First English edition of Op. 37, published by Alfred Novello in London in late December 1837 or early January 1838. The title page reads: 'Three / Preludes & Fugues / Composed for / The Organ, / and Dedicated to Thomas Attwood Esqre / Composer To Her Majesty's Chapels Royal, / By / Felix Mendelssohn Bartholdy. / Op. [37]. / N.° 1[2, 3]—Ent. Sta. Hall.—Pr. 3. Each / London, / J. Alfred Novello, / Music Seller (by special Appointment) to Her Majesty, / 69, Dean Street, Soho. / Leipsic, bei Breitkopf & Härtel. / This Work is Copyright.' The edition bears the plate number 505.[4]

Previous attempts to deal with the editorial problems posed by the preludes of Mendelssohn's Op. 37 have been forced to rely on the only autograph manuscript then known, source *B*. However, this manuscript not only poses serious problems of clarity and legibility, but also in many places transmits a completely different reading than that provided in the Breitkopf and Novello editions. In the absence of other possible resources, there has been a tacit assumption that the German edition possessed a certain greater authority than its English counterpart (see Fig. 2.1 for a *stemma codicum* summarizing this approach to the sources). This assumption leads to several problems, however. Most importantly, there is some doubt whether *B* generated both *BH* and *N* or only *BH*. If the latter is true, then *N* must have been generated by a third, unidentified source.

Recently, however, I had the good fortune to discover such a source (source *R*). This new source offers a solution to these questions and contributes to a better understanding of the different stages in the genesis of the editions of these preludes. Like the Berlin autograph, *R* transmits only the three preludes, but it also provides several further important points of information concerning the editorial problems of the works.

---

[4] One edition of *N* was examined for this study. Held in GB-Ob (shelf mark Mus. Instr. I, 7 [1]), it was evidently part of Mendelssohn's own collection (information kindly provided by Peter Ward Jones).

FIG. 2.2. Modified *stemma codicum* for sources of Preludes to
Mendelssohn's Op. 37

First of all, *R* is a fair copy based on *B*. In *R* Mendelssohn changes from systems embracing two staves in *B* to systems of three staves, with the pedal part
written separately on the third stave. This clarifies the reading of some of the
more cluttered passages in *B*, and also shows that *R* represents a further stage
in the evolution of the composition. More important is that *R* served as the
engraver's copy (*Stichvorlage*) for the Breitkopf & Härtel edition. This is confirmed by a sequence of numbers in another hand (probably that of the engraver)
that occur throughout the score, and that appear to mark the editorial layout
of bars per page. Specifically, these numbers count the number of staves to be
laid out on each printed sheet, so that each number written follows the last bar
of each system as printed in *BH*. Moreover, since the layout of *N* is different
from that of *BH*, it follows that *R* most likely was not the *Stichvorlage* for *N*.

The *stemma codicum* sketched above can, therefore, be revised as shown in
Fig. 2.2. This necessitates three further observations:

1. *R* is clearly more important than *B*, since it reproduces the composer's
   subsequent amendments and also exists as a source in its own right. As
   the source prepared by Mendelssohn to be used as the textual basis of the
   edition, it was understood by him to be the definitive version.
2. The use of *R* as the *Stichvorlage* for *BH* seems to confirm the authority of
   BH over *N*.
3. The question of the origin of the variants present in *N* remains unanswered. What was the source from which the English edition derives?

I know of no significant manuscripts to which we can refer in answering this last
question. We can, however, make good use of Mendelssohn's correspondence.

COMPOSITIONAL HISTORY

The preludes of Op. 37 were written separately from the fugues. Mendelssohn composed the fugues individually between March 1833 and December

1836[5] and considered publishing them as early as January 1837; in March of that year he offered all three to Breitkopf for publication.[6] Having accepted Mendelssohn's offer for an edition of the fugues, however, the publisher suggested that they be paired with preludes.[7] The composer accepted the invitation, but had to delay work on the preludes because of his many engagements, which included a performance of *St Paul* in Leipzig on 17 March and his marriage in Frankfurt am Main on 28 March. The three preludes were actually written—much to Mendelssohn's satisfaction—during the composer's honeymoon, in a burst of creativity between 2 and 6 April.[8] In the meantime, he had received the first proofs of the fugues; he returned these corrected proofs to Breitkopf & Härtel on 17 April:

I am sending per express mail the manuscript of the three preludes for the three fugues for the organ, per your request. I am very pleased that you wished to have these, for I like them much better [in this form] than I did the fugues when they were originally supposed to appear alone. Because of this [the addition of the preludes] the whole collection will be more than twice as long, and so I hope it is what you said you wanted in the note I received the morning before I left Leipzig. Since you told me in that note that the three fugues would appear so short when they were engraved, I immediately set about writing the preludes, which I had [already] resolved to do anyway. . . . Concerning the date of publication, please be so good as to write to me in Frankfurt am Main in care of Mr. J. Herz, and to send a copy before the works' release to J. Alfred Novello in London, also informing him of the title (the German of which I have given to you in the form I wish). Please note that on the reverse of this page there are some corrections to the manuscript of the fugues which I wish to have incorporated, and I hope that you will heed these

---

[5] For a more detailed examination of the works' genesis, see Zappalà, 'I *Preludi*', esp. 288–93.

[6] Letter of 11 Mar. 1837 from Mendelssohn to Breitkopf & Härtel, quoted from Elvers, *Verleger*, 58: 'Now I wish to publish along with the piano fugues [Op. 35] or shortly after them three bigger ones for the organ . . . If you are amenable to this, I could still provide you with the manuscript of the organ fugues before my departure . . . but for both works I want to reserve the English copyright for myself' ('Ich wünsche jetzt mit den Clavierfugen zugleich oder doch bald nach ihnen drei größere für die Orgel drucken zu lassen . . . Wenn Ihnen dies recht ist, da könnte ich Ihnen das Manuscript der Orgelfugen noch vor meiner Abreise zustellen . . . Von beiden Werken wünsche ich jedoch das Eigenthumsrecht für England mir vorzubehalten.'

[7] This may be inferred from Mendelssohn's letter written in Freiburg im Breisgau on 17 Apr.; see below.

[8] The dates of composition are confirmed by source *B*; see the description above. For Mendelssohn's views on the new works, see his letter of 9 Apr. 1837 written from Strasburg to his mother, quoted in Elvers, *Briefe*, 198–200: 'And tell her [i.e. Fanny] that in Speyer I composed three organ preludes, among other things, and that I hope that one or maybe two of them will especially please her.' ('Und sag ihr, daß ich in Speyer unter andern 3 Orgelpraeludien componirt habe, von denen ich hoffe, daß eins oder vielleicht zwei absonderlich gefallen werden.') See also Ward Jones, *Honeymoon*, 37, 99, 135, 139.

precisely, so that I do not become involved in another war with the engraver. Please send the last set of proofs to me in Frankfurt.[9]

This letter provides several important insights into the compositional status of Op. 37 as of 17 April. To begin with, it shows that with the proofs of the fugues Mendelssohn also sent off a manuscript of the preludes—not, however, the original autograph (*B*), but rather the fair copy that he had prepared for use as the engraver's proof (i.e. *R*). We may therefore precisely date manuscript *R* as having been written between the date of composition of the last prelude and the date on which the manuscript was sent to the publisher; i.e. between 6 and 17 April 1837. Secondly, the letter shows that Mendelssohn asked Breitkopf & Härtel to send an exemplar to Novello so that the English firm could prepare its own edition. It remains unclear, however, precisely what source Novello would have consulted; the context of the letter would seem to indicate that Mendelssohn was thinking of an advance proof from the German firm.

Most interesting, however, is the reference to the emendations that are introduced to the fugue manuscripts, and to the correction of the fugues' proofs. Since Mendelssohn had left the original manuscript with Breitkopf & Härtel, he must have corrected the proofs from memory. Although the composer certainly undertook these corrections with great care, correcting proofs in this fashion inevitably would leave room for some inaccuracies to creep into the musical text.

Further information regarding the editorial progress of the opus is provided by a letter of 5 August from Mendelssohn to Breitkopf & Härtel:

And I further request that you send to Mr Novello in London as soon as possible the three organ preludes and fugues, which are also supposed to be published by his firm. He recently asked me for them and I could not give them to him, since I kept

---

[9] Letter of 17 Apr. 1837 from Mendelssohn to Breitkopf & Härtel, quoted from Elvers, *Verleger*, 60: 'Übersende ich heut mit der Fahrpost das Manuscript der verlangten Praeludien zu den 3 Fugen für die Orgel. Es ist mir sehr lieb, daß Sie dieselben zu haben wünschten, denn sie gefallen mir jetzt viel besser als die Fugen, die ich ursprünglich allein zur Herausgabe bestimmte. Das ganze Heft wird dadurch mehr als doppelt so stark und so hoffe ich also daß es Ihrem Wunsche genügt, den Sie mir in dem Billet aussprachen, welches ich den Morgen vor meiner Abreise von Leipzig empfing. Da Sie mir darin sagten, daß die 3 Fugen so wenig voluminös im Stich werden würden, so habe ich mich gleich an die Praeludien gemacht, die ich mir ohnehin vorgenommen hatte, . . . Über die Zeit des Erscheinens sind Sie wohl so gefällig mir nach Frankfurt a/M adr. M. J. Herz zu schreiben, so wie auch ein Exemplar vor dem Erscheinen an J. Alfred Novello in London zu schicken, und seine Firma auf dem Titel (den ich Deutsch, so wie ich ihn angegeben habe wünsche) mit zu bemerken. Einige Correcturen die ich im Manuscript der Fugen nachzutragen bitte bemerke ich hier auf der Rückseite, und hoffe daß es recht genau geschieht, damit ich nicht wieder in einen Krieg mit dem Stecher ziehn muß. Die letzte Correctur bitte ich Sie mir nach Frankfurt zu schicken.'

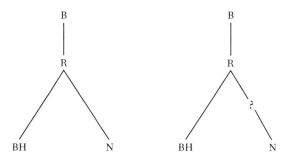

FIG. 2.3. Revised *stemma codicum* for sources of Preludes to
Mendelssohn's Op. 37

no exact copy for myself. If you want to send him the manuscript itself, I will see to it that he immediately sends an exemplar back to you; if not, then send him an exact copy—but in any case I want a manuscript in his hands by the end of this month.[10]

The reference to 'no exact copy' ('keine genaue Abschrift') in this passage underscores that Mendelssohn did not have the fair copy with him. We may thus assert with reasonable certainty that the manuscript the composer had with him was *B*, not *R*. In other words, although he had an exemplar of the composition with him, it was not a completely reliable draft. Further, from the third sentence we may surmise that while the composer encouraged Breitkopf to dispatch a copy of the composition to Novello, he did so on the assumption that he would certainly have the original manuscript by the end of the month. This indicates that *N* was probably produced on the basis of a copy of *R* or, more probably, directly from *R* itself. This is a particularly important point because if the Novello edition derived directly from *R*, then the Novello edition and the Breitkopf & Härtel edition are equally authoritative. This observation makes possible a further revision of the *stemma codicum* (see Fig. 2.3).

The problem of justifying the differences between the two editions thus presents itself anew, albeit now in a new and different way. It is necessary at this point to consider the process of printing and proof-reading, so that we can better understand where discrepancies are the product of errors of transmission (which are mainly due to the actions of the printer) and where they are true and real emendations introduced by the author.

[10] Letter of 5 Aug. 1837 from Koblenz to Breitkopf & Härtel, quoted from Elvers, *Verleger*, 63: 'Ferner bitte ich Sie Herrn Novello in London baldmöglichst die 3 Praelud. und Fugen für Orgel, welche auch bei ihm erscheinen sollen, zukommen zu lassen. Er fragte mich neulich darum und ich konnte sie ihm nicht geben, da ich keine genaue Abschrift behalten hatte. Wollen Sie ihm das Manuscr. selbst schicken, so will ich sorgen daß er Ihnen ein Exemplar sogleich wieder schickt; wo nicht, so schicken Sie ihm wohl eine genaue Abschrift, jedenfalls aber wünsche ich, daß er das Manuscr. bis gegen Ende dieses Monats in Händen habe.'

Unfortunately, Mendelssohn's corrected proofs for Op. 37 seem to have been lost.[11] In addition, the remaining exchange of letters between the composer and his publishers provides little additional information. In one letter of November 1837 he points out more errors in the proofs, and in a second letter from mid-January 1838 he thanks them for the edition.[12] In the second letter the composer is most appreciative of the 'attractive production' ('schöne Ausstattung'), but this of course does not necessarily refer to the correctness of the musical text.

On the basis of this information it is not possible to identify any one of the three extant sources as the 'best text' for Op. 37; indeed, to do so would be methodologically incorrect. If we were to grant that privilege to R because it was the manuscript intended to serve as the definitive text, we would run the risk of underestimating the possible errors in that manuscript itself, as well as ignoring subsequent changes made by the composer, which we know occurred frequently during the various phases of proofs. On the other hand, if we were to resign ourselves to the impossibility of gaining a deeper understanding of the process of the proofs' revision and consequently grant absolute authority to one of the two editions, we would risk overlooking errors that occurred in the final editions (as we likewise know was sometimes the case). We must therefore examine the disparities between the two editions and manuscript R in order to obtain additional guidance.

ANALYSIS OF THE VARIANTS

A detailed analysis of the variants among R, BH, and N leads to some important considerations. On the whole, these variants tend to confirm the hypothesis advanced above on the basis of the composer's correspondence; i.e. that N was probably prepared from either R or a copy of R. At the same time, however, they exacerbate doubts over which should be the accepted final version of the preludes. These variants may be classified into as many as six groups (which may or may not overlap, on a case-by-case basis), as follows.

1. Variants that confirm the derivation of N directly from R or from an intermediate source (*interpositus*). These variants preclude the possibility that N was prepared from a very early prepublication copy of BH. In autograph R the composer originally notated the entry of a new theme in the middle stave,

---

[11] Mendelssohn refers to these corrected proofs in his letter to Breitkopf & Härtel dated 6 Nov. 1837, quoted in Elvers, *Verleger*, 65.   [12] Ibid. 65, 67.

but then cancelled it and (for lack of space) rewrote the line on the pedal stave. He then linked the two segments with a long loop of his pen. This loop was erroneously interpreted as a slur in *N*, but correctly omitted in *BH*.

2. Discrepancies between the two editions. There are at least 120 such general variants, of varying significance. It should be noted that these 120 variants are not all found in only one of the two editions; that is, one edition does not concur fully with the text of *R* while the other is full of disparities. Rather, they are divided almost equally between the two editions: *BH* differs in fifty-six places from *R*, while *N* differs in sixty-four. Before undertaking a more detailed examination of these variants, we should recognize that Mendelssohn was not always as scrupulous a proof-reader as is generally assumed. (This is at least true of the present instance, and his editorial method certainly did not correspond to that required for, e.g., a modern critical edition.) In addition, we must remember that nineteenth-century publication processes hindered the production of a definitive authorial text. And of course, both these considerations may influence the situation of any given work. It thus seems clear that the correct reconstruction of the text of the Op. 37 preludes must depend on a detailed examination of every individual variant in each of the three sources.

3. Minor variants. Of the large number of variants between *BH* and *N*, a first group of some twenty may be classified as improvements that are easily justified if we recognize that the desire for greater legibility or even greater clarity of the musical text occasioned editorial intervention. Most of these variants involve cautionary accidentals and rests that were introduced to clarify the voice-leading. We may hypothesize that similar modifications were made directly by the printer or editor and then approved by Mendelssohn himself; alternatively, they may represent later emendations introduced by the composer. Again, the presence of these 'improvements' in both *BH* and *N* justifies the hypothesis that Mendelssohn considered them minor adjustments that as such did not require an exact correlation between the two editions.

4. Variants of transmission (printer's errors). Another group of about eighty variants seems to suggest that there was ample margin for error during the setting of the musical text onto the printing plate, perhaps because of carelessness on the part of the engraver. It seems very strange that labour such as musical typesetting, which by its nature needs to proceed at a very slow pace, could produce so many misreadings, since errors that are scarcely acceptable in the case of a quick reading are certainly not acceptable in the context of the meticulous scrutiny required to print a manuscript. However, experience teaches that such errors are much more frequent than we would like to think;

errors are often attributed to the poor legibility of the original manuscript, but, realistically, just as many are due to the haste with which the printer must work or to other causes. An example of these problems is evident in bar 13 of the C minor Prelude, where *BH* omits the precautionary natural sign while *N* omits the slur. We must remember that for each 'printer's error' that we are able to identify, the proof-reader must also share the blame for not having identified it when checking the proofs. Therefore, such errors must also be considered the responsibility of Mendelssohn himself.

5. Authorial variants. At the same time, it is important that the philologist not allow printer's errors to become a convenient excuse in such intricate cases. To dismiss all variants as printing errors would, of course, be a methodological error tantamount to an *a priori* assumption that printed copies are exempt from errors just because they follow the author's indications. Even if such an assumption were acceptable, this method would be useless for choosing the more correct of the conflicting readings. In effect, some of these examples could be viewed as authorial variants, which essentially reflect the composer's specific desire to let the work continue to evolve during the long stages of proofs. Although we are now deprived of any such documentation in this specific case, the hypothesis is in itself completely plausible, since there is practical evidence that Mendelssohn continued to revise many of his works through all the stages of printing.

But how can we identify which changes Mendelssohn deliberately made when these are neither documented nor consistently reported in both the editions? How can we distinguish individual instances of printer's errors, deliberate editorial adjustments, corrections made because of a specific change in authorial intent, and even changes that resulted from his substantial disinterest in aspects of production that to us seem decisive, yet for him would have constituted minor details? The cases are at times quite complex. An examination of two particularly significant variants in the Op. 37 preludes will suffice to show how an accurate collation of the available evidence permits the formulation of a final reading.

The first such instance is that of the time signature of the first prelude (see Ex. 2.1). The signature given in *R* and *N* (¢ or cut time) dates from the first manuscript (*B*) and seems, therefore, to have been a firm choice from the very conception of the prelude. If it is difficult to imagine that the printer could have been distracted enough to use the time signature of ¢ (common time) in *BH*, it is still more difficult to hypothesize that Mendelssohn would have imagined a different time signature for the entire prelude at the very late stage of correcting proofs. In this case, therefore, it seems more plausible to accept the reading given in both *R* and *N* over that of *BH*.

Ex. 2.1. Prelude in C Minor, Op. 37 No. 1, bars 1–3 as given in (*a*) source *B*;
(*b*) source *R*; (*c*) source *BH*; (*d*) source *N*

(*a*)

(*b*)

(*c*)

(*d*)

Ex. 2.2. Prelude in C Minor, Op. 37 No. 1, bars 118–20 as given in (*a*) source *R*;
(*b*) source *BH*; (*c*) source *N*

A more difficult case is shown in Ex. 2.2. The reading of this passage in *BH* normalizes the melodic line to conform to the typical contour of the opening theme, in which the second group of four eighth notes in the middle voice is not stepwise; this reading would seem to be preferable, since it permits a third literal repetition of the sequence. But the reading given in *N* instead offers the formation of a group of four conjunct eighth notes—a reading that is also entirely plausible, since it adumbrates the groups of four notes in the highest part of the upper stave in the following bar. Paradoxically, this reading could be even more plausible than that of *BH* because it alters the otherwise too mechanical repetition of the progression and ties its last segment to the following figuration. I should mention that in the first version of the prelude (that given in source *B*) the sequence of two stepwise quadruplets generally occurs more frequently than in the final version, in which the sequence of one conjunct and one disjunct quadruplet predominates.

To examine this passage more closely: in *B* Mendelssohn wrote the progression exclusively using stepwise quadruplets, while in *R* he copied them in the same way but then intervened (as the manuscript shows) to modify the second quadruplets according to the non-scalar configuration, so that they acquire a greater affinity with the melodic profile of the theme. The corrections provide little clear information concerning the second quadruplet of the phase of the sequence, which is the same as *R*; here, Mendelssohn added the precautionary note 'es gilt'. Unfortunately, this note in itself is ambiguous, since it might equally well mean 'stet' or 'E♭ stays'. I personally prefer the second interpretation, because the first would still be imprecise: which note should we use, the C or the E♭? In other, analogous parts Mendelssohn wrote only 'stet' ('gilt') for unambiguous corrections, or the exact names of the valid notes in the case of multiple and, therefore, ambiguous corrections. What is more, to indicate note names Mendelssohn uses Roman script rather than the German script he otherwise usually employed; here 'es' is clearly written in Roman script, while 'gilt' is in German script. If this hypothesis is correct, then the proper reading for this last quadruplet should be a stepwise sequence of four eighth notes, with the possible stylistic legitimation mentioned already. Everything becomes plausible and comprehensible, apart from one last mystery: how was it that the English printer was able to understand the precautionary note added at that point by Mendelssohn (and written in German) better than his German counterpart was?

To inspect all the variants would greatly exceed the scope of this chapter. We have examined two of the most striking cases. But there are many more, some even more ambiguous, and they alternate between interesting authorial variants and mere typographical misprints. These leave the philologist with considerable difficulties in deciding which reading to follow.

6. Hidden variants. One last consequence occasioned by the rediscovery of *R* deserves mention here: namely, the possibility of identifying errors of transmission that are present in both the first editions, and therefore seemingly so verified that they would have remained hidden despite the most detailed investigation. The one modern edition that is based on only *BH* and

Ex. 2.3. Prelude in D Minor, Op. 37 No. 3, bars 48–50 as given in (*a*) source *R*;
(*b*) source *BH*; (*c*) source *N*

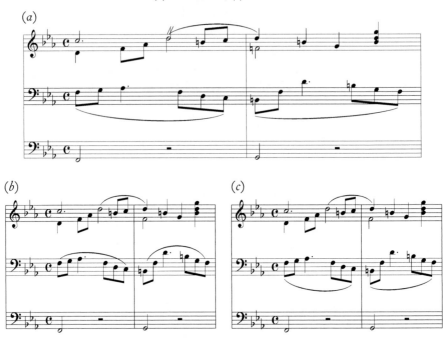

N and assigns the same authority to both[13] could not have reconstructed the
original text as foreseen by Mendelssohn for these passages. Of the six cases
that I have identified, the one given in Ex. 2.3 will suffice to describe these
cases. In this passage, the upper D (*d″*) in the left hand is slurred in all the versions. In *R*, however, it is clear that the D of bar 17 was originally written for
the uppermost voice and thus was tied to the D in the following bar; but
Mendelssohn later reassigned this note to the voice below—without, however, deleting the tie. The tie was therefore retained in error in the manuscript
and in both editions.

[13] Felix Mendelssohn Bartholdy, *Orgelstücke, nach Autographen, Abschriften und Erstausgaben*, ed. Wolfgang Stockmeier (Munich: Henle, 1988). The next year witnessed the appearance
of another modern edition, Felix Mendelssohn Bartholdy, *Three Preludes and Fugues, Opus 37,
Duets, and Preludes and Fugues*, ed. Wm. A. Little (Complete Organ Works, 1; London:
Novello, 1989), in which the editor recognizes that *N* is closer to the manuscript tradition (i.e. to
B, since *R* was still unknown at that date), and therefore prefers *BH* as the basis for his edition,
interpreting it as a later version, 'thus probably reflect[ing] more specifically the composer's final
wishes' (Critical commentary, p. viii).

Obviously, one might argue that in these six cases the variants could just as plausibly be verified as authorial variants, provided by the editions alone and not the manuscript; in this case, *R* would actually represent the earlier version and therefore be less trustworthy. Such an objection is not only possible, but also methodologically correct and proper. In this case, however, the significance of the variants mentioned is such as to make us consider *R* the more likely text.

CONCLUSIONS

What has been the effect of the rediscovery of source *R*? It has given us many answers, while at the same time raising new questions. Among the answers we should include the rehabilitation of the Novello edition as a reliable source and the confirmation of the necessity of collating all three sources (*BH*, *N*, and *R*) in order to achieve a correct definition of the text of the preludes as Mendelssohn wanted it. On the other hand, unresolved questions are raised by all those variants in which the two printed editions differ from their archetypal manuscript—variants that, given the lack of other proven documentation, remain somewhere between typographical misprints and authorial variants.

The investigation of these numerous variants nevertheless has its benefits, since it has cast new light on a series of factors that previously had not been identified, and that have now, after a great deal of attention, been subject to some examination. Among these, we may again number the following:

1. The limits of editorial activity: the varying level of professionalism of the printers and therefore the degree of errors caused by them; the commercial needs of the publishing houses and, therefore, the working times and opportunity, or lack of it, to respect the corrections requested by the author.
2. Mendelssohn's attitude during the production of the proofs: the degree of precision he demanded in the printing of his manuscript; his meticulousness in the correction of the proofs of his own music; his level of interest in correlating the musical text of two divergent editions of the same work; his ability to make changes during the editorial process—i.e. to demand that the editor respect his requests.
3. External factors: the personal circumstances that surrounded Mendelssohn's correction of proofs (his honeymoon, the frequent moving around, the great number of compositions with which he was engaged in that period, his workload, and his changing role in Leipzig).

In the absence of other sources, and in the hope that more sources will some day turn up, little advice can be offered to the modern editor other than to consider all the variables that affect the complex operation that is involved in producing an edition (whether historic editions—i.e. those of Mendelssohn's day—or modern ones, such as critical editions), and then to proceed with a grain of salt in choosing which variants to accept.

3

Mendelssohn's Two *Infelice* Arias: Problems of Sources and Musical Identity

JOHN MICHAEL COOPER

ONE of the central issues that has emerged in the resurgence of Mendelssohn scholarship since the Second World War is the need for critical editions of the composer's complete works. The decades immediately following Mendelssohn's death witnessed not only new editions of works that had been published during his lifetime, but also first editions of many previously unpublished compositions; all were ultimately included, along with still more works not previously released, in the series of *Mendelssohns Werke* published by Breitkopf & Härtel between 1874 and 1877 under the general editorship of the composer's friend Julius Rietz. For decades this series was considered a complete and reliable source for Mendelssohn's compositions; indeed, it is still treated as such in many quarters.

Unfortunately, the publication of the *Werke* created almost as many problems as it solved. Most works were edited according to policies that have since been rejected, and some editions were based on autographs whose authority has since been questioned.[1] Further, the groupings, serial numbers, and opus

Thanks are due to Hans-Günter Klein and the Staatsbibliothek zu Berlin — Preußischer Kulturbesitz for permission to study and edit the autograph of the 1834 manuscript. In addition, I wish to thank Dr Robin J. Arrigo for her assistance in preparing the music examples for this article.

[1] Besides the obvious example of the 'Italian' Symphony, these works include the B flat major String Quintet, Op. 87, and the *Deutsche Liturgie*. See Friedhelm Krummacher, 'Mendelssohn's Late Chamber Music: Some Autograph Sources Recovered', in Jon W. Finson and R. Larry Todd (eds.), *Mendelssohn and Schumann: Essays on their Music and its Context* (Durham, NC: Duke University Press, 1984), 77–80; Hans-Günter Klein, 'Korrekturen im Autograph von Mendelssohns Streichquartett Op. 80: Überlegungen zur Kompositionstechnik und zum Kompositionsvorgang', *Mendelssohn-Studien*, 5 (1992), 113–22; and David Brodbeck, '*Eine kleine*

numbers applied to the new publications distorted the chronology of Mendelssohn's works—both among the newly printed compositions and between them and their previously published counterparts. This situation, in turn, misrepresented his growth as a composer. And perhaps most importantly, the series of collected works, because of its proximity to the comparatively scholarly collected editions of Bach, Mozart, Beethoven, and Schumann, implied a comprehensiveness and editorial authority that were at best exaggerations.

The authority almost unquestioningly accorded to the *Werke* in the first half of the twentieth century has since been diminished by the publication of numerous pieces that were omitted from that series; by new, critical editions of many works that were included in less authoritative editions in the original publications; and by research documenting the existence of an astonishing number of otherwise unknown works (*Jugendarbeiten* and mature compositions alike). These more recent developments have themselves provided much-needed impetus for a revival not only of scholarly investigation into the composer's musical output, but also of general interest in his works among a music-loving public that once believed enough was known about Mendelssohn. The time is thus ripe for the appearance of the newly revived Leipzig *Gesamtausgabe der Werke von Felix Mendelssohn Bartholdy*.[2]

Yet one further problem remains virtually unaddressed, both in our more authoritative editions of Mendelssohn's works and in the critical literature concerning the composer: the fact that the standard generally applied as the fundamental editorial criterion in these editions—that of the *Fassung letzter Hand*, or latest authorial version—is one that was by no means universally accepted in Mendelssohn's day, and is ill-suited to many of Mendelssohn's works and their source situations.[3] Since this editorial philosophy ultimately centres around the nature of musical identity, in Mendelssohn's œuvre as elsewhere, this problem is one that must be addressed as we continue revising our image of this composer and his music.

Kirchenmusik: A New Canon, a Revised Cadence, and an Obscure "Coda" by Mendelssohn', *Journal of Musicology*, 12 (1994), 179–205. On the 'Italian' Symphony, see, most recently, the commentaries in Felix Mendelssohn Bartholdy, *Sinfonie A-dur op. 90, 'Italienische': Alle eigenhändigen Niederschriften in Faksimile*, ed. John Michael Cooper and Hans-Günter Klein (Wiesbaden: Dr. Ludwig Reichert, 1997), i. 1–46; ii. 7–29.

    [2] Concerning the new Gesamtausgabe, see Christian Martin Schmidt, 'Konzeption und Stand der Mendelssohn-Gesamtausgabe', in *Felix Mendelssohn — Mitwelt und Nachwelt: 1. Leipziger Mendelssohn-Kolloquium am 8. und 9. Juni 1993* (Wiesbaden: Breitkopf & Härtel, 1996), 131–4.

    [3] For a brief overview of the philosophy of the *Fassung letzter Hand*, see Georg von Dadelson, 'Die "Fassung letzter Hand" in der Musik', *Acta musicologica*, 33 (1961), 1–14.

In this chapter I shall examine two little-known concert arias for female voice and orchestra—*Infelice! / Ah, ritorna, età dell'oro*, completed in Düsseldorf in April 1834, and *Infelice! / Ah, ritorna, età felice*, completed in Leipzig in January 1843—as examples of the problems of musical identity encountered in Mendelssohn's œuvre, and of the serious problems created when the editorial philosophy of the *Fassung letzter Hand* is employed uncritically as a primary standard of musical identity and authority. These arias suggest that more flexible and context-related concepts must be employed if we are to approach Mendelssohn's works and their sources in a fashion that is consistent with the composer's own views.[4]

GENESES AND PERFORMANCE HISTORIES
OF THE ARIAS

Scholars and performers have generally treated Mendelssohn's two *Infelice* arias as a single work whose genesis spanned a decade.[5] The assumption is understandable: the two are in the same key; are scored for similar ensembles;[6] employ largely identical texts for the recitative, share essential melodic elements of the Andante along with some other musical features, and are contemporaneous with the first and revised versions of *Die erste Walpurgisnacht* —a work that Mendelssohn clearly considered an early version and revision of a single compositional concept.[7] Because of these similarities and shared

[4] For an examination of the ways in which circumstantial documents (specifically, *Albumblätter*) can contribute meaningful insights into the compositional history of a work, see Ralf Wehner, ' ". . . ich zeigte Mendelssohns Albumblatt vor und Alles war gut." Zur Bedeutung der Stammbucheintragungen und Albumblätter von Felix Mendelssohn Bartholdy', in Schmidt, *Kongreß-Bericht*, 37–63.

[5] Peter Ward Jones has recently commented that the differences between the 1843 and its 1834 counterpart rendered it 'virtually an entirely different composition'; see Peter Ward Jones, 'Mendelssohn Scores in the Library of the Royal Philharmonic Society', in Schmidt, *Kongreß-Bericht*, 74. Evidently the only other scholar not to conflate the compositional histories and identities of the two arias is Marcia Citron, who recognized from the programmes of the Philharmonic Society that the text of the Andante in the 1834 aria differed from that of Op. 94; see Citron, *Letters*, 131, 149–50. Unaware of the existence of the autograph for the 1834 aria, Citron stated (p. 150) that it might be lost.

[6] There is no timpani part in the 1843 aria. It is worth noting that the timpani part of the 1834 aria is exceptional, if not unique, in its use of two drums tuned to D and E♭.

[7] On the genesis of the *Walpurgisnacht*, see Christoph Hellmundt, 'Mendelssohns Arbeit an seiner Kantate *Die erste Walpurgisnacht*: Zu einer bisher wenig beachteten Quelle', in Schmidt, *Kongreß-Bericht*, 76–112; further, Douglass Seaton, 'The Romantic Mendelssohn: The Composition of *Die erste Walpurgisnacht*', *Musical Quarterly*, 68 (1982), 398–410. See also Julie D. Prandi's essay in this volume, Ch. 6.

features, the two arias have always been construed as different manifestations of a single musical identity and edited according to the philosophy of the *Fassung letzter Hand*. The 1843 aria, published posthumously in 1851 as Mendelssohn's Op. 94, has been treated as a revision or reworking of the 1834 aria, which, for its part, has remained unpublished.

A closer examination of the two arias and of Mendelssohn's correspondence concerning them clearly reveals that this approach is misguided, or at best an oversimplification. In fact, the works represent not a continuing evolution of a single musical and textual concept, but rather two musically, textually, and circumstantially autonomous approaches to a single compositional task: the creation of an *abbandonata*-style Italian concert aria.

The story began in November 1832, when the Philharmonic Society of London commissioned from Mendelssohn a symphony, an overture, and a vocal piece for the 1832–3 season.[8] The timing of the offer could hardly have been better; yet it also could hardly have been worse. On the one hand, Mendelssohn had completed a stellar education, had attracted considerable attention as a composer through such early masterpieces as the Octet for Strings and the *Midsummer Night's Dream Overture*, and had achieved international celebrity through his ground-breaking performances of Bach's *St Matthew Passion* in Berlin and his trip to England in 1829; clearly, he needed to establish his reputation as an independent professional musician rather than simply a prodigy. On the other hand, the winter of 1832–3 was an extraordinarily busy, difficult, and painful time for him. The completion of this major international commission was to occur while he was also conducting a series of formidable concerts in support of his candidacy for the Directorship of the Berlin Singakademie; completing the first version of *Die erste Walpurgisnacht* and the reworking of the 'Reformation' Symphony; composing an invited composition[9] for the Stadttheater in Düsseldorf (where he had some hopes of securing a position after his humiliating defeat at the Singakademie); preparing to conduct the Lower Rhine Music Festival in Düsseldorf; and attempting to recover from a deep depression induced by the deaths in 1832 of his best friend Eduard Rietz, and of his mentors and teachers Zelter and Goethe.[10] Because of

[8] Letter of 5 Nov. 1832 from William Watts (secretary of the Philharmonic Society of London) to Mendelssohn (GB-Ob, GB II/72). For a detailed exploration of Mendelssohn's fulfilment of the terms of the commission, see Ward Jones, 'Mendelssohn Scores', 70–4.

[9] The still-unpublished incidental music to Karl Immermann's translation/adaptation of Caldéron de la Barca's *El príncipe constante*. The autograph, dated 18 Mar. 1833, is part of Vol. 56 of the former *Mendelssohn Nachlaß* (now in D-B, Ms.mus.autogr. F. Mendelssohn Bartholdy 56).

[10] The standard account of this period is that provided by Eric Werner, based largely on Eduard Devrient's memoirs; see Devrient, *Erinnerungen*, 145–57, and Werner, *New Image*, 227–51. For a reappraisal of Werner's interpretation, see Wm. A. Little, 'Mendelssohn and the Berlin Singakademie: The Composer at the Crossroads', in *MHW*, 65–85.

these circumstances, in the spring of 1833 Mendelssohn was able to complete only one new work—the A major Symphony—in response to the commission, and that only at the last minute. As compensation for his failure to deliver the commissioned vocal piece, which he promised would be completed shortly, he offered the Society its choice of two overtures (neither of which was truly 'new').[11]

But circumstances conspired against serious work on the vocal piece. The composer spent most of the summer of 1833 in London, where he was fêted by all of musical society—including one soirée at which famed soprano Maria Malibran (1808–36) and her lover, virtuoso violinist Charles de Bériot (1802–70), were featured, and at which Mendelssohn improvised on themes from the arias Malibran had sung.[12] In early September he relocated to Düsseldorf, where he plunged immediately into his duties as the newly appointed Municipal Music Director, as well as a time-consuming collaboration with Karl Immermann and the Stadttheater. Not until early 1834 was he able to devote any energy to the commissioned vocal work. He wrote to his family on 16 January that he would begin work on it soon, and on 5 February he was able to report to Eduard Devrient that he was actively working on 'the vocal scena for the Philharmonic concert';[13] two days letter he wrote to Ignaz and Charlotte Moscheles that he feared the piece would be 'all too tame' ('allzuzahm').[14]

His work then began to progress quickly. He again reported on the composition on 19 February, this time providing several useful details:

I am working very busily now and am getting into quite a good mood for composing . . . ; my vocal scena for the Philharmonic will be finished in a few days. The text is the most beautiful nonsense by Metastasio (recitative, adagio, and

[11] Letter of 27 Apr. 1833 from Mendelssohn to William Watts, quoted in Myles Birket Foster, *History of the Philharmonic Society of London, 1813–1912* (London: John Lane, 1913), 118. Traditionally scholars have assumed that the two overtures were the C major ('Trumpet') Overture and the *Meeresstille und glückliche Fahrt* Overture, but Peter Ward Jones has recently suggested that the second work was in fact the *Fair Melusine* Overture; see Ward Jones, 'Mendelssohn Scores', 71–4.

[12] See Mendelssohn's letter to his family dated 16 Jan. 1834, quoted in n. 13, below. For an account of this evening including Abraham Mendelssohn's letter to his family and the remarks of other sources, see Howard Bushnell, *Maria Malibran: A Biography of the Singer* (University Park: Pennsylvania State University Press, 1979), 161–2.

[13] Devrient, *Erinnerungen*, 171. Perhaps significantly, at least one letter contemporaneous with the beginning of work on the piece recalls the soirée with Malibran the previous summer. Explaining to his family in 1834 that he had decided to improvise at a soirée in Cologne, the composer wrote that nothing special had come of the recent improvisation: 'still, since I had not improvised in the longest time (since the evening at Novello's with Malibran, I believe), it was good for a long time nonetheless.' ('indessen da ich seit längster Zeit gar nicht mehr phantasirt hatte (seit dem Abend bei Novello mit der Malibran, glaub' ich), so war es doch lange gut'). Unpublished family letter dated 16 Jan. 1834, held in US-NYp.

[14] Letter of 7 Jan. 1834, in Moscheles, *Briefe*, 74–5.

allegro) assembled from four different operas—but all that should be made good
again by a solo violin that accompanies the voice, and for which I'm speculating on
de Bériot.[15]

The composer's elder sister, Fanny Hensel, provided a bit of complementary
(and punning) information in her response, dated 28 February: 'Concerning
your vocal scena you write only that it contains an obbligato violin part for
Beriot [*sic*]; from that we surmise that you're thinking of Malibran as the
soprano. Does the key fit?'.[16]

Mendelssohn completed the aria on 3 April 1834—though the extremely
untidy autograph suggests that he may have made a subsequent pass through
for revision—and issued one final report to Fanny a few days later:

[N]ow there is an American girl here . . . and also an English girl from whom I
borrowed an English Bible back when I still did not know what sort of vocal piece I
was going to write for the Philharmonic (the Italian one with the *Violino obligé*
is finished; some passages are so completely flat and terrible in *my* manner that
you would have to laugh—the winds do this ♪ and more such things—and so I
am happy that you will not get your hands on it to see it), and then there are two
sopranos in the Singverein whom I am supposed to promote . . .[17]

Mendelssohn sent the aria to the Philharmonic Society by way of his friend
Klingemann on 13 April.[18] He continued to speak jokingly of the piece.
Klingemann's evident enquiry as to the identity of the intended soloist met
with the response: 'Who will sing my scena? You sing it! At the end you will
do it better than all the Grisettes and Masurs in the world would, for you so
enjoy doing that.'[19] On 14 May Klingemann wrote to Mendelssohn that he

[15]   Letter of 19 Feb. 1834, held in US-NYp: '[I]ch bin jetzt sehr fleißig und komme wieder in
recht gute Schreiblaune . . . ; meine Gesangscene fürs Philharmonic wird in ein Paar Tagen fertig sein. Die Worte sind der allerschönste Unsinn von Metastasio, Recitativ, Adagio u Allegro
aus vier verschiedenen Opern zusammengestellt, aber das soll alles eine solo Geige wieder gut
machen, die die Stimme begleitet, und bei der ich auf de Bériot speculire.'

[16]   Translated from Citron, *Letters*, 456 (original in GB-Ob, GB III/78): 'Du schreibst über
Deine Gesangscene nur, daß eine obligate Violine für Beriot dabei sey, daraus schließen wir auf
einen Sopran für die Malibran. Paßt der Schlüssel?'

[17]   Unpublished letter from Mendelssohn to Fanny Hensel dated 7 Apr. 1834 (D-B,
Depositum Berlin 2,2): '[U]nd dann ist eine Amerikanerin hier . . . und dann eine Engländerin,
von der ich mir eine englische Bibel geliehen habe, als ich noch nicht wußte, was ich fürs
Philharmonic für ein Gesangstück componiren sollte (das italienische mit *Violino obligé* ist
fertig, u. einige Stellen so gar matt u. so schrecklich in *meiner* Manier, daß du lachen müßtest,
weshalb ich mich freue, daß Du es nicht zu sehen kriegst, Blasinstrumente, die so machen ♪ u.
d.gl.) und dann sind im Singverein 2 Sopranisten, die ich protegiren soll.'

[18]   Letter of 13 Apr. to Klingemann, in Klingemann, *Briefwechsel*, 126.

[19]   Letter of 14 May 1834 to Klingemann (ibid. 131): 'Wer meine Szene singen soll? Sing' Du
sie. Machst es doch noch am Ende besser, als alle Grisetten und Masuren der Welt, denn Du tust

liked the piece, that there would be a rehearsal the following day, and that Maria Caradori-Allan (1800–65) would be the soloist.[20] The première was given at the Philharmonic Society's concert on 19 May 1834, with Caradori-Allan in the soprano role; the violin obbligato was presumably entrusted to concertmaster J. D. Loder, and Thomas Cooke conducted.[21] A second performance, given on 11 April 1836 with the same orchestra and soloists under the direction of Ignaz Moscheles, was the last in the composer's lifetime. By the early 1840s the autograph was bound together with a number of other works from 1832–7 in what became Vol. 28 of the *Mendelssohn Nachlaß* (now Staatsbibliothek zu Berlin — Preußischer Kulturbesitz, Ms.mus.autogr. F. Mendelssohn Bartholdy 28).[22] The score Mendelssohn had sent to the Society is today housed in the library of the Royal Academy of Music in London (MS 171).[23]

Thus, despite the important role they played in its conception, Malibran and de Bériot never performed the 1834 aria.[24] Although it most likely was in good hands in its performances by Caradori-Allan,[25] she possessed neither the brilliant technique nor the popular fame of the soloists Mendelssohn had been 'speculating' on when he wrote the piece. Moreover, the well-known adulterous romance between Malibran and de Bériot would have granted the aria an undeniable topical appeal—especially since Mendelssohn went to considerable lengths in the work to develop an elaborate and obviously amorous

es gern.' The reference to 'Grisette' is most likely a jocular diminutive reference to renowned prima donna Giulia (Giuletta) Grisi (1811–69), who performed Italian numbers by Rossini and Mozart with the Philharmonic Society on several occasions in 1834 and 1835 and was quite popular on the operatic stage in London and Paris between 1832 and 1847; see Foster, *History*, 127, 129, 135; and Elizabeth Forbes, 'Grisi, Giulia', in *New Grove Dictionary of Opera*, ed. Stanley Sadie (London: Macmillan, 1992), ii. 549–50. (The reference to 'Masuren' remains unclear.)

[20] Unpublished letter to Mendelssohn (GB-Ob, GB III/145): 'Tomorrow there is a rehearsal, and your scena will be played, sung by Caradori. I like it [or her] a great deal for this sort of piece.' ('Morgen ist Rehearsal, u Deine Scena wird gemacht, u gesungen von der Caradori. Sie gefällt mir sehr, für seine Art Musikstück.') [21] Foster, *History*, 128.

[22] See App. A ('Mendelssohn's 1844 List of His Music') in Peter Ward Jones, *Catalogue of the Mendelssohn Papers in the Bodleian Library, Oxford*, iii: *Printed Music and Books* (Tutzing: Hans Schneider, 1989), 283–302, esp. 291.

[23] For a closer description of this manuscript see Ward Jones, 'Mendelssohn Scores', 74.

[24] Mendelssohn's statement that he was 'speculating' on de Bériot's participation (see above, n. 15) evidently was entirely accurate: there is no indication that he ever made arrangements to have the piece performed by those two soloists, and Malibran was in Italy at the time of the aria's première.

[25] According to Julian Marshall, '[h]er voice, though not very powerful, was exceedingly sweet and flexible, and her style almost faultless. . . . She always pleased though she never astonished her audience.' Julian Marshall, 'Caradori-Allan, Maria' in *Grove's Dictionary of Music and Musicians*, 5th edn., ed. Eric Blom (New York: St. Martin's, 1955), ii. 56–7.

relationship between the two soloists that in some ways would have paralleled their real-life relationship (see the discussion below).

By contrast, documentation pertaining to the 1843 aria is sparse. The autograph score held in Vol. 38² of the former *Mendelssohn Nachlaß* (now in the Biblioteka Jagiellońska, Kraków) bears the date 15 January 1843. The work is mentioned in a letter from the composer to his brother Paul written two days later, on 17 January:

I want to tell you about the programmes of our upcoming concerts; perhaps one or another of them will appeal to you or Albertine [Paul's wife]. Please share them with Fanny as well, since I promised them to her. . . . On 9 February there is the concert by Mlle [Sophie] Schloß in which Mme [Clara] Schumann and [Gewandhaus concertmaster Ferdinand] David will also perform, individually and together, and in which a new concert aria by me which I have written for Mlle Schloß will be given, and probably also my *Meeresstille* . . .[26]

The work was indeed performed at Sophie Schloß's 'Extraconcert' in the Gewandhaus on 9 February 1843. Mendelssohn referred to it briefly—and ambivalently—in a letter to Ferdinand Hiller dated 3 March 1843.[27] Although no programme from the concert has been available, contemporary reviews and Alfred Dörffel's *Geschichte der Gewandhausconcerte zu Leipzig* clearly refer to the aria as 'new'; since Dörffel's tables of programmes are based on the original ones and the reviewers were clearly responding to information provided in the programme itself, we may safely conclude that the work was billed as 'new' at the time.[28]

Two more performances of the 1843 aria were given during Mendelssohn's lifetime. The first of these was on 26 May 1845, with Moscheles conducting the Philharmonic Society of London, and the second was in Leipzig on 29 October 1846, with the Leipzig Gewandhaus Orchestra under Mendelssohn's direction; both featured Sophie Schloß as soloist.[29] The work was posthumously published in 1851 by Breitkopf & Härtel in Leipzig (with Italian and German text) and Ewer & Co. in London (with Italian and English text).

---

[26] Unpublished letter to Paul Mendelssohn Bartholdy, held in US-NYp: 'Ich will dir unsere nächsten Concertprogramms herschreiben, vielleicht reizt dich oder Albertine doch eins oder das andre; theil sie auch Fanny mit, der ichs versprochen habe. . . . Am 9ten Febr. ist das Concert von Dem. Schloss in dem Mme. Schumann und David jeder einzeln u auch zusammen spielen, in dem eine neue Concert-Arie von mir vorkommt, die ich für Dem. Schloss gemacht habe, u wahrscheinlich auch meine Meeresstille.'

[27] See Ferdinand Hiller, *Felix Mendelssohn-Bartholdy: Briefe und Erinnerungen* (Cologne: M. DuMont-Schauberg, 1874), 170.

[28] Alfred Dörffel, *Geschichte der Gewandhausconcerte zu Leipzig vom 25. November 1781 bis 25. November 1881* (Leipzig: Breitkopf & Härtel, 1884), 215.

[29] Foster, *History*, 191; Dörffel, *Geschichte*, 115.

TWO SINGERS

Mendelssohn's letter of 17 January 1843 is the primary surviving epistolary reference to the 1843 aria, but contemporary reviews and notices provide important information concerning its reception. The anonymous critic of the *Neue Zeitschrift für Musik* devoted most of his review of Schloß's 'Extra-concert' to the other works on the programme, but concluded his remarks by noting that 'the aria by Mendelssohn that Miss Schloß performed was new, and worthy of its master'.[30] In the 'Correspondenz' of the same periodical Ferdinand Präger reported of the 1845 London performance that 'Miss Schloß performed the aria *Unglückselige*, composed especially for her, with excellent expressiveness and her own special energy.'[31] And the Leipzig 1846 perform-ance was reviewed by both the *Neue Zeitschrift* and the *Allgemeine musikalische Zeitung*. Writing for the former, Franz Brendel stated that 'Mendelssohn's aria composed for Miss Schloß' was among the 'most successful' pieces she had performed—also noting, however, that in her performances 'one often com-plains, not without justification, of a lack of warmth in presentation, [and] likewise a purity of intonation in the case of several notes, especially *e″* and *f″* and indeed in passages ascending to the higher notes'.[32] But the most detailed critique was presented by the anonymous reviewer for the more conservative *Allgemeine musikalische Zeitung*:

The aria by *Mendelssohn Bartholdy* possesses a truth of expression, is pleasing to the ear, and is gratifying for the singer. These three attributes, realized fully, comprise the ideal of the German aria. Odd, that German composers most seldom achieve the easiest of these—idiomatic vocal writing—without which the other two cannot reach fulfilment. Fräulein *Schloß*, who is occasionally too calm for artistic achieve-ments, performed this aria with greater warmth of heart, and therefore warmed [the audience] more.[33]

---

[30] 'Concert von Frl. Sophia Schloß', *NZfM* 18 (6 Mar. 1843), 80: 'Die Arie von Mendelssohn war neu und ihres Meisters würdig.'

[31] F[erdinand] Pr[äger], 'Aus London', *NZfM* 23 (28 Oct. 1845), 140: 'Frl. Schloß sang Mendelssohn's für sie eigens componirte Arie "Unglückselige" mit vorzüglichem Ausdruck und der ihr eigenen Energie.'

[32] Fr[anz] Br[endel], 'Leipziger Musikleben', *NZfM* 25 (28 Nov. 1846), 177: 'Wärme des Vortrags vermißt man öfter nicht mit Unrecht, eben so Reinheit der Intonation, was bei einigen Tönen, besonders dem *e* und *f* der zweigestrichenen Octave, und zwar bei Hinaufsteigen in die Höhe, der Fall ist. Zu den gelungensten Leistungen zählen wir den Vortrag der für Frl. Schloß componirten Arie Mendelssohn's . . .'.

[33] [Leipzig] *AMZ* 48 (28 Oct. 1846), col. 734: 'Die Arie von *Mendelssohn Bartholdy* hat Wahrheit des Ausdrucks, ist angenehm dem Ohr, und dankbar für die Sängerin. Diese drei Eigenschaften, in höchster Potenz gedacht, bilden das Ideal der deutschen Arie. Seltsam, dass die deutschen Componisten gerade die leichteste davon, die Gesangmässigkeit, am Seltensten

These remarks provide two key bits of information regarding the 1843 aria. First, they confirm that it was regarded as 'new'—i.e. not a revision of the 1834 aria—by the composer and his contemporaries. Particularly important, then, is Mendelssohn's reference to 'a new concert aria', for (as is well known) he typically went out of his way to make it known that a project represented a revision of something previously composed. And while there are references to revisions that were so extensive that the work became 'completely new' ('ganz neu'), these are always firmly ensconced in the language of revision;[34] the composer's keen awareness of the *Revisionsteufel* or *Revisionskrankheit* that plagued him evidently compelled him to make light of his predilection for extensive revision. That he simply refers to the 1843 aria as 'new' is therefore telling—especially since the earlier aria to which it might be related had been discussed with the family.

Equally important is the phrase 'which I have written for Mlle Schloß' ('die ich für Dem. Schloß gemacht habe'). This phrase clearly shows that the 1843 aria was written with Sophie Schloß in mind and suggests that its music might in some way be tailored to Schloß's abilities and reputation, much as the 1834 aria was musically influenced by its intended association with Malibran and de Bériot. The fact that all three performances of the 1843 aria given during the composer's lifetime featured Schloß as soloist suggests that she (and perhaps Mendelssohn) considered the 1843 work in some sense 'hers'—and contemporary reviewers obviously considered it so.

Now we may assume that Mendelssohn's having written the two arias for different soloists naturally would have affected the music of the works, unless the two sopranos possessed virtually identical voices and techniques. But contemporary accounts portray Maria Malibran and Sophie Schloß as substantially different talents. The Spanish Malibran was celebrated for her dramatic stage presence and the extraordinary strength and flexibility of her voice; parts adapted for her by Bellini and Donizetti show that she commanded the range of g to e'''.[35] She sang alto as well as soprano and male as well as female

erreichen, ohne welche doch die beiden ersten zur vollen Wirkung nicht gelangen können. Fräul. *Schloss*, zuweilen etwas zu ruhig für Kunstleistungen, trug diese Arie mit mehr Wärme des Herzens vor, und erwärmte daher auch mehr.'

[34] For example, his remark to Klingemann on 16 Feb. 1835 that 'I am also struggling with the first movement of the A major Symphony and cannot get it right; it must in any case become completely different—perhaps entirely new . . .' ('Auch am ersten Stück der a-dur Sinfonie knabbere ich und kann es nicht recht kriegen — ganz anders werden muss es auf jeden Fall — vielleicht ganz neu . . .'); Klingmann, *Briefwechsel*, 171. See also his remarks on the *Lobgesang*, quoted below.

[35] See Elizabeth Forbes, 'Malibran [née García], Maria(-Felicia)', in *New Grove Dictionary of Opera*, iii. 166.

parts in a total of thirty-five operas, and was at home in comic as well as tragic roles. Her strongly extroverted personality and her well-publicized affair with de Bériot (whom she married just a few months before her death of complications from a horse-riding accident in 1836) made her the archetypal prima donna—the sort of figure whose personality and exploits fascinate the public as well as the critics. She was a particular favourite in England from 1833, when (singing in English) she introduced Bellini's *La sonnambula* to London audiences.[36] Mendelssohn's own description of her, written after their introduction during his stay in London in 1829, provides ample evidence of his admiration for her talent: 'Malibran can never be praised enough. There are voices the very tone of which can move one to tears, and she has such a voice. With it she sings seriously and passionately and tenderly, and she acts well, too. You should see her!'[37]

Sophie Schloß, on the other hand, was a far different sort of talent. A native of Cologne, Schloß had been introduced to Mendelssohn while he was in Düsseldorf in 1836 for the première of *St Paul*.[38] Although she was barely 14 years old at the time, the composer was able to respond to her father's request for an evaluation of her talent as follows:

Mlle Schloß . . . possesses an exceptionally pretty, strong, resonant mezzo-soprano voice that leaves little to be desired in purity and solidity of tone. Since she has not yet had a complete training of this fine instrument, one could only wish her an opportunity to perfect her skills in matters of technique as well as presentation and pronunciation. . . .[39]

Clearly, Mendelssohn found potential in the young singer's voice; and clearly, he considered her a mezzo-soprano, not a soprano. This assessment evidently endured for the remainder of their relationship: in May 1839 she sang the alto part in Handel's *Messiah* at the Lower Rhine Music Festival in Düsseldorf,

[36] See Elaine Brody, 'Foreword' to Bushnell, *Malibran*, pp. [xi]–xix.

[37] Translated from Devrient, *Erinnerungen*, 80: '[D]ie Malibran [ist] nie genug zu preisen. Es giebt Stimmen, deren bloßer Ton Einen zum Weinen stimmt, eine solche hat sie, und singt damit sehr ernsthaft und feurig und zart, und kann auch spielen. Du solltest sie sehen!'

[38] The following description is adapted from Ulrich Tank, *Die Geschwister Schloss: Studien zur Biographie der Kölner Altistin Sophie Schloss (1822–1902) und zur Geschichte des Musikalienverlages ihres Bruders Michael (1823–1891)* (Beiträge zur rheinischen Musikgeschichte, 115; Cologne: Arno Volk, 1976), 2–24.

[39] Letter of 7 Aug. 1836, quoted from Tank, *Die Geschwister Schloss*, 2–3: 'Dlle. Sophie Schloß . . . besitzt eine ausgezeichnet schöne, kräftige, wohltönende Mezzosopranstimme, die an Reinheit und Gediegenheit des Klanges wenig zu wünschen übriglassen dürfte. Da es ihr bisjetzt noch an völliger Ausbildung dieses schönen Organs gefehlt hat, so wäre ihr nur die Gelegenheit zu wünschen, sich im Technischen des Gesanges, sowol was Fertigkeit als was Vortrag und Aussprache betrifft, noch zu vervollkommnen.'

and later that year Mendelssohn had her engaged as 'zweite Sängerin' of the Gewandhaus—emphasizing, however, that she was qualified only for the position of second singer, not first.[40] For the remainder of his career he continued to programme her for alto parts—most prominently, that in the première of *Die erste Walpurgisnacht* on 2 February 1843, just a week before the première of the 1843 aria. Contemporary accounts further confirm that Schloß cultivated as her speciality Italian cavatinas and vocal scenas, and that she was a mezzo-soprano whose voice tended towards the alto range.[41]

Not surprisingly, the music of the two arias clearly reflects that Mendelssohn was thinking of these two singers as he wrote them. As stated above, there are pronounced and important musical similarities. But while the 1834 aria seems to exploit the versatility, power, and range of Malibran's voice, the 1843 aria is in many ways written to capitalize on the strengths of a more limited soloist. The 1834 aria requires considerable stamina on the part of the soprano, but the 1843 aria is substantially more compact, both in its entirety and in the individual sections. The 1834 aria requires a greater range of dynamics across the tessitura, while the 1843 aria carefully prepares and supports each dynamic change. The 1834 aria continually explores the full vocal tessitura, including the upper fourth to bb'', while the 1843 aria deliberately emphasizes repeated notes in the middle of the register (especially bb'— evidently a good note for Schloß's voice). And while both arias include a long bb'' as the final climax of the work (just before the closing ritornello), the 1843 aria generally avoids or deals gingerly with pitches above f'' (see Brendel's review, quoted above), while its 1834 counterpart celebrates the brilliance and power of that upper register.[42]

These circumstances and comparisons strongly suggest that the differences between the earlier and later aria were not the result of any dissatisfaction with the earlier work, but rather responses to different circumstances, different performers, and different compositional goals. A closer examination of the two compositions corroborates this observation.

---

[40] Letter from Mendelssohn to Kistner and the Directors of the Gewandhaus concerts, 17 June 1839, in Elvers, *Verleger*, 306–7.

[41] See e.g. the review in the Leipzig *AMZ* 41 (29 Apr. 1840), cols. 371–2, of Schloß's performance of 22 Apr. 1840 in the Gewandhaus. The reviewer praises her progress and her diligent study, but continues that 'the voice of Miss Schloss is a mezzo-soprano, which, incidentally, tends strongly towards the alto range, for the lower notes are relatively fuller, more powerful, and generally healthier than the higher ones' ('Die Stimme der Fräul. Schloss ist Mezzo-Sopran, der sich übrigens schon sehr zum Alt neigt, denn die tiefern Töne sind im Verhältniss voller, kräftiger, überhaupt gesunder als die höheren').

[42] This consideration may explain the 1843 aria's otherwise disappointing omission of the leap to g'' in the third bar of the main theme of the Andante; cf. Exx. 3.5 and 3.15, below.

TEXT AND MUSIC OF THE 1834 ARIA

As shown above, Mendelssohn related to Fanny Hensel in February 1834 that he had compiled the text of his aria from 'the most wonderful nonsense of Metastasio' found in four different operas by that master of *opera seria* libretti; the resulting text and its sources are provided in Table 3.1. This composite text reveals that in seeking his material Mendelssohn was clearly proceeding from the *abbandonata* prototype: in the recitative, the speaker laments her betrayal by her lover and the pains engendered by false love, and in the lyrical andante sostenuto, she wistfully recalls their time together and longs for a return of that 'bell'età'. The ensuing allegro vivace is characterized by vacillation among various emotional extremes: first, the speaker scorns her betrayal and laments the ephemerality of happiness; then she recalls the tender pastoral imagery of the andante; and she ultimately returns to the emotional turbulence of the two primary stanzas of the Allegro vivace. Since Metastasio's librettos typically reveal a characteristically Baroque stasis of affect over considerable expanses of verse, we may surmise that Mendelssohn assembled his texts from four different operas precisely in order to maximize the affective variety of these textual sources—i.e. that such dramatic emotional extremes played a central role in his concept of the work.

Not surprisingly, the music of the aria vividly reflects these widely varying affects (see Table 3.2 and Ex 3.1). The work begins in B flat major with a brief,

TABLE 3.1. Text, text sources, and translation for *Infelice!* / *Ah, ritorna, età dell'oro* (1834)

[1.] Recitativo (Allegro vivace)

[*Unidentified source*:]

1	Infelice!	Wretched one!

From Il Trionfo di Clelia, III/3 [*Larissa sola*]:

2	già dal mio sguardo si diliguò! [. . .]	Already he has vanished from my sight!
3	Partì! La mia presenza	He is gone! The guilty one could not
4	l'iniquo non sostenne!	bear my presence!

From Romeolo ed Ersilia, III/5 [*Valeria*]:

5	Rammenta al fine [. . .] i falli,	Remember to the end his wrongdoings,
6	i torti suoi.[a]	his misdeeds.
7	Risveglia la tua virtù!	Summon up your virtue!
8	Scordati l'empio traditor![b]	Forget the cruel traitor!

TABLE 3.1. *continued*

From Giustino IV/7:

9   Amante sventurata[c] —   Betrayed lover —

[*Unidentified source:*]

10   E l'amo pure!   And yet I love him!

From Giustino IV/7:

11   Così, fallace amore, le tue promesse   Is this, false love, how you keep your
       attendi?   promises?

12   Tu non mai rendi la rapita quiete![d]   You will never return to me my stolen
                                             peace!

13   Queste son le speranze, e l'ore   So much for hopes and happy
       liete . . .   hours . . .

[2.] Andante sostenuto

From Il Trionfo di Clelia, III/3:

14   Ah, ritorna, età dell'oro   Ah, return, golden days,

15   alla terra abbandonata,   to this abandoned land,

16   se non fosti immaginata,   if you were not simply imagined

17   nel sognar felicità!   in a happy dream!

From Giustino IV/7:

18   Fu il mondo allor felice   The world was happy then,

19   che un tenero arboscello,   when a tender shrub

20   un limpido ruscello [. . .]   [and] a limpid brook

21   le genti alimentò.   nourished the people.

[3.] Allegro vivace

From Giustino IV/7:

22   D'amor nel regno   In the kingdom

23   non v'è contento   there is no contentment

24   che del tormento   that is not less

25   non sia minor.   than our torment.

26   Si scorge appena   One hardly feels

27   felice speme   happy hope

28   che nuova pena   before a new pain

29   la turba ancor.   disrupts it again.

---

[a]   Metastasio: tuoi.

[b]   Metastasio: Scordati un empio!

[c]   Metastasio: Oh sventurati amanti!

[d]   Metastasio: Nè mai gli rendi la rapita quiete?

TABLE 3.2. Structure of *Infelice!* / *Ah, ritorna, età dell'oro* (1834)

R = Ritornello. For themes, see Ex. 3.1.

Tempo	*Allegro vivace*			*Andante sostenuto*		*Allegro vivace*				
Theme	R(a)	R(b)	Recit.	And. 1	And. 2	R(c)	A1	A2	B1	B2
Key	B♭	B♭→g	g→d: V	d: V→B♭: I	B♭: I-I	g: V→i	g: i→c: i	c: i→g: V	B♭: V^7/ii→I	B♭: I-I
Bars	1	2–18	18–41	42–69	70–141	142–58	158–74	175–86	186–96	197–216

Tempo	(*Allegro vivace*)					*Allegro vivace*			
Theme	R(a)′	R(b)′	Recit.	'Reminiscence'	R(c)′/(A1′)	A2	B1	B2	C
Key	B♭	B♭→F	F	d: i^6_4→F/f	f: i→c: i^6	c: i→g: V	B♭: V^7/ii→I	B♭: I-V	B♭: I-I
Bars	216–17	218–27	227–42	243–58	258–76	277–86	286–96	297–312	312–28

Tempo	(*Allegro vivace*)	*Andante come 1ma*	*Allegro come 1ma*			
Theme	R(b)‴	And. 2′	B1′	R(a)‴	R(b)‴	R(a)⁗
Key	B♭: I→I^6_4	B♭: I→V	B♭: V→I	B♭: I-I	B♭: I-I	B♭: I-I
Bars	328–38	338–43	343–61	361–2	363–6	366–9

Ex. 3.1. *Infelice! / Ah, ritorna, età dell'oro* (1834): (*a*) first main theme group;
(*b*) second main theme group; (*c*) third main theme

sharply defined rhythmic motif and a running figure of doubled eighth notes
stated in imitation in the strings, complemented by a counter-idea consisting
of quarter notes leading to each down-beat. With a dramatic crescendo, this
introduction veers into G minor to prepare the entry of the solo voice, the
scene-setting exclamation of 'Wretched one! Already he has vanished from
my sight! He is gone; the guilty one could not bear my presence!' ('Infelice! già
dal mio sguardo si diliguò! Partì! La mia presenza l'iniquo non sostenne!');
see Ex. 3.2. The unsettled character suggested by the running doubled eighth
notes begins to change to one of resignation as the speaker implores 'Is this,
false love, how you keep your promises?' ('Così, fallace amore, le tue pro-
messi attendi?'), and a modulation to D minor occurs as she despairs of any
future 'hopes and happy hours' ('Queste son le speranze, e l'ore liete'); see
Ex. 3.3.

The Andante further extends this process of musical characterization, suggesting that the persona of the speaker represented by the solo soprano is complemented by that of her former lover, symbolized by the obbligato violin.
Beginning with a series of exchanges between the woodwind choir and the

EX. 3.2. *Infelice! / Ah, ritorna, età dell'oro* (1834), introduction and
beginning of recitative, bars 1–20

solo violin, with the former adumbrating the main theme of the Andante and
the latter answering with a series of ascending arpeggios, this introduction
modulates from D minor to the dominant of B flat major, ending with a fermata on a half cadence with the solo violin perched on the dominant in its
highest, sweetest register (Ex. 3.4, bars 46–50). The violin then states the main
theme of the andante over a simple accompaniment of strings and sparse
woodwinds (Ex. 3.4, bars 51 ff.) and cadences in B flat major, whereupon the

Ex. 3.2. *continued*

theme is restated by the soprano solo over similar accompaniment, but without the solo violin, in bar 70 (Ex. 3.5). In bar 78 the violin re-emerges with a
countermelody derived from that presented in bar 58 by the woodwinds, and
the two personae appear together, but initially with little direct musical interaction, with a new theme at the pastoral imagery of 'the world was happy then,
when a tender shrub [and] a limpid brook nourished the people' ('Fu il mondo
allor felice, che un tenero arboscello, un limpido ruscello le genti alimentò').
They then engage in a closely intertwined exchange on this pastoral imagery
in bars 95 ff., and the section closes with a finely wrought dialogue/duet on
the main theme of the Andante (Ex. 3.6).

The elaborate development involved in this marvellously crafted passage
deserves attention for two reasons. First of all, in creating two different
personae—the one associated with the solo soprano, the other with the solo
violin—Mendelssohn obviously reinforced the association of the work with
its intended performers, for the interest of its intended audience; for although,
as mentioned above, Malibran and de Bériot were not yet married in 1834,
their affair was quite well known, and a performance of the work featuring the
two of them in such conspicuously amatory solo roles inevitably would have

Ex. 3.3. *Infelice! / Ah, ritorna, età dell'oro* (1834), end of recitative, bars 27–41

Ex. 3.4. *Infelice! / Ah, ritorna, età dell'oro* (1834), end of
introduction to Andante sostenuto, bars 46–69

benefitted from the public's awareness of their personal romantic relationship. Secondly, since the development of the lovers' relationship graphically
depicted in the andante is entirely absent (or at best an undeveloped thing of
the past) in the text, the creation and development of that relationship was
obviously an important consideration in Mendelssohn's composition of the
aria—a typically romantic act of musical intervention, intended to add a
dimension that did not exist or was only implied in the original source. Such
interventions are by nature assertions of a composer's identity, confirmations

Ex. 3.4. *continued*

of a romantically individualized reinterpretation of an original that otherwise would have been familiar to the public only in a substantially different guise, if at all.

Initially, the ensuing allegro vivace returns to the more straightforward style of text setting established in the opening recitative (see Ex. 3.7). The opening rhythmic motif returns, now stated in G minor, *piano*, and in imitation at the fifth, followed by a return of running doubled eighth notes in the strings (a different figure, but nevertheless clearly allusive because of its scoring, scalar nature, and rhythmic character). This figure serves as the basis of a crescendo leading to the first stanza of the allegro vivace, also in G minor; the emotional agitation characteristic of the allegro as a whole is again vividly reflected in the string figurations and the harmonic instability of this passage. At bar 158 the soprano re-enters, beginning *piano* (*agitato*) and realizing a crescendo leading to bar 166; a series of *sf–p* climaxes on V⁹ chords, first in D minor and then in C minor, tonally underscores her emotional turmoil, and the affective turbulence of this passage is further enhanced by the emphasis on melodic diminished fifths (see bars 167, 169, 171, 173, and 181 of the vocal part in Ex. 3.7). The stanza concludes with a half-cadence in G minor, at the

Ex. 3.5. *Infelice! / Ah, ritorna, età dell'oro* (1834), Andante sostenuto,
bars 70–96

Ex. 3.5. *continued*

forceful homophonic setting of 'Non sia minor!', whereupon the second primary text stanza begins with the dominant-seventh harmony of C minor (supertonic in the new key of B flat; see Ex. 3.7, bars 186–8). This stanza, too, is set as an increasingly agitated crescendo; ultimately, it confirms the main key of B flat major with a modified return of the opening ritornello in bar 216—thus marking the mid-point of the aria.

The second half initially increases the drama by restating the first two lines of the primary stanza ('D'amore nel regno' etc.) with a new, broadly arching theme in a key possessed of greater tonal tension, F major (Ex. 3.8). The dramatic urgency subsides, however, with a momentary discursion into D minor—a 'reminiscence episode' in which the solo violin and soprano in alternation take up again the pastoral idea of the Andante wherein they were first joined: 'the world was happy then, when a tender plant [and] a limpid

Ex. 3.5. *continued*

brook nourished the people' (see Ex. 3.9).[43] The reminiscence implicitly becomes more real as the music returns to F major, the key from which it initially departed, with clear cadences in bars 253–4 and 257–8. But the cadence in bar 258 abruptly turns to F minor, and the resumption of the *agitato* running doubled eighth notes in the strings reveals that the episode was only a fleeting daydream, not an actual return of the longed-for times past.

The end of the reminiscence episode seems to mark a crucial recognition for the speaker and a dramatic turning point in the composition, for the *agitato*

[43]   That this episode represents a reminiscence (utterly absent in Metastasio's text) is confirmed by the unexpected return of the violin solo; what is more, the melodic idea exchanged between the soprano and the solo violin at the beginning of this passage strongly resembles the melody assigned to 'e l'ore liete' at the end of the recitative (cf. bars 245–50 of Ex. 3.9 and bars 40–1 of Ex. 3.3).

Ex. 3.6. *Infelice!* / *Ah, ritorna, età dell'oro* (1834), Andante sostenuto,
bars 115–41

Ex. 3.6. *continued*

Ex. 3.6. *continued*

mood prevails to the end. The text with which the Allegro vivace began ('D'amore nel regno', etc.) is now set as a series of short, breathless, modulatory phrases rather than a bona fide melody; the restatements of sections A2, B1, B2, and C (see Ex. 3.1) are all modified to heighten tension, primarily through increased harmonic instability; and the final statement of section C dissolves into a crescendo based on the turbulent material of the opening ritornello—with the quarter-note counter-idea now entrusted to the solo soprano, who repeatedly exclaims 'disrupts it again' ('la turba ancor'). The climax of this protracted *Steigerung*—a tonic 6/4 chord with a fermata (a clear opportunity for a cadenza by Malibran)—is followed by a brief return of the Andante featuring the solo soprano and solo violin—a reflective entreaty for a return of that 'bell'età' (see Ex. 3.10). The plea remains unanswered, however, and the aria closes with a series of reiterated cries of 'Ah, ritorna!', set to a modified version of B1 (Ex. 3.10, b. 343) and followed by a final turbulent statement of the doubled-eighth-note figure (Ex. 3.10, b. 363).

Two further observations regarding the 1834 aria should be offered here. First, while it is considerably more ambitious in scope, scoring, and affective range than Mendelssohn's most important previous concert aria, *Ch'io t'abbandono*,[44] it further corroborates the earlier aria's demonstration of Mendelssohn's mastery of styles and techniques evocative of the warm lyricism of Italian opera. Secondly, several striking musical features suggest that it took

[44] Composed in 1825 for baritone and piano and based on a text by Metastasio and still unpublished; the autograph survives as MS 1444a of the Heinemann Collection in US-NYpm.

Ex. 3.7. *Infelice! / Ah, ritorna, età dell'oro* (1834), Allegro vivace,
bars 142–91

Ex. 3.7. *continued*

as its prototype Beethoven's concert aria *Ah, perfido! / Per pietà, non dirmi addio*, a well-known *abbandonata* aria with which Mendelssohn certainly was familiar. The directness of some of the allusions clearly invites such a comparison. Although broad similarities such as both arias' abrupt recollection of their respective slow themes at the end might be dismissed as coincidental, the strong motivic orientation of Mendelssohn's aria certainly suggests a relation to Beethoven's. Moreover, such similarities are less easily dismissed in view of the striking resemblance between the opening ritornellos and recitatives of the two arias (cf. Ex. 3.2, above, and Ex. 3.11).

Ex. 3.7. *continued*

TEXT AND MUSIC OF THE 1843 ARIA

As stated above, most previous commentators on Mendelssohn's 1843 *Infelice* aria have treated it as an extension of the 1834 aria, explaining its compositional history by relying on the Philharmonic Society commission of November 1832 and Mendelssohn's 1834 correspondence. Yet the composer's letter concerning the 1843 aria clearly shows that he viewed it as a 'new' piece composed for Sophie Schloß rather than for Malibran, de Bériot, and the London orchestra. This autonomy is also reflected in the substantially

Ex. 3.7. *continued*

different texts and textual sources employed, especially after the recitative (see Table 3.3).

Considered more closely, too, the 1843 aria proves to be substantially less directly related to the 1834 one than has previously been assumed. Although the opening ritornello clearly takes its 1834 counterpart as a point of departure (see Ex. 3.12), there as in the main Allegro the *agitato* character is achieved primarily through throbbing repeated notes, used in place of the cascading doubled eighth notes and widely arching melodies of the earlier aria (cf. Ex. 3.2, above, and Ex. 3.13). The recitative emphasizes different lines via repetition than does the recitative in the earlier aria, and inserts 'and yet I cannot hate him' ('e pur odiar nol posso ancor') while downplaying 'and yet I love him' ('e l'amo pur?'). The Andante does not present a graphic development of the lovers' past relationship, but remains firmly grounded in the present; rather than becoming lost in her memories, as seems to be the case in the 1834 Andante, the speaker is consciously aware that she is reminiscing: 'Ah, if I look around I am always reminded of the day he vowed to be true to me' ('Ah! Se volgo gli occhi intorno mi rammento sempre il giorno che riceve la sua fè'). And the main allegro is based on three ideas that admit little relation to the five ideas of the Allegro of the 1834 aria (cf. Ex. 3.1, above, Table 3.4, and Ex. 3.14).

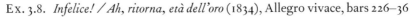

Ex. 3.8. *Infelice! / Ah, ritorna, età dell'oro* (1834), Allegro vivace, bars 226–36

Each of these differences affects a fundamental aspect of the 1843 aria. First of all, in the ritornello and subsequent passages the replacement of running melodic lines and expansively crafted melodies with repeated notes appreciably diminishes the lyricism of the composition as a whole. Secondly, the more modest scenic import of the Andante eliminates the need for the elaborate development of the lovers' relationship that characterized the 1834 Andante; although the violin obbligato part certainly would have been in good hands at the 1843 aria's first performance, featuring Ferdinand David in the solo role,[45]

---

[45]   Indeed, in the letter in which he mentions the aria Mendelssohn also points out that the concert featured David as soloist and with Clara Schumann; see above, at n. 26.

Ex. 3.9. *Infelice! / Ah, ritorna, età dell'oro* (1834), Allegro vivace, 'reminiscence episode' (bars 240–58)

the creation of such a symbolic solo persona would have been counterproductive to the more restrained character of the episode in the later work (see Ex. 3.15). Third, in dispensing with the affective extremes that so strongly influenced the music of its 1834 counterpart, the text of the 1843 aria requires a more stylistically consistent musical language in the main Allegro; consequently, the three ideas that convey the two textual stanzas of the main Allegro are more homogeneous. In addition, since the 1843 text continually emphasizes the speaker's enduring fury and her longing for a consolation hitherto denied, all the themes of the 1843 aria retain the sense of dramatic urgency created by persistent repeated notes in the accompaniment, and all are characterized by a certain tonal ambivalence, employing internal modulations without prominent cadential gestures.

Ex. 3.9. *continued*

Still more important is that the different text for the last stanza of the 1843 aria makes possible a final resolution entirely absent in its 1834 counterpart: 'And yet just the memory of those love-filled days can soothe this bitter grief!' ('e pur la memoria dei giorni d'amore l'amaro dolore può sol consolar'). Mendelssohn must have recognized that these lines carried within them the seed of resolution. Consequently, during the first part of the aria he created and exploited a musical style that treated that resolution as only a potentiality, but after the return of the Andante he musically depicted the consolation that, according to the text, was possible simply because of the memory of that time: theme B from the main Allegro, formerly in G minor, is now presented firmly in B flat major, as the subject of the coda (cf. bars 124 ff. of Ex. 3.13, below, and Ex. 3.16). The consolation so emphatically denied in the 1834 aria is thus

Ex. 3.10. *Infelice! / Ah, ritorna, età dell'oro* (1834), conclusion (bars 329–69)

granted in the 1843 aria—again, a romantic interpretative intervention that transforms the work's essentially static composite text into an end-weighted gesture whose goal and culmination is the resolution of the speaker's emotional conflicts in the final bars of the work.

Finally, the 1843 aria represents a substantially different assertion of authorial identity. Although the more modest demands of the vocal part may be due largely to differences between the two soloists' techniques and abilities, the elimination of the musically and scenically effective violin obbligato must

Ex. 3.10. *continued*

represent an independent compositional decision on the part of the composer, at least in part a response to the different text of the Andante. The choice of texts itself reflects the emphasis on resolution of conflict that had become a central part of Mendelssohn's cultural agenda by the early 1840s.[46] And while the allusions to Beethoven's *Ah, perfido!* may still be obliquely present, the musical style of the 1843 aria reveals little of the self-conscious attempt to

---

[46] See Leon Botstein, 'The Aesthetics of Assimilation and Affirmation: Reconstructing the Career of Felix Mendelssohn', in *MHW*, 5–42.

Ex. 3.10. *continued*

evoke Italianate lyricism that characterizes the 1834 composition.[47] In short, while *Infelice! / Ah, ritorna, età dell'oro* impresses as a deliberate attempt to invite association with a number of other personalities and issues (Malibran, de Bériot, and their romance; contemporary Italian opera; and Beethoven),

---

[47] It is perhaps significant that in the early 1830s, when he composed *Infelice! / Ah, ritorna, età dell'oro*, Mendelssohn still seems to have been considering composing Italian opera, while any such plans had been long since set aside when he composed the 1843 aria; see R. Larry Todd,

Ex. 3.11. Beethoven, *Ah, perfido! / Per pietà, non dirmi addio*, bars 1–16

Infelice! / Ah, ritorna, età felice reveals few such allusive gestures. Rather, the 1843 aria proceeds from its own circumstances and reflects the general cultural values that by the 1840s had emerged as central to Mendelssohn's compositional personality.

'On Mendelssohn's Operatic Destiny: *Die Lorelei* Reconsidered', in Schmidt, *Kongreß-Bericht*, 113–40, esp. 138–9. See also Monika Hennemann's discussion of the role of national identity in Mendelssohn's search for a suitable operatic subject, in her essay in this volume, Ch. 9.

TABLE 3.3.   Text, text sources, and translation for *Infelice! / Ah, ritorna, età felice* (1843)

[. . .] = textual deletion from 1834 aria; _____ = textual addition to 1834 aria; **[*text*]** = textual replacement

[1.] Recitativo (Allegro vivace)

[*Unidentified source:*]

1	Infelice!	Wretched one!

From Il Trionfo di Clelia, III/3 [Larissa sola]:

2	già dal mio sguardo si diliguò! [. . .]	Already the wicked man has vanished from my sight!
3	[. . .] La mia presenza	The guilty one could not
4	l'iniquo non sostenne!	bear my presence!

[*Unidentified:*]

5	E pur odiar nol posso ancor!	And yet I cannot hate him!

From Romeolo ed Ersilia, III/5 [Valeria]:

6	Rammenta al fine [. . .] i falli,	Remember to the end his wrongdoings,
7	i torti suoi.ᵃ	his misdeeds.
8	Risveglia la tua virtù!	Summon up your virtue!
9	Scordati l'empio traditore!ᵇ	Forget the cruel traitor!

From Giustino IV/7:

10	Amante sventurataᶜ –	Betrayed lover –

[*Unidentified source:*]

11	E l'amo pur?	And yet I love him!

From Giustino IV/7:

12	Così, fallace amore, le tue promesse attendi?	Is this, false love, how you keep your promises?
13	Tu non mai rendi la rapita quiete!ᵈ	You will never return to me my stolen peace!
14	Queste son le speranze, e l'ore liete . . .	So much for hopes and happy hours . . .

[2.] Andante sostenuto

From Il Trionfo di Clelia, III/3:

15	Ah, ritorna, età felice,	Ah, return, happy days,

[*Unidentified:*]

16	*Quando accanto del mio bene*	***when, at my lover's side,*
17	*non conosci queste pene,*	*I knew nothing of this pain,*
18	*quando a me fù fido ancor.*	*when he was still faithful to me.*
19	*Ah, se volgo gli occhi intorno*	*Ah, if I look around myself*

TABLE 3.3. *continued*

20	*mi rammento sempre il giorno*	*I am always reminded of the day*
21	*che riceve la sua fè,* **	*on which he promised to be true to me,* **

From Giustino IV/7:

22	***che 'l** tenero arboscello,*	*when a tender shrub*
23	***che 'l** limpido ruscello [. . .]*	*[and] a limpid brook*

**[*Unidentified:*]

24	*parlami del suo amor.* **	*spoke to me of his love.*

[3.] Allegro vivace

**[*Unidentified:*]

25	[*Invan! Invano!*	**[*In vain! In vain!*

[*From Giustino IV/7:*]

26	*non v'è contento*	*there is no contentment*
27	*senza tormento*	*without torment*
28	*nell'amor.*	*in love.*

[*Unidentified:*]

29	*E pur la memoria*	*And yet the memory*
30	*dei giorni d'amore*	*of those love-filled days*
31	*l'amaro dolore*	*alone can soothe*
32	*può sol consolar.*]**	*this bitter grief.*]**

---

[a] Metastasio: tuoi.
[b] Metastasio: Scordati un empio!
[c] Metastasio: Oh sventurati amanti!
[d] Metastasio: Nè mai gli rendi la rapita quiete?

CONCLUSIONS: IDENTITY

Clearly, the relationship between these two works is more complicated than the conventional interpretation admits. Although the commonalities listed above (key, ensemble, shared passages of text and music, proximity to another important act of compositional revision) are obvious and important, they are also elusively general—for the most part, matters of gesture more than of substance. After all, by publishing neither aria Mendelssohn granted definitive authority to neither. Moreover, the two arias were obviously written for entirely different soloists and orchestras, and their composition was invited by different circumstances in different countries, a

Ex. 3.12. *Infelice! / Ah, ritorna, età felice* (1843), introduction
and beginning of recitative, bars 1–25

decade apart. In connection with its intended vocal soloist, the later work
was described by the composer and his contemporaries as 'new'. The two
arias employ substantially different texts, taken from different sources. The
music to which these texts are set differs greatly. And the works' large-scale
dramatic gestures differ fundamentally: the early aria celebrates the affective
extremes occasioned by a consolation that is emphatically denied, while
the later aria dwells on a single affect, explores that affect while striving
relentlessly for consolation, and ultimately does achieve consolation. For
all their textual and musical overlappings and general stylistic similarities,

EX. 3.12. *continued*

therefore, I am uncomfortable describing these two arias as anything more
—or less—than closely related but autonomous responses to a single general compositional challenge. They are thus more obviously parallel to, for
example, Mendelssohn's settings of Psalm 42 and Psalm 43[48] in the nature

[48] In the Lutheran Bible, Psalms 42 and 43 share verses 12 and 5 respectively (verses 11 and 5
in the Authorized Version): 'Was betrübst du dich, meine Seele, und bist so unruhig in mir?
Harre auf Gott; denn ich werde ihm noch danken, daß er meines Angesichts Hilfe und mein Gott
ist' ('Why art thou cast down, O my soul? And why art thou disquieted within me? Hope thou
in God: for I shall yet praise Him who is the health of my countenance, and my God').
Mendelssohn's setting of Psalm 42 (composed in 1837 and published as Op. 42 in 1838/9) and his
setting of Psalm 43 (composed in 1844 and posthumously published as Op. 78 No. 2 in 1849) likewise share this text and use the same music for all shared material.

Ex. 3.13. *Infelice! / Ah, ritorna, età felice* (1843),
Allegro assai vivace, bars 99–128

of their interrelationship than they are to the 1832 and 1843 versions of the *Walpurgisnacht.*

If one accepts that the relationship between the arias is indeed more nuanced and complex than has been previously assumed, several other issues necessarily arise. The first of these concerns the relationship between authorial identity and musical identity. Clearly, Mendelssohn hinged his suggestion of his own authorial identity and authorial intention on different circumstantial considerations in each of these two works—or, to put it differently, each

Ex. 3.13. *continued*

was critically influenced by such considerations. The 1834 aria was the work of an unknown (if also prodigious) quantity in European musical life, a musical *Wunderkind* who, confined to his newly acquired post in the sleepy Rhineland province of Düsseldorf, stood only to benefit from association with international celebrity. By contrast, the 1843 aria was written at the early height of Mendelssohn's professional prestige, a point at which he hardly needed to stand on the shoulders of other giants. Writing for a talented younger singer whom he had endorsed for nearly a decade, he penned an aria that corresponded to Schloß's area of specialization—an aria that was not only more compact and in no way dependent on the sharing of soloistic

Ex. 3.13. *continued*

Ex. 3.14. *Infelice! / Ah, ritorna, età felice* (1843):
(*a*) first main theme; (*b*) second main theme; (*c*) third main theme

TABLE 3.4. Structure of *Infelice!* / *Ah, ritorna, età felice* (1843)

R = Ritornello. For themes, see Ex. 3.14.

Tempo	Allegro vivace			Andante	Allegro assai vivace			
Theme	R(a)	R(b)	Recit.	And.	R(c)	A	B	C
Key	Bb	Bb→g: V	g: i→d: V→Bb: V	Bb: I→V	g: V→i	g: i→V	g: i→Bb: V	Bb: V⁷/IV→I
Bars	1–2	3–15	15–48	49–98	99–108	109–24	125–40	141–63

Tempo	(Allegro assai vivace)					Andante	Allegro assai vivace	
Theme	R(c)'	R(c)"/(c)	A	B	C	And.	B'	R(a)'
Key	Bb: I→g: V	g:–i⁶→V⁷	g:V⁷–V⁷	g: i→Bb: V	Bb: V/IV→vii°⁷/V	Bb: V⁷–V⁷	Bb: V⁷→I	Bb: I–I
Bars	163–71	172–9	180–200	201–18	219–35	236–41	242–63	264–70

Ex. 3.15. *Infelice! / Ah, ritorna, età felice* (1843),
Andante con moto, bars 49–73

Ex. 3.15. *continued*

display with a violinist, but also better suited to her strengths and acknowledged limitations.

   In short, these two works were not just influenced by contextual or circumstantial considerations; they were *defined* by them. They do not essentially
share a single identity and represent varying, and variously authoritative,
manifestations of that identity, as the conventional interpretation assumes.
Rather, they are autonomous works whose respective identities derive
from the circumstances under which they were composed, the performers
for whom they were written, and the composer's awareness of those factors.
This observation has important ramifications because it explicitly contradicts
a primary tenet of the editorial philosophy of the *Fassung letzter Hand*:

Ex. 3.16. *Infelice! / Ah, ritorna, età felice* (1843),
conclusion (bars 227–70)

the notion that the latest authorial version, regardless of the context in which it was created, represents the best (or at any rate 'most authorized') version.

The latter point is also supported, in Mendelssohn's case at least, by the issue of public vs. private dissemination. Since in the nineteenth century the printing of a musical artwork represented a crucial step in transforming it from a private creation to public property, the step of publication was by its nature one that had to be taken seriously. (Certainly this accounts at least partially for Mendelssohn's reported reference to his *Heidenrespekt vor dem*

EX. 3.16. *continued*

Druck,[49] his insistence that one should publish only if one was able to keep a steady stream of quality compositions before the public and his resulting refusal to talk his sister Fanny into publishing,[50] and his release of few of his mature compositions in print.) But a composer's failure to publish a given

[49] See Devrient, *Erinnerungen*, 76.

[50] This is of course among the thorniest issues in the Mendelssohn siblings' biographies; it is worth mentioning that my phrase 'talk his sister Fanny into publishing' reflects Mendelssohn's use—and underscoring—of the German verb *zureden*. The word does mean 'to persuade', as previous translations have always rendered it, but (unlike, for example, *überzeugen*) it is used only when one expects to encounter opposition—i.e. when one has to talk someone else into doing something. For a new examination of this situation, see Marian Wilson Kimber, ' "For Art

Ex. 3.16. *continued*

piece indicates only that he did not consider it appropriate for general dissemination in association with his public persona at the time of publication.[51] It does not belie the fact that many such works were privately disseminated *with* his authorization, nor does it necessarily imply any intrinsic deficiency in the works and variants that were privately disseminated, posthumously published, or not printed at all.

Finally, there is the issue of the relevance (or lack thereof) of latest authorial versions—the core of the editorial philosophy of the *Fassung letzer Hand*. The concept that the latest version of an artwork was the definitive one emerged only in the second decade of the nineteenth century and was not generally accepted until the last third of the century. The external force that prompted the emergence of this editorial philosophy was the necessity of editorial choice, created by the vast expansion of the publishing industry, in

Has the Same Place in your Heart as Mine": Family, Friendship, and Community in the Life of Felix Mendelssohn', in *Companion*, 29–85. See also the essays by R. Larry Todd and Françoise Tillard in this volume, Chs. 12 and 14.

[51] On this point, see especially Douglass Seaton, 'The Problem of the Lyric Persona in Mendelssohn's Songs', in Schmidt, *Kongreß-Bericht*, 167–86, esp. 179–86. For a useful case study of this issue vis-à-vis Mendelssohn's *Two Byron Romances*, see Monika Hennemann, 'Mendelssohn and Byron: Two Songs almost without Words', *Mendelssohn-Studien*, 10 (1997), 131–56.

music as elsewhere, in the nineteenth century.[52] With the (reluctant) exception of Goethe,[53] the intellectual environment of Mendelssohn's upbringing was predominantly opposed to such a concept; in this view, publication reified the essence of the artwork (or text) and divorced it of the contextual considerations that occasioned it and constituted its aesthetic validity.[54]

The criterion of the *Fassung letzter Hand* therefore remains an anachronistic one—an editorial, not authorial, construct that removes from consideration *a priori* the artist's own understanding of the nature and aesthetic validity of an artwork and its various sources. It functions primarily as a criterion for textual critics and editors who feel compelled to produce a single, authoritative (if not always authorized) version of the text of an artwork. It is a theoretical framework that predetermines the way in which the historical reality represented by various works' different compositional histories will be interpreted.

Since the editorial philosophy of the *Fassung letzter Hand* gained widespread acceptance only well after Mendelssohn's death, we must recognize that it need not bear on our understanding of the relative authority of any variant versions of any of his works—or those of any other early nineteenth-century composer.[55] It is a philosophy whereby theoretical consistency (the

---

[52] For a brief overview of the history of this philosophy and an exploration of some important problems occasioned by it, see Allan C. Dooley, 'Varieties of Textual Change in the Victorian Era', *Text: Transactions of the Society for Textual Scholarship*, 6 (1994), 225–47; further, Jerome J. McGann, *A Critique of Modern Textual Criticism* (Charlottesville: University Press of Virginia, 1992); and several essays in Gunter Martens and Hans Zeller (eds.), *Texte und Varianten: Probleme ihrer Edition und Interpretation* (Munich: C. H. Beck, 1971).

[53] Although Goethe did participate in the production of some volumes of the *Ausgabe letzter Hand* of his works, he was keenly aware of the organic development of works over time, taking care to preserve the earlier versions along with their later counterparts, and thus providing substantially more information regarding the compositional histories of many of his works than most writers do. My thanks to Julie D. Prandi for her useful insights regarding Goethe's attitudes towards publishing and variant versions of his works.

[54] The classic study of the ramifications of printing and publishing for the nature of a text and the relationship between authors and their readers, Elizabeth Eisenstein's *The Printing Press as an Agent of Change: Communications and Cultural Transformations in Early Modern Europe* (Cambridge: Cambridge University Press, 1979), suggested that fixity was a virtually immediate consequence of print cultures. This suggestion has recently been eloquently challenged by Adrian Johns in *The Nature of the Book: Print and Knowledge in the Making* (Chicago: University of Chicago Press, 1998). Johns's documentation of the fact that textual fixity and the consequent fixity of authorial identity were comparatively recent developments with serious detractors further buttresses the view that such deep-seated reservations were part and parcel of Mendelssohn's aesthetic outlook.

[55] Jeffery Kallberg has already explored the implications of this situation in the œuvre of Frédéric Chopin; see Jeffery Kallberg, 'Are Variants a Problem? "Composer's Intentions" in Editing Chopin', *Chopin Studies*, 3 (1990), 257–67; repr. as 'The Chopin "Problem": Simultaneous

highly questionable notion that the latest version of an artwork is always the one that the author considered best or most successful) assumes priority over the often complicated realities posed by the various sources for an artwork. The question begs: are chronology, authority, and quality quite so synonymous? (I, for one, would hesitate to suggest that the 1834 *Infelice* is substantively inferior to its 1843 counterpart—and there certainly is no clear evidence that Mendelssohn felt it was.)

The answers to this question involve issues of circumstantially defined authorial intention, circumstantially imparted aesthetic integrity, and circumstantially defined artistic identity—and they suggest that the largely anachronistic editorial philosophy of the *Fassung letzter Hand* is inadequate for dealing with at least some of Mendelssohn's works and their sources. In so doing, they argue for a more nuanced procedure in evaluating the authority of Mendelssohn's compositions, as well as the autonomy of variant readings. It thus seems advisable to differentiate among three classes of compositions as we edit and perform his works.

First, and most straightforward, are the instances in which Mendelssohn explicitly rejected one version of a work in favour of another version or expressed his preference for one version or the other. Among such compositions is the symphony-cantata *Lobgesang*.[56] After the second performance the composer decided that the work required revision and asked the intended English publisher, Vincent Novello, to delay the work's printing until the revisions had been made. Novello, however, arranged for a performance of the first version by the Philharmonic Society of London. Furious,

Variants and Alternate Versions', in Jeffrey Kallberg, *Chopin at the Boundaries: Sex, History, and Musical Genre* (Cambridge, Mass.: Harvard University Press, 1996), 215–28; further, 'Chopin in the Marketplace', ibid. 161–214. Of course, if one sees the issue of performance medium as a criterion for identity in nineteenth-century music, then the vast sea of arrangements and transcriptions—many of which were prepared, authorized, and published by their composers—for different instruments (especially piano and piano duet, with or without one or more obbligato instruments) becomes unavoidable. No work has been done on this issue in connection with Mendelssohn, although both cello sonatas (Opp. 45 and 58) were also published as violin sonatas a year after their original appearance and the 'Ave Maria' Op. 23 No. 2 was published in a second edition with written-out organ part and added parts for clarinets, bassoons, cello, and bass, in the event the organ was not used. A similar situation obtains in Robert Schumann's œuvre, as is evident from the existence of the *Adagio and Allegro*, Op. 70, and the *Fantasiestücke*, Op. 73 in versions for cello as well as their original media (horn and clarinet, respectively, with piano), and of the Cello Concerto in an equally authorized version for violin; see Joachim Draheim, ' "Dies Concert ist auch für Violine transscribirt erschienen": Robert Schumanns Cellokonzert und seine neuentdeckte Fassung für Violine', *NZfM* 148 (1987), 4–10.

[56] For a more detailed discussion of the '*Lobgesang* affair' see Peter Ward Jones, 'Mendelssohn and his English Publishers', in R. Larry Todd (ed.), *Mendelssohn Studies* (Cambridge: Cambridge University Press, 1992), 240–55, esp. 249–50.

Mendelssohn demanded that Novello return the score of the original version to Klingemann, and wrote:

You cannot believe how terribly angry such a performance would make me, since you do not know the new pieces. With them the whole thing becomes a totally different work, and comes so much closer to my original conception and expresses it so much more clearly, that any repetition of the old version is a real injustice and an insult to me.[57]

In the absence of later variant readings (which must be considered on their own terms), cases such as this clearly should be approached according to the criterion of the *Fassung letzter Hand*—for Mendelssohn explicitly rejected the earlier variant, even as he granted it status as 'a totally different work'.[58]

More problematical from an editorial standpoint are works that survive in multiple chronologically discrete versions, but for which we do not have an explicit rejection of the earlier version(s) from the composer himself. The most obvious candidates for this class of composition are the many Lieder that Mendelssohn wrote out on various occasions in different versions, sometimes varying only in 'accidentals'[59] and sometimes more substantively. Since works and variant readings in this class are authorized and not rejected, each surviving version possesses its own validity that was never repudiated by the composer. Applying the theory of the *Fassung letzter Hand* to such works amounts to denying the validity of Mendelssohn's own judgement that each version was successful and worthy of presentation.[60]

Finally, there are the works Mendelssohn left unpublished at his death. These works are the ones most notoriously fraught with peril for the editor, since Mendelssohn granted definitive authority to none of them and to no version of any of them. It is in these cases that issues of musical identity and

---

[57] Letter to Karl Klingemann of 15 Mar. 1841, translated from Klingemann, *Briefwechsel*, 260: 'Du glaubst nicht, wie mich eine solche Aufführung so schrecklich ärgern würde, weil Du die neuen Sachen nicht kennst. Das ganze Stück wird dadurch wirklich ein andres, und kommt meiner ursprünglichen Idee so viel näher, drückt sie so ungleich deutlicher und besser aus, dass mir jede Wiederholung des alten, ein wahres Unrecht, eine wahre Beleidigung antut.'

[58] Obviously, this category pertains primarily to works published by Mendelssohn himself, although similar considerations would also preclude a performance of, for example, the original reading of posthumously published works such as the 'Reformation' Symphony. For new perspectives on the deleted material in Op. 107 and its significance, see Wolfgang Dinglinger's essay in this volume, Ch. 5.

[59] I use the term in its broader sense, corresponding to its application to matters of punctuation, capitalization, and format in literary texts. In evaluating musical texts, the term may be understood to denote any or all of the following: tempo, phrasings and articulations, dynamic and expressive indications, and even beamings and voice-leadings.

[60] For a discussion of the aesthetic problems posed by 'occasional' or 'complaisance' works and a case study in their relationships to other pieces, see Christoph Hellmundt's essay in this volume, Ch. 8.

autonomy are most complex and most pressing, and precisely for that reason it is imperative that such cases not be approached blindly with the anachronistic theoretical precept of the *Fassung letzter Hand* as the sole or primary tool for evaluating the nature and autonomy of each surviving text. As mentioned above, the best-known problematical cases in this category are the 'Italian' Symphony and the B flat major String Quintet, Op. 87; other appropriate works include most of the posthumously published compositions.

In short, I believe that we can no longer rely primarily on the sweeping general assumptions of the *Fassung letzter Hand* theory to guide us as we reassess Mendelssohn's œuvre as a whole. Certainly this philosophy is appropriate for some works, and it would in any case be neither feasible nor desirable to publish every variant and every *Albumblatt* for every work. But we can scour the composer's voluminous correspondence and scores for indications of any real rejections and preferences, rather than simply assuming that the latest surviving versions of related compositional endeavours are the best and/or most authorized. We can, in the case of many smaller works for which there is no surviving indication of such preference or rejection, print several parallel and substantively divergent versions. And, perhaps most importantly, we can cease to assume that Mendelssohn always regarded early variants as intrinsically inferior to their later counterparts. If nothing else, the similarities and divergences between the two *Infelice* compositions compellingly demonstrate that circumstantial or topical considerations can beneficially influence musical artworks.

But the latter statement should be applied here only with caution—for the issue of the *Fassung letzter Hand* is ultimately irrelevant to these arias. In fact, these two works provide a conspicuous example of the problems produced by the unquestioning application of that textual philosophy to Mendelssohn's œuvre. This is not just an instance in which inappropriate editorial assumptions have led to the erroneous confusion of a set of mostly general compositional gestures with the issue of specific musical identity. It is, more importantly, a lesson in the ways in which such assumptions can obscure rather than explain relationships among compositions and sources—and a case that has deprived the musical world of Mendelssohn's first masterful essay in the early nineteenth-century Italian operatic style.[61]

---

[61] At the time of writing two recordings of *Infelice! / Ah, ritorna, età dell'oro*, both based on my edition, have appeared. For the Swiss firm of Claves Records (CD 50–9912) the aria has been recorded by Francine van der Heijden, with Ingo Caetani conducting the Robert-Schumann-Philharmonie, Chemnitz (this recording also includes the revised version of the A major Symphony and the concert aria *On Lena's Gloomy Heath*, with baritone Boris Statsenkow as soloist). Van der Heijden also performs the solo role in a recording made by Steven W. Eggleston with the Ensemble Tactus for Novitas Records (MM509804); this recording likewise includes the 1834 revision of the A major Symphony.

PART II

Individual Works

4

Mendelssohn's First Composition

PETER WARD JONES

W HAT is Mendelssohn's first original extant composition? The earliest musical notation in his hand that we know of is that contained in the volume of harmony and counterpoint exercises done under the supervision of Carl Friedrich Zelter.[1] As Larry Todd has indicated in his edition of this volume, the first entries were probably made in August or September 1819, although the advanced nature of the initial exercises in the book suggests that others, no longer extant, would have preceded them, perhaps done on loose sheets or possibly in another exercise book.[2] Certainly Mendelssohn had been receiving tuition from Zelter since at least July 1819, and perhaps earlier.[3] A number of original compositions are to be found amongst the formal exercises in thoroughbass, counterpoint, and canon, but the earliest of these exercises dates from July 1820, by which time there is plenty of evidence of compositions elsewhere.

Mendelssohn's earliest known composition has hitherto been regarded as the 'Lied zum Geburtstag meines guten Vaters, den 11ten December'. The single-page manuscript of this short simple song in G major beginning 'Ihr Töne schwingt euch' was placed by Mendelssohn at some time into the album he presented to his fiancée, Cécile Jeanrenaud, as a Christmas present in 1836, now in the Bodleian Library.[4] No year is given on the manuscript, but a companion song by his sister Fanny, setting the same text, is firmly dated 1819; this manuscript is now on deposit in the Staatsbibliothek zu Berlin — Preußischer Kulturbesitz.[5]

---

[1] GB-Ob, MDM c. 43.

[2] R. Larry Todd, *Mendelssohn's Musical Education* (Cambridge: Cambridge University Press, 1983), 95.

[3] Todd suggests (pp. 11–12) that it may have begun as early as 1817 or 1818, although this seems rather unlikely.

[4] GB-Ob, MDM c. 21, fo. 107.   [5] D-B, MA Depos. Berlin MS 3.

Ernst Wolff in his Mendelssohn biography of 1906 was the first to establish the status of Felix's 'Lied' and to reproduce it in much reduced facsimile.[6] Since then this was commonly accepted as Mendelssohn's first work right through to and including the *MGG* article by Eric Werner.[7] By some misfortune, however, the *New Grove* Mendelssohn article[8] named and reproduced the first page of an instrumental 'Recitativo' dated 7 March 1820 as Mendelssohn's first composition. Rudolf Elvers pointed out the error in his review-essay on the article,[9] and the revised reprint in *The New Grove Early Romantic Masters 2* of 1985 correctly describes the piece as simply 'one of the earliest extant attempts at composition'.[10] This 'Recitativo' occurs as the first item in the first volume of the Berlin Mendelssohn autographs. John Warrack, in his essay on 'Mendelssohn's Operas', has suggested that this work is 'dramatic by intention, if not in fulfilment', and further suggests that the following texted aria 'Quel bonheur pour mon coeur' and other short movements in dramatic style belong with it.[11] Whether the aria really belongs with the 'Recitativo' may be questioned, but it seems not unlikely that the 'Recitativo' and/or the French songs may have been intended for some little entertainment (dramatic or otherwise) for his mother's birthday, which was on 15 March. Since Felix had already composed a song for his father's birthday, it is not improbable that he would also have written something for Lea's. The 'Recitativo' has hitherto been described by most writers as a piece for piano solo, though the revised *New Grove* work-list also mentions a later version with strings. But in reality it was never a solo piano work; it was conceived from the outset as a concertante piece for piano and strings, as is clear from the two pages of string parts in score which immediately follow the piano part in the Berlin manuscript.[12]

[6] Ernst Wolff, *Felix Mendelssohn Bartholdy* (Berlin: Harmonie, 1906), facing p. 13.

[7] Eric Werner, article 'Mendelssohn', in *MGG* ix. 59–98.

[8] *New Grove*, Felix Mendelssohn Bartholdy article by Karl-Heinz Köhler, with work-list and bibliography by Eveline Bartlitz (xii. 134–59).

[9] Rudolf Elvers, 'Verlorengegangene Selbstverständlichkeiten: Zum Mendelssohn-Artikel in *The New Grove*', in J. Schläder and R. Quandt (eds.), *Festschrift Heinz Becker zum 60. Geburtstag* (Laaber: Laaber, 1982), 417–21. Elvers suggests that the error was probably taken over from Peter Ranft, *Felix Mendelssohn Bartholdy: Eine Lebenschronik* (Leipzig: Deutscher Verlag für Musik, 1972).

[10] John Warrack, Hugh Macdonald, and Karl-Heinz Köhler, *The New Grove Early Romantic Masters 2: Weber, Berlioz, Mendelssohn* (London: Macmillan, 1985), 203.

[11] 'Mendelssohn's Operas', in Nigel Fortune (ed.), *Music and Theatre: Essays in Honour of Winton Dean* (Cambridge: Cambridge University Press, 1987), 263–97.

[12] The manuscript (D-B, Ms.mus. autogr. F. Mendelssohn Bartholdy 1, pp. 1–3) opens with the piano solo part on two pages, dated 7 Mar. It is complete with Tutti and Solo indications, and is immediately followed by two pages of the string parts in score, in which the piano part is merely cued in, and which must date from the same time. The date of 22 Apr. for the 'version with strings' given in the work-list in *The New Grove Early Romantic Masters 2* (p. 273) derives

It is, however, not with either of these compositions, the 'Lied' or the 'Recitativo', that this chapter is concerned, for I should like to propose that there is another work which has a strong claim to be regarded as Mendelssohn's earliest surviving composition. In Mendelssohn's youthful letter of 1 November 1819 addressed to his childhood horn-playing friend, Rudolph Gugel, and first published by Elvers in 1962,[13] the composer says that 'I have not given you a reply about the matter because I have had so much to do recently that I seemed to be constructed of Latin, French, and Arithmetic myself. A double sonata which I composed came on top of that, and so I was rarely finished before half past eight.'[14] 'Double sonata' ('Doppelsonate') can only really mean in this context a sonata for two pianos. Now just such a three-movement sonata in D major is to be found, unattributed, in the Deneke Mendelssohn collection in the Bodleian Library, in the miscellaneous volume MS M. Deneke Mendelssohn b. 5 (fos. 42–9). It is written in a gathering of music paper consisting of five bifolia plus one single leaf, which contains in addition to the sonata a further single movement in G minor (with an implied Allegro tempo), also for two pianos (fos. 49ᵛ–52).[15] At the end of this second work occurs the only date, 'd. 21sten Februar', tantalizingly given without any year.

In the second volume of the *Catalogue of the Mendelssohn Papers in the Bodleian Library, Oxford*, Margaret Crum included these pieces as works of Mendelssohn, describing them, slightly inaccurately, as '[t]wo very early sonatas for two pianos' and suggesting a date of '1821 or earlier'.[16] They do not appear in the *New Grove* work-list, but are in the revised list in *The New Grove Early Romantic Masters 2*, where they are dated as '? before 1821', but also have

from that found on the separate string parts, which are in the Bodleian Library (MS MDM b. 5, fos. 198–200, violin II, viola, and bass parts only), but this date should in any case be 12 Apr.; '22' is a typographical error in the published Bodleian catalogue (see *Catalogue II*, 10). In copying the parts Mendelssohn made one or two minor alterations compared with the score. The 12 Apr. date may indicate that the work was not performed until about that time, and perhaps therefore did not feature on Lea's birthday.

[13] Rudolf Elvers, 'Ein Jugendbrief von Felix Mendelssohn', in *Festschrift für Friedrich Smend zum 70. Geburtstag* (Berlin: Merseberger, 1963), 93–7. I am grateful to Dr Elvers for discussion of the problem of Mendelssohn's first composition over the past few years.

[14] 'Ich habe dir darum nicht geantwortet weil ich dieser Tage so viel zu thun gehabt habe, da ich selbst vom Latein französisch und Rechnen zusammengebaut war. Eine Doppelsonate, die ich componirte, kam dazu und so wurde ich selten vor halb 9 Uhr fertig.' See Elvers, 'Jugendbrief', 95.

[15] The paper measures 340 × 240 mm and has a 'C & I HONIG' watermark. The two works have now been published as *Zwei Stücke — Sonate D-dur, Sonatensatz g-moll — für zwei Klaviere*, ed. Joachim Draheim (Wiesbaden: Breitkopf & Härtel, 1998).

[16] *Catalogue II*, 7.

PL. 4.1. GB-Ob, MS M. Deneke Mendelssohn b. 5, fo. 42.
Bodleian Library Oxford

the authorship queried by the comment 'attrib. Mendelssohn'.[17] It is a resolution of these questions that is addressed in this chapter.

An examination of the first page of the Sonata (Pl. 4.1) shows a script that at first sight appears utterly unlike the familiar Mendelssohn hand. A later page (Pl. 4.2) also demonstrates how rough and crude this script often is. But if this is compared with the composer's hand in the first volume of the Berlin autographs (works of 1820), then it soon becomes clear that this is indeed one and the same hand. Characteristic are the sloping treble clefs, the long thin sharps, the rests, and the writing of the word 'Primo'. The young Mendelssohn also has the habit, when writing octaves that require sharps or flats, of making do with a single accidental, usually placed before the upper note. This is also occasionally found in contemporary printed scores, so it is not simply a youthful aberration on Mendelssohn's part—Fanny also has the same habit.

The manuscript is also clearly a compositional manuscript—the crossings out and other changes of mind seen in Pl. 4.2 are sufficient evidence of that. Here, I would suggest, is the young Mendelssohn in the full rush of exuberant creative activity, and feeling under no constraint to write neatly. By comparison, the hand in the Zelter exercise book (and the song for his father's birthday) is far neater, but this is only to be expected. Zelter was a stickler for old-fashioned virtues and would have demanded a tidy hand in material presented to him. In fact we know from his comments in the book that on occasion he rebuked Felix for his hastiness, and insisted that exercises originally done in pencil should be gone over in ink before proceeding further. In such discipline undoubtedly lay the roots of the elegance of his mature musical hand, but in this sonata Felix was a free spirit.

If the hand and the nature of the manuscript suggest that these two pieces are undoubtedly early works of Mendelssohn, can the matter of dating be taken further? As mentioned, the only date on the manuscript itself is that of 21 February, added at the end of the G minor movement. Although no year is given, I would suggest that the February in question can hardly be anything other than that of 1820. Several pieces of evidence point in this direction, starting with the stave ruling of the paper. What is most striking about this manuscript is that Mendelssohn is trying to write the work on fifteen-stave paper—ideal for a song or a violin sonata, but most unsuitable for a two-piano work. Mendelssohn has the choice of either contenting himself with only three systems per page and thus wasting three staves on each page, or else trying to compress one system of four staves into three. With evidently nothing more

PL. 4.2. GB-Ob, MS M. Deneke Mendelssohn b. 5, fo. 44.
Bodleian Library Oxford

suitable to hand, and being economically minded, he chose the latter option.[18] Occasionally he adds in an extra hand-drawn stave, but usually he manages to make do with what is provided.

Because all four hands are rarely over-busy simultaneously, this is not quite the obstacle that it might have been, although it is not always clear exactly what notes each instrument are meant to be playing. The foot of the first page provides a good example of what Mendelssohn has to resort to. At the end of the third system the Secondo part has the most important role, so Mendelssohn allots it the top two of the three staves remaining for the last system and accommodates the Primo part on the bottom stave. But from the second bar the Primo resumes the predominance, so Mendelssohn reverses the instruments from this bar onwards. What is not clear is just what the left hand of the Primo part is intended to play in bar 1. A close inspection of the beginning of the bottom stave shows that it actually incorporates both a treble and a bass clef, with both sets of accidentals. This might seem to imply that the left hand doubles the right hand an octave lower, but this then results in it dipping below the bass line of the Secondo left hand in a not altogether convincing manner. Still, with a 10-year-old all things are possible! It should be noted that although it is most often the lowest system of the page that receives this treatment, this is not invariably the case. Mendelssohn clearly had the work largely in his head before committing it to paper (a state of affairs common even in his early works, as Fanny testified),[19] and where he saw that one of the upper systems could happily accommodate the next four or five bars on three staves, he would write it out accordingly (see Pl. 4.2).

The relevance of all this from the point of view of dating is simple. From March 1820 Felix had a bound music manuscript book uniformly ruled with sixteen staves (now volume 1 of the Berlin autographs). When this was filled he continued in a similar book (volume 2) started in December 1820. Certainly until the middle of 1821 virtually all his compositions were apparently entered into these books, with the exception of such little pieces as appear in the Zelter exercise book, and the two Singspiels for his parents' birthdays (*Die Soldatenliebschaft* for Abraham's in December 1820, and *Die beiden Pädagogen* for Lea's in March 1821). Thus, if the two-piano works had

---

[18] It is interesting to note that in the summer of 1819 Felix had asked his father to send (? or bring) him some music paper from Paris, and his father asked him in return what sort of paper he wanted—see Abraham's letter of 2 July 1819 to Fanny with a postscript to the other children: 'You, my dear Felix, must state exactly what kind of music paper you wish to have; ruled or not ruled, and if the former you must say distinctly how it is to be ruled' (Sebastian Hensel, *The Mendelssohn Family* (London: Sampson Low, Marston, Searle, & Rivington, 1881), i. 78).

[19] See Fanny's statement of 1822 concerning Felix, quoted in Sutermeister, *Briefe*, 299: 'So habe ich zum Beispiel seine Opern auswendig gewußt, noch ehe eine Note aufgeschrieben war.'

originated in the winter of 1820/21, they would surely have been entered into the Berlin books, which apart from anything else were ruled with much more suitable paper. It is interesting to note that Fanny was also presented with a music manuscript book at the same time as Felix in March 1820—evidently her first, notwithstanding her superior age. If she had an exercise book similar to that of Felix for her studies with Zelter, this has not survived. Whereas Felix's book is of upright format with sixteen staves, Fanny's is of oblong format with only eight staves—a format she continued to favour throughout her life, just as her brother normally used upright paper. Whether this choice of format influenced (or reflected) the types of composition that Fanny mainly cultivated is an interesting topic, but beyond the present discussion.[20] From volume 3 of Felix's Berlin autographs onwards, volumes containing several works are convolutes—i.e. they are later bindings-up of originally discrete unbound manuscripts.

The style of Mendelssohn's notation in this Sonata also very much favours an 1819/20 date. Besides its evident childlike quality, there are occasional faults in the notation which point to inexperience. Thus in Pl. 4.1 at the opening, the upbeat triplets of the Primo's right hand are accompanied by half-measure rests in the other parts, instead of a quarter-note rest. In bar 3 Mendelssohn has shown the three beats rest in the Primo left hand as a quarter-note followed by a half-note rest rather than the other way round (although this is a point of musical grammar that he normally observes correctly elsewhere in the manuscript). After the modulation to the dominant, A major, later in the movement, he often forgets that he does not actually have three sharps in the key signature, and many necessary accidentals are omitted. That said, it is a matter for wonder that Mendelssohn had already mastered so many of the notational niceties at this age.

If the G minor movement is to be dated with a certain degree of confidence as being composed in February 1820, what about the preceding D major Sonata? Its very proximity—the Sonata ends on the recto of fo. 49, and the G minor movement begins on the verso—might make one argue for a close date, perhaps in the New Year. But from Felix's letter to Gugel of 1 November 1819 we must infer that the 'Doppelsonate' mentioned there was composed around October of that year. It is just possible that Felix composed more than one such work over these months, and that the D major Sonata is a later work than the 'Doppelsonate' of the letter. It is, however, not entirely fanciful to see a slightly surer touch at work in the G minor movement, which may argue for a time gap between them. In the absence of further documentary evidence to

---

[20] On this point, see Hans-Günter Klein's essay in this volume, Ch. 11.

support the idea of additional unknown works, I would propose that the D major Sonata may probably be identified with that of the Gugel letter; this would make it the 10-year-old Mendelssohn's earliest surviving work. We of course have no knowledge of what attempts at composition he may have made before the autumn of 1819. It seems not at all unlikely that the lessons with Zelter were begun because Mendelssohn was already actively composing, and his parents decided that it was time that he learned the disciplines of the craft.

Two further small points are worth making. First, if the Sonata was actually performed, as surely it would have been, with his sister playing the other piano part, then presumably there must have existed at one time another copy of the score, or at least a copy of one of the piano parts, but this has not survived (it is of course quite possible that Felix himself played from memory). Secondly, the manuscript now forms part of MS M. Deneke Mendelssohn b. 5. This volume was originally a loose portfolio of miscellaneous manuscripts of various origins, mostly in Mendelssohn's hand, but including some items that were probably treasured by the family for their personal associations. Thus Mendelssohn's last composition, the *Alt-Deutsches Frühlingslied*, is in the same volume (fo. 40). It may just be that the two-piano Sonata is present here because it was seen as special and regarded as the earliest of his surviving juvenilia. But not too much importance should be attached to this evidence, since the contents of b. 5 have a rather obscure history.[21]

So much for the externals. What about the music itself? The Sonata consists of three movements: a sonata-form Allegro in D major of 114 bars; a Menuetto and Trio (the minuet in D major, the trio in B major); and a concluding Prestissimo in D major of ninety-four bars. In performance they take about 3½, 2, and 2¼ minutes, excluding all but the customary minuet and trio repeats.

In the first movement both halves are marked to be repeated, but the exposition is by far the longest portion (71 of the 114 bars). The development section consists of just six bars of modulatory work based on the first subject and then eight bars of dominant preparation for the recapitulation, in which the first theme of the second subject does not reappear at all. Combined with a strong monothematic character, the movement is very similar to Mendelssohn's other early attempts at sonata-form movements in what Larry Todd has characterized as 'the novice struggling to acquire mastery of form'.[22] But for a 10-year-old the energy and achievement is considerable, despite certain crudities and miscalculations. Incidentally, the slightly later G

---

[21] For further particulars of this volume see *Catalogue II*, 6–10.
[22] Todd, *Mendelssohn's Musical Education*, 79.

Ex. 4.1. Mendelssohn, Sonata in D Major for Two Pianos, first movement, bars 35–42

minor movement already displays more balanced proportions; within its 110 bars, the exposition occupies forty bars, the development twenty-one bars, and the recapitulation and coda forty-nine bars.

In the first movement of the Sonata the two pianos share the limelight to a surprising degree, and Mendelssohn has no trouble in letting the instruments exchange themes and short phrases. The Minuet and Trio is more Primo dominated, with the Secondo mainly filling out the accompaniment. More equality returns in the finale, though it remains more Primo-led than the opening movement.

What were the influences on the work? Tracing such influences of course can be an elusive game, especially in the case of someone like Mendelssohn, who as a child would have been receptive to all sorts of music by composers major and minor. As a medium the two-piano repertoire immediately suggests the great D major Sonata of Mozart, K. 448, which would almost certainly have been known in the Mendelssohn household.[23] Yet apart from the manner of some of the exchanges of themes between the two instruments, perhaps the momentary lyricism of the first theme of the second subject in the first movement (Ex. 4.1), and one or two of the cadential phrases and harmonies, the spirit of Mozart does not predominate.[24] Haydn seems at least as close an influence, especially if we consider the rugged Minuet, and the last movement —another monothematic sonata movement, notwithstanding the rondo character of its opening theme, complete with repeat (Ex. 4.2). Haydnesque too are some of the surprise dynamic effects—Mendelssohn takes care to write these in, although in many other places dynamic indications are lacking,

---

[23] A copy of the Piano 1 part only of the work in Cahier 14 of the Breitkopf & Härtel *Oeuvres complettes* is in the Bodleian Library (Deneke 199), and may possibly have been a Mendelssohn copy. A complete set of the *Oeuvres complettes* owned by Mendelssohn is now in the Firestone Library, Princeton University Library, though the parts are later issues (up to 1842) rather than the original 1798–1806 edition.

[24] This is not true of the G minor movement, where there are distinct echoes of Mozart's G minor Symphony, K. 550.

Ex. 4.2. Mendelssohn, Sonata in D Major for Two Pianos:
(*a*) Menuetto, bars 1–8; (*b*) Finale, bars 1–8

Ex. 4.3. Clementi, Sonata in D Major, Op. 25 No. 6, first movement, bars 1–8

and a certain imagination on the part of the performer has to be brought into play.

For the basic three-movement structure with a central minuet and no slow movement, there are no parallels in Mozart, but again it is not uncommon in the Haydn piano sonatas. But I would also suggest that Muzio Clementi's influence is perhaps not far away. Four of his piano sonatas (Op. 8 No. 3, Op. 10 Nos. 1 and 3, and Op. 28 No. 3) have similar movement patterns, and the start of the Sonata in D major, Op. 25 No. 6, is in a strikingly similar vein to Mendelssohn's own opening (Ex. 4.3). It is also interesting to note that Clementi was one of the few other composers of the time to have written a sonata for two pianos—although in B flat rather than D major. When we remember that Mendelssohn's own piano teacher, Ludwig Berger, had been a pupil of Clementi, it seems likely that the latter's music would have formed an important part of the young pianist's musical diet.[25]

Other idioms, such as the mixture of triplets and eighth notes and the semitonal inflections (also seen in the birthday song), can also be found in Clementi's works, but are of course very much part of the common currency of the time. Not so perhaps the swing from D major straight to B major between the Minuet and Trio—a bold move, but quite in keeping with some of the harmonic experiments that Mendelssohn indulges in the first volume of the Berlin manuscripts, and again certainly with precedents in Haydn (String

---

[25] The Mendelssohn family music library also included a Sonata for Two Pianos in C major by F. H. Himmel (Vienna: Hoffmeister, 1801), which shows no sign of having influenced Felix, and a set of variations for two pianos in E flat by Zelter (in manuscript). See Rudolf Elvers and Peter Ward Jones, 'Das Musikalienverzeichnis von Fanny und Felix Mendelssohn Bartholdy', *Mendelssohn-Studien*, 8 (1993), 85–103.

Quartet, Op. 74 No. 1, and, with less suddenness, Symphony No. 99). But if the positive influences are hard to define precisely, it is easier to see what is not there, and that is most obviously J. S. Bach and Beethoven, neither of whom had as yet impinged on Mendelssohn's compositional process.

The interest and importance of this Sonata, I would argue, lies not just in its chronological precedence. It also offers us a glimpse of Mendelssohn the composer before the effects of Zelter's teaching had become really apparent —before all that contrapuntal discipline had taken hold—when he was basically reflecting the music he had absorbed in four or so years of piano tuition. There is scarcely a hint of counterpoint here, whereas in the slightly later G minor movement, imitative technique can already be seen to be creeping in, even if only occasionally; this is even more obvious in later works of 1820 such as the F major violin sonata.[26] If my interpretation of the evidence is correct, then surely we have here a remarkable and revealing first glimpse of the powers of youthful genius.

---

[26] Modern edition, *Sonate F-Dur für Violine und Klavier*, ed. Renate Unger (Leipzig: Deutscher Verlag für Musik, 1977).

5

The Programme of Mendelssohn's 'Reformation' Symphony, Op. 107

WOLFGANG DINGLINGER

THE notion that part of Mendelssohn's 'Reformation' Symphony fails to follow a clear programme is central to the conventional wisdom concerning this composition, and despite several excellent recent attempts to answer this question the situation has changed little.[1] The problem lies in an ostensible discrepancy in the programme between the outer movements and the middle ones.[2] The assertion that there is a gaping hole in the work's programme, encountered even in recent studies,[3] differs but little from that of Hermann Kretschmar, who declared already a century ago that the work was a 'half-serious contribution to programme music'.[4] This view supposes that Mendelssohn did not satisfactorily address his challenge in writing the work, even though he initially attempted to perform and publish it and therefore must have been convinced that he had fully realized his ideas in the work as a whole.

---

[1] See e.g. Judith Silber, 'Mendelssohn and the "Reformation" Symphony: A Critical and Historical Study' (Ph.D. diss., Yale University, 1987); ead., 'Mendelssohn and his "Reformation" Symphony', *Journal of the American Musicological Society*, 40 (1987), 310–36; Judith Silber Ballan, 'Marxian Programmatic Music: A Stage in Mendelssohn's Musical Development', in R. Larry Todd (ed.), *Mendelssohn Studies* (Cambridge: Cambridge University Press, 1992), 149–61; and Ulrich Wüster, ' "Ein gewisser Geist": Zu Mendelssohns "Reformations-Symphonie" ', *Die Musikforschung*, 44 (1991), 311–30.

[2] For example, Silber, 'Mendelssohn and his "Reformation" Symphony', 313: 'The middle movements, less obviously programmatic . . .'.

[3] Thomas Christian Schmidt, *Die ästhetischen Grundlagen der Instrumentalmusik Felix Mendelssohn Bartholdys* (Stuttgart: M & P Verlag für Wissenschaft und Forschung, 1996), 272.

[4] Hermann Kretschmar, *Führer durch den Konzertsaal, 1. Abtlg.: Sinfonie und Suite*, 6th edn. (Leipzig: Breitkopf & Härtel, 1921), 315: '[The work's] clearest reference to the Reformation itself occurs in the last movement, at the centre of which is the chorale "Ein feste Burg".'

The finding that the outer movements of the symphony contain musical gestures that permit convincing evidence of their programmes, while the inner movements do not,[5] rests upon the search for musical features that might suggest a plot. There are in fact musical features that make it possible to decode such a plot in part, but their absence in certain sections of the symphony has always frustrated attempts to discern an overall programme. Without more easily identifiable pointers, however, it is difficult to formulate any reasonably clear idea of the compositional intention behind the symphony and its relationship to the Reformation; yet the features that *are* identifiable are so compelling that they link the symphony to a specific intention with a directness rarely encountered in Mendelssohn's works.

But the presence of these programmatically direct musical gestures should not prevent us from entertaining the possibility that despite some identifiable musical features it is not a programme (in the sense of an extra-musical plot) that constitutes the content of the symphony, but another, more general, concept. Although such a concept might be realized in the structures of all parts of the symphony, the work's indeterminate character would require explanations as to its general nature. These explanations might be offered through a variety of features—the title, the chorale, and so on—that would indicate the general direction we should follow in interpreting the work as a whole.

Furthermore, an interpretation of the partial lack of a programmatic connection that is suggested by a strict division between 'absolute' and 'programmatic' musical elements is convincing only when qualified. As Carl Dahlhaus emphasized:

The attempt to position various kinds of 'painterly', 'poetic', and 'characteristic' music on a continuum between absolute and programme music . . . directly contradicts the historical fact that 'middle stages' and 'modified forms' were cultivated earlier than the extremes. The term 'absolute' music was just as alien to the eighteenth and early nineteenth centuries as was the idea to which it aspires.[6]

What *was* discussed in Mendelssohn's day was a different problem, as a definition provided by Robert Schumann demonstrates:

A composition possesses character—musical character—if a mood predominates so persistently that no other interpretation is possible . . . Characteristic music differs from painterly (or picturesque) music in that the former represents states

---

[5] See Silber, 'Critical and Historical', 204.
[6] Carl Dahlhaus, 'Thesen über Programmusik', in Dahlhaus (ed.), *Beiträge zur musikalischen Hermeneutik* (Regensburg: Gustav Bosse, 1975), 193.

of the soul, whereas the latter represents states of life; most often, the two are mixed together.[7]

Schumann's point is that the firmness of external references in a composition stands alongside the composer's inner creative urges; each influences the other. He proclaims no opposition between programme music and absolute music, nor does he mention what later became the hallmark of absolute music because it is taken for granted. We must therefore consider here the characteristic and picturesque manifestations of a programme, rather than positing an opposition between absolute and programme music that culminated in the factional arguments of the later nineteenth century.

Any doubt that at least the second movement is tied to a programme is dispelled by a letter of 15 June 1830 from Mendelssohn to his family that describes a Corpus Christi procession in Munich:

I recently wished that you all were with me as I was wandering around among the people during the procession, when I looked around me a great deal and felt very satisfied with the first movement of my 'church symphony'—it never would have occurred to me that the contrast between the first two movements[8] would still be so appropriate today. But if you had heard how the entire crowd intoned the prayer in a singsong voice and then how one hoarse priest occasionally cried out or another read the Gospel aloud, and how all of a sudden in the middle of this a merry piece of military music with trumpets interrupted, and how the clerical banners waved back and forth, and how choirboys were draped with golden tassels, then I believe you would have praised me as I praised myself and enjoyed myself.[9]

Mendelssohn's surprise that this contrast was 'still so appropriate today' reveals that he clearly intended to present an historical contrast in the first two movements of the D minor Symphony. He then adds a possible interpretation of this vivid description of the procession. The letter does not say, however, which particular *musical* features are to be contrasted; it mentions only the 'contrast between the first two movements'. Thus, the description is retroactively tied to this contrast, and the opposite—a description in which the contrast is tied to the description—is inappropriate. To search the first two

---

[7] Robert Schumann, 'Character, musikalischer', in *Damen-Conversations-Lexikon*, ed. K. B. S. Herloßson (Leipzig: Fr. Volckmar, 1834), ii. 330.

[8] Movements (*Sätze*), not pieces (*Stücke*). Judith Silber Ballan has pointed out that the original word 'Stücke' was crossed out and replaced by 'Sätze'; see Silber Ballan, 'Critical and Historical', 222. Thomas Christian Schmidt's reading of this passage, which suggests that the reference is to the introduction and exposition of the first movement, thus needs to be amended; see Schmidt, *Grundlagen*, 272 n. 106.

[9] First published in Silber, 'Critical and Historical', 221–6.

movements for identifiable figures corresponding to the images described in this scene would thus be a fruitless task.[10]

This specific contrast, and further general ideas as well, are achieved through the use of formal conventions in the symphony—this much is obvious. The conventions themselves, however, are filled with elements that are (to borrow Schumann's terms again) specifically either 'characteristic' or 'picturesque'. The 'picturesque' elements have been identified often enough[11] —among other things, the clearly programmatic aspects of the title, the chorale, and the Catholic elements. Less accessible are those elements that Schumann describes as 'characteristic'. The key to these elements seems to reside in the transition between the third and fourth movements—a passage that Mendelssohn deleted in his 1832 revision of the symphony.[12]

This deleted passage is divided into three sections: an instrumental recitative played by the solo flute;[13] a short recollection of the Andante of the third movement; and a more animated *crescendo* in dynamics and instrumentation that prepares the chorale that opens the Finale. Judith Silber Ballan—the first to publish and discuss these twenty-eight bars[14]—noted that Beethoven's Ninth Symphony was a possible structural model, with its instrumental recitatives that introduce the finale by presenting material from preceding portions of the work; she further pointed out certain structural congruities between the

---

[10] That Mendelssohn had the scene before his eyes may be considered highly likely, since this is entirely consistent with his manner of composition; see Wolfgang Dinglinger, *Studien zu den Psalmen mit Orchester von Felix Mendelssohn Bartholdy* (Cologne: Studio, 1993), 78–9. However, it is impossible to speculate precisely what image Mendelssohn actually envisaged when he conceived the work; certain only is that it must have concerned historical contrasts.

[11] A detailed presentation is found in Silber, 'Historical and Critical'.

[12] The first version, which was finished on 12 May 1830, and the revised ending, completed on 11 Nov. 1832, are contained in Volume 26 of the original *Mendelssohn Nachlaß* (D-B, Ms.mus.autogr. F. Mendelssohn Bartholdy 26).

[13] That the whole 'vocal' part of the recitative—continued over the entire twenty-eight bars—is entrusted to the flute may be only one aspect of Mendelssohn's instrumentation of this passage, since he decided on the flute only as an afterthought. In the autograph the beginning of the recitative is written in the clarinet stave, and it was reassigned to the flute only later. One possible association might be that Luther was a flautist as well as a lutenist. For humanists of Luther's time, the lute was the universally symbolic instrument for all presentations of music and music-theoretical problems, while mastery of the flute was something exceptional; indeed, the Great Reformer's appellation as the 'Wittemberg Nightingale' refers to his facility on the flute. More important than this possible association, however, is Thomas Ehrle's assertion of the timbre of the flute as an adumbration of a fortuitous development, as at the end of the first part of the *Meeresstille und glückliche Fahrt* Overture; see Thomas Ehrle, *Die Instrumentation von Felix Mendelssohn Bartholdy* (Wiesbaden: Breitkopf & Härtel, 1983), 36. In the 'Reformation' Symphony, too, the flute follows the reserved third movement as prefigurer of the 'victory symphony' of the finale, the opening of which (the first stanza of the chorale 'Ein' feste Burg') is again presented by the solo flute.   [14] Silber, 'Historical and Critical', 128.

Ex. 5.1. Thematic relationships in 'Reformation' Symphony: (*a*) deleted flute
recitative in bridge to Finale, bar 1; (*b*) 'Gregorian' motif from slow introduction
to first movement; (*c*) 'wind chorale' from slow introduction to first movement;
(*d*) incipit from main theme of first movement

two works. Yet the extent to which such correspondences are evident even in
the details of every movement of the two symphonies remains remarkable.[15]
The deleted passage begins with two unmeasured recitative bars for solo flute
(see Exs. 5.1 and 5.2), comprising: (1) the 'Gregorian' motif, which opens the
slow introduction to the first movement and whose old-fashioned counterpoint simulates the 'church style'; (2) the 'postlude' to this contrapuntal part
of the introduction, characterized by an upwards leap of a sixth followed by a

---

[15] To list only the most striking parallels: *First movement*: the idea of beginning the movement by gradually developing the main theme, which itself is a complex of several ideas; *Second
movement*: the absence of the designation 'Scherzo', the trio section's anticipation of the main key
of the finale; and the creation of a 'complementary relationship' to the first movement by beginning directly rather than emerging gradually; *Third movement*: the recitative or arioso character
of the Violin 1 part; the abrupt allusion at the end of the movement to a musical figure from the
first movement; the use of the winds first to echo material already presented by the strings, and
later to anticipate material in the strings; *Fourth movement*: both works first introduce the trombones in the finale.
  Judith Silber Ballan has pointed out that there was no necessity for Mendelssohn to have the
chorale sung in his finale, since it was so well known that listeners would have automatically
associated the tune with the familiar text, but this is precisely the reason why the idea of
Mendelssohn's chorale should be considered a derivation of the model of Beethoven's Ninth.
The features of the chorale passage that Silber Ballan points out support this interpretation: a setting in the church style which relies on contemporary hymnals (perhaps that of August Wilhelm
Bach); the suggestion of congregational participation through irregular rests between the
phrases; and the suggestion of a cantor and the subsequent entrance of the choir. See Silber,
'Critical and Historical', 127.

Ex. 5.2. Thematic relationships in 'Reformation' Symphony: (*a*) deleted flute recitative in bridge to Finale, bar 2–4; (*b*) cadence of chorale; (*c*) first movement, bassoon solo in bars 162, etc.; (*d*) second movement, cello solo in bars 79–81; (*e*) third movement, violin recitative, bars 2–3

descending scale;[16] (3) the rising fifth that signals the main theme of the first movement; (4) simultaneously, allusions to the chorale 'Ein feste Burg', as variants of characteristic melodic turns of the chorale melody sound; and (5) the characteristic cadential turn of the solo cello from the trio of the second movement, which in turn is derived from the incipit of the main theme of the first movement. Furthermore, a motif from the second subject of the first

---

[16] This is a passage in the style of a 'wind-instrument chorale', although in the introduction the crescendos on each note also prominently recall the sound of an old and 'drafty' organ. That the composer intended to suggest the sound of an organ seems to be confirmed by a letter from Munich to his father dated 16 Sept. 1831 (information kindly provided by Dr Rudolf Elvers, Berlin). Reporting on the planned rehearsals for a performance of the 'Reformation' Symphony that was later cancelled, Mendelssohn also reports on the registrations he used to perform Bach's chorale 'Schmücke dich, o liebe Seele' (BWV 654) in St Peter's Cathedral. He continues: 'For I always use the same voicings in one of my new sacred pieces, *Verleih' uns Frieden*; yesterday I tried it with the beginning of the "Reform[ation]" Symphony. For the wind instruments [here there is a musical example showing bars 23–4 of the slow introduction] I used my manual with the reed registers—but with all of them, and that includes a thirty-two-foot bassoon, a sixteen-foot viola, and a couple of [other] low reed stops. The thing sounded powerful and indeed terribly serious.' ('Mit denselben Stimmen spiele ich denn immer eine meiner neuen Kirchenmusiken "Verleih uns Frieden", gestern habe ich den Anfang der Reform. Symphonie versucht; hatte zu den Blaseinstrumenten [bars 23–4] wieder mein Clavier mit den Zungenstimmen, aber mit allen, und da ist noch ein Fagott 32 Fuß, eine Bratsche 16' und ein paar tiefe Schnarrstimmen dabei, da klang das Ding mächtig und gar entsetzlich ernsthaft.')

movement (b. 162, where the solo bassoon is marked *espressivo*) is taken up several times by the solo flute, *con espressione*, in the subsequent course of the deleted passage.

One distinctive feature of the deleted passage makes perfectly clear that Mendelssohn's adaptation was far more than just a structural one. After a number of motifs from the preceding movements have sounded, the scoring gradually expands to a *tutti*. Within this gradual build-up, more and more instruments intone the chorale 'Allein Gott in der Höh' sei Ehr', which came into existence in the early years of the Reformation as the German 'Gloria',[17] and which even today remains at the core of the Protestant hymn repertoire. Two quotations of the hymn by solo instruments[18] are followed by two *tutti* statements that present the chorale in a fashion that unmistakably recalls the instrumental movements of J. S. Bach, as well as Bach's ways of moulding chorales into florid orchestral textures.[19] This is the only passage of the sort in the entire symphony (Ex. 5.3).

Mendelssohn would also employ this chorale in his oratorio *St Paul*. While in the oratorio it represents 'one heart and one soul'[20] confessed by the persecuted congregation of Christians,[21] in the 'Reformation' Symphony it leads the people out of the misery of oppressive contrasts, concentrating on the fundamental issue: 'To God alone be the Glory'. This design parallels that of the baritone recitative in the Ninth, which forges new paths in a similar musical context: 'O Freunde, nicht diese Töne, sondern laßt uns angenehmere und freudenvollere anstimmen' (O friends, not these tones, but let us sing more more pleasing and more joyous ones). Paralleling this passage in the Ninth,

---

[17] The chorale is by Nikolaus Decius (*c*.1485–after 1546), a German cantor who wrote the texts and tunes for the chorales that replaced the Latin versions of the Credo, Sanctus, and Agnus Dei in the Mass.

[18] Oboe (beginning on *g'*), clarinet (beginning on *g*), and bassoon (beginning on *e*). The last two quotations are abbreviated, limited to the first five notes, which span the rising fifth that acts as a signal in many ways in this symphony. Each time, the solo flute stops its ascending lines in order to make way for the quotation.

[19] This is accomplished by sixteenth-note movement in parallel thirds and sixths in the upper voices and eighth-note movement outlining chords in the middle voices and the bass, which possesses the character of a continuo line. The first block is a dominant-seventh chord based on A, with D major as its goal, and the second block is a dominant-seventh chord based on D, with G as its goal. In this key, the characteristic subdominant of the symphony's main key of D major, there finally follows the chorale 'Ein feste Burg', which opens the finale. The gesture of the ascending fifth that opens 'Allein Gott in der Höh' sei Ehr' '—which again should be considered extremely closely related to 'Ein' feste Burg' and the germinal motivic language of the entire symphony—is expanded to describe a minor seventh in the 'Bachian' portions of the passage.

[20] Soprano recitative (No. 3), 'Die Menge der Gläubigen war ein Herz und eine Seele'.

[21] The chorale (No. 2) following the opening chorus, which had introduced the persecution of the Christians at the hands of the pagans.

Ex. 5.3. Chorale derivations in 'Reformation' Symphony: (*a*) chorale 'Allein Gott in der Höh'' (Sulzbach chorale book 1820 and elsewhere); (*b*) oboe solo from deleted recitative; (*c*) 'Bach' variation from deleted recitative

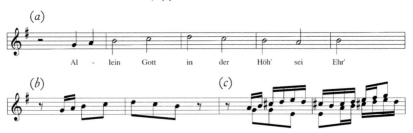

the confessional 'Allein Gott in der Höh'' in the 'Reformation' Symphony leads directly to the intonation of the chorale 'Ein feste Burg' and to the triumphal music of the finale. Mendelssohn's reliance on Bach's musical processes can hardly be coincidental, since for Mendelssohn—and not only for Mendelssohn—Bach was the 'musical representative of Protestantism'.[22]

There can be little doubt that considerations of congruent content led Mendelssohn to adapt Beethoven's Ninth Symphony as a model in the 'Reformation' Symphony, for he criticizes empty imitations as 'lifeless repetitions of what has already been done'.[23] Concerning the imitation of content without form, he writes: 'in such a case I would not be able to finish any composition, because of the emptiness of the task and my aversion to it'; and he justifies obvious similarities between his own works and those of other composers equally fervently, by referring to comparable feelings stimulated by a similar object.[24]

Our investigation of Mendelssohn's intention regarding the content of the 'Reformation' Symphony thus also must entail a consideration of his understanding of Beethoven's symphony. In the absence of definite remarks by Mendelssohn himself on the subject, such a task can be carried out only indirectly, by considering how Beethoven was received in Berlin in the second half

[22] Letter of 10 Mar. 1835 from Abraham Mendelssohn Bartholdy to Felix, quoted from *Briefe 1830–47* (1875), ii. 53: 'That Bach is the musical representative of Protestantism, which first became clear to me at the [performance of the *St Matthew*] *Passion*, is evident to me in every piece by him that I encounter—most recently the Mass [BWV 232], which I heard in the [Sing-]Akademie and which seems to me decidedly anti-Catholic' ('Was mir zuerst bei der Passion klar wurde, daß Bach der musikalische Repräsentant des Protestantismus sei, wird mir bei jedem neuem Stück, das ich von ihm höre, . . . evident, — so neulich durch die Messe, die ich in der Akademie hörte und die mir auf's Entschiedenste antikatholisch vorkommt . . .').

[23] Letter of 18 Dec. 1830 from Mendelssohn to Carl Friedrich Zelter (*Briefe 1830–47*, i. 72).

[24] Letter of 13 July 1831 to Eduard Devrient, quoted from Devrient, *Erinnerungen*, 115.

of the 1820s.[25] Particularly important are the views of Adolph Bernhard Marx, who was very close to Mendelssohn in the 1820s and strongly influenced him. In the *Berliner Allgemeine musikalische Zeitung*, which he edited, Marx carefully laid the groundwork for the first Berlin performance of Beethoven's Ninth Symphony.[26] Numerous criticisms of the work, in which the stumbling block was the choral finale, prompted Marx to pen an interpretation that was designed to prepare the way for the work;[27] he published these remarks just before the performance. We know that Mendelssohn was familiar with precisely this interpretation, since he explicitly referred to Marx and Marx's interpretation of the Ninth when he reported concerning the symphony's première in Stettin: 'All Stettin is topsy turvy about the Beethoven symphony! O Marx! Marx! What a disaster he has created! Here they find his view of the symphony entirely wrong.'[28] The reference to the disaster created by Marx refers not directly to Marx's interpretation of the Ninth, but rather to the fact that he had published his interpretation; for this essay spurred the citizens of Stettin to pen their own odd interpretative attempts, which Mendelssohn ridiculed.

Marx explained the Ninth as autobiographically inspired: the heroic Beethoven had forged paths to new realities. According to Marx, the deep immersion in instrumental music represented by the first three movements made Beethoven the undisputed master of the instruments, but it also made him a human who lived in isolation. With the finale, however, Beethoven freed himself from this situation. Since this idea determined every movement of the work, Marx said, it alone could explain and justify the division of the symphony into two parts, one instrumental and symphonic, the other vocal and cantata-like. The idea that Marx supposed to underlie the work granted to the last movement 'the character of an end result' ('finalen Resultatcharakter') and explained 'the unity of the work, which derived from a dramatic arch of tension that spanned the entire work and had as its goal the last movement'.[29]

---

[25] A number of studies dealing with this and related issues have appeared recently: Silber Ballan, 'Marxian Programmatic Music'; Elisabeth Eleonore Bauer, *Wie Beethoven auf den Sockel kam: Die Entstehung eines musikalischen Mythos* (Stuttgart: J. B. Metzler, 1992); Andreas Eichhorn, *Beethovens Neunte Symphonie: Die Geschichte ihrer Aufführung und Rezeption* (Kassel: Bärenreiter, 1993).

[26] Adolph Bernhard Marx, 'Etwas über die Symphonie und Beethovens Leistungen in diesem Fache', *Berliner Allgemeine musikalische Zeitung*, 1 (1824), 165–8, 173–6.

[27] Adolph Bernhard Marx, 'Symphonie mit Schlußchor über Schillers Ode an die Freude', *Berliner Allgemeine musikalische Zeitung*, 3 (1826), 373–8.

[28] 'Ganz Stettin steht auf dem Kopfe über die Beethovensche Symphonie. O Marx! Marx! Welch Unglück richtet er an . . . Hier findet man seine Ansicht von der Symphonie ganz falsch.' (Quoted from Silber, 'Marxian Programmatic Music', 157.)

[29] '[D]ie Geschlossenheit des Werkes aus einem werkübergreifenden und auf den letzten Satz zielenden dramatischen Spannungsbogen' (Eichhorn, *Beethovens Neunte*, 211).

Since Marx not only identifies as the fundamental idea of the symphony the 'decisive separation of two realms of the world of tones',[30] but also singles out the last movement as the 'triumph over the world of instruments',[31] Mendelssohn had the possibility of a direct transferral: the progress of Beethoven's Ninth towards the finale was directly tied to the representation of victory. And there is more: Marx considered the finale significant because it 'opened up and conquered new realms for the human spirit'.[32]

Marx expressed his conviction that the immediate intelligibility of a composition was directly related to its proximity to current ideas, and concluded that the more temporally removed an artwork was, the more it had to accomplish 'in order to overcome the distance': 'The only work of art that is truly profound and meaningful is one that opens up a new idea, a new sphere of life—that is, one that extends beyond the present horizon and only now and then can be grasped only by the few who are lucky enough to be able to adopt this new idea.'[33]

By emphasizing the necessity of an act of recognition for a true understanding of the Ninth, Marx surrounds the work with the aura of the 'sublime', for: 'music can achieve sublimity only when it exceeds the imagination's ability to comprehend it, [when it] seems too grand and meaningful, too strange and wonderful, to be easily appropriated'.[34] Thus, the inaccessibility of the work borders on the sublime. As Ferdinand Hand emphasized, because the sublime, as 'the direct representation of the idea and of the infinite in finite form', possesses a symbolic character, it 'permits interpretation—and this interpretation will remain unintelligible to anyone who does not already understand such writing'.[35] The special unwieldiness of the Ninth Symphony resided in its finale, and because Beethoven's idea is emphatically articulated in the finale Marx felt that the idea of the sublime was central to the idea of the work as a whole. Because Mendelssohn orients himself to the Beethoven symphony that is most resistant to unmediated understanding, he transports the aura of the sublime by taking over those musical features that necessitated interpretation. This aura would seem just as appropriate to the object it aimed

[30] Marx, 'Symphonie', 374.   [31] Ibid. 375.   [32] Ibid.

[33] Adolph Bernhard Marx, 'Über die Form der Symphonie-Cantate, auf Anlass von Beethoven's neunter Symphonie', *AMZ* [Leipzig], 49 (1847), col. 491; quoted from Eichhorn, *Beethovens Neunte*, 215.

[34] Conrad Friedrich Michaelis, 'Einige Bemerkungen über das Erhabene in der Musik', *Berliner Allgemeine musikalische Zeitung*, 1 (1805), 180; quoted from Eichhorn, *Beethovens Neunte*, 214.

[35] Ferdinand Hand, *Aesthetik der Tonkunst*, i (Leipzig: C. Hochhausen & Fournes, 1837). This and all other citations from Hand's treatise are quoted from Eichhorn, *Beethovens Neunte*, 198.

to evoke (the Reformation) as it was for Marx's interpretation of Beethoven's Ninth.[36] Fundamental to Mendelssohn's attitudes as a whole was a striving towards all that was highest and greatest,[37] and Marx was hardly the only person who viewed the Ninth Symphony as the summit of musical achievement.[38] Moreover, Mendelssohn had an opportunity to draw a parallel between the two victorious emergences of something new, the historical event of the Reformation and the idea Marx had read into the Ninth: fighting one's way through in order 'to open up and conquer new realms for the human spirit'.[39]

But Mendelssohn avoided the problems that Beethoven's symphony had created: he did not employ a chorus, and the undisputed quality and authority of the Lutheran chorale he cites—this 'principal requisite of the idea behind the programme'[40]—eliminated the possibility of any accusations of triviality. Precisely these were the main charges against Beethoven's Ninth that Marx had tried to refute: that the choral finale violated conventional boundaries among genres, and that the melody to which he set Schiller's poem was banal and entirely inappropriate. If the aura of the sublime, which clings to these intensely difficult specific structural features of the Ninth, seemed to be lessened by the absence of a choral finale in Mendelssohn's 'Reformation' Symphony, this was compensated for by the chorale.[41] The church style was a sublime one, according to Hand, 'because of its relation to a higher world and

---

[36] The grandeur of idea of the Reformation and the circumstance that it was about a single individual fighting alone and succeeding despite all odds may be seen as parallels. Such themes also figure in Mendelssohn's oratorios *St Paul* and *Elijah*, and with those works he obviously aroused a strong public interest. The journalist Karl Gutzkow (1811–78), in his reminiscences of his youth in Berlin, which coincided with Mendelssohn's time there, wrote in his remarks on religious and moral models that Luther represented the combination in a single personality of everything that was expected of a prophet. See Karl Gutzkow, *Aus der Knabenzeit*, in *Gutzkows Werke, Siebenter Teil*, ed. Reinhold Gensel (Berlin: Bong, 1910), 97.

[37] A motto and educational principle of Abraham Mendelssohn Bartholdy that Mendelssohn thoroughly internalized was 'Aut Caesar, aut nihil'; see Eric Werner, *Mendelssohn: Leben und Werk in neuer Sicht* (Zurich: Atlantis, 1980), 49. Rather than carrying on traditional strands in a direct line, Mendelssohn establishes ties to the recognized classical masters in the various areas of his activity. (Dahlhaus reserved the concept of the 'classici auctores' for Mendelssohn; see Carl Dahlhaus, 'Mendelssohn und die musikalische Gattungstradition', in *Problem Mendelssohn*, 55–60.)

[38] '[T]hus we recognize in this [the Ninth Symphony] the greatest and boldest intention and disposition ever accomplished in the realm of instrumental music' ('[S]o erkennen wir hierin [9. Symphonie] die größte und kühnste Intention und Disposition, die im Gebiete der Instrumentalkompositon gefaßt worden ist'); Marx, 'Symphonie', 377.

[39] Ibid. 375.   [40] Wüster, ' "Ein gewisser Geist" ', 320.

[41] The chorale is presented in even note values; it is in a slow tempo; and it has a chordal setting. Judith Silber Ballan has explored the parallels between Mendelssohn's setting of this chorale and those given in August Wilhelm Bach's chorale book of 1830; see Silber, 'Historical and Critical', 106–9.

to the Godhead; it possesses a dignity that gives rise especially to feelings of religious devotion'.[42] This, according to Hand, was especially true of chorales set in the church style, which lend sublimity because of the 'symbolic power that acts directly on the emotions'.[43] Despite all modifications, Mendelssohn presents the chorale 'Ein' feste Burg' in this same church style in the 'Reformation' Symphony.[44]

Marx found the Ninth Symphony especially appealing because it 'achieved a particular purport along with its general expressiveness'; because Beethoven had 'made his own artistic individuality the content of the artwork'—an achievement that was 'all the more significant because the greater the man is who offers himself to us in [the artwork], *the more the features of his portrait can be discerned again in other composers, each according to his relationship with him who is the model for his contemporaries in life and art*'.[45] According to Marx, therefore, other composers' significance may also be measured by the extent to which Beethoven's influence is evident in their works.

This challenge did not escape Mendelssohn's notice. Fanny Hensel interpreted her own and her brother's compositional styles with the remark that 'I believe it results from the fact that we were young precisely during Beethoven's last years, and it was thus reasonable for us to absorb his way of doing things.'[46] Particularly notable is her continuation of this observation: 'You've lived through it and progressed beyond it in your composing, and I've remained stuck in it . . .'.[47]

The idea that, according to Marx, was the foundation of the Ninth Symphony was carried over by Mendelssohn into the inner and outer movements,

---

[42] Hand, *Ästhetik der Tonkunst*, i. 442; quoted from Ulrich Wüster, *Felix Mendelssohn Bartholdys Choralkantaten: Gestalt und Idee — Versuch einer historisch-kritischen Interpretation* (Frankfurt am Main: Peter Lang, 1996), 380–1. Wüster examines the ways in which the chorale was associated with the sublime, summarizing: 'The chorale simply became a symbol for the musical expression of religious exaltation. Its even note values moving slowly forwards and homorhythmic texture were perceived as musical symbols of a universal and enduring validity. As such a potent small form, the chorale fulfilled all the postulates of the sublime.'

[43] Wüster, *Choralkantaten*, 381.

[44] Silber, 'Critical and Historical', 106–9. Mendelssohn's chorale setting corresponds even in its details to the chorale settings published by (for example) his organ teacher, August Wilhelm Bach, in his chorale book (Berlin: Trautwein, 1830/34).

[45] '[J]e größer der Mann ist, der sich in ihnen uns darbietet und *je mehr die Züge seines Abbildes sich auch an den andern Tonkünstlern — je nach ihrer Verwandtschaft mit ihm, dem Vorbilde seiner Zeit- und Kunstgenossen — wiederfinden*' (Marx, 'Symphonie', 373).

[46] 'Ich glaube es kommt daher, da wir grade mit Beethovens letzter Zeit jung waren, u. dessen Art u. Weise wir billig, sehr in uns aufgenommen haben.' Letter of 17 Feb. 1835, quoted from Citron, *Letters*, 490. The translation is lightly modified from that given in Citron, p. 174.

[47] 'Du hast Dich durchgelebt und durchgeschrieben, u. ich bin drin stecken geblieben . . .' (ibid. 490).

even into the details of the formal adaptation of his plan in the 'Reformation' Symphony. In describing the overall form of the Ninth as a 'double edifice, [an] intentional and penetrating separation of the two realms of the world of tones, which could be succeeded only by those introductory words "O friends, not these tones" etc.',[48] Marx clearly states that the baritone recitative marks the work's turning point. Mendelssohn's D minor Symphony accomplishes this, adapted to the subject, through the chorale 'Allein Gott in der Höh''. But for Marx the third movement of the Ninth had two functions: it was at once a conclusion and a transition: the Adagio, 'in which the most intimate and profoundest longing and the sweetest calm penetrate the soul in alternation'[49] aspires to reach beyond itself and adumbrate the Finale in what he called its 'longing for true fulfilment';[50] he also speaks of the movement's 'melancholy and devotion', and of 'solemn gravity accompanied by the deepest heartfelt emotion'.[51]

This quality, often described as a 'prayerful character',[52] is taken up by Mendelssohn in his D minor Symphony. It constitutes the closing facet of the conflicting forces that accumulate in the first three movements and push towards resolution. The unbroken connection of the third movement to the finale makes this function unmistakably clear. Here, the parallel to the model is revealed in the characteristic intonation and in its preparatory function, as well as in the details of the movement. For example, the conclusion of the first phrase of the melody in the woodwinds has a clear precedent, even down to the details of the accompanimental parts, in the analogous passage in the third movement of the Ninth (see Ex. 5.4).

Marx interpreted the first two movements of the Ninth as the presentation of the two opposing aspects of a single fact: the powerful mustering of the masses of instruments in the first movement was set against the independent life granted to each individual instrument in the second.[53] The storm conjured up in what he called the 'titanic' first movement[54] was contrasted in the second movement with 'the melodies of all who are entwined in a merry, inexhaustible round dance and enter into the most numerous relationships'.[55] In the letter from Munich cited above, Mendelssohn described the idea of the first two movements of his D minor Symphony as one of contrast, and his statements

[48] Marx, 'Symphonie', 374.   [49] Ibid. 376.   [50] Ibid. 377.

[51] Adolph Bernhard Marx, *Ludwig van Beethoven: Leben und Schaffen* (Leipzig: A. Schumann, 1902), ii. 239 (originally published Berlin: O. Jahnke, 1859).

[52] See e.g. Wilhelm Seidel, '9. Symphonie d-Moll op. 125', in Albrecht Riethmüller, Carl Dahlhaus, and Alexander L. Ringer (eds.), *Beethoven: Interpretationen seiner Werke* (Laaber: Laaber, 1994), ii. 252–71 at 264.

[53] Marx, 'Symphonie', 376.   [54] Ibid.   [55] Ibid.

Ex. 5.4. Comparison of (*a*) Beethoven, Symphony No. 9, third movement,
bars 16–21, and (*b*) Mendelssohn, 'Reformation' Symphony,
third movement, bars 16–21

might suggest that the second movement was something unserious, perhaps
grotesque, or something that perverted the first movement. This fits neatly
with the fact that all the principal themes of the second movement represent,
without exception, to some extent the melodic opposites of the themes of the
first movement. Motifs from the slow introduction, which derive from the
'Catholic' element, appear in the second movement in retrograde, are rhythmically altered, and are otherwise embedded in the melodic fabric (Exs. 5.5,
5.6, 5.7). Assuming the character of a scherzo, they are freed of any serious-
ness of intonation, and they provide the contrast, the transformation into the
opposite, that Mendelssohn mentioned.

Nevertheless, Mendelssohn's construction is a risky one. For Marx, 'the
form of the Ninth Symphony [was] firmly tied to the idea and therefore
unique, unrepeatable, [and] in some sense "spent" '.[56] Any transferral to
another work, therefore, was by definition impossible. Marx stated this
expressly in later writings: 'The form that was assumed by the Ninth Symphony . . . was necessary for Beethoven's personality and for the development
of the art—that is, it was artistically justified. For his successors, it is not.'[57]

---

[56] '[D]ie Form der neunten Symphonie [war] fest an die Idee geknüpft und somit einzigartig,
unwiederholbar, gewissermaßen "verbraucht" ' (Eichhorn, *Beethovens Neunte*, 213).

[57] 'Jene Form der neunten Symphonie . . . war für Beethovens Person und im Gange
der Kunstentwicklung nothwendig, also künstlerisch berechtigt, sie ist es nicht für seine
Nachfolger' (Marx, 'Symphonie', quoted from Eichhorn, *Beethovens Neunte*, 213).

Ex. 5.5. Thematic relationships in 'Reformation' Symphony: (*a*) main theme
of second movement; (*b*) 'Dresden Amen' from slow introduction;
(*c*) 'Gregorian' motif from slow introduction

Ex. 5.6. Thematic relationships in 'Reformation' Symphony:
(*a*) theme from trio of second movement; (*b*) 'wind chorale'
motif from slow introduction to first movement; (*c*) 'wind chorale'
motif from exposition of first movement

Ex. 5.7. Thematic relationships in 'Reformation' Symphony: (*a*) trio of second
movement; (*b*) incipit of main theme from first movement exposition;
(*c*) second phrase of main theme from first movement exposition

Now of course Mendelssohn *does* modify this form in his own D minor Symphony by circumventing the Ninth's principal problem, the choral finale. At the same time, however, his 'virtual' choral finale—a choral finale performed by the instruments—represents a departure only in degree, not in substance.[58]

Thus, by appropriating the model of the Ninth Mendelssohn forced himself to grapple with the uniqueness and exclusive bond represented by its form, at the same time substituting a historical event for the autobiographical statement articulated by that form. According to Marx, Beethoven speaks to us of himself in the Ninth Symphony. But in his own D minor Symphony Mendelssohn speaks to us not of himself, but rather of something that lies outside of him. Beethoven himself speaks, but Mendelssohn assumes the role of a mediator for an external subject. He adopts the model of an escalation of conflict and its resolution, but he has to rid it of all personal utterances, and—despite the obvious and detailed reliances on the Ninth—can appropriate only the general idea of that work. Because of this, he feels compelled to explain what he had in mind with his striking adaptation. The clear and obvious programmatic gestures that have promoted the misguided notion that the programme of the work can be determined from them alone thus emerge as the explanations that Mendelssohn considered pressing and necessary in order to clarify how we should interpret his adaptation of the work's model. Only through this adaption does Mendelssohn's reliance on the model make sense; considered only by itself it cannot be understood.

But this unintelligibility directly contradicts Mendelssohn's later conviction that a good composition is characterized by clarity and intelligibility. In his celebrated letter of November 1842 to Marc-André Souchay, he says:

People usually complain that music is so ambiguous, and what they are supposed to think when they hear it is so unclear, whereas everyone would understand words. But for me it is exactly the opposite—and not just with entire discourses, but also with individual words; these, too, seem to me so ambiguous, so unclear, in comparison with good music, which fills one's soul with a thousand things better than words. What the music I love expresses to me is thoughts not too *unclear* for words, but rather too *clear*.[59]

---

[58] That Mendelssohn's solution at the same time represented an important contribution to the repertoire of end-weighted symphonies has been shown by Reinhard Kapp; see Reinhard Kapp, '*Lobgesang*', in Josef Kuckertz, Helga de la Motte-Haber, Christian Martin Schmidt, and Wilhelm Seidel (eds.), *Neue Musik und Tradition: Festschrift Rudolf Stephan* (Laaber: Laaber, 1990), 239–49, esp. 244.

[59] 'Es wird so viel über Musik gesprochen und so wenig gesagt. — Ich glaube die Worte überhaupt reichen nicht hin dazu, und fände ich, daß sie hinreichten, so würde ich am Ende gar keine Musik mehr machen. Die Leute beklagen sich gewöhnlich, die Musik sei so vieldeutig, es

In this passage Mendelssohn identifies the qualities music must possess in order to speak to him, and, conversely, what is lacking in music if it displeases him: such an unsatisfactory composition conveys only vague ideas, or perhaps no ideas at all. As Dahlhaus explained: 'By *thought* Mendelssohn obviously referred to a representation whose object was primarily a feeling. . . . What is essential . . . is . . . the decisiveness with which Mendelssohn juxtaposed the concept of an "indefinite" feeling . . . with the idea of a feeling . . . that is made "definite" through music.'[60]

In other words, if music articulates definite ideas or feelings, it is clear and requires no explanations—not even 'musical' ones such as those which are so obviously labelled in the 'Reformation' Symphony. Conversely, if such explanations *are* necessary, then something must be wrong with the music. It was for this reason that Mendelssohn wrote to his friend Julius Rietz: 'I can no longer tolerate the "Reformation" Symphony, and of all my compositions it is the one that I would most like to see burnt. It will never be published.'[61] Rietz, Mendelssohn's successor as Municipal Music Director in Düsseldorf, had previously reported to the composer concerning a performance of the D minor Symphony that had been given under his direction on 12 December 1837: 'The "Reformation" Symphony was performed, albeit not with that title, and was enthusiastically received. People were racking their brains trying to figure what it was supposed to mean, and I quietly enjoyed their various conjectures but was careful not to reveal the correct interpretation.'[62]

---

sei so zweifelhaft, was sie sich dabei zu denken hätten, und die Worte verstände doch ein Jeder. Mir geht es aber gerade umgekehrt. Und nicht blos mit ganzen Reden, auch mit einzelnen Worten, auch die scheinen mir so vieldeutig, so unbestimmt, so mißverständlich im Vergleich zu einer rechten Musik, die einem die Seele erfüllt mit tausend besseren Dingen als Worten. — Das was mir eine Musik ausspricht, die ich liebe, sind mir nicht zu *unbestimmte* Gedanken, um sie in Worten zu fassen, sondern zu *bestimmte*.' Quoted from *Briefe 1830–47*, ii. 221.

[60] Carl Dahlhaus, *Klassische und romantische Musikästhetik* (Laaber: Laaber, 1988), 142.

[61] Letter to Julius Rietz dated 11 Feb. 1838 (US-Wc): 'Die Reformations-Symphonie kann ich gar nicht mehr ausstehen, möchte sie lieber verbrennen als irgend eines meiner Werke, soll niemals herauskommen . . .'.

[62] GB-Ob, MDM VII/46: 'Die Reformations-Symphonie ist, wenn auch nicht unter dem Titel, aufgeführt und mit Beifall aufgenommen worden, die Leute zerbrachen sich den Kopf, was sie wohl zu bedeuten habe, und ich hatte im Stillen meine Freude über die verschiedenen Mutmaßungen, hütete mich aber recht, das Rechte zu offenbaren.' Thanks are due to John Michael Cooper for the reference to this performance and this letter. In addition, a short notice of the performance may be found in the [Leipzig] *AMZ*, in one of the periodical's reports on musical life in Düsseldorf (which were quite rare in that journal at the time): 'Der Verein für Tonkunst gibt nämlich vom Herbste bis zum Sommer etwa acht musikalische Aufführungen, in denen die gediegenen Sachen zum Vortrage kommen. Vielseitigkeit der Leistungen ist gleichfalls zu rühmen. Im vorigen und diesem Jahre kamen zum Vortrag Sinfonien: . . . eine in Manuskript von Mendelssohn, die allgemein ansprach . . .' *AMZ* 20 (1838), col. 328.

Rietz's report is surprising in several regards. For one, it indisputably shows that at least one more performance of the symphony was given with Mendelssohn's approval during his lifetime than previous studies have assumed.[63] For another, it demonstrates that the performance was allowed to take place only under strict stipulations: the programmatic title was withheld and nothing could be revealed concerning the work's programme. Mendelssohn thus made clear once again that he perceived a disparity between the challenge undertaken in the work and the actual form of the composition itself. His refusal to let the symphony be presented with clarification of the compositional goal under which it had been created and first performed is his admission that it failed to achieve this goal. Mendelssohn remained silent regarding his intentions in order not to provide a measuring stick by which the clarity not achieved in the music could be made obvious by other means.

Only through a gradually developing, more precise understanding concerning symphonic instrumental music that attempted to convey definite thoughts did it become clear to Mendelssohn that the 'Reformation' Symphony was ambiguous where it should be clear: it did not achieve definition and clarity of thought. If the first movement depicts a struggle, this is not Mendelssohn's own struggle, as the first movement of the Ninth obviously depicts Beethoven's struggle. Nevertheless, Mendelssohn's depiction assumes a form that in its own way is reserved for autobiographical expression, and whose uniqueness, coupled with this content, parallels that emphasized by Marx in his reading of the Ninth. In order that the 'Reformation' Symphony not be misinterpreted as an autobiographical work, Mendelssohn felt compelled to take substantial measures suggesting that the work took another direction, away from himself—and these measures are the conciliatory, obtrusive, and overly obvious programmatic gestures that previous commentators have always focused on.

Such a negative interpretation is justified by Mendelssohn's decision, which he later recognized as misguided, to adapt the model of the Beethoven Ninth. He recognized his misstep already in 1832, when he revised the 'Reformation' Symphony to delete the most obvious reference to the Ninth. The fundamental idea of conflict and resolution remained intact; but the passage corresponding to that in which Marx found the greatest justification for his autobiographical interpretation of the Ninth—the moment where Beethoven announces himself with the words 'O friends, not these tones'—

---

[63] The notion that Rietz may have illegally obtained the performance materials from the Berlin performance of 1832 and somehow performed the symphony without Mendelssohn's knowledge is refuted by the close relationship the two enjoyed; moreover, in such a case Rietz's report would have read much differently.

was eliminated from the 'Reformation' Symphony, since for Mendelssohn the work represented anything but an autobiographical utterance.

In 1841 Mendelssohn wrote to Rietz: 'The fundamental ideas in . . . my "Reformation" Symphony . . . are interesting more for what they mean than for what they are in and of themselves. . . . The two must be allied and melt into one another. . . . For me, the most important thing . . . is to make themes and all such things interesting in their own right.'[64] Evident in this quotation is a relationship between 'fundamental ideas' and musical themes: 'fundamental ideas' may condense into musical ones and thereby undergo a concretization that results in a theme 'and all such things'. What underlies the ideas—and this is also true of their musical embodiment—is interesting and grandly conceived; yet in the 'Reformation' Symphony the immediate effect of these ideas is not absolutely clear: the ideas have not yet *become* music. In the letter to Rietz just cited, Mendelssohn refers to the process of transformation that allows an extramusical idea to become concrete in musical terms. Important is that ideas are formulated musically in such a fashion that a clarity results that makes them musically definite as well. The endeavour is doomed to failure, however, if the 'ideas' are thought out and constructed but are not musically rich enough. If the transformation does not succeed in such a fashion that their intention is clear without explanations, and if the clarity is no more than a roughly accurate translation of an extramusical idea, then the composition has not succeeded and the themes 'and all such things' are not sufficiently interesting musically.

Thus, because the problem in the 'Reformation' Symphony was a fundamental misstep with regard to the concept that underlay the work, there was no prospect for saving the work by revising it again; it would have to be entirely rewritten. And so the fate of the 'Reformation' Symphony was sealed.

—translated by John Michael Cooper

[64] *Briefe 1830–47*, ii. 186. 'Die Grundgedanken in . . . meiner Reformationssymphonie . . . sind mehr durch das, was sie bedeuten, als an und für sich interessant; . . . Beides muß sich verbinden und verschmelzen . . . Ein Thema, oder all' dergleichen, auch an und für sich musikalisch recht interessant zu machen . . ., das, meine ich, ist das Hauptgewicht.'

6

Kindred Spirits: Mendelssohn and Goethe, *Die erste Walpurgisnacht*

JULIE D. PRANDI

IN discussing Felix Mendelssohn's setting of Goethe's 'Die erste Walpurgis-nacht', we have ample opportunity for illustrating the composer's willed affinity with the poet as well as the natural similarity in artistic temperament. There is a remarkable convergence of aesthetic sensibility in the way both artists encompass classical and romantic forms, which can be observed in the close correspondence of Goethe's thought and feeling as expressed in the poem and Mendelssohn's rendering of it in musical terms. But equally if not more important is that Mendelssohn's ethical views correspond so well to Goethe's. An attachment to Enlightenment sensibility leads both men to dignify a pagan religion in the ballad and to dare to show Christians in an unflattering light, although both ultimately work to break down the dicho-tomy of Christian and heathen and point the way to a common humanity.

Mendelssohn was on his grand tour of Italy when he completed the first version of *Die erste Walpurgisnacht*, which he dedicated to Goethe. He notes that he arrived in Rome on the same day Goethe had and that he was reading Goethe's autobiographical *Italian Journey*: 'everything that he describes I also experienced exactly like that, and it's dear to me'.[1] How closely he patterned his own experience of Italy after Goethe's, based on Goethe's book, is well documented.[2] For Goethe the joy of being in Italy was the opportunity it provided for direct study of Greco-Roman antiquity and the advantages of this pagan world-view for human wholeness and happiness. Goethe's ballads dealing with the conflict between Christianity and pagan religion, of which

[1] Letter to his family, 8 Nov. 1830, quoted in *Briefe 1833–47* (1870), i. 45: 'denn alles, was er beschreibt, habe ich genau ebenso erlebt, und das ist mir lieb'.

[2] See Norbert Miller, 'Felix Mendelssohn Bartholdys italienische Reise', in *Problem Mendelssohn*, 23–34 at 23–4.

'Die erste Walpurgisnacht' is one, grew out of his experiences during his stay in Italy.[3] Therefore, although we might well wonder at Mendelssohn's pre-occupation with a poem set in the mountains of central Germany while he savours the southern climate in Italy, it has a certain logic. Like Goethe, Mendelssohn can view both pre-Christian Romans and the Germanic tribes as imbibing of the same happy heathen spirit. On the way to Italy Mendels-sohn had visited Goethe in Weimar, where they had perhaps discussed the Walpurgis ballad in addition to Mendelssohn's Italian itinerary.

As this context shows, the heathen and the Germanic aspects of Goethe's poem probably attracted Mendelssohn. It is distressing to find Mendelssohn's literary taste or musical style being explained as illustrating his Jewishness when he, like Goethe, in addition to being engaged in a universalizing, cos-mopolitan project, is thoroughly grounded in German traditions. Far from being a Jewish protest against the dominion of Christianity[4] or a work prov-ing his 'residual psychological loyalty to his Jewish heritage',[5] Mendelssohn's setting of 'Die erste Walpurgisnacht' illustrates his roots in German intellec-tual life, especially his kinship with Goethe. The plot of the poem deals with Germanic tribes in the Harz mountains. In a letter to his family written just after the overture was completed, the composer called it 'the Saxon A minor overture'.[6] 'Saxon' in this case designates the Germanic tribe represented in Goethe's poem as the druids and their people. The Saxons were forcibly converted to Christianity under Charlemagne, who waged war intermittently for about thirty years to achieve this. Goethe states that the inspiration for his poem came from a book in which the author wanted to give this historical background to the fabled Blocksberg Walpurgis eve celebration.[7] Apparently,

---

[3] Walter Hinck, *Die deutsche Ballade von Bürger bis Brecht* (Göttingen: Vandenhoeck & Ruprecht, 1968), 19; Friedrich Gundolf, *Goethe* (Darmstadt: Wissenschaftliche Buchgesell-schaft, 1963), 512.

[4] Heinz-Klaus Metzger, 'Noch einmal: *Die erste Walpurgisnacht*', in Heinz-Klaus Metzger and Rainer Riehn (eds.), *Felix Mendelssohn Bartholdy* (Musik-Konzepte 14/15; Munich: edition text + kritik, 1980), 93–6 at 94.

[5] Leon Botstein, 'The Aesthetics of Assimilation and Affirmation: Reconstructing the Career of Felix Mendelssohn', in *MHW*, 5–42 at 22.

[6] 'Ferner frägst Du, warum ich die italienische A dur Symphonie nicht componire? Weil ich die sächsische A moll Ouvertüre componire, die vor der "Walpurgisnacht" stehen soll.' Letter to his family, 21 Jan. 1832, in *Briefe 1830–47*, i. 239.

[7] 'So hat nun auch einer der deutschen Altertumsforscher die Hexen- und Teufelsfahrt des Brockengebirgs . . . durch einen historischen Ursprung retten und begründen wollen.' Goethe to Zelter, 3 Dec. 1812, quoted from *Goethes Briefe*, ed. Karl R. Mandelkow and Bodo Morawe (Hamburger Ausgabe in 4 Bände, 2nd edn.; Hamburg: Christian Wegner, 1968–76), iii. 215. According to the 'Anmerkung des Herausgebers' (iii. 599), the article Goethe was referring to has been identified as one by Johann Peter Christian Decker, published in the *Hannöversche Gelehrten Anzeiger* of 1752.

this book makes heroes of the Saxon heathens for their clever ruse to outwit 'their superstitious [Christian] adversaries'.[8] To label his people's choruses (Nos. 6, 7, and 9) Mendelssohn adds the word 'heathen' (*Heidenvolk*)—a word not used in Goethe's poem at all. This highlights his attraction to the pagan aspect.

Aesthetically, the Walpurgis ballad and Mendelssohn's setting of it exemplify the blending of classical and romantic forms and impulses. The cultural reputation of Mendelssohn parallels Goethe's in that the works of both men are assigned alternately or supplementarily to the classical and romantic eras. This has been problematic in Mendelssohn reception, but it need not be, as the example of Goethe shows. Although Goethe is considered the quintessential representative of German classicism in German cultural history, his works, even those of his maturity such as *Wilhelm Meisters Lehrjahre* or the ballad 'Die erste Walpurgisnacht', are often considered romantic by the standards of world literature. What is intensely romantic in Mendelssohn's setting of Goethe's poem is the bold orchestration, the experimental form combining symphonic with choral music, and the juxtaposition of the solemn with the playful and lighthearted in the musical language. While technically classified as one of Goethe's classical ballads,[9] the poem is romantic in its protest against persecution of a people for their customs and beliefs. Yet the controlled form and Enlightenment import of the poem lend it a classicity that is also sensitively reflected in the piece Mendelssohn composed.

Romanticism affects the content of the ballad as well as its sound symbolism. The passion infused into the text, with the wild abandon of the devilish ruse as well as the fervent religious feeling of the pagans, is romantic in quality. The marked musicality in the sound of the words in the poem seems to have attracted Mendelssohn, who claimed: 'one doesn't need to make the music, it is already clearly there, everything resounds already—I always sang the verses to myself without even thinking about it.'[10] Like many of Goethe's ballads, this one features varied repetition as well as a richness of assonance

---

[8] 'Um nun gegen die ausspürenden bewaffneten Bekehrer sicher zu sein, hätten sie für gut befunden, eine Anzahl der Ihrigen zu vermummen, und hiedurch ihre abergläubische Widersacher entfernt zu halten.' Goethe to Zelter, 3 Dec. 1812; *Goethes Briefe*, Hamburger Ausgabe, iii. 216.

[9] In the 1800 and 1806 editions of his collected works, Goethe placed the poem under the rubric 'Balladen und Romanzen', but in the 1815/17 and 1825 editions, the heading became simply 'Balladen'.

[10] '[D]a braucht man gar keine Musik erst dazu zu machen, sie liegt so klar da, es klingt alles schon, ich habe mir immer schon die Verse vorgesungen, ohne daß ich dran dachte.' Letter to Goethe, 28 Aug. 1831, quoted in *Briefe an Goethe*, ed. Karl R. Mandelkow (Hamburger Ausgabe in 2 Bände, 2nd edn.; Munich: C. H. Beck, 1982), ii. 586.

and sound symbolism. For example, the 'ö' vowel characterizes the fear of the fleeing Christians (*Hölle, Wölf-, Getöse, Böse*), whereas the call to the sacrificial fire is painted almost entirely in the back vowels 'a' and 'u' combined with the happier bright diphthong 'ai' (*rein, reinigt, eilen, heilig*). In Mendelssohn's music, the fear expressed in the alto solo as well as by the Christians is rendered with falling chromaticism. The chorus 'Kommt mit Zacken', which Mendelssohn sets with loud bass drum, abrupt crescendos, and unusually pronounced dissonance, has the howl built into its vowels: *Kauz, Eule, Heul, Geheule*. Goethe's romantic word-sound painting becomes romantic tone painting under Mendelssohn's hand.

Lest one get the erroneous impression that Mendelssohn follows too slavishly in Goethe's footsteps, I hasten to add that the composer manifests still another trait cultivated by the grand old man of Weimar: daring and a will to experiment with new forms.[11] Mendelssohn had difficulty in deciding on a designation for this work; he finally settled on the term 'ballad', in line with the classification Goethe gave the poem and as such unique as a genre in Mendelssohn's œuvre. Critics have repeatedly commented on the novelty of the form and the different genre names Mendelssohn considered before settling on 'ballad'.[12] Also, the composer took certain liberties for which the poem provides no basis, notably the long 'Bad Weather' overture, the integration of women in equal measure to men in the choruses, and the creation of a female solo.

Although the poem's length and Mendelssohn's desire to combine symphony and song gave important impetus to the innovations in this piece, I would argue it is the non-liturgical nature of the text, the plot of the ballad, and the vibrancy of the poetic language that ultimately freed Mendelssohn from the yoke of older musical forms and inspired experimentation. Mendelssohn's *Die erste Walpurgisnacht* is a path-breaker for further experiments in combining dramatic choral works with symphonic music in a way much more integrated and successful formally than Berlioz's comparable attempts (most notably, the contemporaneous 'dramatic symphony' *Roméo et Juliette*).

Despite all its romantic aspects, in its basic tendency Goethe's 'Walpurgisnacht' ballad represents the Enlightenment rather than Romanticism, for it lacks the magic element, the eerie quality, the mysterious fog and mist atmosphere that Goethe so expertly evokes in other ballads of his such as 'Erlkönig'

---

[11] See Werner, *New Image*, 205; Wolfgang Stresemann, *Eine Lanze für Felix Mendelssohn* (Berlin: Stapp, 1984), 170.

[12] Arnd Richter, 'Felix Mendelssohn Bartholdy: "Die erste Walpurgisnacht" Op. 60', *NZfM* 11 (Nov. 1986), 33–40 at 37; Douglass Seaton, 'The Romantic Mendelssohn: The Composition of "Die erste Walpurgisnacht"', *Musical Quarterly*, 68 (1982), 398–410.

or 'Totentanz'.[13] The pitchforks and devils are shown from the beginning as a ruse, which is contrary to the folk-ballad tradition. It is the image of the flame, with its Enlightenment implications, that pervades the poem: forms of *Flamme* (flame) occur seven times; *Licht* (light) twice; *Brande* (fire) and *Glut* (glow) once each.

In his treatment of the word *Licht*, which he invests with sustained note values and puts at the crest of several vocal phrases, Mendelssohn evokes the Enlightenment side of the poem. That he is philosophically drawn to fire as a metaphor for spiritual enlightenment is hardly surprising when we consider the dramatic weight and symbolic value of light in two of his other major choral works, *St Paul* and the *Lobgesang*. In the symphony-cantata *Lobgesang*, which shares aspects of its musical language with *Die erste Walpurgisnacht*,[14] the most important poetic image is the coming of light to end a long period of darkness.[15] Paul's conversion, the central dramatic event in part I of Mendelssohn's oratorio, is dramatized in a long elaborate chorus 'Mache dich auf, werde Licht' (No. 15), which focuses obsessively on the word *Licht*.

Ethically, Goethe and Mendelssohn were men of courage and conviction, which they were able to convey artistically. Whereas in February 1831 Mendelssohn wrote to his family saying he had composed the music to the Goethe poem in his head, but had 'no courage to write it down',[16] in August of the same year he wrote to Goethe on the latter's birthday that he had had 'the temerity to compose your "Erste Walpurgisnacht"; now I have finished it in Milan'.[17] Daring was necessary not only because of the musical form but also because of the content of Goethe's poem.

Why were people not more outraged by this text and its patently anti-Christian, pro-pagan sentiment? It will not do to write off this aspect of Goethe's text as mere anticlericalism, as 'a mild satire on medieval church bigotry'.[18] Although Goethe's word *Pfaffenchristen*, a derogatory word coinage for Christians dominated by parsons or priests, seems to point to

---

[13] See Gundolf, *Goethe*, 507.

[14] Carl Dahlhaus, ' "Hoch symbolisch intentioniert": Zu Mendelssohns "Erster Walpurgisnacht" ', *Österreichisches Musikzeitschrift*, 36 (1981), 290–7 at 291. What Seaton, 'Vorwort', *Lobgesang*, *op. 52* (Carus, 1990), p. v, says of the symphony cantata, i.e. that phrases first sung by a soloist are then taken up by the chorus, repeated and developed, has also been said by Richter, ' "Walpurgisnacht" ', 34, regarding the ballad.   [15] Seaton, 'Vorwort', p. v.

[16] ' "Die erste Walpurgisnacht" von Goethe habe ich seit Wien halb componirt und keine Courage, sie aufzuschreiben.' To his family, 22 Feb. 1831, quoted from *Briefe 1830–47*, i. 93.

[17] 'Da ich die Kühnheit gehabt habe, Ihre "erste Walpurgisnacht" zu componiren, schrieb ich Ihnen schon von Rom aus; nun habe ich sie in Mailand fertig gemacht.' Letter to Goethe, 28 Aug. 1831; quoted from *Briefe an Goethe*, ed. Mandelkow, ii. 586.

[18] Werner, *New Image*, 203.

anticlericalism, a knowledge of Goethe's views on Christianity as well as a reading of that word in context makes the anti-Christian thrust quite clear. In the poem there are no Christian priests, only warriors killing the pagans. No distinction is made between the doctrine of Christianity and its practitioners, or between its priests and ordinary Christian people.

Goethe's ballad originated in the 1790s, the decade when the most anti-Christian statements flowed from his pen. Poems from this era include the tragic ballad 'Die Braut von Korinth', which, like 'Die erste Walpurgisnacht', deals with the clash of pagan and Christian world-views, much to the disadvantage of the latter.[19] The theologian Julius Schubring, librettist for *St Paul* and *Elijah*, well understood the anti-Christian jibes in Goethe's text, as he showed by sardonically nicknaming Mendelssohn's *Walpugisnacht* his 'Blocksberg Cantata'.[20] The fabled site of the witch's Sabbath, the Blocksberg, is located in the heartland of the ancient Saxons, who so resisted Charlemagne's Christianization campaigns; the medieval Church hardly existed at that point in history.

The combined cultural authority of Goethe and the highly successful conductor and composer Mendelssohn might have disarmed the critics of the 1840s. However, in searching for explanations why *Die erste Walpurgisnacht* is so seldom performed today, one might well consider possible objections to its depiction of Christian cruelty and cowardice. As the alto solo intones, the Christians 'slaughter on the embankment our fathers, our children!'[21] What has been called the most provocative verse of the poem[22] receives a peculiar emphasis since it is the only instance of a recitative in the entire work:

> These dismal cleric-Christians,
> Let's go outwit them boldly!
> We'll scare them with the devil
> Whom they themselves invented.[23]

---

[19] Compare Albert Bielschowsky, *Goethe: Sein Leben und seine Werke* (Munich: Beck, 1920), ii. 386; Dahlhaus, ' "Hoch symbolisch" ', 291; Julie Prandi, '*Dare To Be Happy': A Study of Goethe's Ethics* (Lanham, Md.: University Press of America, 1993), 4, 99.

[20] Quoted after Werner, *New Image*, 460.

[21] 'Ach, sie schlachten auf dem Walle unsre Väter, unser Kinder!' Goethe's ballad has a male druid speak these words. When Mendelssohn changed the sex of the speaker, he also changed 'wives' (*Weiber*) to 'fathers'.

[22] Richard Hauser, ' "In rührend feierlichen Tönen": Mendelssohns Kantate *Die erste Walpurgisnacht*', in Metzger and Riehn, *Felix Mendelssohn Bartholdy*, 83.

[23] 'Diese dumpfen Pfaffenchristen, lasst uns keck sie überlisten! Mit dem Teufel, den sie fabeln, wollen wir sie selbst erschrecken.' Mendelssohn follows Goethe's text here to the letter.

A Viennese censor felt compelled to change this last line a bit to remove the idea that the devil was a fabrication of the Christians.[24] Dramatically the recitative is the turning point from the *pianissimo* 'im Stillen' at the end of Number 4 to the increasing excitement in Number 5, which boils over into the *forte* of the devil's masquerade of Number 6.

In calling his ballad 'a poetic fable',[25] Goethe implies that it has a moral. However, in his letter to Mendelssohn explaining the poem, he says little to disclose what the moral was. Certainly there is nothing that would indicate that the moral concerned the struggle for religious freedom, as has been suggested.[26] Goethe writes only of the old displacing the new: 'an old, established thing . . . is shoved aside, pushed, displaced by emerging innovations'.[27]

Is the moral of this fable that the people espousing the old belief can resist creatively, as Goethe says: 'a joyous, indestructible enthusiasm flared up once again in dazzling clarity'?[28] Perhaps, but in the end the old beliefs are 'if not suppressed, then forced into the narrowest confines'.[29] Just as important in Goethe's poem is the insistence on the original purity of an old belief—one that became perverted into what we now associate with Walpurgis eve only in the course of prolonged persecution. The attraction Mendelssohn felt for his *Erste Walpurgisnacht*, demonstrated by his frequent allusions to its text and music in his correspondence, confirms his intellectual bond with Goethe and the breadth of the composer's religious views: sins may have been committed in the name of Christianity, a fact which, if it does not discredit Christianity, sharply relativizes it by hinting that a pagan religion can have just as much truth to it. No, the *Allvater* of the ballad is not, as one critic argued, Mendelssohn's stand-in for the God of the Jews,[30] but rather a sign that truth and nobility of feeling are not the monopoly of any one religion: even pagans can know and honour the deity and the light of reason. This enlightened view in religious matters matches Mendelssohn with his mentor, Goethe.

If it seems odd 'to find the devout Mendelssohn writing an anti-Christian piece',[31] perhaps a comparison with Goethe will make this easier to understand.

---

[24] Hensel, *Familie* (1880), i. 312.

[25] '[I]ch habe diese fabelhafte Geschichte wieder zur poetischen Fabel gemacht.' *Goethes Briefe*, iii. 216.   [26] Seaton, 'Romantic Mendelssohn', 404.

[27] '[D]a ein Altes, Gegründetes . . . durch auftauchende Neuerungen gedrängt, geschoben, verrückt . . . werde.' *Goethes Briefe*, ed. Mandelkow and Morawe, v. 447.

[28] '[E]in freudiger unzerstörbarer Enthusiasmus lodert noch einmal in Glanz und Klarheit hinauf.' *Goethes Briefe*, ed. Mandelkow, iv. 447–8.

[29] 'wo nicht vertilgt, doch in den engsten Raum eingepfercht werde'. *Goethes Briefe*, iv. 448.

[30] Metzger, 'Walpurgisnacht', 96; Botstein, 'Aesthetics of Assimilation', 23.

[31] Lawrence Kramer, ' "Felix culpa": Goethe and the Image of Mendelssohn', in R. Larry Todd (ed.), *Mendelssohn Studies* (Cambridge: Cambridge University Press, 1992), 64–79 at 78.

Although a self-declared 'heathen', Goethe respected Jesus as a teacher and honoured individual Christians and their beliefs, even if he was at times critical of Christianity. In addition, both Mendelssohn and Goethe had a penchant for seeing things from opposite points of view without feeling any contradiction. In his collected poems Goethe pointedly placed his hymn 'Ganymed', portraying love for Zeus, side by side with his hymn 'Prometheus', attacking and scorning Zeus. 'Heidenröslein', depicting an aggressive male lover, and 'Das Veilchen', exhibiting the male lover as passive victim, also appear together by Goethe's own design. The first draft of the Walpurgis scene in *Faust*, in which the celebrants were ghoulish and lascivious, originated in 1797; Goethe was still at work on it when he composed the 'Walpurgisnacht' ballad, with its noble, virtuous pagans, in 1799. During the years 1831–2, at the same time Mendelssohn was working on *Die erste Walpurgisnacht*, he drew up the first plans for the *St Paul*. And when Mendelssohn was revising the *Walpugisnacht* a decade later, he was also busy with piously Christian oratorios and psalms.[32]

As for the symbolic meaning of *Die erste Walpurgisnacht*, we know that Mendelssohn, at the head of the 1843 revised score, quoted Goethe's explanation to him of the old and tested being pushed aside by the new.[33] Evidently this sort of historical conflict stirred Mendelssohn profoundly. His comments about his experience at Pompeii, recorded in the same letter in which he talks of throwing himself into composing *Die erste Walpurgisnacht*, may shed some light on how he views the relationship of past and present. He found the scene at Pompeii 'the most unhappy that I have had up to now in Italy'.[34] Everything, he continued, pointed to another religion, a different life. To have tourists roaming these ruins, 'cheerfully climbing around on them', seems to have disturbed him, since he wrote: 'once again it is the old tragedy of past and present which in my life I can't get over'.[35] Indeed. It is not a question of Jew versus Gentile, but rather the conflict between old and new that is central in this Pompeii experience, as in the *Walpurgisnacht* and again in *St Paul* and still again in *Elijah*.

---

[32] See Hauser, 'In feierlichen Tönen', 76–7.

[33] See Lawrence Kramer, '*Felix culpa*: Mendelssohn, Goethe, and the Social Force of Musical Expression', in id., *Classical Music and Postmodern Knowledge* (Berkeley: University of California Press, 1995), 122–42 at 138.

[34] '[D]er Eindruck [war] eigentlich der traurigste, den ich bis jetzt in Italien gehabt.' Mendelssohn to his family, 27 Apr. 1831; quoted from *Briefe 1833–47*, i. 115.

[35] '[D]och zeigt wiederum fast Alles auf eine andere Religion, anderes Leben, kurz auf 1700 vergangene Jahre hin; und dazu klettern denn Franzosen und Engländerinnen munter drauf umher . . . — es ist wieder einmal das alte Trauerspiel von Vergangenheit und Gegenwart, über das ich in meinem Leben nicht wegkomme.' Mendelsson to his family, 27 Apr. 1831; quoted from *Briefe 1833–47*, i. 115.

The music of the overture, in which wintry weather seems to contest with spring for mastery, has been gauged as an attempt to reflect a historical dialectic, a conflict of old and new.[36] There is tragedy for Mendelssohn in the fact that the pagans, who triumph over their Christian adversaries in the poem, are doomed in the long run to fail. This is reflected symbolically in the music by parallels in the 'Saxon' overture and the 'Kommt mit Zacken' chorus (No. 6). As Mendelssohn pointed out, 'the overture, like the witches' song, was from the beginning in A minor, and concerning the theme and physiognomy, entirely the same'.[37] By using the same key and a similar musical language, Mendelssohn created an arc from the overture to the climax of the vocal segment.[38] Thus inscribed into the music we find a Germanic tribe, dynamically asserting its religion, but tragically destined to go under in the dialectics of history, just as the 'Bad Weather' in the overture, metaphorically equivalent to the Saxon tribe, gives way to the thaw in the 'Transition to Spring'.

The irony of the poem is connected to the strategy of the druids and the relation of the title to the content as well as to the historical situation. As Goethe pointed out: 'they [the heathens] considered it prudent . . . to complete the purest worship ceremony protected by devils' masks'.[39] This constitutes a shocking breakdown of the dichotomy between demons and divine service. By using the term 'Walpurgisnacht' in his title, Goethe leads the reader to suspect the satanic mass so familiar in German folklore; but what he delivers instead is fervid devotion, pure hearts, and praise of a father of all. As Mendelssohn's friend Adolf Marx noticed, 'Goethe attributes to the original inhabitants . . . a belief that is actually characteristic of Christendom—namely, the striving for eternal light.'[40] Not only do the heathens become the good guys, but more profoundly, the whole assumed dichotomy of heathen and Christian religious feeling is overthrown. As we shall see, this impulse to break down dichotomies is translated on several levels into Mendelssohn's musical setting of the poem.

A radical and Romantic aspect of Mendelssohn's *Erste Walpurgisnacht* is that it undermines not only the opposition of heathen and Christian, but also the conventional distinction between sacred and secular music. The opposition between heathen and Christian is destabilized where the pagan priests are

[36]   Dahlhaus, ' "Hoch symbolisch" ', 291–2.

[37]   '[D]ie Ouvertüre wie der Hexenchor waren von jeher in a-moll, und was Thema und Physiognomie betrifft, ganz dieselben.' Quoted from Klingemann, *Briefwechsel*, 290.

[38]   Richter, 'Walpurgisnacht', 39.

[39]   'Sie [hätten] für gut befunden . . . beschützt von Teufelsfratzen den reinsten Gottesdienst zu vollenden.' To Zelter, 3 Dec. 1812; quoted from *Goethes Briefe*, iii. 216.

[40]   'From the Memoirs of Adolf Bernhard Marx', trans. Susan Gillespie, in *MHW*, 217.

given the same dignity in orchestration and vocal line that was ordinarily reserved for church music.[41] Despite the conventional classification of this piece as 'secular', it is 'sacred' in that it gives priests the leading role as organizers of a religious service that is the focus of the poem. Mendelssohn changed Goethe's designation of 'a druid' in Numbers 1, 7, 9 to 'a priest', which emphasizes the sacred aspect of this piece.

Continuing his subversion of dichotomies, Mendelssohn's music also mixes the serious, potentially tragic situation of the pagan people with playful and light-hearted moments. While enumerating the scenes his music would present before he actually wrote out the complete score, Mendelssohn moves quickly through contrasting moods that seem to weigh equally in his mind:

The thing [*Die erste Walpurgisnacht*] . . . can be really fun; for at the beginning there are plenty of spring songs and such; then, when the watchmen raise a ruckus with their pitchforks and spikes and owls, the witches' spook is added, and you know I have a particular weakness for that. Then the druids, ready to sacrifice, come out in C major with trombones, then again the watchmen . . . and finally at the end the complete sacrificial song.[42]

It appears that the combination of these disparate elements, transgressive of genre, was very likely a major attraction the *Walpurgisnacht* held for Mendelssohn. He includes it among those pieces that he composed 'with the least consideration for people', and which for precisely that reason 'always please people best'.[43] In another letter the composer sets the 'monsters' of the witches' chorus and the 'bearded druids' side by side: 'The monsters and the bearded druids . . . are royal fun for me.'[44]

The boundary between pleasure and play on the one side and serious religious feeling on the other is also deconstructed in Mendelssohn's *Walpurgisnacht*. The priests invoking their communal religious rite are given serious music, which has elsewhere been compared to that of Sarastro in the *Magic*

---

[41] Kramer, '*Felix culpa*: Goethe and the Image of Mendelssohn', 78.

[42] 'Das Ding ["Die erste Walpurgisnacht"] . . . kann sich ganz lustig machen; denn am Anfang giebt es Frühlingslieder und dergl. vollauf; — dann, wenn die Wächter mit ihren Gabeln und Zacken und Eulen Lärm machen, kommt der Hexenspuk dazu, und Du weißt, daß ich für den ein besonderes *faible* habe; dann kommen die opfernden Druiden in C dur mit Posaunen heraus; dann wieder die Wächter . . . und endlich zum Schluß der volle Opfergesang.' Letter to his family, 22 Feb. 1831, quoted in *Briefe 1830–2* (1882), 125.

[43] '[W]ie ich bis jetzt die Erfahrung gemacht habe, daß die Stücke, die ich mit der wenigsten Rücksicht auf der Leute gemacht hatte, gerade den Leuten immer am besten gefielen, so, glaube ich, wird es auch mit diesem Stücke gehen.' Letter to Eduard Devrient, 15 July 1831, quoted ibid. 215.

[44] 'Das Ungethüm und der bärtige Druide mit seinen Posaunen . . . macht mir königlichen Spaß.' Mendelssohn to his family, 14 July 1831; quoted from *Briefe 1830–47*, i. 152.

Flute and to sacred music.[45] While the flute and oboe passages in the orchestra make a joke of the terrified Christians in Number 8,[46] the pleasure songs (*Lustgesänge*) of the women's chorus greeting the spring suggest a connection between the pagan ceremony and fertility rites.[47] Pleasure becomes part of a religious celebration. In any case, *Lust* is one of only four words in the entire score that Mendelssohn renders with a melisma.[48]

Another melisma word is *Herz*—a key word for both Goethe (it occurs twice in the poem) and Mendelssohn, and for similar reasons. Not only is the heart the seat of emotion, a central focus of Mendelssohn's musical aesthetics, but it also has positive natural ethical connotations. The concept of 'heart' in this poem unites the aesthetics of Romanticism with the ethics of the Enlightenment in a way both Goethe and Mendelssohn reflect in their work. The sacrifice on the mountain 'elevates the heart' in Number 1; Mendelssohn repeats this line five times in the score, with *Herz* thrice repeated each time. In Number 7 the people are instructed that day will dawn as soon as one brings to the *Allvater* 'a pure heart'. Elevation and purity emphasize the ethical dimension of 'heart'.

In summary, Mendelssohn sought not only to experience Italy through Goethe's eyes, but also to approach his feeling for pagan virtue by composing music to Goethe's poem while actually in Italy. The combination of technical perfection, clarity, and complexity of form together with a particular dynamism, exuberance, daring, and inspired use of form: these are characteristic of Goethe as well as of Mendelssohn. If both Goethe's and Mendelssohn's works are hard to cubbyhole as either classic or romantic, this should in no way be interpreted as a demerit; on the contrary, it is not seldom the mark of the greatest artistic geniuses. The image of Mendelssohn as a careful reviser of his works, as a man who left many unfinished torsos, is also surprisingly consistent with Goethe's artistic practice. Mendelssohn completely rewrote his *Erste Walpurgisnacht* a decade after his first version; Goethe did likewise for such important works as *Faust* and *Wilhelm Meister's Apprenticeship Years*.[49]

There is a romantic rebellion in Mendelssohn's choice of this pro-pagan poem as well as in his formal musical experimentation, which juxtaposes

---

[45] Kramer, '*Felix culpa*: Goethe and the Image of Mendelssohn', 78.

[46] Werner, *New Image*, 205, finds 'the caricaturing tone of Italianized *opera buffa*' in the music of the fleeing Christians.

[47] Kramer, '*Felix culpa*: Goethe and the Image of Mendelssohn', 77.

[48] The four melismas on the words *Lust*, *Herz* (No. 1), *Falle* (No. 2), and *Rundgeheule* (No. 6) are each three notes long.

[49] See John Michael Cooper's essay in this volume, Ch. 3, for an exploration of the problems of identity and authorship posed by Mendelssohn's and Goethe's œuvres.

seeming opposites of sacred and secular, mocking and solemnity, pleasure and religion. Yet, like Goethe, a man for many reasons his kindred spirit, Mendelssohn is able to turn a pagan, localized celebration into one that appeals to all of humanity, regardless of religious tradition; and to reconcile the opposites in order to forge in his music a new, classical unity of symphony, drama, and song.

7

Just how 'Scottish' is the 'Scottish' Symphony? Thoughts on Form and Poetic Content in Mendelssohn's Opus 56

THOMAS SCHMIDT-BESTE

FELIX MENDELSSOHN BARTHOLDY'S Third Symphony in A Minor, Op. 56 is—and always has been—the 'Scottish' Symphony: this idea seems to be one of the eternal truths of Mendelssohn scholarship, so obvious that any discussion about it would appear superfluous. Until very recently, every study dealing with the work has taken the title and all its associations for granted, not only as a label but as a starting point for any number of theories concerning the programmatic or poetic content of the piece—some rather generic, others quite detailed, treating the piece movement by movement.[1]

It may come as something of a surprise, therefore, that Mendelssohn never authorized the title and that the work was published and long performed simply as the 'Third Symphony in A Minor, Op. 56'. In fact, during Mendelssohn's lifetime and for years after his death, no mention was made of any supposed association with Scotland in the literature concerning the symphony. To put it quite simply, no one seems to have been aware of it. Even Robert Schumann, very close to Mendelssohn especially in the late

---

[1] See—apart from practically all biographies—the following studies on programmatic content in Op. 56: Ludwig Finscher, ' "Zwischen absoluter und Programmusik": Zur Interpretation der deutschen romantischen Symphonie', in Christoph-Hellmut Mahling (ed.), *Über Symphonien: Beiträge zu einer musikalischen Gattung. Festschrift Walter Wiora zum 70. Geburtstag* (Tutzing: Hans Schneider, 1979), 103–15, esp. 113–15; and Martin Witte, 'Zur Programmgebundenheit der Sinfonien Mendelssohns', in *Problem Mendelssohn*, 119–27, esp. 122–6. The recent full-scale study of the Mendelssohn symphonies likewise reports the 'Scottishness' of the symphony as an unchallenged fact; see Wulf Konold, *Die Symphonien Felix Mendelssohn Bartholdys: Untersuchungen zu Werkgestalt und Formstruktur* (Laaber: Laaber, 1992), 223.

1830s and early 1840s, did not refer to the work as 'Scottish'—on the contrary, his review contains the famous error of treating the 'Scottish' as the
'Italian', according to information which he had reportedly received 'third
hand'.[2]

As is the case with the 'Italian' symphony,[3] only the secondary biographical literature brought the ostensibly 'correct' association to light. Let us start
with England, the country for which the piece was written, and to whose ruler,
Queen Victoria, it was dedicated. From the very beginning, the A minor
Symphony was enormously popular in England, where—or so one might
expect—allusions to Scotland would be particularly certain to be noticed.
Alas, the reviews of the first performance and publication know nothing of
such a connection. George Alexander Macfarren, himself well acquainted
with Mendelssohn and instrumental in introducing many of the composer's
works to the reading public, wrote an extensive review of the symphony's first
English performance on 13 June 1842, which appeared three days later in the
Musical World. Macfarren is, of course, full of praise for the new masterpiece,
almost ecstatic; but he mentions no programmatic context of any kind.[4] The
same journal published another large piece reviewing the publication of the
four-hand piano reduction (London: Ewer, 1843); again, the writer expresses
unmitigated enthusiasm for the work and praises its 'abounding beauty'
and 'consummate mastery', but gives not a hint of Scotland.[5] And finally, the
obituary for Mendelssohn that appeared in the *Musical World* after the composer's death in 1847 again allots considerable space to the symphony, but—
in contrast to the *Hebrides* overture, whose topographical connotations are
duly noted—once more mentions no programmatic association for the symphony.[6] Other papers are no different in this respect: the *Musical Examiner*
comments on the failed performance in Paris on 14 January 1844, and most

---

[2] 'Wir wissen's durch dritte Hand, daß die Anfänge der neuen Symphonie zwar auch in eine
frühere Zeit, in die von Mendelssohn's Aufenthalt in Rom fallen; die eigentliche Vollendung
geschah aber erst in jüngster Zeit.' Robert Schumann, 'Symphonien für Orchester', in *NZfM* 18
(15 May 1843), 155 (review of the four-hand piano reduction). See also Finscher, '"Zwischen
absoluter und Programmusik"', 106.

[3] The 'Italian' features of the A major Symphony and their reception have been examined in
John Michael Cooper, 'Felix Mendelssohn Bartholdy and the *Italian* Symphony: Historical,
Musical, and Extramusical Perspectives' (Ph.D. diss., Duke University, 1994), 268–334; but
whereas Cooper postulates that Mendelssohn did in fact intend the work to be understood as an
'Italian' symphony, there is—as in the case of Op. 56—no evidence that it was received as such
until after the composer's death; see Thomas Christian Schmidt, *Die ästhetischen Grundlagen der
Instrumentalmusik Felix Mendelssohn Bartholdys* (Stuttgart: M & P Verlag für Wissenschaft und
Forschung, 1996), 275–7.

[4] *Musical World*, 17 (16 June 1842), 185–7.   [5] *Musical World*, 18 (5 Jan. 1844), 4–5.

[6] *Musical World*, 22 (13 Nov. 1847), 718–20.

extensively on the London performance in the Hanover Square Rooms in June 1844 in equally generic terms.[7]

The first source to mention the 'Scottish' character of the A minor symphony is isolated and quite peculiar: the anonymous reviewer of the first English performance in the journal *Athenaeum* is, as are all his colleagues, full of enthusiasm.[8] After extolling the 'picturesque beauty and poetical colour' of the work in general, he comments on the Scherzo as follows: 'The style of its melody is Scottish, without the slightest servility of imitation'. The finale ('Allegro guerriero') evokes similar associations: 'A gleam of the same northern wildness which we ventured to ascribe to the first *allegro* is observable in it, which (in default of a more precise definition) recalled to us the *colour* of the composer's overture to the "Isles of Fingal", though nothing can be more dissimilar than the forms of the two compositions.' Most interestingly and in marked contrast to all later sources, the author makes no mention of Mendelssohn's trip to Scotland in 1829 as a possible source of inspiration, nor does he include the introduction and first movement—later to be labelled the most 'Scottish' part of the entire composition—in his remarks. He appears almost hesitant to suggest that the composer consciously intended topographical associations and ascribes the poetic images that the music generated within him (he even apologizes for his 'vagueness of language') to a general atmospheric similarity to the *Hebrides* overture. As interesting as it is to note that a contemporary listener was apparently able to hear the Nordic colour of the work as 'Scottish' without any information about the composer's biography and supposed intention, this nevertheless remains an isolated incident; no one—inside or outside England—appears to have taken up the suggestion or have commented upon it.

The first source to cite Scotland specifically as fount of inspiration for Op. 56 is not a review, but a book: the *Sketch of the Life and Works of the Late Felix Mendelssohn Bartholdy* published by Jules Benedict in 1850. Benedict, who had known the composer during his lifetime and was intimately acquainted with many of his English friends, obviously had access to many previously unknown and unpublished sources, and is—not only in the case of the A minor Symphony—a most valuable source of information otherwise unavailable before his monograph appeared; the first reference to the A major Symphony as 'Italian' stems from the same source.[9] Already in his account of Mendelssohn's Scottish journey, Benedict refers to Holyrood Castle as the place where Mendelssohn received his first inspiration for the A minor

[7] *Musical Examiner*, 67 (10 Feb. 1844), 414; 87 (29 June 1844), 651–3.

[8] *Athenaeum*, 764 (18 June 1842), 549.

[9] See Cooper, 'Felix Mendelssohn Bartholdy and the *Italian* Symphony', 270.

Symphony (the classic account of this inspiration—in Mendelssohn's own words—is that found in Sebastian Hensel's family history, first published in 1879):

The splendid Overture to 'Fingal's Cave' was the only immediate result of these impressions; but even the greatest of his instrumental works, the Symphony in A minor, though not completed until *fourteen* years later, may be said to have had its origins in the sombre inspirations of ancient Holyrood, as beheld in the still gloom of evening.[10]

In his description of the symphony proper, Benedict again refers to this source of inspiration:

He now [in 1842] executed a design long cherished by him, namely—that of commemorating, by the aid of music, the impressions gathered during his visit to Scotland in 1829. This . . . 3rd Symphony descants upon the theme of the Scottish Highlands. The first movement is obviously suggestive of their wild scenery, with all its associated incidents. The gathering and dispersion of a storm is next described, and in a manner which has no affinity with any preceding model. In the scherzo, the familiar tones of the bagpipes at once indicate the rude merriment of a mountaineer's feast—again, in listening to the melancholy wail and funereal dirge of the adagio, one may easily conjure up to view the mournful procession that follows some departed friend to the grave; whilst the last movement, the fiery 'Allegro guerriero', bears the true impress of the afterlife of war and peril eagerly embraced by many as a distraction under an irretrievable loss.[11]

Only after this description of the A minor Symphony as 'Scottish' did other writers and reviewers begin to comment on the association. On the occasion of a concert of the Philharmonic Society under Michael Costa in July 1852, the *Musical World* reviewed 'The A minor symphony (the "Scotch symphony", as it is called)',[12] whereas the knowledge of Benedict's book does not seem to have reached the countryside yet, since a review of a performance at the Hereford Festival later in the same year contains no such reference.[13] A few months later, then, the nicknames of both the A minor and A major Symphonies begin to be taken for granted, as a review of a concert given by Adolphe Jullien and the New Philharmonic Society featuring the A major Symphony demonstrates:

The symphony in A . . . is generally known as the Italian Symphony, from the last two movements being founded on themes in imitation of two popular dances—the

---

[10] Jules Benedict, *Sketch of the Life and Works of the Late Felix Mendelssohn Bartholdy* (London: John Murray, 1850), 14–15.

[11] Ibid. 38–9.   [12] *Musical World*, 30 (3 July 1852), 419.

[13] *Musical World*, 30 (25 Sept. 1852), 614.

saltarello and the *tarantella*. Though for years laid aside by the society, it was at length resuscitated, and at this time bids fair to rival, if not surpass, in popularity the great symphony in A minor, ordinarily styled the 'Scottish Symphony'.[14]

From this point onwards, the use of a title for the A minor Symphony was widespread, if not universal, in English and American publications.

In Germany, however, 'recognition' of the title was delayed even further: not only the often-quoted Schumann review, but all other early writings that document the reception of the work show not negligence, but simple unawareness of a presumed title or programmatic point of reference. Schumann's misunderstanding aside, the reviews of the first performances are almost unanimous in their praise for the long-awaited first major instrumental symphony by Mendelssohn, but no sources allude to anything more than a general folk-like atmosphere—a 'Volkston'—in the work.[15] The first Mendelssohn biographies to appear immediately after his death know nothing of a 'Scottish' symphony. Wilhelm August Lampadius, whose *Felix Mendelssohn Bartholdy: Ein Denkmal für seine Freunde* appeared in 1848, instead falls into the trap Schumann had laid, although he does express some misgivings about an 'Italian' symphony in A minor:

It is said that the earliest beginnings of this symphony can be dated as early as Mendelssohn's sojourn in Rome, and one has tried to find a special southern flair in it. I confess that I cannot quite share this opinion, and I believe that somebody who did not know of the work's origin in Rome would not be able to discover much of any southern fire in it.[16]

The work catalogue prepared by the composer's friend Julius Rietz and published in 1853 lists the piece simply as 'Dritte Sinfonie / für Orchester.

---

[14] *Musical World*, 30 (11 Dec. 1852), 787.

[15] See the performance reviews in *NZfM* 16 (1 Apr. 1842), 108; *AMZ* 44 (23 Mar. 1842), 257–60; the reviews of the printed edition in *AMZ* 45 (10 May 1843), 341–4 (by A[ugust] K[ahlert]); and *Allgemeine Wiener Musik-Zeitung*, 3 (5 Dec. 1843), 615, 619, 622–3, 626. For further references to early reviews, all equally 'un-Scottish', see Konold, *Die Symphonien*, 230–3.

[16] Wilhelm Adolf Lampadius, *Felix Mendelssohn-Bartholdy: Ein Denkmal für seine Freunde* (Leipzig: Hinrichs, 1848), 124: 'Man sagt, die frühesten Anfänge dieser [A-moll] Symphonie datiren schon von Mendelssohns Aufenthalt in Rom, und man hat demnach auch ein besonderes südliches Colorit in ihr finden wollen. Ich gestehe, daß ich diese Meinung nicht ganz theilen kann, und glaube, daß Jemand, der von dieser Entstehung in Rom nichts wüßte, auch von südlicher Gluth wenigstens kaum etwas in ihr entdecken würde.' There is an unwitting double irony in Lampadius's account: the piece performed on 13 Mar. 1848 was in fact not the 'Scottish', but the 'Italian' symphony (see Cooper, 'Felix Mendelssohn Bartholdy and the *Italian* Symphony', 342–3); the music that Lampadius had in mind, however, was undoubtedly that of Op. 56.

Part[itur]. (A moll)'.[17] Not until the 1861 edition of Mendelssohn's travel letters,[18] in which the composer several times refers to a 'Scottish' symphony in A minor (as opposed to the A major 'Italian' symphony), does the topographical reference became public knowledge on the Continent. Only after that point do references to a 'Scottish' symphony appear in reviews and literature, often specifically recalling the pertinent quotes from the travel letters. In 1867 August Reissmann described the symphony 'that had already been inspired by his journey to Scotland in 1829, and that he had called "Scottish Symphony" several times in his travel letters, but that was not written down before his time in Berlin'.[19] Eduard Devrient, in his memoirs of the composer published in 1869, speaks simply of 'the so-called Scottish symphony'.[20] However, it was only after Sebastian Hensel's family biography of 1879—which describes the journey to Scotland in detail—that the title was universally acknowledged.[21] Elisabeth Polko, as late as 1868, knows nothing of a 'Scottish' symphony,[22] nor does Julius Rietz, in his edition of the symphony in the *Mendelssohns Werke* published in 1875, mention such a nickname: the Symphony is titled simply 'Dritte Symphonie / von / Felix Mendelssohn Bartholdy / Der Königin Victoria von England gewidmet. / Op. 56'.

From Hensel's time onwards, the designation appears to need no further explanation. In 1880 George Grove can call the work 'Scotch' in his Mendelssohn article without discussing the provenance of the title;[23] and in the third edition of the work catalogue in 1882, the entry for Op. 56 reads: 'Dritte Symphonie / Victoria od[er] auch schottische S[ymphonie] genannt (écossaise)'.[24] All subsequent biographies, beginning with the second edition

[17] *Thematisches Verzeichnis der im Druck erschienenen Compositionen von Felix Mendelssohn Bartholdy* (Leipzig: Breitkopf & Härtel, [1853]), 33.

[18] *Briefe 1830–47* (1882), i. 89, 95. (The *Reisebriefe* constituting the first volume were originally published in 1861.)

[19] 'Außer mehreren Liedern mit Worten . . . und ohne Worte, hat Mendelssohn in dieser Zeit nur noch jene A-moll-Symphonie (Op. 56) geschaffen, welche bereits durch seine Reise in Schottland (1829) angeregt worden war, die er auch mehrmals in seinen Reisebriefen als "Schottische Symphonie" erwähnt, deren Ausarbeitung jedoch erst in Berlin erfolgte.' August Reissmann, *Felix Mendelssohn-Bartholdy: Sein Leben und seine Werke* (Berlin: Guttentag, 1867), 252.   [20] Devrient, *Erinnerungen*, 228.

[21] Hensel, *Familie*, ed. Feilchenfeldt, 268–302, *passim*. A number of the relevant letters from Scotland have been newly edited in Elvers, *Briefe*, 78–85.

[22] Elise Polko, *Erinnerungen an Felix Mendelssohn-Bartholdy: Ein Künstler- und Menschenleben* (Leipzig: F. A. Brockhaus, 1868), 99.

[23] George Grove, 'Mendelssohn', in *A Dictionary of Music and Musicians*, ed. George Grove (London: Macmillan, 1880), ii. 279.

[24] *Thematisches Verzeichnis* (3rd enlarged edn., Leipzig: Breitkopf & Härtel, 1882), 34.

of Lampadius's in 1886,[25] tell the story of the inspiration in Holyrood Castle at sunset, all very obviously drawing on the sources printed by Sebastian Hensel. It had thus taken the musical world about forty years to 'catch on'.

Now it could be argued that the public and the critics of Mendelssohn's time had just been too obtuse to realize what the composer had in mind or—as for example in the case of Schumann's 'Spring' Symphony—that the composer had supplied the symphony with a 'hidden' programme,[26] a set of references accompanying the creative process and not meant for a general public, but rather intended just for himself and possibly for his closest circle of family and friends (although in this case it obviously had not included Schumann). This appears to be the position that most scholars in the past have taken, since they usually either overlook the composer's failure to perform or publish the work with a title, or do not attribute any special significance to it. Martin Witte, for example, conceded that 'Mendelssohn, in view of the kind of reception he desired for his works, decided not to reveal the specific "programme" to his audience'[27] but still postulated that 'every single movement is subject to a specific programme',[28] a theory that he bases on the (inaccurate) observation that the 'titles' for Mendelssohn's symphonies 'originate without exception with the composer himself. All of them already appear with the very first thematic inventions and drafts and go on to accompany the entire creative process throughout. Therefore, the validity of the respective title always extends to all four movements.'[29]

Conventional wisdom thus holds that Mendelssohn did indeed intend the work to be the 'Scottish' symphony, only that his attitude towards the public in general and his suspicion of written programmes or even titles in his later life caused him to suppress the 'real' meaning of the piece, which was thus left for posthumous scholarship to unearth. In view of Mendelssohn's attitude towards the public and particularly to musical journalism, this explanation would not even seem unlikely: after all, Mendelssohn considered all attempts to describe music through the written word as futile and potentially dangerous,

---

[25] Lampadius, *Felix Mendelssohn-Bartholdy* (2nd edn., Leipzig: F. E. C. Leuckart, 1886), 78, 281–2.   [26] See Finscher, ' "Zwischen absoluter und Programmusik" ', 108–12.

[27] 'daß Mendelssohn aber mit Rücksicht auf einen von ihm gewünschten Apperzeptions-prozeß darauf verzichtet hat, die "Spezialprogramme" mitzuteilen.' Witte, 'Zur Programmge-bundenheit', 120–1.

[28] 'Ich gehe also . . . davon aus, daß jedem einzelnen Satz der drei Sinfonien ein spezielles Programm zugrundeliegt.' Ibid. 120.

[29] 'Die Titel . . . stammen ausnahmslos von Mendelssohn selbst. Sie tauchen immer schon im Zusammenhang mit den allerersten thematischen Erfindungen bzw. Entwürfen auf und begleiten dann kontinuierlich den gesamten Entstehungsprozeß. Die Gültigkeit des jeweiligen Titels erstreckt sich somit immer auf sämtliche vier Sätze.' Ibid. 119.

since no text or single word could even begin to explain the 'meaning' of a piece of instrumental music.[30] To repeat the composer's often-quoted opinion, expressed in the famous letter to Marc-André Souchay and elsewhere: music was too 'definite', too specific for words, as words denoted only generalized points of reference, not specific individual feelings and images.[31] The danger, from Mendelssohn's point of view, would have been that everyone would have expected references to Scottish folklore or what was considered to be such; after all, he had heard the real thing on his journey and had learnt to view it with healthy scepticism.[32] They would have imagined reading Ossian and Walter Scott while sitting comfortably in their salons, but they never would have felt what he had felt when he had actually been there.[33] Mendelssohn would have wanted the listener to experience the same feelings and same ideas that he had experienced when he had been in Scotland, the 'schottische Nebelstimmung' as he called it; whether in doing so they had Scotland in mind or something completely different was of absolutely no consequence. To quote once more Mendelssohn's letter to Souchay:

Resignation, melancholy praise of God, a *par force* hunt: one person does not think of these in the same way as another. What for one person is resignation is melancholy for another; to a third person neither suggests anything truly vivid. Indeed, if a person were by nature an enthusiastic hunter, for him the *par force* hunt and the praise of God could be pretty much the same thing, and for him the sound of horns would truly be the proper way to praise God. We would hear nothing but the *par force* hunt, and if we were to debate with him about it we would get absolutely nowhere. The words remain ambiguous, but we all understand the music properly.[34]

The attempts of modern-day musicologists—at times bordering on the desperate—to find the 'Scottish' elements in the symphony would probably have reinforced Mendelssohn in his decision to suppress the title.

[30] Schmidt, *Die ästhetischen Grundlagen*, 196–200.

[31] Letter from Felix Mendelssohn Bartholdy to Marc-André Souchay, 15 Oct. 1842, quoted in *Briefe 1830–47*, ii. 221–2. See further Schmidt, *Die ästhetischen Grundlagen*, 155, 172–9.

[32] Schmidt, *Die ästhetischen Grundlagen*, 96–101; see also Roger Fiske, *Scotland in Music: A European Enthusiasm* (Cambridge: Cambridge University Press, 1983), 141–2.

[33] Ludwig Finscher even dubs the A minor Symphony a 'Walter Scott symphony'; see Finscher, ' "Zwischen absoluter und Programmusik" ', 114–15.

[34] 'Resignation, Melancholie, Lob Gottes, par force Jagd, — der Eine denkt dabei nicht das, was der Andere; dem Einen ist Resignation, was dem Andern Melancholie; der Dritte kann sich bei beiden gar nichts Lebhaftes denken. Ja, wenn Einer von Natur aus ein recht frischer Jäger wäre, dem könnte die par force Jagd und das Lob Gottes ziemlich auf eins herauskommen, und für den wäre wirklich und wahrhaftig der Hörnerklang auch das rechte Lob Gottes. Wir hörten davon nichts als die par force Jagd, und wenn wir uns mit ihm darüber noch so viel herumstritten, wir kämen nicht weiter. Das Wort bleibt vieldeutig, und die Musik verständen wir beide doch recht.' *Briefe 1830–47*, ii. 222.

This interpretation might sound quite credible; however, there is one minor problem: there is little or no evidence that Mendelssohn himself, by the time he had actually finished the piece, thought of his symphony as 'Scottish' in the sense of a piece 'about' Scotland. To demonstrate this, let us review very quickly its genesis.

It all begins with the well-known scene in Holyrood Castle in Edinburgh on 30 July 1829: Mendelssohn is overwhelmed by the quintessentially Romantic castle ruin with all its nature-related and historical implications, and exclaims: 'I think that here and today I have found the beginning of my Scottish symphony.'[35] A sketch from the same day of the introduction of what was to become the A minor Symphony proves that this was indeed the case.[36] In the following months and years he did mention the piece occasionally, with the intention of finishing it at the same time as the 'Italian' Symphony for his journey to England in 1833; at the time, he called the piece alternatively 'symphony in A minor'[37] or in fact 'Scottish symphony'.[38] During his stay in Italy in the winter and spring of 1831, he specifically complained that he could not re-envisage the 'schottische Nebelstimmung'—the 'foggy atmosphere of Scotland'—and therefore felt unable to get into the right mood even to begin to write down the symphony.[39] However, the last letter that specifically mentions a 'Scottish' A minor Symphony dates from 5 December 1832;[40] afterwards, between 1833 and 1835, we just hear of the 'symphony in A minor' as he repeatedly declares his intention finally to write the piece down.[41] When he did get around actually to doing so during the autumn and winter of

[35] '[A]m zerbrochenen Altar wurde Maria zur Königin von Schottland gekrönt. Es ist das alles zerbrochen, morsch und der heitere Himmel scheint hinein. Ich glaube, ich habe heut da den Anfang meiner Schottischen Symphonie gefunden.' Hensel, *Familie*, i. 271.

[36] The sketch is today in D-B, N.Mus.ms. 111; for a reproduction, see Hans Christoph Worbs, *Felix Mendelssohn Bartholdy mit Selbstzeugnissen und Bilddokumenten* (Reinbek bei Hamburg: Rohwolt, 1974), 98.

[37] See letter to his family, 11 Aug. 1830, in Elvers, *Briefe*, 117; letter to Fanny and Rebecka, 22 Nov. 1830, ibid. 129.

[38] See letter to his father, 10 Dec. 1830, in Sutermeister, *Briefe*, 89; further, Mendelssohn's letter to his sister Rebecka of 24 Jan. 1831 (US-NYp): '[T]hen I also still have to write the two symphonies and something for piano, and if I want to finish all that within two months I have to stick to it, even if I write down just one of the symphonies (the Scottish one)' ('[D]ann habe ich noch die beiden Sinfonien und etwas fürs Clavier zu machen, und wenn ich das Alles in 2 Monaten fertig bringen will, so muß ich mich dran halten, sogar auch wenn ich nur eine von den Sinfonien (die schottische) hier aufschreibe').

[39] 'Vom 15ten April bis 15ten May ist die schönste Jahreszeit in Italien — wer kann es mir da verdenken, daß ich nicht in die schottische Nebelstimmung mich zurückversetzen kann? Ich habe die Sinfonie deshalb für jetzt zurücklegen müssen . . .'. Letter to his family, 29 Mar. 1831, quoted from Sutermeister, *Briefe*, 123.

[40] Letter to Karl Klingemann, 5 Dec. 1832, quoted in Klingemann, *Briefwechsel*, 103.

[41] Letter to Klingemann, 20 Feb. 1833, ibid. 112; letter to Ignaz Moscheles, 13 Aug. 1835, in Moscheles, *Briefe*, 121. For more references see Konold, *Die Symphonien*, 226–7.

1841–2, he reverted to calling it just the 'great symphony'[42] or 'the symphony'.[43] Since the A minor Symphony was the only symphony he was working on at the time, there was no longer any need to distinguish between an 'Italian' or A major symphony and a 'Scottish' or A minor Symphony. One even wonders if the two nicknames were little more than labels pinned on the two compositional projects, merely referring to the places where the inspiration, the first sketches, and the first reports of each had originated, in order to make it easier to tell them apart in letters and conversations.

Particularly remarkable in this respect is that even in the letters to his closest artistic confidants (i.e. his family and very close friends) Mendelssohn never mentioned a 'hidden' poetic title or programme. Only in the summer of 1842, when he decided to dedicate the piece to Queen Victoria of England, did Mendelssohn call the topographical association to mind again: in a letter from London to his mother dated 19 July 1842 he explained this decision: 'Furthermore, I have to add that I requested permission to dedicate the A minor Symphony to the Queen, because it was really only for her that I undertook the journey and because the English name fits the Scottish piece twice as nicely.'[44] This does sound like confirmation that the symphony can and should justifiably be called the 'Scottish' with all its ramifications, but in the actual dedication letter to Queen Victoria, Mendelssohn further specified how he wanted this to be understood:

Thus, it was my desire to present that piece to Your Majesty which had been the reason for my last visit to England, and His Royal Highness Prince Albert had the good grace to give permission in the name of Your Majesty. The Symphony is enclosed; may Your Majesty accept it graciously and kindly! It belongs to Your Majesty in every respect, since the first idea for it came about during my earlier journey through Scotland, and since it brought me the pleasure after its completion to accompany Your Majesty singing my own songs.[45]

---

[42]   Letter to Klingemann, 6 Sept. 1841, in Klingemann, *Briefwechsel*, 266.

[43]   Letter to Ferdinand David, 16 Feb. 1842, in Felix Mendelssohn Bartholdy, *Briefe aus Leipziger Archiven*, ed. Hans-Joachim Rothe and Reinhard Szeskus (Leipzig: Deutscher Verlag für Musik, 1972), 175.

[44]   'Noch habe ich nachzutragen, daß ich mir die Erlaubnis ausbat, der Königin die A-Moll-Symphonie zuzueignen, weil die doch eigentlich Veranlassung meiner Reise gewesen und weil der englische Name auf das schottische Stück doppelt hübsch paßt.' Hensel, *Familie*, 651.

[45]   'Da war mir es nun Bedürfniß E[uer] Maj[estät] das Stück zu Füßen zu legen, welches die Veranlassung meines letzten Engl[and]-Besuches gegeben hatte, und S[eine] Kön[igliche] Hoh[eit] Pr[inz] Alb[ert] geruhte mir in E[urer] Maj[estät] Namen die Einwilligung dazu zu ertheilen. Die Symphonie erfolgt hiebei, mögen E[ure] Maj[estät] sie gnädig und freundlich aufnehmen! Sie gehört E[urer] Maj[estät] in jeder Beziehung an, da der erste Gedanke dazu auf einer frühern Reise durch Schottland entstanden ist, und da sie mir nach ihrer Vollendung das Glück verschaffte E[urer] Maj[estät] meine Lieder begleiten zu dürfen.' GB-Ob, MDM c. 32, fo. 50 (draft).

The operative phrase in this sentence, in my opinion, is 'the first idea' ('der erste Gedanke'). Back in 1829, the ruins of Holyrood inspired the composer to write a 'Scottish' symphony, but in 1842 that inspiration was no more than a fond memory of youthful enterprises and ideas. 'The first idea' came in Scotland, but there is no evidence that any part of the later stages of composition are directly or even indirectly influenced by it.[46] The references to Scotland in the letters to his mother and to Queen Victoria remain isolated; nowhere else in the years following 1842 does he call his symphony anything other than the 'A minor Symphony'.

The musical sources point in the same direction. The only material extant from the very early stages of composition is the sketch of the introduction mentioned above. The remaining material pre-dating the finished score is considerably later. It consists of a single-page continuity draft for parts of the first movement, held today in the Staatsbibliothek zu Berlin — Preußischer Kulturbesitz (shelfmark Mus.ms.autogr. F. Mendelssohn Bartholdy 19, p. 51), which is written on paper that Mendelssohn only began to use late in the year 1836.[47] All other surviving sketches or drafts were written in the immediate context of the finished version, that is, from the autumn and winter of 1841–2, either in the form of score drafts or in the form of pages removed from the autograph itself.[48] Moreover, the written references from the years 1829 to 1832 almost without exception mention not that he was actually working on the symphony, but either his intention or his inability to do so.[49] Only once, in July 1830, did the composer state that he had actually done 'a little' work on it: 'Apropos—Delphine [von Schauroth] copied a Lied ohne Worte in E major

[46] Note that Reissmann, too, had taken the quotes from the Mendelssohn letters literally and differentiated between the 'inspiration' in Scotland and the actual 'writing down' in Berlin in 1841–2; see above.

[47] Douglass Seaton had originally dated the sketch as 'after 1834' (see 'A Draft for the Exposition of the First Movement of Mendelssohn's "Scotch" Symphony', *Journal of the American Musicological Society*, 30 (1977), 129–35); however, Mendelssohn began to use this particular type of paper in larger quantities only in the autograph of the *3 Preludes and Fugues* for organ Op. 37, composed in Dec. 1836 and Jan. 1837; it seems unreasonable to assume that he should have used a single page of it much earlier than that. Full details will be given in the author's edition of the A Minor Symphony in the *Leipziger Ausgabe der Werke Felix Mendelssohn Bartholdys*, in press.

[48] The sketch collection in which the draft for the first movement (Staatsbibliothek zu Berlin, vol. 19) is bound also contains nine pages of full-score draft for the third and fourth movements (pp. 55, 59–66) and, in addition, a sketch of the second theme of the finale on the top of p. 66; the paper and page layout are identical to that of the autograph score. The same is true for two single folios apparently removed from that score, the first surviving as pp. 53–4 of the same volume (from the first movement), the second in GB-Ob, MDM c.22/6, fo. 18; see *Catalogue II*, 12 (from the finale, not from the third movement, as Crum states).

[49] '[W]enn ich doch nur eine von den beiden Sinfonien hier fassen könnte, die italiänische will und muß ich mir aufsparen, bis ich Neapel gesehen habe denn das muß mitspielen, aber auch die andere läuft weg, je näher ich ihr kommen möchte . . .'. Letter to Fanny Hensel, 1 Mar. 1831, quoted in Sutermeister, *Briefe*, 113.

into my *Stammbuch*. Apropos E major—O Fanny, I worked a little on my Scottish symphony.'[50] This 'little work', however, remained isolated and without consequences: in March 1831, for example, the A minor and A major symphonies were both still 'far afield' ('in weitem Felde')—which is Mendelssohn's way of saying that nothing or almost nothing had been written down yet.[51] Even in December 1832 he claimed that he wanted to 'write' the symphony, not continue writing it or finish it.[52]

Furthermore and most importantly, the composer wrote to Klingemann in September of 1841 that he had *begun* to write 'a great symphony', without any reference to any earlier work on the same piece.[53] The 1829 sketch of the Introduction is therefore the only music that can be linked to Scotland and its 'Nebelstimmung' with any certainty. Even the first movement itself, which might be considered appropriate in general mood and character, is not documented in written form until a sketch datable no earlier than late 1836 and possibly much later. On the other hand, to turn the argument around, if Mendelssohn primarily associated 'Nebelstimmung' with Scotland—and who could blame him, considering the miserable weather he and Klingemann experienced during their trip of 1829?[54]—it seems hardly likely that the cheerful Scherzo or the lyrical Andante were indeed representative of what the composer or his contemporaries might have considered typically 'Scottish'.

It should be noted in this context that the years around 1829 and 1830 are also what might be called the peak of Mendelssohn's 'programmatic' period. While the 'Scottish' Symphony was being planned, the great concert overtures (except the *Melusina* Overture) were finished or in progress; the 'Reformation' Symphony was finished; and last—but not least—the great 'Italian' Symphony was in full progress.[55] A case in point, little noticed so far, is that Mendelssohn in his letter from Holyrood Castle wrote that he has found the beginning of *his* Scottish symphony and not *a* Scottish symphony—that is to say, he had come to Scotland with the firm idea in mind that he *wanted* to write a Scottish symphony. The earlier letters referring to his travel plans are

---

[50] 'à propos Delphine hat ein Lied ohne Worte aus e dur in mein Stammbuch geschrieben. à propos e dur o Fanny ich habe an meiner Schottischen Sinf. ein wenig gearbeitet.' Letter to Lea Mendelssohn, 23 July 1830 (US-NYp).

[51] Letter to Fanny Hensel, 1 Mar. 1831, quoted in Sutermeister, *Briefe*, 117.

[52] Klingemann, *Briefwechsel*, 103.   [53] See above, n. 42.

[54] See Bärbel Pelker, ' "Zwischen absoluter und Programmusik": Bemerkungen zu Mendelssohns Hebriden-Ouvertüre', in Annegrit Laubenthal and Kara Kusan-Windweh (eds.), *Studien zur Musikgeschichte: Eine Festschrift für Ludwig Finscher* (Kassel: Bärenreiter, 1995), 560–71.

[55] See Judith Silber Ballan, 'Marxian Programmatic Music: A Stage in Mendelssohn's Musical Development', in R. Larry Todd (ed.), *Mendelssohn Studies* (Cambridge: Cambridge University Press, 1992), 149–61; further, Schmidt, *Die ästhetischen Grundlagen*, 330–2.

full of references to Scottish folk music and the (supposedly) musically inspiring nature and history of Scotland. In March 1829 he wrote to Klingemann that he wanted to travel to Scotland 'with a rake for folk melodies';[56] to Zelter he wrote that he longed for Scotland 'because I intend to compose many things there',[57] and from London he commented on his tendency to seasickness 'because I love the sea very much from ashore and I even want to use it for a symphony with Scottish bagpipe'.[58] His later disillusionment with actual Scottish folklore or folklore in general[59] might well have contributed to his inability to write down the symphony in the following years, when it was doubtless still intended to be 'Scottish'. Thirteen years later, the memory was still there—nostalgically tinged over time, no doubt—but only as a starting point for a cyclical and poetical framework that far exceeded the simple topographical association.

On the other hand, the 1830s show a growing tendency on Mendelssohn's part to view musical forms and the development of musical ideas themselves as a carrier of 'meaning', gaining more and more importance as opposed to 'extramusical' meaning expressed in titles and tone-painting. His teacher Carl Friedrich Zelter had always been critical of such 'characteristic' compositions; as early as in 1826 he had criticized the *Midsummer Night's Dream Overture*—a bit unfairly—because 'the main idea lies outside of the music . . . one *has* to know the stage play'.[60] And in later years—specifically, in the year in which he finished his A minor Symphony—Mendelssohn himself looked upon his 'Reformation' Symphony less favourably. In April of 1842 he wrote to Julius Rietz that 'its basic ideas . . . are more interesting for what they mean than for themselves'.[61]

[56] 'Nächsten August reise ich nach Schottland mit einer Harke für Volksmelodien . . .'. Letter to Karl Klingemann, 26 Mar. 1829, in Klingemann, *Briefwechsel*, 51; see also Schmidt, *Die ästhetischen Grundlagen*, 93–6.

[57] 'Ich habe mir eine große Reisecarte gekauft und suche den Weg nach Schottland, wohin mich sehr verlangt, weil ich mancherley zu componiren denke; die Dudelsäcke und die Echos sollen sich ganz wunderlich ausnehmen.' Letter to Carl Friedrich Zelter, 23 June 1829 (D-B, MA Ep. 7).

[58] '[W]eil ich das Meer auf dem festen Lande sehr liebe und es sogar zu einer Sinfonie mit Schottischer bagpipe gebrauchen will.' Letter to Abraham Mendelssohn, 29 May 1829 (US-NYp).

[59] See e.g. the letter to Abraham Mendelssohn, 25 Aug. 1829, in Elvers, *Briefe*, 85–6; see also Schmidt, *Die ästhetischen Grundlagen*, 96–9; Fiske, *Scotland in Music*, 141–2.

[60] 'In dem Sommernachtsstücke, liegt der Hauptgedanke ausser der Musik. Mann soll das Stück selbst kennen, man muß es kennen.' Letter to Felix Mendelssohn Bartholdy, 18 Sept. 1826 (draft), ed. in Thomas Schmidt-Beste, ' "Alles von Ihm gelernt?" Die Briefe von Carl Friedrich Zelter an Felix Mendelssohn Bartholdy', *Mendelssohn-Studien*, 10 (1997), 25–57 at 44.

[61] '[D]ie Grundgedanken . . . meiner Reformationssymphonie . . . sind mehr durch das, was sie bedeuten, als an und für sich interessant'; letter to Julius Rietz, 23 Apr. 1842, quoted in *Briefe 1830–47*, ii. 187. See also Wolfgang Dinglinger's essay in this volume, Ch. 5.

The paramount task of the composer is rather to make 'a theme, or anything of the sort, in and of itself really interesting as music'.[62]

The genre of the symphony presented a special problem for Mendelssohn as for anyone else at the time, since it occupied an uneasy middleground in respect to programmaticism. At least since Beethoven, the genre represented the highest challenge of instrumental composition, the yardstick by which a composer's achievement was measured. It was therefore expected to be much more sophisticated technically than, say, a concert overture, much less a *Lied ohne Worte*. Yet a symphony could not rely on thematic process alone, as chamber music could; it had to have some sort of 'poetic' meaning.[63] Michael Cooper has shown how Mendelssohn, struggling with these 'requirements' already in the 'Italian' Symphony, tried to achieve unity of musical and poetical meaning through use of cyclical motifs in the revision of the work.[64] And by now it will hardly come as a surprise that here, too, he dropped the label 'Italian' along the way, never to use it again.

It therefore hardly seems exaggerated to claim that in the mature Mendelssohn's symphonic writing, at least the primary layer of musical meaning is to be found in the development of musical ideas; the 'narrative', if one wishes to call it that, rests primarily on the 'forms of sound in motion', as Eduard Hanslick would put it,[65] and not on a progression of extramusical associations.

If, then, we accept that the A minor Symphony might not necessarily be '*the* "Scottish" Symphony', and if we accept that for Mendelssohn meaning was not restricted to extramusical associations, where does the A minor Symphony stand? On the one hand, it would seem preposterous to declare the work to be 'absolute music', for there are too many folkloric elements, too many spheres of association, too many *topoi* that would have carried 'meaning' for the audience; these include the 'Nebelstimmung' of the Introduction (set suggestively with just the low woodwinds, horns, and violas); the 'storm scene' in the coda of the Allegro; the horn signals in the Andante; the 'Allegro guerriero' of the finale; and finally the 'male chorus' of the epilogue.

This concluding *Männerchor*, however, once again throws into high relief the problem of topographical association: as Peter Mercer-Taylor has quite

---

[62] 'Ein Thema, oder all dergleichen, auch an und für sich musikalisch recht interessant zu machen, . . . das, meine ich, ist die Hauptwichtigkeit . . .'. *Briefe 1830–47*, ii. 187.

[63] See Carl Dahlhaus, 'Die Symphonie nach Beethoven', in id., *Die Musik des 19. Jahrhunderts* (Neues Handbuch der Musikwissenschaft, 6; Wiesbaden: Akademische Verlagsgesellschaft Athenaion, 1980), 125–32.

[64] Cooper, 'Felix Mendelssohn Bartholdy and the *Italian* Symphony', 179–211.

[65] Eduard Hanslick, *Vom Musikalisch-Schönen* (Leipzig: R. Weigel, 1854; repr. Darmstadt: Wissenschaftliche Buchgesellschaft, 1991), 32.

convincingly shown, the male chorus carries with it a very specific sphere of association, but it is that of German patriotism, not Scottish folklore.[66] It seems difficult, if not impossible, to combine the different 'poetic' aspects into a topographically coherent picture—much less a Scottish one. The problem, if one comes right down to it, is that there really were no specifically 'Scottish' topoi in the musical language of the time, nor was there a *Nationalton* in the sense of the 'Bohemian' and 'Russian' tone exemplified later in the works of Dvořák and Glinka. A more general 'Nordic' tone was just establishing itself, corresponding to some degree to what Mendelssohn calls 'Nebelstimmung'; he himself had contributed to it with his *Hebrides* Overture, and the introduction and first movement of the A minor Symphony would certainly qualify. But there were no specific musical elements that a listener would have been able to identify as typically 'Scottish' without being so instructed. Instead, the symphony had to acquire coherence—meaning, if one so desires—in a quite different way: through a very intricate and all-encompassing network of cyclical themes and motivic relationships.

For once, we might listen to contemporary criticism, but not only to Schumann's famous 'Italian' review. From the very beginning, two elements were invariably defined as main characteristics of the A minor Symphony: folklore and cyclical form. To quote from the review of the première published in the Leipzig *Allgemeine musikalische Zeitung*:

Although the symphony is similar in layout and form to those so far introduced into this genre, the important difference is that the single movements—as in the symphony-cantata [Op. 52]—are not independent, self-sufficient pieces, but are intimately connected to one another and thus form just one large movement, an uninterrupted and undivided tone painting. Its character—with the possible exception of the Adagio, which as an uplifting focal point is intimate and elegiac— is folkloric almost throughout, and it seems as if the symphony were based on the image of a grandiose, lively, serious, and meaningful folk scene.[67]

---

[66] Peter Mercer-Taylor, 'Mendelssohn's "Scottish" Symphony and the Music of German Memory', *Nineteenth-Century Music*, 19 (1995/96), 68–82.

[67] 'Die Anlage und Form der Symphonie gleichen zwar in ihrer Ausführung der bisher in dieser Kompositionsgattung eingeführten, doch mit dem sehr wesentlich Unterschiede, dass die einzelnen Sätze, wie in der Symphonie-Cantate, nicht selbständig in sich abgeschlossene Musikstücke sind, sondern mit einander in unmittelbarer Verbindung stehen und somit zusammen nur einen grossen Satz, ein durch nichts unterbrochenes oder getheiltes Tongemälde bilden. Der Character desselben hat, mit Ausnahme vielleicht des Adagio, das als erhebender Mittelpunkt sehr innig und elegisch gehalten ist, fast durchweg etwas Volksthümliches und es scheint, als ob der Symphonie das Bild einer grossartigen, vielbewegten ernst- und bedeutungsvollen Volksszene zum Grunde läge.' *AMZ* 44 (23 Mar. 1842), col. 258.

August Kahlert, in his review of the piano-duet reduction in the same journal, wrote in a similar vein. His observations on programme music in general are especially noteworthy because they appear to be rather close to Mendelssohn's own. Kahlert first comments on the nature of the symphonic genre:

Everyone who has any musical sense at all knows how inadequate words are in this respect. Serious, serene, angry, yearning, playful, all these words give a most vague kind of definition that encompasses the most different things, which at best excites curiosity, but can only deliver a most incomplete picture. One should not rob instrumental music of that aspect which is not definable in words, because that would mean to limit it. Therefore it seems that the most dangerous kind of criticism is that which immediately underlays specific images and thoughts in an instrumental piece that intensely moves the listener; such criticism easily becomes arbitrary and is often just ridiculed by the composer.[68]

Concerning the A minor Symphony in particular, he concludes: 'The whole work is characterized by an inner equilibrium, by a finely intelligent connection of all ideas, by firmly delineated forms.'[69]

The second movement in particular attracted the attention of the critics. Kahlert writes:

After a short fermata, we arrive at the second section of the work, in F major, in which key a Vivace non troppo, a scherzo, scorning the usual scherzo type derived from the minuet, transports us into a merry bustle, yet containing more harmless serenity than passionate joy. The piece . . . builds on a songlike motif that moves almost like a folksong, naively and without any pretensions. . . . The fact that the clarinet in particular takes up this cheerful song also points in the direction of folk-life, as the clarinet is especially authorized as a folk instrument.[70]

---

[68] 'Wie arm hier das Wort ist, weiß jeder wirklich musikalische Mensch. Ernst, heiter, zornig, wehmütig, scherzhaft, alle dieser Worte schweben in einer allgemeinen, auf das Verschiedenste immer noch passenden Bestimmungsweise, die höchstens zur Neugier reizt, aber immer nur das unvollständigste Bild zu liefern vermag. Gerade dieses durch Worte Unbestimmbare sollte man der Tonkunst nicht rauben, weil dies sie beschränken heisst. Darum scheint jene Art der Kritik, welche sogleich dem den Hörer mächtig anregenden Instrumentalstück bestimmte Bilder und Gedanken unterlegt, die gefährlichste, die sehr leicht in Willkür verfällt, und vom Componisten häufig nur ausgelacht wird.' *AMZ* 45 (10 May 1843), col. 341.

[69] 'Das ganze Werk ist von innerlichem Ebenmaasse, feinem geistreichen Zusammenhange aller Ideen, sicher gezeichneten Formen.' *AMZ* 45 (10 May 1843), col. 344.

[70] 'Wir gelangen nach kurzer Fermate in die zweite Abtheilung des Werks und zwar nach F dur, in welcher Tonart ein Vivace non troppo, ein Scherzo, das den altherkömmlichen Weg der aus der [*sic*] Menuett erwachsenden Scherzi verschmäht, uns in ein lustiges Treiben versetzt, das aber mehr harmlose Heiterkeit, als Jubel der Leidenschaft enthält. Dieses Stück hat gleichfalls ein liedähnliches Motiv, das beinahe wie ein Volkslied, naiv und ohne alle Ansprüche seinen Weg geht. . . . Auch dass die Clarinette gerade dieses scherzhafte Lied anstimmt, deutet auf Volksleben, da die Clarinette als Volksinstrument besonders autorisiert ist.' *AMZ* 45 (10 May 1843), cols. 342–3.

Or, to quote the review of the première once more:

In many respects, this movement is perhaps the most ingenious and witty of the entire symphony, almost bursting with technical intricacies and characteristic allusions, to an extent that many of them may remain hidden even to the most trained and educated ear after only one hearing.[71]

What, then, are the 'technical intricacies and characteristic allusions' of the Scherzo? Quite obvious, and much commented upon, are of course the 'characteristic allusions', beginning with wind calls over string tremolos (half a century later, Mahler was to call a similar passage in his First Symphony 'Wie ein Naturlaut'). The clarinet—as the quintessential 'nature instrument', in Kahlert's words, 'especially authorized as a folk instrument'—plays a pentatonic melody (derived, of course, from the rising opening motif of the symphony), joined later by other 'nature instruments', flutes and horns. The phrases fall in neat groups of four or eight measures, typical not necessarily of 'real' folk music, but very much so of the German 'Volkston'. The stage is set for a perfectly pastoral movement, and indeed the movement has been compared to the Scherzo of Beethoven's 'Pastoral' Symphony.[72]

Still, Mendelssohn chooses a quite unusual path to realize his 'folk-scene'. The most obvious solution would have been simply to write a regular scherzo dance movement—the traditional place for folklore in the symphony, used programmatically as such in Beethoven's 'Pastoral' Symphony. Mendelssohn, however, wrote a 'Scherzo' in 2/4 time, undoubtedly dance-like in character, but far from a regular Scherzo or any other traditional dance movement. In form, too, it is highly unusual. There is no trace of the traditional scherzo–trio–scherzo dance form; instead, it is an irregular sonata form with elements of a rondo.[73] In terms of a sonata form, the first thematic group consists of three groups of eight bars, with the first phrase comprising the pentatonic theme, the second a literal repetition of the first, and the third a retransition with falling sixteenth-note figures in the strings. The whole—rather extended—thematic complex is very straightforward tonally and in phrase structure. It is striking that the whole first group is heard three times in

---

[71] 'Dieser Satz ist in vieler Hinsicht vielleicht der genialste und geistreichste der ganzen Symphonie, von technischen Feinheiten und charakteristischen Andeutungen fast überfüllt, so dass viele bei einmaligem Hören auch dem geübtesten Ohr verborgen bleiben können.' *AMZ* 44 (23 Mar. 1842), col. 259.

[72] See Witte, 'Zur Programmgebundenheit', 124; Konold, *Die Symphonien*, 308.

[73] I shall treat the movement as a sonata form, but it is also possible to describe it as a heavily modified 'sonata rondo', with the refrains beginning in bars 1, 105, and 183/193. I am very grateful to Friedhelm Krummacher for pointing out the alternative formal interpretation of the Scherzo as a rondo.

almost literal repetition, in the same key, but in different instrumentations. It is progressively shortened, however, from sixteen to eight bars. The resulting effect is a three-stage dynamic climax culminating in a full-orchestra *fortissimo* in bar 49. In terms of texture and 'drama', the passage is singularly effective, but at the same time it remains seemingly 'naive and without pretensions', as Kahlert would have it, in melody and harmony. Both the second and third theme are equally dance-like in character and layout, with clearly delineated four- or eight-bar phrases.

Yet, the naivety exists only on the surface. Already in the exposition and much more so in the development, Mendelssohn demonstrates the contrapuntal techniques for which he is so justly famous, layering the themes or parts thereof on top of one another in the most diverse combinations, aided of course by the above-mentioned harmonic and melodic simplicity of the thematic material. The song-like character therefore serves a dual function, on the one hand underlining the 'folkloric' character of the movement, on the other supporting the permutations and layering techniques so beloved of the composer.

Equally remarkable is the retransition to the highly condensed recapitulation. After a false reprise of the first half of the first theme in E flat, the second half re-enters on the 'correct' pitches in bar 183 in the oboes and violins, but the harmonic progression reaches the tonic F major only with the entrance of the second theme ten bars later. The entire sixty-three-bar exposition of the first thematic group is thus reduced to some counterpoint in the woodwinds (bb. 195–6) accompanying the second theme. The displacement of the second theme also effects a change in its character and texture. After having appeared only sparsely instrumented thus far, *piano* and *pianissimo*, it now marks the recapitulation in a *fortissimo* for the full orchestra. Again, the illusion of simplicity is maintained on a superficial level—phrase structure and melody as such are largely intact—yet in the context of a highly original elaboration of the sonata form.[74] In the movement as a whole, Mendelssohn thus demonstrates the far from simple skill of combining the most sophisticated of classical forms with the 'poetic' image of dancing on a village green.

I have tried to show with just these few remarks how the Scherzo seems paradigmatic for Mendelssohn's mature symphonic style, and in keeping with his own ideals and the demands of tradition. The blend of poetic elements is connected with a definite yet verbally unspecified mood or sphere of association; with a thematic process equally compelling in the movement itself and in

---

[74] On this matter see also Greg Vitercik, *The Early Works of Felix Mendelssohn: A Study in the Romantic Sonata Style* (Musicology: A Book Series, 12; Philadelphia: Gordon & Breach, 1992), 294–6.

the whole cycle, therefore acquiring a meaning of its own; and lastly with a formal design intended to reflect clearly both poetic and thematic process while at the same playing with tradition in a strikingly imaginative way.

The A minor Symphony—the first 'real' symphony of the mature Mendelssohn—was published as his first purely instrumental symphony since the C minor Symphony, Op. 11 of 1824 (published in 1833). It became immensely popular almost at once and remains so to this day. Yet, as we have seen, it is more than problematic to view it as the precursor of the pro-grammatic symphonies of the later half of the century, or even the 'National-symphonie', as has been done occasionally;[75] it rather seems the other way around—as if precisely this search for 'national identities' in instrumental music posthumously provided a location which the composer of this A minor Symphony had long since left behind.

---

[75] Thus e.g. in Wolfram Steinbeck, 'Der klärende Wendepunkt in Felix' Leben: Zu Mendelssohns Konzertouvertüren', in Schmidt (ed.), *Kongreß-Bericht*, 232–56. On p. 242, Steinbeck proposes that the *Hebrides* Overture and the 'Scottish' Symphony were to become the 'essence of national romanticism' ('Inbegriff der Nationalromantik').

PART III

Repertoires

8

'Indessen wollte ich mich Ihnen gern gefällig beweisen': On Some Occasional Works, with an Unknown Composition by Mendelssohn

CHRISTOPH HELLMUNDT

MY investigation was prompted by a composition by Mendelssohn that has remained virtually unknown until now, and which in my estimation should be considered an 'occasional work'. What does this term mean? In general, one designates as 'occasional works' compositions written for a specific occasion (usually rather hastily) and which achieve no great significance, either in the composer's œuvre or in musical life in general. Sometimes these are large-scale works, but usually they are smaller. If the suggestion or request for the composition comes from an external source, the composer's own personal impetus plays a subordinate role, since he feels obligated to compose something. What is more, such works usually are given only to the person or institution that commissioned them—not to a publisher for dissemination in printed form. Public performance is of course not ruled out—it actually is the purpose of larger works—but usually these performances are isolated events associated with a single specific occasion. A survey of the musicological

Only during the editing process of this volume did the author become acquainted with a publication that answers some questions in connection with this composition: Arsenius Noggler, 'Das Schicksal einer Komposition Felix Mendelssohn-Bartholdys', in *Programm des öffentlichen Obergymnasiums der Franziskaner zu Bozen: Veröffentlicht am Schlusse des Schuljahres 1907–08* (Bozen: Selbstverlag der Anstalt, 1908), 1–11. For further information concerning Mendelssohn's relationship to Christanell (the commissioner of the work discussed in this chapter), see my 'Anton Christanell und seine Beziehungen zu Felix Mendelssohn Bartholdy', *Mendelssohn-Studien*, 11 (1999), 77–102.

literature, however, reveals that there are widely varying, and even contradictory, definitions of the term 'occasional work'. One author may consider certain of Mendelssohn's compositions 'occasional works', while other authors suggest that he wrote no such works. Thus Eric Werner writes confidently: 'Of the occasional composition *An die Künstler* (*To the Artists*, Schiller) and similar purely ephemeral pieces, let us observe that they have all remained in manuscript—and rightly so.'[1] And Rudolf Elvers writes of the Overture and Romanze to *Ruy Blas*: 'for [Mendelssohn] both pieces remained occasional works'.[2] On the other hand, Wulf Konold writes of the *Lobgesang*:

In the Mendelssohn literature this large-scale work almost always receives poor marks; it is dubbed an occasional work, a hastily written complaisance piece. But anyone who has studied Mendelssohn and his working method more intensively should know that for him there were no 'occasional works' or hastily written complaisance pieces . . .[3]

Such an interpretation naturally does not reject the concept of 'occasional works' altogether, but rather only its application to Mendelssohn's compositions.

If I subscribed to this opinion, I could dispense with this study immediately. But I believe that one can be rather flexible in this matter. We cannot overlook the fact that in Mendelssohn's œuvre there are certain compositions that can be considered occasional works. Among them are works that were written in response to an external request, as well as others that were written at Mendelssohn's own initiative. To the latter group belong works such as various birthday compositions, the unpublished *Wedding Cantata* (1820),[4] and the posthumously published Liederspiel *Die Heimkehr aus der Fremde*, Op. 89 (1829)[5]—that is, works of Mendelssohn's youth. But there are also works such as the *Abschiedstafel*, Op. 75 No. 4—a song for male chorus that Mendelssohn wrote in 1844 as an expression of his gratitude for being inducted as a member of a choral society. On the other hand, the choral *Festgesang* 'Möge das

---

[1] Werner, *New Image*, 417.

[2] '[F]ür ihn blieben beide Stücke Gelegenheitswerke.' Elvers, *Verleger*, 350.

[3] Wulf Konold, *Die Symphonien Felix Mendelssohn Bartholdys: Untersuchungen zu Werkgestalt und Formstruktur* (Laaber: Laaber, 1992), 100: 'In der Mendelssohn-Literatur erhält dieses großangelegte Werk fast durchweg schlechte Noten; man bezeichnet es als Gelegenheitsarbeit, als schnell geschriebenes Gefälligkeitsstück. Dabei sollte doch jeder, der sich etwas intensiver mit Mendelssohn und seiner Schaffensweise auseinandergesetzt hat, wissen, daß es für ihn weder "Gelegenheitswerke" noch schnell geschriebene Gefälligkeitsstücke gab.'

[4] The cantata 'In rührend feierlichen Tönen' for four solo voices, four-part chorus, piano, and harpsichord (D-B, Mus. ms. autogr. F. Mendelssohn Bartholdy 2, pp. 94–106).

[5] See Thomas Krettenauer, *Felix Mendelssohn Bartholdys 'Heimkehr aus der Fremde': Untersuchungen und Dokumente zum Liederspiel op. 89* (Augsburg: Dr. Bernd Wißner, 1994).

Siegeszeichen' of 1838 is a work written in response to an external request—
a work first published late in 1996 and first posthumously performed in
March 1997, at the Mendelssohn/Hensel festival hosted by Illinois Wesleyan
University.[6]

It is worth noting that when Mendelssohn sent commissioned works to
their recipients, on several occasions he stipulated that the work was not to
be printed or published. Some individuals adhered strictly to this stipulation;
in these cases it is entirely possible that the compositions have remained
unknown from Mendelssohn's day into our own time. Such is the case for
the *Festgesang* 'Möge das Siegeszeichen'. In his letter accompanying the
manuscript for this work, Mendelssohn wrote: 'But I certainly count on you to
consider the work strictly as your private property, and to make it public in
no way other than by performance—not by publication. It is important to
me that you comply with this stipulation, and I am sure that I can trust you
to do so.'[7]

A similar situation obtains for a composition Mendelssohn sent to a collector in Vienna. In that case, he clearly directed that the work 'not be let out
of [the collector's] hands', and that it was written 'not for the public and only
for the album'.[8] In another case he stated in the accompanying letter: 'I cannot
consent to the publication in print or facsimile of the little song I wrote
for you, for I made it completely for you and absolutely not for it to be made
public. I therefore ask you never to make it available for such purposes.'[9] In
this case, however, the composition, the song 'Lieben und Schweigen' written
for Constantin von Tischendorf, did not remain unknown for as long as the
Festgesang has; it was published in 1872—after Mendelssohn's death, but one
year before Tischendorf's death.

Mendelssohn also specified that the 'Lied für die Deutschen in Lyon'
should not be published. To Eduard Dürre he wrote: 'I beg you please to

---

[6] A different work from the *Festgesang* 'An die Künstler' published in 1846 as Mendelssohn's
Op. 68.

[7] Letter to Anton Christanell, 30 Mar. 1838 (RUS-SPsc, Department of Manuscripts, Nem.
F XII No. 35, fo. 7): 'Ich rechne aber sicher darauf, daß Sie das Stück nur als Ihr Privateigenthum
betrachten u. in keinem Falle anders als durch Aufführung öffentlich bekannt machen, nicht
durch den Druck. Die Erfüllung dieser Bedingung ist mir wichtig, u. ich bin überzeugt, daß ich
Ihnen darin vertrauen darf.'

[8] Letter to Johann Vesque von Püttlingen, 7 Apr. 1844 (A-Ws, in Album v. Püttlingen):
'nicht außer Händen zu geben', 'nicht für die Oeffentlichkeit und nur für das Album bestimmt'.

[9] Letter to Constantin von Tischendorf, 14 Oct. 1842, quoted from Otto Haas, London,
Catalogue No. 1 (1936), lot 221: 'Zur Herausgabe oder Facsimilierung des kleinen Liedchens,
welches ich Ihnen schrieb, kann ich meine Einwilligung nicht geben, da ich es ganz u. gar für Sie
gemacht habe, und durchaus nicht für eine öffentliche Bekanntmachung. Ich bitte Sie daher
niemals zu einer solchen die Hand zu bieten.'

stipulate to the Society that this song may in no way be published or printed.'[10]
The song was first published posthumously, as Mendelssohn's Op. 76 No. 3.

In a number of other cases Mendelssohn's wishes were already violated
during his lifetime. This is true, for example, of the 'Chor der Wäscherinnen'
from *Ruy Blas*. In 1839 Mendelssohn sent the autograph score of the piano-
vocal reduction of this chorus to Karl Dräxler, who had translated the play
into German; he asked that the music not be published.[11] Despite this request,
the piano-vocal score was published by the end of the same year.[12]

Now we turn to the above-mentioned *Festgesang*—a work not previously
considered by research. It has been housed in a library that had owned it since
before 1917,[13] and that library by no means kept the piece under wraps. In
1938 the Saltykov Shchedrin Public Library in Leningrad (now the National
Library of Russia, with the RISM siglum RUS-SPsc), published in Russian a
catalogue edited by Andrei Rimsky-Korsakov entitled *The Musical Treasures
of the Manuscript Division*. Although this catalogue mentioned the autograph
for the *Festgesang*,[14] linguistic and political barriers are probably responsible
for its having escaped substantive scholarly attention.[15]

Mendelssohn wrote this work at the commission of a well-to-do amateur
music lover who lived in the little-known place of Schwaz in the Tyrol (near
Innsbruck). The commissioner, Anton Christanell (1801–82),[16] was not a

---

[10] Letter of 11 Oct. 1846 (IL-J, Manuscripts and Archives Department, Collection Otto
Lobbenberg, 55, Album No. 34): 'Eins bitte ich Sie der Gesellschaft zur Bedingung zu machen,
daß nämlich das Lied auf keine Weise veröffentlicht oder dem Druck übergeben wird.'

[11] Letter to Karl Dräxler, 3 May 1839. See Elvers, *Verleger*, 350; cf. Hauswedell Auction Cat.
63 (2 Dec. 1955), lot 383.

[12] As the fourth *Notenbeilage* in *Orpheus: Musikalisches Taschenbuch für das Jahr 1840*, ed.
August Schmidt (Vienna: Riedl, and Leipzig: Liebeskind, [Dec. 1839]).

[13] It bears a stamp of the 'Imperial Library' in St Petersburg.

[14] A. N. Rimsky-Korsakov, *Muzykal'nye sokrovishcha Rukopisnogo otdeleniya Gosudarstvennoy Publichnoy Biblioteki imeni M. E. Saltykova-Shchedrina: Obzor muzykal'nykh rukopisnykh
fondov* (Leningrad: Izdanie Gosudarstvennoy Publichnoy biblioteki, 1938), 28: 'Mendelssohn
Bartholdy, Felix, 1809–1847. Piece "Festgesang" for piano and four-part chorus with a letter
to the person in whose honour it was composed. Shelfmark: Nem. F XII No 35.' (The title
'Festgesang' is in German; all the rest is in Russian.) This description may be the source of erroneous information provided in a German publication which states that in Leningrad there is
an autograph for the Op. 68 *Festgesang* 'An die Künstler' that previously had been located in
the archives of the Simrock publishing house in Bonn; see Rudolf Elvers, 'Auf den Spuren
der Autographen von Felix Mendelssohn Bartholdy', in Günther Brosche (ed.), *Beiträge zur
Musikdokumentation: Franz Grasberger zum 60. Geburtstag* (Tutzing: Hans Schneider, 1975),
83–91 at 86.

[15] I discovered the autograph in 1993 in connection with my investigation of Mendelssohn
manuscripts in Russian libraries for the new *Leipziger Ausgabe der Werke von Felix Mendelssohn
Bartholdy*.

[16] Research concerning Christanell's personal life has yielded little information. For some
personal data (about his various functions in Schwaz and about his wife and three children) I owe

personal acquaintance of Mendelssohn, though he had already written to him several times. In one of those letters Christanell described himself as an 'art-loving musical dilettante' (*kunstliebender Musikdilettant*);[17] in another, he presented himself as a 'tradesman and property owner' (*Handelsmann und Güterbesitzer*).[18] He occupied various offices in Schwaz, among other things serving as mayor, and organized musical events as a pastime. In April 1837 he asked Mendelssohn to send him metronome markings for *St Paul*,[19] and in October of the same year he asked him to prepare a piano-solo arrangement of the overture from that oratorio.[20] He planned a performance of the work, but the correspondence does not clarify whether he was only the organizer or—perhaps more likely—a musical contributor, perhaps as conductor or pianist.

In the meantime, Mendelssohn had sought information about Christanell. He asked the composer Ferdinand Hiller, his friend who was travelling through Austria, to make inquiries about Christanell in Innsbruck.[21] Hiller travelled directly to Schwaz, visited Christanell on 22 September 1837, and wrote with some amusement and in great detail to Mendelssohn about the experience. He closed his account by remarking: 'He loves music with all his heart and soul, and it is almost moving that a private citizen is making such efforts to perform oratorios in Schwaz. We parted on very friendly terms.'[22] Christanell also wrote to Mendelssohn, and said that he felt very honoured by Hiller's visit.[23]

On 7 March 1838 Christanell asked Mendelssohn to set to music a text for the occasion of the birthday of Emperor Ferdinand I on 19 April of that year— just about six weeks later; Christanell wanted to have the piece performed for the benefit of the poor in Schwaz. He further explained that Schwaz recently

a debt of gratitude to Herr Oberamtsrat Hans Sternad, chronicler of the city of Schwaz. Inquiries in the Tyrol Landesmuseum Ferdinandeum and the Tyrol Landeskonservatorium in Innsbruck likewise produced no more specific information, particularly concerning the concerts Christanell produced and the location of his estate.

[17] Letter to Mendelssohn of 12 Apr. 1837 (GB-Ob, GB VI/31).

[18] Letter to Mendelssohn of 7 Mar. 1838 (GB-Ob, GB VII/83).

[19] Letter to Mendelssohn dated 12 Apr. 1837 (GB-Ob, GB VI/31).

[20] Letter to Mendelssohn of 11 Oct. 1837 (GB-Ob, GB VI/82). As Mendelssohn failed to answer for a while, Christanell repeated his petition on 7 Jan. 1838 (GB-Ob, GB VII/195).

[21] Letter of Mendelssohn from London of 1 Sept. 1837 to Hiller in Innsbruck: 'Erkundige Dich doch in Inspruck, ob jemand weiß, wer Herr Christanell in Schwatz ist, der zwei Mal an mich geschrieben, sich einen großen Musikliebhaber nennt und von dem ich wohl sonst etwas wissen möchte.' See Ferdinand Hiller, *Felix Mendelssohn Bartholdy: Briefe und Erinnerungen* (2nd edn., Cologne: DuMont-Schauberg, 1878), 85–6; original in Historisches Archiv der Stadt Köln, Best. 1051, vol. 23, 1055–1058 (No. 245); cf. Ferdinand Hiller, *Mendelssohn: Letters and Recollections*, trans. M. E. von Glehn (London: Macmillan, 1874), 100.

[22] Letter of 25 Sept. 1837: 'An der Musik hängt er wirklich mit ganzer Seele u. die Bemühungen eines Privatmannes in Schwaz Oratorien aufzuführen sind fast rührend. Wir schieden sehr freundlich . . .' (GB-Ob, GB VI/70).

[23] Letter to Mendelssohn of 11 Oct. 1837; see above, n. 20.

had experienced a considerable number of misfortunes, and that the number of needy citizens was therefore greater than usual.[24] Christanell requested a work for chorus with piano accompaniment, with which he would dedicate a newly received grand piano. He gave Mendelssohn the following text to set:

Möge das Siegeszeichen des lebendigmachenden Kreuzes Dich und Deine hohe Nachkommenschaft gegen sichtbare und unsichtbare Feinde für und für begleiten. Amen.

May the symbol of victory of the life-giving Cross protect you and your august progeny against enemies visible and invisible for ever and always. Amen.

Christanell did not reveal the authorship of the text; he had found the words in the *Schlesisches Kirchenblatt* (Breslau) 3 (1837), 89. According to this Catholic religious periodical, they were spoken by the patriarch John from the Armenian monastery of Etchmiadzin to the Russian czar Nicholas I during a visit when presenting him with a small piece of the Holy Cross as a relic.[25] Mendelssohn must have received the commission on 15 March, the day on which the baptism of his eldest son, Karl (1838–97), took place. Many guests were present—among them, for one week, Mendelssohn's brother Paul and his wife, Albertine, from Berlin. Since the Leipzig Mendelssohn household was filled with lively goings-on for quite a while, Mendelssohn had no time to think of composing. Not until the end of the month could he return to work; however, he had announced that a new composition by him would be performed at the Gewandhaus concert of 2 April, and he still had to compose this piece. The work in question was the *Serenade and Allegro giojoso*, which was completed only one day before the première, on 1 April 1838, and was published as Mendelssohn's Op. 43 in 1839.[26]

The *Festgesang* 'Möge das Siegeszeichen' was also composed during this time period. The autograph score is dated 'Leipzig, 30 March 1838', and because this is a small-scale work compared with the *Serenade and Allegro giojoso* we may assume that Mendelssohn began and completed it that same day. He mentioned the piece in a letter to his mother dated 2 April 1838: 'But dear Mother, please tell Paul that I have actually composed the choral piece for Mr. Christanell, "Möge das Siegeszeichen", and already sent it to Schwaz the day before yesterday.'[27] This passage indicates that the two brothers had discussed

---

[24] Letter to Mendelssohn; see above, n. 18.   [25] See Noggler, 'Schicksal', 1–2.
[26] See Marian Wilson [Kimber], 'Felix Mendelssohn's Works for Solo Piano and Orchestra: Sources and Composition' (Ph.D. diss., Florida State University, 1993), 385–449.
[27] 'Erzähle doch Paul, liebe Mutter, ich hätte den Chor für Hrn. Christanell "möge das Siegeszeichen" wirklich componirt, u. vorgestern bereits nach Schwaz abgeschickt . . .' (US-NYp).

the commission, but that Felix had not yet begun the composition when Paul left Leipzig on 22 March.[28] The phrase 'actually composed' seems to suggest that Mendelssohn initially doubted whether he really would complete the commissioned work. Perhaps he then decided to complete the work because it was commissioned not only for the occasion of the Emperor's birthday, but also for the benefit of the poor. As now is well known, Mendelssohn was always receptive to such social concerns—although Christanell probably did not know of this predilection and would not have taken advantage of it.

The score of the *Festgesang* arrived in Schwaz on 9 April.[29] Christanell himself wrote out the parts,[30] and ten days later the work was premièred according to plan; it probably was also performed repeatedly in Schwaz in the following years. Already on 11 April Christanell wrote in his letter of gratitude to Mendelssohn:

In order to move the hearts of many to make a small donation for the benefit of our numerous needy citizens (about 1,500), . . . this piece will be heard not only this year, but *every* year. It shall ring out repeatedly, at the same celebration and for the same purpose—at least so long as we are able and I have a say-so in these concerts.[31]

Evidently Mendelssohn wrote out the score only once, keeping no preliminary manuscripts for himself. Likewise, we know of no sketches or drafts; the sole source is the autograph score sent to Christanell, which, although neatly written, reveals numerous corrections and therefore should be considered a first notation. Today it is housed in the Manuscript Department of the National Library of Russia in St Petersburg (shelf mark Nem. F XII No 35, fos. 1–6). In the above-cited letter accompanying the score, the composer admitted that the commission had cost him considerable effort;[32] at the same time, however, he wanted to support Christanell's project and wrote that he 'nevertheless wanted to oblige [him], and'—as Christanell said—'contribute [his] bit to the festival held in the mountains of Tyrol'. He concluded: 'So please accept it as it is.'[33] Mendelssohn's word *gefällig* shows he is doing

---

[28] On 29 Mar., in a letter to Paul, Felix looked back on the visit, writing that it had been nice to visit with him a week ago (US-NYp).

[29] See Christanell's letter to Mendelssohn dated 11 Apr. 1838 (GB-Ob, GB VII/122).

[30] Letter of 11 Apr. 1838 (see above, n. 29).

[31] 'Aber nicht allein heuriges Jahr wird dieser Gesang erschallen, um die Herzen vieler zu einer milden Spende zu stimmen für unsere zahlreichen Ortsarme (*circa* 1500), . . . sondern alljährlich, wenigstens so lange als ich bei diesen Musiken das Wort zu führen habe, nach möglichsten Kräften, zum gleichen Fest und Zwecke wi[e]derholt erschallen' (letter of 11 Apr. 1838; see above, n. 29). [32] Letter of 30 Mar. 1838 (see above, n. 7).

[33] Ibid.: '[I]ndessen wollte ich mich Ihnen gern gefällig beweisen, u. wie Sie sagen zu dem Fest in Tyrols Bergen mein Scherflein beitragen, also nehmen Sie es hin, wie es geworden ist.'

Christanell a favour, and authorizes us to call this work an occasional or complaisance piece.

What caused Mendelssohn problems was the original text. He wrote to Christanell that 'it was no small thing to set these exact words to music; yet I could not help but change one small thing, for I simply could not make do with the "hohe Nachkommenschaft" [august progeny]'.[34] For the words 'Dich und Deine hohe Nachkommenschaft' ['you and your august progeny'] he substituted the more general phrase 'Dich und die Deinen' ['you and yours', or 'you and your kin'] in his setting. That he was not quite comfortable with the text as a whole is evident from some other remarks in the letter to his mother cited above, in which he continues: 'And as odd as the words were, the chorus using them turned out quite nicely—to my own surprise.'[35] In this statement the German word *toll* is ambiguous today; it may mean 'odd', 'strange', 'mad', or 'crazy'. We cannot know for certain whether Mendelssohn used it in a decidedly pejorative sense.

This work has remained unknown because of the stipulation of the composer (see above): Christanell was to consider the work solely as his private property and under no circumstances to have it published. In his letter of gratitude Christanell assured Mendelssohn that he could count on him to comply with this condition, and he obviously remained true to his word. Because of this, no performance materials are known to have survived either in Schwaz or in Innsbruck (the regional capital of Tyrol). Such materials must have remained in the exclusive possession of Christanell and been so carefully guarded in his estate that nothing but the autograph was able to reach the outside world. In this connection the question of how the autograph score and the accompanying letter travelled together to Russia must, for the time being, remain open,[36] as must the question of why no further material from

---

[34] Letter of 30 Mar. 1838: 'Es war keine leichte Aufgabe, grade diese Worte in Musik zu setzen, und allerdings habe ich eine kleine Abänderung machen müssen, weil die "hohe Nachkommenschaft" mir gar nicht passen wollte.'

[35] Letter from Mendelssohn to his family, 2 Apr. 1838 (US-NYp): '[U.] so toll die Worte waren, so ists wahrhaftig zu meinem eignen Erstaunen ein ganz netter Chor daraus geworden.'

[36] On 22 Apr. 1854 Christanell himself sent the autograph score and Mendelssohn's letter to the Russian prince Alexei Lvoff, who was a composer and the director of the Imperial Court Chapel in St Petersburg. Christanell asked Lvoff to present the score to Tsar Nicholas I, hoping that the work would be published in Russia. His wish was not fulfilled, but for unknown reasons neither did he get the score back. The score and letter eventually were transferred to the Imperial Library in St Petersburg, probably after the death of Lvoff in 1870. See Noggler, 'Schicksal', 6–9. The present location of the rest of Mendelssohn's letters to Christanell is, for the time being, unknown. In 1908 important parts of the estate of Anton Christanell apparently were located in Bozen (Bolzano, South Tyrol, Italy, at that time Austria); see Noggler, ibid. 10.

Ex. 8.1. *Festgesang* 'Möge das Siegeszeichen', prelude (bars 1–8)

Christanell's estate could be found.[37] At least one set of choral parts must have existed at one time.

The autograph for the *Festgesang* comprises twelve neatly written pages on printed sixteen-stave paper. The title page bears the inscription: 'Festgesang / für den Herrn Anton Christanell / in Schwaz / componirt / von / Felix Mendelssohn Bartholdy'. This page is followed by eleven written pages of music. The work as a whole is in G major, and it consists of a march-like Prelude for piano in 3/4 time and marked *Allegro Maestoso alla marcia*, followed by a somewhat slower section for chorus with piano accompaniment written in 4/4 time and designated *Moderato*.

Occupying the first page of the autograph, the piano prelude comprises sixty-two notated measures, of which the first twenty-five are repeated; the word 'Allegro' in the tempo designation was added retroactively. This prelude serves two functions: on the one hand, it sets the mood for the following vocal section; on the other, it unfolds with a certain—modest—pianistic virtuosity that obviously proceeds from Mendelssohn's consideration of Christanell's desire to show off the sound of the new piano. The prelude is characterized by the chordal texture that lends the entire work its weighty majesty and by the march-like rhythms, which attain an especially solemn character in 3/4 time (see Ex. 8.1).

The choral part of 133 bars is divided into two sections, one predominantly homophonic with a march-like theme, and the other fugal (see Exs. 8.2 and

[37] According to Noggler (pp. 10–11), in 1908 a letter by Mendelssohn dated 18 May 1837 and an otherwise unknown autograph piano solo reduction (two hands) of the overture to *St Paul* were in the possession of Christanell's descendants.

Ex. 8.2. *Festgesang* 'Möge das Siegeszeichen', main theme of choral section

Ex. 8.3. *Festgesang* 'Möge das Siegeszeichen', fugal theme of choral section

8.3). This section is worked out so that it is gradually combined with the march theme. The work is crowned with a hymn-like, homophonic coda.

Particularly noteworthy is the theme with which the choral section begins. When Mendelssohn wrote this theme it was new to him. Today, however, we hear in it the beginning of a prominent theme from another, more familiar, and larger work: the beginning of the symphony-cantata *Lobgesang*, Op. 52.

Ex. 8.4. Symphony-Cantata *Lobgesang*, motto theme

Al - les, was O - dem hat, lo - be den Herrn
All that has life and breath, sing to the Lord

In the *Lobgesang*, this theme is also subsequently taken up by the chorus and sung to the words 'Alles was Odem hat, lobe den Herrn' ('All that has life and breath, sing to the Lord') (see Ex. 8.4).

The differences between these two themes are minimal: in the first bar there is a small rhythmic difference, resulting from the divergent text, and in the second bar there is a melodic development through the insertion of a new note. Nevertheless, these small differences hardly change the overall impression of the melodic structure of the motto of the *Lobgesang*.

How did this striking similarity arise? We know of no statements from the composer on the subject. We may assume that it is no coincidence, however. Conceivably Mendelssohn was so taken with the melodic idea that occurred to him in the *Festgesang* that he wanted to do more with it. Several letters of 1838 and 1839[38] and sketches that must date from the same years[39] confirm that at the time Mendelssohn was working on a symphony in B flat major. Evidently he dropped this idea later on, but in 1840 he completed a symphony-cantata in B flat titled *Lobgesang*. Although the theme in question does not occur in the sketches for this work,[40] Mendelssohn must have had it in mind—for he sketched only *new* compositional ideas.

I should also like to point out another spot that is not as significant, but nevertheless noteworthy. In the extended piano prelude to the *Festgesang* one passage (bb. 22–5 and 44–6) is not at all unrelated to the *Lobgesang*—specifically, the tenor solo 'Stricke des Todes hatten uns umfangen' (No. 6, 'The sorrows of death had closed all around us'), the oft-repeated passage bearing the text 'Ich will dich erleuchten', or 'I will be to thee light'; cf.

---

[38] See Max Friedländer, 'Ein Brief Felix Mendelssohns', *Vierteljahrsschrift für Musikwissenschaft*, 5 (1889), 483–9, esp. 486–7; Stuart Douglass Seaton, 'A Study of a Collection of Mendelssohn's Sketches and other Autograph Material, Deutsche Staatsbibliothek Berlin Mus. ms. autogr. Mendelssohn 19' (Ph.D. diss., Columbia University, 1977), 110–11; R. Larry Todd, 'An Unfinished Symphony by Mendelssohn', *Music & Letters*, 61 (1980), 293–309.

[39] D-B, Mus. ms. autogr. F. Mendelssohn Bartholdy 19, pp. 36–48. While some of these sketches may be assigned to the *Lobgesang*, others that are mingled among them and are primarily in B flat major or related keys could not be identified; see Seaton, 'Study', 9–10.

[40] Ibid. 183.

Ex. 8.5. Symphony-Cantata *Lobgesang*, 'Ich will dich erleuchten'

Ex. 8.6. *Festgesang* 'Möge das Siegeszeichen', prelude (bars 22–5)

Exs. 8.5 and 8.6). This latter resemblance may be coincidental; the first, however, concerning the central motif of the *Festgesang*, must have represented a deliberate reminiscence in the *Lobgesang*.[41]

Certainly the *Festgesang* Mendelssohn wrote for Christanell is no masterpiece. Unlike most of the still-unknown youthful compositions that the composer kept in his cabinets as exercises, however, it is the work of the mature master. Mendelssohn himself considered it an occasional composition, but the work may certainly find its interested and attentive listeners even today—and even in regions other than the 'mountains of Tyrol'—more than one hundred and fifty years after the composer's death.

—translated by John Michael Cooper

[41] Concerning the *Festgesang* see also my Preface to the first edition, Chor-Bibliothek 5279 (Wiesbaden: Breitkopf & Härtel, [1997]).

9

'So kann ich es nicht componiren': Mendelssohn, Opera, and the Libretto Problem

MONIKA HENNEMANN

'I CANNOT compose it like that'[1]: Felix Mendelssohn's typical reaction to opera libretti presented to him goes some way to account for his failure to complete a mature opera and thus even suggests that a more accurate title of this chapter might read 'Mendelssohn, no opera, and the libretto problem'. It might initially seem odd to discuss the relationship to opera composition of a composer who never completed mature work in the genre. However, Mendelssohn's attempts at opera composition constitute such a significant part of his compositional career that they deserve to be investigated, particularly when we take into account his constant preoccupation with this challenge and his promising start in the genre. By the age of 20, he had seen a total of six of his own *Singspiele* and *Liederspiele* performed, and definitely planned to compose further dramatic works. In the course of the following years, he considered more than fifty subjects,[2] was in contact with prospective librettists, and received a large number of unsolicited libretti. There was never a period in his life during which his mind was not occupied with opera composition. Why he remained unsuccessful in these endeavours despite his interest is a very complex issue that requires a thorough investigation of all available sources.

---

[1] Felix Mendelssohn's comment about Emanuel Geibel's libretto for *Die Lorelei*, quoted in Devrient, *Erinnerungen*, 279.

[2] For a preliminary inventory, see R. Larry Todd, 'Mendelssohn's Operatic Destiny: *Die Lorelei* Reconsidered', in Schmidt, *Kongreß-Bericht*, 113–40, esp. 138–9. I am also grateful to Ralf Wehner for additional information.

It would be helpful if we had at our disposal a variety of musical examples taken from unfinished operas by Mendelssohn; unfortunately, however, very little music was actually written down. From an early age, it was Mendelssohn's habit to wait for his libretti to be completed and adjusted to his taste before he started to compose, as is exemplified in a letter of March 1824 to the librettist of *Die Hochzeit des Camacho*, Friedrich Voigts: 'I await the second act the more anxiously, as I cannot start to compose before I have it, in order to get an overview of the complete text.'[3] Similar statements exist for other opera projects. The single exception to this manner of proceeding seems to be an opera project on Edward III that Mendelssohn discussed with James Robinson Planché in 1838. The composer wrote to William Chappell about the libretto: 'It suggested to me in several places musical ideas which I noted down while reading, and found then how adapted to music these flowing and expressive verses are.'[4] Unfortunately, the musical drafts mentioned here have not yet resurfaced.

Notwithstanding the lack of musical evidence, the topic of Mendelssohn as an opera composer is a fascinating one, providing insight into his views on opera, his self-image, and his working process. What makes this issue more broadly significant is that Mendelssohn's individual problem is symptomatic of a general one, namely the struggle to create 'German' opera in the first half of the nineteenth century. Many composers tried to define and contribute to a genre that, despite many locally produced and performed operas, did not really exist as such. In response to the absence of political unity in Germany, 'German' opera was expected to help achieve a sense of national unity through common cultural values and a common musical language. There is, however, one fundamental difference between Mendelssohn and other composers attempting to create 'German' opera, such as Beethoven, Schumann, and Brahms: as opposed to these other composers, Mendelssohn in his adolescence had already produced a series of dramatic compositions that he himself was partial to and that were well received by his audience, which makes his later difficulties even harder to comprehend.

Any investigation of Mendelssohn's operatic endeavours must rely on contemporary accounts and on published and unpublished parts of the immense

---

[3] 'Ich erwarte den 2ten Act um so sehnlicher, als ich nicht eher zu componiren anfangen kann, als bis ich ihn habe, um das Ganze übersehen zu können.' Letter from Mendelssohn to Friedrich Voigts, Berlin, 13 Mar. 1824, quoted in Rudolph Elvers, *'Nichts ist so schwer gut zu componiren als in Strophen': Zur Entstehungsgeschichte von Felix Mendelssohns Oper 'Die Hochzeit des Camacho'* (Berlin: Mendelssohn-Gesellschaft, 1976), 14.

[4] Memorandum of Mendelssohn to William Chappell, 29 Dec. 1838, quoted in James Robinson Planché, *The Recollections and Reflections of J. R. Planché* (London: Tinsley Brothers, 1872), 311. For a discussion of this memo, see below.

corpus of letters to and from the composer. The ongoing publication of Mendelssohn's correspondence and the rediscovery of material presumed lost continue to reveal evidence of still more unrealized operatic schemes. Here, I shall discuss only a few of the most significant projects, focusing on two aspects that seem particularly relevant for the understanding of Mendelssohn's 'virtual' operatic career: the questions of national identity and of genre. This approach allows us to go beyond description and speculation and to demonstrate a connection between the operas Mendelssohn contemplated and the development of his ideas.

MENDELSSOHN'S OPERA ATTEMPTS AND NATIONAL IDENTITY

Mendelssohn's 'youthful operas', increasingly long stage pieces written for specific festivities in the Mendelssohn home, were performed under the direction of the composer with family members and friends as singers and instrumentalists, supplemented by hired professional musicians. Five of these works were written in a popular form of the day, the *Singspiel*, a term that usually refers to a type of opera in German with a comic or sentimental plot with spoken dialogue and often comprising only one or two acts. His last completed stage work, *Die Heimkehr aus der Fremde*, is a *Liederspiel*—a predominantly locally successful genre established by the Berlin composer Johann Friedrich Reichardt and consisting of a series of solo Lieder. The genre was familiar to Mendelssohn through the *Liederspiel* composition of, among others, one of his earliest music teachers, Ludwig Berger.[5] However, Mendelssohn went beyond Reichardt's and Berger's models by including ensemble numbers in addition to solo Lieder.

The libretti of the first four *Singspiele* (*Die Soldatenliebschaft*, 1820; *Die beiden Pädagogen*, 1821; *Die wandernden Komödianten*, 1822; *Die beiden Neffen, oder Der Onkel aus Boston*, 1823–4) were written by a family friend, Dr Ludwig Casper, and are based on French vaudevilles. The fifth libretto, *Die Hochzeit des Camacho*, Op. 10 (1824–5), by Friedrich Voigts, is based on Ludwig Tieck's German translation of *Don Quixote*; this was the only opera publicly performed and published during Mendelssohn's lifetime. The composer's friend Karl Klingemann produced the lyrics to the last completed dramatic work, the *Liederspiel Die Heimkehr aus der Fremde*, Op. 89, which

---

[5] Berger had composed the *Liederspiel Die schöne Müllerin* on texts by Wilhelm Müller in 1818.

was performed in 1829 on the occasion of the silver wedding anniversary of Mendelssohn's parents. Though Mendelssohn declined to have the work performed publicly despite his family's pressure,[6] he was very fond of it: 'You know the details about the play for the festivity already from Klingemann, it has become one of our most precious memories and, I think, my best composition.'[7] Mendelssohn never discussed the style and form of these works, nor did he experiment with other ones.

In summary, these youthful works represent a typically German (and in case of *Die Heimkehr aus der Fremde* specifically Berlin) style of operatic composition. In their form and textual origin, as is characteristic of this style, they are strongly based on French light stage pieces of the time. Perfectly suited for the teenage Mendelssohn, they are reminiscent of Mozart's early operas. Unfortunately, *Die Soldatenliebschaft*, *Die wandernden Komödianten*, and *Der Onkel aus Boston* remain unpublished. Commercial recordings are available of *Die beiden Pädagogen*, *Die Heimkehr aus der Fremde*, and *Die Hochzeit des Camacho*.[8]

Mendelssohn's focus on a single style of operatic composition ended in the early 1830s. During his travels to France and Italy he was able to gain first-hand knowledge of these countries' national operatic styles in their original shape. As a result, he began to consider writing operas particularly for France that were to be adjusted to the local audience's taste. One purpose of Mendelssohn's exposure to new musical styles during his extensive journey was, as he put it, that 'I should choose a place where I want to live, which I accomplished, at least in a general sense.'[9] The young composer absorbed new artistic

[6] See Devrient, *Erinnerungen*, 94–5: 'They pressed him to have the *Liederspiel* performed in public; especially his mother clung to the wish vividly and for a long time. At first out of considerations of reverence, Felix refused to surrender to the public the work that he only provided for a family celebration sacred to him.' ('Man drängte ihn, das Liederspiel öffentlich aufführen zu lassen, besonders seine Mutter hielt lange und lebhaft an dem Wunsche fest. Felix sträubte sich, zunächst aus Pietätsrücksichten, das Werk, das er nur für das ihm heilige Familienfest gedacht, der Oeffentlichkeit preiszugeben.')

[7] Letter from Mendelssohn to Friedrich Rosen, Berlin, 9 Apr. 1830, quoted in Klingemann, *Briefwechsel*, 78: 'Von dem Festspiel weisst Du schon durch Klingemann das Nähere, es ist eine unserer liebsten Erinnerungen geworden und ich denke, es ist meine beste Komposition.'

[8] Felix Mendelssohn, *Die beiden Pädagogen*, cond. Heinz Wallberg, Münchner Rundfunkorchester, Chor des Bayerischen Rundfunks, cpo, 1980 (cpo 999); Felix Mendelssohn Bartholdy, *Die Heimkehr aus der Fremde*, cond. Heinz Wallberg, Münchner Rundfunkorchester, Chor des Bayerischen Rundfunks, cpo, 1978 (cpo 999 555–2); Felix Mendelssohn Bartholdy, *Die Hochzeit des Camacho*, cond. Jos van Immerseel, Anima Eterna, Der Junge Chor Aachen & Chor Modus Novus, Channel Classics, 1993 (CCS 5593).

[9] Letter from Mendelssohn to his family, Paris, 21 Feb. 1832 (GB-Ob, MDM d. 13, fo. 107ᵛ): 'Aber auch die andre Absicht, da ich mir einen Ort aussuchen solle, wo ich leben möge, ist, wenigstens im Allgemeinen, mir gelungen . . .'. In many cases, the printed versions of letters differ from the originals. Wherever possible, the manuscript version is quoted with reference to the printed version; the present letter is also given in *Briefe 1830–2* (1862), 322.

influences quickly and did not hesitate to offer his sharp criticism in the letters to his family. His commentaries on the opera performances he attended are enlightening with regard to his views on French and Italian opera.

For example, Mendelssohn's letters from Paris suggest that when he considered writing an opera in French style, he rejected the *opéra comique* in favour of grand opera. He claims that two reasons prevented him from pursuing this idea: the low quality of French libretti and the fear that his opera would not be of high quality, but nevertheless successful:

This is my reason for not applying for an opera here [in Paris]. If I write fairly good music, just like it should be nowadays, it will be understood and loved in Germany (as has been the case with all good operas). If I produce mediocre music, it will be forgotten in Germany; here, however, it would be often performed, praised, sent to Germany, and performed there due to the authority of Paris, as we can see daily. I do not want this, and if I were unable to create good music I would not want to be praised for it.[10]

Mendelssohn clarified his view on French opera even more explicitly in the continuation of this letter:

[Parisian] *opéra comique* is as degenerate and bad as only few of the German theatres are; it falls into one bankruptcy after another. If one asks Cherubini why he does not allow his operas to be performed there, he answers: 'Je ne fais pas donner des opéras sans choeur, sans orchestre, sans chanteurs et sans décorations.' [I don't put on operas without a [decent] chorus, orchestra, singers, or scenery.] He has already arranged the programme for the grand opera house for the next few years, and one could only get a contract three or four years in advance.[11]

Not surprisingly, Mendelssohn chose not to apply for a contract under those circumstances.

In addition to these obvious (and admitted) obstacles, the most honest reason for Mendelssohn's hesitation to write a French opera was his moral views:

---

[10] 'Das ist auch der Grund warum ich mich hier [in Paris] um keine Oper bewerbe; wenn ich eine rechte, gute Musik mache, wie sie heut sein muß, so wird sie in Deutschland auch schon verstanden und geliebt; (es ist mit allen ihren guten Opern so gewesen;) wenn ich eine mittelmäßige Musik mache, so wird sie in Deutschland vergessen, hier aber würde sie doch oft gegeben, gelobt, nach Deutschland geschickt, und dort auf die Pariser Autorität hin gegeben, wie wir es täglich sehen; das will ich aber nicht, und wenn ich keine gute Musik habe machen können, so will ich auch nicht dafür gelobt sein.' Letter from Mendelssohn to his family, Paris, 21 Feb. 1832 (GB-Ob, MDM d. 13, fo. 108ʳ; also in *Briefe 1830–2*, 322).

[11] Ibid.; also in *Briefe 1830–2*, 322–3: 'Zudem ist die *opéra comique* hier so verfallen und schlecht, wie wenig deutsche Theater, ud. sie fällt von einem Bankrott in den andern; wenn man Cherubini fragt, warum er seine Opern nicht dort zu geben erlaubt, so antwortet er *je ne fais pas donner des opéras sans choeur, sans orchestre, sans chanteurs & sans décorations*, die große Oper hat aber schon auf Jahre hinaus schon bestellt, und man könnte nur auf 3, 4 Jahre hin einen Auftrag erhalten.'

I am convinced that every single one of the new texts here, if staged for the first time in Germany, would have not the slightest chance of success. In addition, the main point for all of them is one of those that one should be explicitly opposed to (even if I understand that one has to go with the times, not against them), namely that of immorality . . . [W]hen in another opera a girl undresses and simultaneously sings a song about how she will be married tomorrow at this time, it made an effect, but I have no music for it because it is vulgar. And if this were what today's times would require and find necessary, then I want to write sacred music.[12]

Modern French opera, focusing more on stage effects than on music or quality of content, did not agree with Mendelssohn's moral values. When he realized this, he quickly ceased to consider French opera as a possibility. The only exceptions to this are two stage works on libretti by Eugène Scribe, the first initiated in 1842 for a performance in Berlin, and the second (which will be discussed in more detail below) commissioned for the London stage in 1847 with an option for a Paris performance in the following year.

Critical voices, such as the one of Heinrich Heine in the *Augsburger Zeitung* of 25 April 1844, did not attribute Mendelssohn's choice to refrain from composing French opera to a genuine decision on the composer's part, but doubted his capability to compose a grand opera for Paris and expected him to be 'old and grumpy before bringing something grand onto the stage'.[13]

The situation in Italy was very similar to that in France: despite their low quality, most works were successful in pleasing on a superficial level. The resulting audience expectation irritated Mendelssohn, as is obvious in his report of the première of Pacini's *Il corsaro* on 15 January 1831:

Then lots of numbers followed, and the thing became boring; the audience thought so, too. When Pacini's grand finale started, the people in the parterre stood up, began to talk loudly and to laugh, and turned their back to the stage; . . . I would have been upset if the music had made a great impression, because it is pitiful,

---

[12] Letter from Mendelssohn to his father, Paris, 19 Dec. 1831 (GB-Ob, MDM d. 13, fo. 96^r; also in *Briefe 1830–2*, 287–8): 'Jeder der neuen hiesigen Texte, zum erstenmale in Deutschl. auf die Bühne gebracht, würde, meiner Ueberzeugung nach, nicht den geringsten Erfolg gehabt haben. Dazu kommt noch, daß der Hauptpunkt bei ihnen allen, gerade einer von denen ist, in denen man, wenn sie auch die Zeit verlangt wenn ich auch vollkommen einsehe, daß man mit ihr, nicht gegen sie gehen müsse sich der Zeit geradezu entgegen stellen soll: es ist der der Unsittlichkeit. . . . [W]enn in einer anderen Oper das Mädchen sich auskleidet und dabei ein Lied singt, wie sie morgen um diese Zeit verheiratet sein werde — es hat Effect gemacht, aber ich habe keine Musik dafür. Denn es ist gemein, und wenn das heut die Zeit verlangte ud. nothwendig fände, so will ich Kichenmusik schreiben.'

[13] 'Mendelssohn wird vielleicht alt und mürrisch werden, ohne etwas wahrhaft Großes auf die Bretter gebracht zu haben.' Heinrich Heine, 'Musikalische Saison in Paris', 25 Apr. 1844, quoted in Heinrich Heine, *Werke, Briefwechsel, Lebenszeugnisse*, ed. Lucienne Netter, x (Berlin: Akademie-Verlag, 1979), 229.

beneath criticism. But I get equally aggravated that they suddenly turn their back on Pacini, whom they wanted to crown on the Capitol, and that they mock his melodies and sing them in caricature; it proves how low such a musician stands in the public opinion.[14]

Mendelssohn believed that this unpredictable and irresponsible audience behaviour invited composers to write low-quality operas, for which the case of Donizetti provided him with another example. In a letter of 6 January 1831, the young composer attacked the older one's negligent attitude towards opera composition and his sacrifice of quality for the sake of leisure time, quickly earned money, and superficial audience satisfaction:

This is why Donizetti finishes an opera in ten days; the audience hisses at it, but that does not matter, since he gets paid for it and can take another stroll. If his reputation were finally in danger he would have to work too much, and that would be uncomfortable. This is why he writes one opera every three weeks, puts a bit of effort into some of the pieces so that they will please the audience, and then he can go for more walks for a while and continue to compose poorly.[15]

This type of behaviour was again very different from Mendelssohn's own work ethics, exemplified in the extensive and often lengthy revision process for many of his major pieces, and his careful consideration about what to publish.[16] It does not come as a surprise that there was but one short-lived intention to write an opera on an Italian libretto in his later career: Felice Romani, one of the leading Italian librettists of the time who provided texts for Donizetti, Bellini, and Verdi, had originally agreed to deliver a libretto for the *Tempest* project for Covent Garden in 1847. It seems to have been

---

[14] Letter from Mendelssohn to his family, Rome, 17 Jan. 1831 (GB-Ob, MDM d. 13, fo. 35ᵛ; also in *Briefe 1830–2*, 95): '[D]ann kamen noch viele Stücke ud. die Sache wurde langweilig, das fand das Publicum auch ud. als Pacini's großes Finale anfing, so stand das Parterre auf, fing an sich laut zu unterhalten, zu lachen ud. drehte der Bühne den Rücken zu; . . . [H]ätte die Musik Furore gemacht, so hätte mich es geärgert denn sie ist unter aller Kritik jämmerlich, aber daß sie nun dem Liebling Pacini den sie auf dem Capitol kränzen wollten auf einmal den Rücken drehn, den Melodien nachäffen und sie karikirt nachsingen, das ärgert mich auch wieder, ud. es beweist wie tief ein solcher Musiker in der allgemeinen Meinung steht . . .'.

[15] Letter from Mendelssohn to his parents, Rome, 6 June 1831 (GB-Ob, MDM d. 13, fo. 61ᵛ; also in *Briefe 1830–2*, 160): '[D]aher macht Donizetti eine Oper in zehn Tagen fertig, sie wird ausgezischt, aber das thut ihm gar nichts; denn er bekommt dafür bezahlt ud. kann wieder spazieren gehn, sollte aber seine Reputation endlich gefährdet werden, so würde er wieder zuviel arbeiten müssen, ud das wäre unbequem; darum schreibt er einmal eine Oper in drei Wochen, giebt sich zu ein Paar Stücken Mühe, damit sie recht gefallen, ud kann wieder eine Weile spazierengehen ud schlecht schreiben!'

[16] That Mendelssohn hesitated to publish his works hastily is shown e.g. in Devrient, *Erinnerungen*, 76, where he is quoted as saying, 'Ich habe einen Heidenrespekt vor dem Druck' ('I have a holy terror of respect for printing').

Mendelssohn's explicit wish, however, to have this libretto prepared by Scribe instead. Despite his reservations, Mendelssohn's concert arias on Italian texts give ample evidence that he possessed the musical abilities necessary to produce a work in the Italian style. His most prominent composition in this genre is the concert aria *Infelice! Ah, ritorna, età felice*, Op. 94 (1843), but there are also much earlier concert arias on Italian texts, namely *Che vuoi mio cor?* (1823?), *Chio t'abbandono* (1825), and *Infelice! / Ah, ritorna, età dell'oro* (1834), long assumed to be an earlier version of Op. 94.[17]

All the perceived obstacles in France and Italy that kept Mendelssohn from composing operas in those countries nevertheless helped him to develop his identity as composer. As a result of his travels and his contact with different cultures, he realized that he wanted above all to be a German composer writing for a German audience, which naturally affected his viewpoints on opera and plans for working in the genre. Though his goal was still to establish himself as an opera composer, he took a different course, initiated by a commission to write an opera for Munich in 1831, which seemed to have come to him unexpectedly and by coincidence: 'I also received my Munich commission without taking even the first step to that end, namely after my concert.'[18] The commission for Munich was supposed to be only the beginning of a career in Germany, with a production in Stuttgart to follow: 'If I succeed with the opera in Munich, then I take it to Stuttgart, where Count Leutrum made the friendliest proposals to me; all this is for next year, and if that comes to pass, then something else will turn up for the following year.'[19] These commissions confirmed Mendelssohn's decision to start his professional career in Germany:

I could not follow this path [of composing for Paris or London], because my first opera is ordered for Munich. I therefore want to try it out in Germany, and will live and work there as long as I am able to work and survive there; because this is certainly the first duty. If I cannot succeed there, I have to leave again for London or Paris, where it is easier. However, if I succeed in Germany, I am still aware how one gets paid and honoured better elsewhere, how one lives more easily and freely, and how one always has to move forwards and labour in Germany and can never rest.[20]

---

[17] See John Michael Cooper's essay in this volume, Ch. 3.

[18] Letter from Mendelssohn to his family, 21 Feb. 1832 (GB-Ob, MDM d. 13, fo. 107ᵛ; also in *Briefe 1830–2*, 321–2): '[M]einen Münchner Auftrag habe ich ebenfalls bekommen, ohne den geringsten ersten Schritt zu thun, und zwar erst nach meinem Concert . . .'.

[19] Letter from Mendelssohn to his father, Frankfurt, 13 Nov. 1831 (D-B, N. Mus. ep. 1288, fo. 2ʳ): 'Gelingt mir die Oper in München, so gehe ich damit nach Stuttgart, wo mir Graf Leutrum die freundlichsten Anträge dazu gemacht hat; das ist Alles für das nächste Jahr, und geht das in Erfüllung so wird sich für das darauf folgende schon wieder etwas Anderes gefunden haben.'

[20] Letter from Mendelssohn to his father, Paris, 19 Dec. 1831 (GB-Ob, MDM d. 13, fo. 96ʳ; also in *Briefe 1830–2*, 286–7): '[I]ch könnte ihn [den Weg über Paris und London] auf keinen

He communicated the same to his former teacher Zelter: 'I will stay with what you and my parents have taught me to love, and will therefore be categorized as part of the *école Allemande* right away.'[21]

For the commission in Munich, Mendelssohn's father suggested a French libretto, but the composer clearly disagreed.[22] Instead, he chose Immermann as his librettist for an opera based on Shakespeare's *Tempest*, explaining his decision by stating that he had already come to an agreement with Immermann before he got to know his father's opinion.[23]

This decision against his father's will indicates that Mendelssohn had matured enough during his absence from home to push his ideas through. Still, he seems to have needed further arguments to convince his father. On the one hand, he refers to his mother's support for his plans,[24] and on the other hand he quoted a letter from the commissioner, Baron von Poissl (who proposed to ask a German author for a libretto[25]) to reinforce his point.

Fall einschlagen, da meine erste Oper für München bestellt ist und ich den Auftrag angenommen habe. Versuchen will ich es in Deutschland, und dort bleiben ud wirken, so lange ich da wirken und mich erhalten kann. Denn das ist freilich die erste Pflicht ud. kann ich das nicht, so muß ich wieder fort ud. nach London oder Paris, wo es leichter geht; aber kann ich das in Deutschland so sehe ich freilich, wie man anderswo besser besteht, mehr geehrt, lustiger ud. freier lebt, wie man aber dort immer fortschreiben, arbeiten, niemals ausruhen muß.'

[21] Letter from Mendelssohn to Carl Friedrich Zelter, Paris, 15 Feb. 1832, quoted in Elvers, *Briefe*, 153: 'Ich bleibe nun bei dem, was Sie und die Eltern mich lieben gelehrt haben, bin also gleich in die école Allemande einrangirt.'

[22] Letter from Mendelssohn to his father, Paris, 19 Dec. 1831 (GB-Ob, MDM d. 13, fos. 95^r + 96^r; also in *Briefe 1830–2*, 284 and 286): '[I hope] you will allow me now as previously to speak my opinion openly about this point. This concerns your idea, which you proposed to me, that I should have a text written for me by a French librettist and then compose it for the stage in Munich in translation. . . . For a number of reasons, it does not see feasible to me to compose a French text in translation.' ('[Ich hoffe, daß] du mir erlaubst, wie bisher auch darüber meine Ansicht gerade hinzusagen. Es betrifft dies nämlich, die Idee, die Du mir angiebst, mir von einem französischen Dichter einen Text machen zu lassen, und ihn übersetzt für die Münchner Bühne zu componiren. . . . Einen französischen Text übersetzt zu componiren scheint mir aus mehreren Gründen nicht ausführbar.')

[23] See *Briefe 1830–2*, 286–7.

[24] Letter from Mendelssohn to his father, 19 Dec. 1831, quoted in *Briefe 1830–2*, 285: '[T]hat he [Immermann] has chosen a subject that I have had on my mind for a long time and that—if I am not wrong—Mother had wished to be turned into an opera.' ('[D]aß er [Immermann] ein Sujet genommen hat, welches mir lange schon im Sinne war, und welches auch (wenn ich nicht irre) Mutter zu einer Oper sich gewünscht.')

[25] In a letter of 13 Nov. 1831 to his father, Mendelssohn quoted the proposal of Baron von Poissl: 'If you already possess a libretto that you are intending to compose, I ask you to share it with me for examination; if this is not the case, please feel free to start negotiations with any German poet of reputation in which you trust . . .' ('Wenn E.W. schon ein Buch, das Sie zu komponiren beabsichtigen, besitzen, so bitte ich mir selbes zur Einsicht mitzutheilen wenn dies nicht der Fall ist, so gefälligen Sie mit irgend einem deutschen Dichter von Reputation auf den Sie Ihr Vertrauen setzen, in Unterhandlung zu treten . . .'). D-B, N. Mus. ep. 1288, fo. 2^r.

Other major composers of the time shared Mendelssohn's feeling of obligation to their mother country and his desire to contribute to the development of a distinctly 'German' opera; one example is Robert Schumann: '[My] prayer from morning to evening [was] called German Opera. It must be a reality.'[26] Though nowhere defined explicitly,[27] 'German' opera implied not only opera in the German language and on German themes, but also in a musical style and form that differed considerably from the Italian and French models and would be recognized as being 'German' by the audience.

It becomes evident that Mendelssohn's expressed desire to create a German opera was not the product of homesickness during the young composer's travels. Relatively late in his career, in 1845, he still had the same goal, as he wrote in a letter to Eduard Devrient: 'Especially when I (as here this winter) listen to new German and other operas, then I feel as if I were obliged to give a hand and put my judgement into a score—and I am indeed obliged, but it [the realization of his plan] does not depend on me.'[28] He proceeded to define his requirements for a libretto, again stressing the importance of 'Germanness' in regard to language and subject matter: '[The opera scenario] would have to be German, noble and cheerful, whether a Rhenish folk tale or otherwise a genuine national event or fairy tale, or a good basic character (as in *Fidelio*).'[29]

Mendelssohn's rejection of French and Italian operatic style and his decision to contribute to German opera did not influence his attitude towards composing an opera for England. This seems to have been an entirely different issue, primarily because there was no distinctly 'English' opera style.[30] In

[26]   Robert Schumann, quoted in Aubrey S. Garlington, 'Mega-Text, Mega-Music: A Crucial Dilemma for German Romantic Opera', in Nancy Kovaleff Baker and Barbara Russo Hanning (eds.), *Musical Humanism and its Legacy: Essays in Honor of Claude V. Palisca* (Stuyvesant, NY: Pendragon, 1992), 381–93 at 384.

[27]   The character of the desired German national opera may be best described by Carl Maria von Weber: 'die gern von Fremden lernt, aber es in Wahrheit und Eigentümlichkeit gestaltet wiedergibt' ('which eagerly learns from foreign influences, but renders them truthfully and genuinely shaped'). Quoted in Anna Amalie Abert, 'Oper, C. Die romantische Oper', *MGG* x, col. 48.

[28]   Letter from Mendelssohn to Devrient, 26 Apr. 1845, in Devrient, *Erinnerungen*, 250: '[B]esonders wenn ich (wie hier diesen Winter) neue deutsche und andere Opern höre, daß mir dann sei, als wäre ich verpflichtet, auch mit anzufassen und mein Votum in Partitur zu setzen — und dazu bin ich auch verpflichtet, aber dennoch hängt es nicht von mir ab.'

[29]   Letter from Mendelssohn to Devrient, 26 Apr. 1845, ibid. 251–2: 'Deutsch müßte es sein, und edel und heiter; sei es eine rheinische Volkssage, oder sonst ein ächt nationales Ereigniß oder Mährchen, oder ein rechter Grundcharakter (wie im *Fidelio*).'

[30]   That English opera houses wanted to establish a geniune tradition is expressed, for example, in a report about Her Majesty's Theatre in *The Times* of 21 Jan. 1847, p. 5: '[The programme for the Italian opera house] is especially distinguished by setting forth the circumstance, that the

addition, Mendelssohn had specific reasons for considering opera projects for England. First, his relationship to England was particularly close, and he was highly admired by the English public. Secondly, four of the operas he intended to write for England were commissioned, which is exceptional among his opera projects.

Mendelssohn made a first attempt at English opera in 1829, and his commentary shows how different the attitude of the London audience was from that in Italy and France: 'I shall write an opera for *Covent Garden*, if the texts they want to give me here are satisfactory. They have offered me conditions that are honourable, pleasant, and to my advantage, and on the whole, the people here like me because of my music and honour me because of it; this makes me extraordinarily happy.'[31] The specific details of this project remain unknown, as does the answer to the question why he never followed through with it.

Mendelssohn's reasons for accepting a commission for an opera in English were quite different for the next attempt, this time with a libretto by Planché on the subject of Edward III and the Siege of Calais. He returned to the idea of composing for England because his attempts to find a suitable German libretto had been fruitless, as shown in his remarks to Johann Gustav Droysen: 'As I fear (after many, often unpleasant, experiences) that I will not find a proper libretto in Germany, I accepted a commission to compose for England a while ago. It was very hard for me to accept this, but I had no choice.' He quickly added that he 'certainly planned to have the verses translated into German first, because I actually am hardly able to compose English ones (nor do I want to).'[32]

---

metropolis of England is no longer dependent on foreign theatres for a supply of operas, but that foreign composers deem the London public of sufficient importance to justify the composition of operas for this country expressly.'

[31] Letter from Mendelssohn to Devrient, 19 [*sic*] June 1829, in Devrient, *Erinnerungen*, 84: 'For Coventgarden schreibe ich eine Oper, wenn die Texte, die man mir hier geben will, genügend sind. Sie haben mir Bedingungen gemacht, die ehrenvoll, angenehm und vortheilhaft sind, und im Ganzen sind mir die Leute hier meiner Musik wegen gut, und achten mich deshalb; das freut mich ganz außerordentlich.' As pointed out in J. Rigbie Turner, 'Letters to Eduard Devrient', in R. Larry Todd (ed.), *Mendelssohn Studies* (Cambridge: Cambridge University Press, 1992), 200–39 at 207, the correct date of this letter is 17 June 1829.

[32] Letter from Mendelssohn to Droysen, Leipzig, 24 Jan. 1838, quoted in Gustav Droysen, 'Johann Gustav Droysen und Felix Mendelssohn-Bartholdy', *Deutsche Rundschau*, 28 (1902), 107–26, 193–215, 386–408 at 211–12: 'Da ich nach vielen oft unangenehmen Erfahrungen fürchtete, in Deutschland keinen ordentlichen Operntext zu bekommen, so habe ich vor einiger Zeit allerdings den Auftrag angenommen, für England zu componieren. Es fiel mir sehr schwer, das einzugehen, aber es blieb mir weiter nichts anderes übrig. . . . Freilich habe ich mir vorgenommen, die Verse erst deutsch übersetzen zu lassen, da ich wirklich englisch kaum componieren kann (geschweige mag).'

Clearly, Mendelssohn had given up hope of finding an appropriate German text and had decided to follow the alternative direction he had mentioned in the letter to his father in 1831 (i.e. if being unsuccessful in Germany, to retreat to London or Paris for better conditions). The quality of Planché's libretto came as a pleasant surprise, quickly changing Mendelssohn's attitude and even inspiring him to write down musical drafts, as has been discussed earlier.[33] Indeed, Mendelssohn's reaction to Planché's text was overwhelmingly positive: 'I must also thank you for the beautiful verses, which are so truly musical, that I have nothing more to wish in that respect; and upon the whole there are so many so great beauties in this work, and I so fully appreciate them, that I anticipate the greatest delight from the composition, and I wish I might soon be able to begin it.'[34] However, Planché's resistance to several substantial changes Mendelssohn requested—such as the addition of a comic character to this 'serious' opera in order to provide more entertainment for the audience—led the composer to change his mind once more. In 1840, he wrote to Klingemann:

For the last [parcel], for example, I had to pay more than a Thaler postage, and very unfortunately the poem is not worth it, because I am afraid it will never turn into something usable and I agree with you completely on that point. It is neither cold nor warm, and the man is not willing to understand that the mistake lies in the whole, except for the subject, which could have been turned into something.[35]

The project remained unrealized; by the time Planché finally offered to make the requested changes, Mendelssohn had lost interest.

Mendelssohn's third and most momentous attempt to write an opera for England was initiated in early 1847, when he again considered composing an opera based on *The Tempest*—this time using a libretto by Eugène Scribe (evidently, he had overcome his prejudice against French librettists), adapted by Benjamin Lumley. This project was of particular interest for Mendelssohn because Jenny Lind was contracted to perform in this opera. The excitement of the commissioners resulted in an immediate public announcement of the work in all major London newspapers, as well as in the programmes issued by the theatre. However, Mendelssohn could not be persuaded by such publicity.

---

[33] See above, n. 4.

[34] Letter of Mendelssohn to Planché from Leipzig, 12 Aug. 1838 (US-Wc, Whitall Collection), quoted in Planché, *Recollections*, 287.

[35] Letter of Mendelssohn to Klingemann, Leipzig, 2 Jan. 1840, in Klingemann, *Briefwechsel*, 241–2: '[I]ch habe für das letzte [Paket] z.B. über einen Thaler Porto zu zahlen gehabt, und leider, leider ist das Gedicht das nicht wert; denn ich fürchte, es wird nimmermehr etwas Gescheutes daraus, und bin darüber ganz Deiner Meinung. Es ist nicht kalt und nicht warm, und der Mann will nicht verstehn, dass der Fehler eben am Ganzen liegt, wobei ich freilich das Sujet ausnehme, aus dem etwas zu machen gewesen wäre.'

Insulted by the crude attempt to force his hand, he promptly refused to participate. He also privately admitted his dislike of Lumley's libretto: 'I have since read it often and carefully—have almost concluded that I cannot compose it until some (even if utterly distant) point in this year's season—have not written a single note—isn't that 'much ado about nothing' instead of *The Tempest*?'[36] It remained that way, and so Mendelssohn's most promising attempt at English opera was also destined to fail.

MENDELSSOHN'S OPERA ATTEMPTS AND THE ISSUE OF GENRE

Closely related to the question of national styles and equally relevant for Mendelssohn's contemplated opera projects is the issue of genre. Again, Mendelssohn's own struggle is representative of a general one that occupied German composers of the time. As part of their striving for 'German opera', composers in the first half of the nineteenth century experimented with approaches to opera composition that would replace the predominant Italian and French forms with a distinctly German one. In an effort to support these attempts, German opera houses were opened alongside Italian ones, and the latter were increasingly closed down (for example 1826 in Munich, 1828 in Vienna, and 1832 in Dresden).[37] Court opera houses were supplemented or replaced by private or state theatres. Hand in hand with these important changes, new target groups emerged—a development that required new criteria for selecting the repertoire and that provided composers, librettists, and performers with opportunities for experimentation.

The operatic repertoire in Germany at that time consisted of a huge variety of new operas that enjoyed limited local success. Instead of contributing to a 'German national opera style', the composers tailored these works to their specific performance situations and did not attempt to make them part of a national tradition. On the one hand, about 600 operas were composed in Germany between 1820 and 1850,[38] most of them imitating either successful

[36] Letter of Mendelssohn to Klingemann, 18 Feb. 1847, in Klingemann, *Briefwechsel*, 321: '[I]ch habe ihn [Lumleys Text] seitdem oft und aufmerksam gelesen — bin fast zur Gewissheit gekommen, dass ich ihn nicht komponieren kann bis zu einer (wenn auch noch so entfernten) Zeit der diesjährigen Saison — habe noch keine Note daran geschrieben — ist das nicht statt des Tempest "much ado about nothing"?'

[37] For a more detailed description of this development, see Siegfried Goslich, *Die deutsche romantische Oper* (Tutzing: Hans Schneider, 1975), esp. 121–6. Goslich also makes the point that the leading positions in important opera houses were increasingly occupied by Germans (e.g. Weber and Wagner in Dresden, Spohr in Kassel, and Marschner in Hannover).

[38] Ibid. 125.

foreign operas or the compositions of Marschner and Weber. On the other hand, an account of 1849 lists only nine operas by living German composers as being famous beyond their local area of production.[39]

The experimentation with form and departure from French and Italian models was most prominently undertaken in the operas of Ludwig Spohr, who introduced musical connections between the numbers of his opera *Faust* (1813–15) and continued to develop the idea of 'reminiscence motifs' in later works. His *Jessonda* (1821, premièred in 1823) is probably the first through-composed German opera. This form, however, had not yet become a guiding principle; Spohr returned to number opera and alternated between the two approaches in his later works.

Carl Maria von Weber, the creator of what could be called the only manifestation of 'the German opera', also deviated from the form of *Der Freischütz* (1821), a *Singspiel*, in his later works. His next opera, *Euryanthe* (1823), is through-composed in the sense that it consists of scenic units.[40] Other composers offering new approaches to opera composition were Marschner and Spontini. The general tendency of the times was to move away from *Singspiel* to opera, and to 'Germanize'[41] French styles. The development of new forms and the use of previously neglected subjects ultimately resulted in Wagner's creation of the music drama, which revolutionized opera composition after 1850; it was he who finally provided a consistent approach, intended to be (and perceived as such by many of his contemporaries and successors) distinctly German.

In theory, Mendelssohn participated in this development. He began his career in the *Singspiel* tradition, in which he considered dialogues necessary for practical reasons, as is seen in a letter by Voigts, the librettist of *Die Hochzeit des Camacho*: 'Do not make the dialogue between the musical pieces too short. Singers, orchestra, and audience must be able to catch their breath. I think a few words between the vocal pieces are absolutely necessary. . . . The dialogue must not be left out . . . so that the audience can rest a little.'[42]

---

[39] See J. Cornet, *Die Oper in Deutschland und das Theater der Neuzeit: Aus dem Standpunkte practischer Erfahrungen* (Hamburg: Meißner & Schirges, 1849), 56.

[40] For an interesting discussion of this work and Weber's involvement with German opera, see Michael C. Tusa, *Euryanthe and Carl Maria von Weber's Dramaturgy of German Opera* (Oxford: Clarendon Press, 1991).

[41] I use the term 'Germanization' to summarize various attempts to develop a distinctly German operatic tradition with German libretti on German subjects in a form that differed significantly from the French models.

[42] Letter from Mendelssohn to Voigts from Berlin, 16 Jan. 1824, in Elvers, *'Nichts ist so schwer'*, 8–9: 'Machen Sie doch ja keinen zu kurzen Dialog zwischen den Musikstücken. Sänger, Orchester, und Zuhörer müssen sich verpusten können. Ich halte ein paar Worte zwischen den Gesangstücken für höchst nothwendig. . . . [D]er Dialog [muß] nicht fehlen damit der Zuhörer sich . . . etwas ausruhen kann.'

In 1824, at the age of 15, Mendelssohn proved that he was well aware of his abilities and limits. When Eduard Devrient, his friend and most consistent goad to composing an opera, suggested an Italian drama (*Olinde and Sophronia* from Tasso's *Gerusalemme liberata*) as a source for a libretto to be prepared by him, the young composer admitted that 'he [did] not dare to compose such a serious subject'.[43]

In their increasing length and complexity Mendelssohn's youthful operatic works reveal a progression in his compositional abilities that culminated in *Der Onkel aus Boston*; it includes two ballet scenes and has a performance time of about two and a half hours. The form and content of these works clearly stay within the conventions of *Singspiel*. Yet strikingly, Mendelssohn made no more attempts at 'comic opera' in his later life. Devrient's opinion that Mendelssohn should try a 'higher' genre makes clear that there was a de facto hierarchy of operatic genres. It also reveals that operas were categorized not only as serious or comic, but that there were other sub-genres as well. Many of Mendelssohn's later operatic attempts can be divided into certain categories according to their subject matter. The largest category is that of 'historical opera', represented for example by *Edward III and the Siege of Calais* (1838), *Otto III* (1840), *Barbarossa in Suʒa* (1843), *Otto und Adelheid* (1843), and *Der Bauernkrieg* (1844 and 1846). A second group of opera projects is based on literature. The most prominent examples are *The Tempest* (1831, 1844, and 1847, after Shakespeare), *Kenilworth* (1840, after Sir Walter Scott), *Der Cid* (1840 and 1842, based on a Spanish romance), *Die Jungfrau von Orleans* (1843, after Schiller), *King Lear* (1843, after Shakespeare), *Faust* (1843, after Goethe), and *Hamlet* (no date, after Shakespeare).

A genre explicitly rejected by Mendelssohn is that of magic opera: 'As a start, I do not want a magic opera, or rather, I do not believe that I have enough talent in that area, whereas I would work with more confidence in the serious or purely comic style. If you have a serious, historical, caballing or completely jolly human subject in mind, I beg you, please let me know of it.'[44] He was even more explicit about a subject recommended to him by Devrient on *Die Insel der Glückseligkeit* in 1843: 'Magic and miracles do not constitute

---

[43] 'Felix meinte: er möchte sich an einen so ernsten Gegenstand noch nicht wagen.' Devrient, *Erinnerungen*, 24.

[44] Letter from Mendelssohn to Eduard von Bauernfeld in Vienna, 28 Apr. 1838, quoted in Ludwig Nohl, *Musikerbriefe* (2nd edn., Leipzig: Duncker & Humblot, 1873), 329: 'Ich wuensche mir zum Anfang keine Zauber-Oper, oder vielmehr traue ich mir in diesem Fache nicht genug Talent zu, waehrend ich im ernsten oder rein heiteren Styl mit mehr Zuversicht arbeiten wuerde. Schwebt Ihnen nun ein ernster, historischer oder ein intriganter oder ganz heiterer menschlicher Stoff vor, so bitt ich Sie, theilen Sie ihn mir mit.'

what is operatic in my view, and I do not find much of the purely human, noble, and all-animating there, which does constitute it.'[45] A biblical subject, *Lazarus*, proposed by Chorley in 1840, did not win his approval either, although Mendelssohn's oratorios have often been called 'substitute operas' and have even been staged.

The subject that finally met with Mendelssohn's approval in *Die Lorelei* (with different potential librettists in 1844, 1845, and 1846–7) was a German folk legend, as were other potential libretti, including *Das Nibelungenlied* (1840 and 1846) and *St Genoveva* (1842 and 1846). *Die Lorelei*,[46] which had turned up as early as 1829 as a potential subject for an opera by Fanny,[47] seemed to provide the right mixture of dramatic development, diversity of characters, morality, and 'Germanness' (the story had been created by Clemens Brentano in the manner of German fairy tales in 1801 in a successful attempt to make it part of the German cultural legacy) to be approved by Mendelssohn. The libretto, collaboratively prepared by the poet Geibel and the experienced dramatist Devrient, promised to be an effective combination of beautiful verse and stage-worthiness.

In addition to a genre distinction based on subjects, it is important to consider formal elements. All Mendelssohn's youthful operas and the subsequent projects until 1840 were in all likelihood to have dialogue and consist of two or three acts, as is expressed in a letter to Planché in which Mendelssohn listed his requirements of a 'good, truly poetical libretto which inspires me at once':[48] 'I dislike the five acts as you do: there should be three or two. I prefer three acts, but I think there could be a subject that would have to be divided into two; and then I should have no objection.'[49] A period of formal indecisiveness followed, as is evident in a letter to Fürst of 1840: 'This scenario can be lengthy or short, detailed or only sketchy; I won't presume to decide this, likewise whether the opera should be in three, four, or five acts. If it is good as it is, eight acts are not too many and one is not too few. I also cannot decide for or against [the inclusion of] a ballet—only whether it suits my disposition

---

[45] 'Zauberei und Wunderquellen machen das Opernhafte, wie ich mir's denke, nicht, und das rein Menschliche, Edle, Alles Belebende, was es macht, habe ich darin nicht sehr gefunden.' Letter of Mendelssohn to Devrient, 28 June 1843, quoted in Devrient, *Erinnerungen*, 233–4. Turner (in 'Letters', 231) gives the original version of this quote as follows: 'Die Nymphe der Poesie, der Musik, der Baukunst &c., der Gott der Zephyr, die Mutter der Winde, Zauberei Wunderquellen &c, &c, — das alles macht das Opernhafte . . . nicht.'

[46] Alternatively spelled 'Loreley'.

[47] See Droysen, 'Johann Gustav Droysen und Felix Mendelssohn-Bartholdy', 126 and Eva Weissweiler, *Fanny Mendelssohn: Ein Portrait in Briefen* (Frankfurt: Ullstein, 1985), 91.

[48] Letter of Mendelssohn to Planché, Leipzig, 12 Feb. 1838, quoted in Planché, *Recollections*, 281.   [49] Ibid.

(musical or otherwise).'[50] A few years later, in 1843, the composer had found a new formal prototype that he (from all we know) favoured for the rest of his life: 'I cannot approve of the whole [libretto by one of Devrient's friends] because I am generally opposed to the form of a five-act opera with spoken dialogue. In general, I would not like to compose such an opera with dialogue, and I would like to see dialogue disappear even from operas with fewer acts; but it seems to me that through-composed music is explicitly required for five-act operas.'[51] The structure of the fragments of *Die Lorelei*, especially the layout of the finale, also suggests that Mendelssohn's final attempt at opera was intended to be through-composed.[52]

MENDELSSOHN'S FAILURE: LOSS OR GAIN?

It is striking that despite his lack of success as opera composer, the public expected Mendelssohn to compose an opera as much as he did himself. But even on those occasions when he did find a libretto that he did not reject immediately, he gave preference to working on other compositions, particularly his oratorios and symphonies, as is evident in a letter to Carl Gollmick: 'You have chosen and implemented a highly interesting subject, and I share your opinion that the opera must be very effective on stage, if put to music with dignity and spirit. . . . I am at present so occupied with another large instrumental work that will most likely keep me busy until next year that I am unable to keep the text for myself, as much as I would like to, since it is completely uncertain when I would find time for such a significant work.'[53]

---

[50] Letter from Mendelssohn to J. Fürst, Leipzig, 4 Jan. 1840, in *Briefe 1833–47* (1864), 219–20: 'Dies Scenarium mag nun ausführlich oder kurz, detaillirt oder angedeutet sein, darüber maße ich mir keine Entscheidung an. Und ebenso wenig darueber, ob die Oper in 3, 4 oder 5 Acten sein soll; ist sie gut so, wie sie ist, so sind mir 8 nicht zu viel, und einer nicht zu wenig. Und ebenso wenig über das Ballet und nicht Ballet. Nur darüber, ob sie meinem musikalischen und sonstigen Wesen zusagt oder nicht . . .'.

[51] Letter from Mendelssohn to Devrient, Leipzig, 28 June 1843, quoted in Devrient, *Erinnerungen*, 233: 'Aber das Ganze [Operngedicht eines Freundes von Devrient] ist mir schon aus dem Grunde nicht vollkommen zusagend, weil die Form einer fünfactigen Oper mit gesprochenem Dialog mir widerstrebt. Ueberhaupt würde ich ungern eine Oper mit dergleichem Dialog componiren, und möchte ihn sogar aus denen mit wenigen Acten lieber verschwinden sehen; aber bei einer fünfactigen scheint mir durchgehende Musik geradezu nothwendig.'

[52] For an in-depth discussion of *Die Lorelei*, see Todd, 'Mendelssohn's Operatic Destiny'.

[53] Letter from Mendelssohn to Carl Gollmick in Wolfsburg, Leipzig, 17 July 1840, US-Wc, Whitall Collection: 'Sie haben einen höchst interessanten Stoff gewählt und durchgeführt, und ich bin mit Ihnen der Meinung, daß die Oper auf der Scene von großer Wirkung sein muß, wenn

Mendelssohn's attraction to musical genres combining words and music was obvious, but he found ways to explore this interest through experimenting in other venues than opera, as in *Die erste Walpurgisnacht*[54] or in the incidental music to Sophocles' *Antigone*. When we consider Mendelssohn's consciousness of musical tradition and his attempt to continue it, it is not surprising that he failed in a genre in which there was no distinct German tradition, as opposed to symphony, oratorio, and lied, to name the most significant ones. Nevertheless, neither his potential librettists nor his audience ever gave up on him. In 1838 he wrote to his sister Rebecka: 'Four opera subjects were sent to me last week, each even more ridiculous than the last—this will make nothing but enemies for me. This is why I write instrumental music and long for the unknown poet who might live next door or maybe in Timbuctu, what do I know?'[55] With regard to the expectations of the audience, Klingemann wrote in 1838: 'Another main reason why I hope that you and the opera will come off together is again a selfish one: namely that I can get rid of the annoying but irrepressible question of the terribly large number of people with whom I talk (willingly or not) about you and your gifts: "Why doesn't M. write an opera?" or its occasional variant, "When will etc.?" '[56]

Another expression of public anticipation is found in an article published in the *Neue Zeitschrift für Musik* of 18 February 1840 by Eduard Krüger:

We have but *one* singer left of German birth, German frame of mind, German art, the only rightful heir to the heroes of the past century. In him rests our hope that music is not yet facing ruin: in him we find an independent, new song full of sensuous beauty and intellectual depth, and the pathos of our artistic period, in which he is great, has not yet swallowed his ethos. I will not name him; words fail me to praise him rightly. May heaven and the muses grant that his fine powers are guided away from the area of oratorio, in which he is not completely at home, towards that of

sie würdig und mit Geist in Musik gesetzt wird. . . . [I]ch bin im Augenblick mit einer anderen größeren Instrumental-Arbeit, die mich bis zum nächsten Jahre in Anspruch nehmen dürfte, so beschäftigt, daß ich den den Text leider nicht für mich behalten kann, so gern ich es thäte, da es noch ganz unbestimmt ist, wann ich zu einer so bedeutenden Arbeit Zeit gewinne.'

[54] See Julie D. Prandi's essay in this volume, Ch. 6.

[55] Letter of Mendelssohn to Rebecka Dirichlet, [?] Feb. 1838, quoted in *Briefe 1833–47*, 167: 'Vier Opern-sujets habe ich in der vorigen Woche zugeschickt bekommen, eins war immer lächerlicher als das andere, — das giebt nun lauter Feinde. So schreibe ich Instrumentalmusik, und sehne mich nach dem unbekannten Dichter, der vielleicht hier nebenan wohnt oder in Timbuctu, was weiß ich?'

[56] Letter from Klingemann to Mendelssohn, London, 6 Apr. 1838, quoted in Klingemann, *Briefwechsel*, 230: 'Noch ein Hauptgrund, weshalb ich's so wünsche, dass Ihr, Du und die Oper miteinander zustande kommt, ist abermals ein selbstischer, nämlich dass ich dann entsetzlich vielen Leuten gegenüber, mit denen ich mich über Dich und Deine Gaben nolens volens unterhalte habe, die lästige aber unerlässliche Frage loswerde: Warum schreibt M. keine Oper, die sich gelegentlich auch wohl so variiert: Wann wird p. p.?'

opera. But who can advise a genius? It is fortunate enough that we need not despair for today's continuing artistic development on account of [foreign] intruders![57]

Perhaps surprisingly, the genius to which the future of German opera is entrusted here is Mendelssohn. Unfortunately, he could not provide this new path of opera composition. It was left to Richard Wagner to create such an 'independent, new song' (though most likely not in a manner that Krüger would have approved of) by developing his own theoretical framework and by distancing himself from the Romantic opera tradition, announcing in 1851 that he would 'not write operas any more, but will call his works dramas'.[58] Despite the different turn opera composition in Germany took, the public regretted that Mendelssohn did not succeed as an opera composer, even posthumously. *Die Hochzeit des Camacho*, *Die Heimkehr aus der Fremde*, and the *Lorelei* fragments were rediscovered shortly after his death in 1847 and were performed both on stage and in concert halls. Translated into English (all three works), French (the latter two), Swedish, and Hungarian (both *Die Heimkehr aus der Fremde*), they were performed in many European countries[59] and generated much more interest than they had during Mendelssohn's lifetime. A particularly strange manifestation of the audience's desire for an operatic work by Mendelssohn was a *Singspiel* on the life of Heinrich Heine, created by Julius Brammer and Alfred Grünewald in the early twentieth century, supposedly with music by Mendelssohn. As it turned out, this work consists of adapted versions of Mendelssohn's music, mostly songs without words with added transitions, quotes, variations, and free adaptations.[60]

[57] 'Nur *einen* Sänger haben wir noch, deutscher Geburt, deutschen Sinnes, deutscher Kunst, den einzigen rechtmäßigen Erben der Heroen des vorigen Jahrhunderts. In dem ruht unsere Hoffnung, daß die Musik noch nicht zu Grunde gehe: in ihm ist selbstständiger, neuer Gesang voll sinnlicher Schönheit und geistiger Tiefe, und das Pathos unserer Kunstperiode, in dem er groß ist, hat noch nicht das Ethos verschlungen. Ich nenne ihn nicht, die Worte fehlen mir, ihn recht zu preisen. Gäbe der Himmel und die Musen, daß diese schöne Kraft von dem ihr nicht völlig heimischen Gebiete des Oratoriums zur Oper gelenkt würde! Freilich, wer darf dem Genius raten! Glück genug, daß wir nicht brauchen um der Eingedrungenen willen an der Fortentwicklung der Gegenwart zu verzweifeln!' Krüger, 'Ueber die heutige Oper', in *NZfM* 12 (18 Feb. 1840), 58–9.

[58] 'Ich schreibe keine Opern mehr: da ich keinen willkürlichen Namen für meine Arbeiten erfinden will, so nenne ich sie Dramen, weil hiermit wenigstens am deutlichsten der Standpunkt bezeichnet wird, von dem aus Das, was ich biete, empfangen werden muß.' Richard Wagner, 'Mitteilung an meine Freunde', quoted in *Gesammelte Schriften und Dichtungen* (4th edn., Leipzig: C. F. W. Siegels Musikalienhandlung, 1907), 343.

[59] For a list of documented performances, see Alfred Loewenberg, *Annals of Opera*, i (2nd rev. edn., Geneva: Societas Bibliographica, 1955), col. 707 (*Die Hochzeit des Camacho*), col. 893 (*Die Heimkehr aus der Fremde*), and cols. 962–3 (*Die Lorelei*).

[60] See Hellmuth Christian Wolff, 'Zum Singspiel "Dichterliebe" von Mendelssohn', *Mendelssohn Studien*, 6 (1986), 151–62. This work in three scenes was performed in Berlin (1919) and Vienna (1920).

To return to the title of this chapter, 'Mendelssohn, Opera, and the Libretto Problem': there is evidence that some of the libretti and subjects suggested to him were suitable to be set to music, as becomes obvious in the following examples. *Hans Heiling* was successfully composed by Marschner, and Mendelssohn even tried to arrange a performance of that opera in Düsseldorf during his tenure as Municipal Music Director there. His successor at the Düsseldorf theatre, Julius Rietz, also succeeded him in attempting to set Immermann's libretto on *The Tempest*, while Scribe's libretto on this subject was used by Fromental Halévy for an opera premièred at Covent Garden in 1850; Kotzebue's *Pervonte* libretto (on which Klingemann had based his adaptation for Mendelssohn) had already been composed by Peter Joseph von Lindpainter (1811) and Reinacker; the *Nibelungenlied* was quite successfully adapted by Wagner; and *Der Cid*, a libretto by Carl Gollmick, was turned into an opera by Heinrich Neeb and performed in Frankfurt in 1843. Finally, the *Lorelei* libretto was used for two operas, one by Max Bruch in 1860 and the other by the Finnish composer Pacius in the 1880s.

Clearly, then, the ideas and libretti Mendelssohn was unable to set were in fact well suited for opera composition. Perhaps Mendelssohn's problem was not a libretto problem, but a problem of approach and attitude. One would-be librettist, Carl Gollmick, whom Mendelssohn told very openly that they did not share the same work ethics and that he therefore was not willing to consider collaborating with him,[61] later wrote in the *Neue Zeitschrift für Musik*:

A libretto is never good or bad in itself. It becomes either in the hands of the composer, who very often becomes its Proc[r]ustes. It only depends on his ability to indulge in the spirit of his time or in the taste of the audience. A libretto is like a naked doll that acquires value only through its clothes.[62]

Mendelssohn might well have shared this view; since he was careful to avoid producing mediocre music, he waited for the perfect libretto, for which he wanted to provide the proper attire. If Mendelssohn's operatic endeavours

---

[61] In his letter to Gollmick of 17 July 1840 (see above, n. 53), Mendelssohn also wrote: 'I will set this text to music, God and my health permitting; but remind me that I did not agree with your arrangement of it and that we could not resolve our different views.' ('Ich werde diesen Text sicher in Musik setzen, wenn Gott will & ich gesund bleibe; doch erinnern Sie mich daß ich mit Ihrer Bearbeitung desselben nicht einverstanden war, und daß wir unsere Ansichten nicht vereinigen konnten.')

[62] 'Ein Opernbuch ist an sich nie gut oder schlecht. Es wird beides erst unter den Händen des Componisten, der für dasselbe nicht selten zum Proc[r]ustes wird. Es kommt nur darauf an, wie er es versteht, dem Geiste seiner Zeit oder dem Geschmack des Publikums zu fröhnen. Ein Opernbuch ist wie eine nackte Puppe, die ihren Werth erst durch die Gewänder erhält.' Carl Gollmick, 'Glossen über Operntexte, Schluß', *NZfM* 42 (24 May 1842), 165–6.

were hampered by neither his libretti nor his musical ability, we may reasonably conjecture that the expectations of the audience were so high that Mendelssohn was afraid he would not meet them. Since this did not generally stop him composing music, we might then conclude that his lack of success as an opera composer in the long run contributed to his success in other genres—and was not a loss, therefore, but a gain.

10

~~≈~~

Mendelssohn's Cycles of Songs

DOUGLASS SEATON

In the history of the lied it is generally understood that Felix Mendelssohn did not compose song cycles—unlike a number of his immediate predecessors and his contemporaries, most notably Franz Schubert and Robert Schumann.[1] Nevertheless, the issue of cycles among Mendelssohn's songs is one worth opening, and some phantom cycles might be detected from the evidence of the manuscripts, the song texts, and the music itself. The following discussion considers some of the grounds for regarding certain groupings of Mendelssohn's songs as cycles. It begins by taking some straightforward cases among the composer's part songs as models and then proceeds to examine some more problematic cases among his solo Lieder.

---

[1] Lorraine Gorrell, *The Nineteenth-Century German Lied* (Portland, Ore.: Amadeus Press, 1993), 210, for example, flatly states, 'Although Mendelssohn wrote no song cycles, over half of his songs appeared in collections of six, as was customary at that time.' Mendelssohn is not mentioned in the article 'Song cycle' by Luise Eitel Peake in *New Grove*, xvii. 521–3. The otherwise fine survey of the lied edited by Rufus Hallmark, *German Lieder in the Nineteenth Century* (New York: Schirmer, 1996), unfortunately does not include a section on Mendelssohn, and in its discussion of the song cycle, written by John Daverio, suggests that Mendelssohn's sets of songs should be regarded only as 'collections' rather than cycles. Luise Eitel Peake, 'The Song Cycle: A Preliminary Inquiry into the Beginnings of the Romantic Song Cycle and the Nature of an Art Form' (Ph.D. diss., Columbia University, 1968), does not deal with Mendelssohn. Barbara Turchin, 'Robert Schumann's Song Cycles in the Context of the Early Nineteenth-Century Liederkreis' (Ph.D. diss., Columbia University, 1981) does mention Mendelssohn's Op. 9. Interestingly Rufus Hallmark's article 'Song cycle' in *The New Harvard Dictionary of Music*, ed. Don Michael Randel (Cambridge, Mass.: Belknap, 1986), 770–1, does list Mendelssohn as one composer among those who contributed song cycles in the decade of the 1830s, but it is not clear to which songs this refers.

TABLE 10.1. Two cycles of quartet lieder

First line	Subject	Voice	Key
A. *Drei Volkslieder*, Op. 41 Nos. 2–4 ('Liebesgeschichte' in F-Pc, MS 201)			
Entflieh' mit mir	'Come away with me'	Young man as protagonist	E
Es fiel ein Reif	Lovers alone in the world	Narrator	a
Auf ihrem Grab	New couple at the lover's grave	Narrator	E
B. *Der erste Frühlingstag*, Op. 48 Nos. 1–3			
O sanfter, süsser Hauch	Anticipating spring	Nature poet	E
Liebliche Blume	Greeting spring and primrose	Nature poet	A
Süsser, goldner Frühlingstag	Celebration of spring and prayer	Nature poet	E

I

Mendelssohn seemingly did not choose to publish his solo songs as cycles (though in the present study I shall argue that even this claim might have to be qualified). He did so, however, in two different cases among his quartet lieder for soprano, alto, tenor, and bass.[2] Two groups of three quartets within published sets of six explicitly constitute cycles (shown in Table 10.1): the 'Drei Volkslieder' on texts by Heine, Op. 41 Nos. 2–4, which form a narrative (called 'Liebesgeschichte' in one source[3]); and the set of three songs entitled 'Der erste Frühlingstag', Op. 48 Nos. 1–3, which centre on the Romantic response to nature. Several observations should be made about these two cases.

The Op. 41 cycle, though actually written by Heine, is cast in a tetrametric strophic framework and naive style common in German folk poetry. In the first song, which adopts the voice of one of the protagonists in a story, a young lover attempts to convince his beloved to leave the security of her parents'

---

[2] The cycles among the part songs are not discussed in either of the two surveys of this repertoire: Lars Ulrich Abraham, 'Mendelssohns Chorlieder und ihre musikgeschichtliche Stelling', in *Problem Mendelssohn*, 79–87; Wolfgang Goldhan, 'Felix Mendelssohn Bartholdys Lieder für gemischten und Männerchor', *Beiträge zur Musikwissenschaft*, 17 (1975), 181–8.

[3] F-Pc, MS 201.

home and to come away with him. The second song adopts a narrative position as it describes the two young people's departure, separation from their families, and death. The third song, still in the narrative voice, expresses the echoes of sadness in the sounds of nature and the instinctive tears of a new pair of sweethearts at the grave of the former lovers. Although the complete story is thus intended to be understood as a narrative, it demonstrates the possibility of multiple speakers in a song cycle, if all but one of those speakers are understood to be quoted by a single narrative voice.[4]

The three songs form a tonal symmetry in the keys of E major, A minor, and E major. The first, though threatening emotional blackmail (if the maiden does not come, the youth will die, and she will be left alone and feel a stranger even in her own home), adopts the optimistic major mode as a point of departure; it offers no hint of the tragedy to come. The central song, which tells the outcome of the lovers' flight, employs the minor mode to reflect the tragedy of their end. The third song, returning to the key and major mode of the first one, completes the cycle. It introduces a new pair of lovers, who weep at the linden tree by the grave of the former pair, though they do not know why they are weeping. This now places the little cycle's framing tonality in an ironic light, for the key of E major is revealed as only the key of lovers and not, after all, of the optimism that the first song originally suggested. Indeed the implication may be that the cycle of love and fate is merely prepared now to begin again.

The Op. 48 cycle is simpler, with little sense of plot. The first song, on a poem by Uhland, anticipates the arrival of spring and the blooming of violets. The second, by Lenau, greets the primrose as herald of the spring. The final song, again to a text by Uhland, responds to the spring with song, celebration, and prayer.

Despite drawing from poems by two different writers, the songs clearly share a single voice, the conventional voice of the Romantic poet of spring and nature. The ubiquity of poems about nature and springtime among nineteenth-century lieder makes it difficult to argue for or against topical cyclicity. Nature poems were, of course, appropriate for songs 'im Freien zu singen'.[5] In fact, the effect of singing these outdoors, as was intended, is to

---

[4] The ground-breaking study on narrative and persona in the lied, specifically focusing on Schubert's 'Erlkönig', is in the first chapter of Edward T. Cone, *The Composer's Voice* (Berkeley: University of California Press, 1974), 1–19.

[5] The designation 'im Freien zu singen' was a standard one for Mendelssohn's publications of part songs, and common enough in the period. For Mendelssohn's description of one such performance, see his letter to his mother of 3 July 1839, in *Letters of Felix Mendelssohn Bartholdy from 1833 to 1847*, trans. Lady Wallace (Boston: Ditson, 1863), 158–61.

bring the singers into the poet's landscape setting and thus to increase the performers' identification with the lyric persona.

Tonal symmetry is again evident in the Op. 48 cycle, though it certainly does not express irony here. The first and final songs are in E major, which functions simply as the tonic key for the spring songs, the point of anticipation and fulfilment. The key of the middle song, A major, represents only a move within the frame of E—as subdominant, a move towards relaxation.

These sets suggest some criteria for the possible discovery of other cycle-like groupings elsewhere in Mendelssohn's œuvre. Judging by these models, for example, the pattern of sets of three songs might be characteristic. We would not, on the basis of these clearly identifiable cycles, expect Mendelssohn to construct the enormous cycles of the length of twenty or twenty-four songs that Schubert did, or even the twelve- or sixteen-song cycles of Schumann. Mendelssohn's cycles are compact and well focused.

Key planning or other musical connections might also contribute to cyclicity. Both cycles of part songs follow an outline of tonic–subdominant–tonic. We can hardly expect the composer to have limited himself to that plan exclusively, however. Rather, the important issue would be that the keys not simply make for musical symmetry and unity but also engage the content of the texts in some convincing way.

Further, the example of Op. 48 suggests that it is not necessary for a cycle to include songs by only a single poet. More important would be that the poems satisfy the need for continuity of topic and of poetic voice. The spring songs of Op. 48 indicate the possibility that more than one writer can be understood as speaking in the same voice, especially when the voice is one that is conventionally recognized, such as the Romantic poet greeting the spring. The Heine love story of Op. 41 reminds us that the cycle may include a complex of contributing voices—in that case the narrative voice and the quoted voice of one of the protagonists within the story.

The manuscript sources also make clear that a cycle need not be generated at the initial composition of its songs, but rather might be assembled from songs composed at various times (see Appendix). The Heine cycle was composed as a whole, on 22 January 1834. It appears intact in several sources. This is not true, however, of the spring cycle. There, even the two Uhland songs were composed not quickly and in sequence, but nearly six months apart (on 5 July and 28 December 1839, respectively), and they were separated by other compositions for mixed quartet. Indeed, the first of the spring songs was composed shortly after a group of three other songs, from June 1839, including Uhland's 'O Winter, schlimmer Winter', a song that contrasts winter and summer and that might have served to launch a seasonal cycle.

II

This last observation might help to open our next line of thought. We might, in fact, scan Mendelssohn's song output for phantom cycles—groupings that do not appear as such in the published collections but that might have been conceived as cycles at some stage in their composition. In this we would be pursuing a tactic recently proposed by Richard Kramer in Schubert research.[6] Collation of Mendelssohn's song compositions by their dates of composition and by their juxtaposition in various original sources reveals groupings that deserve study in this regard.

To demonstrate how such research would proceed, we can look to Mendelssohn's complete output of part songs for mixed voices, since they form a more manageable body of music and of manuscripts than do his solo songs. (For a listing of all the autograph manuscripts of the mixed-quartet songs in chronological order by date, see Appendix.)

Some of the songs, such as the last one in the Appendix, 'Deutschland' by Geibel, clearly stand apart from any groupings, but this is relatively rare. The songs beginning with the three composed on 23–4 November 1837 show Mendelssohn mixing and matching songs from a limited selection. The songs were repeatedly copied out in pairs and threes. In the latter cases we find one song for men's voices conjoined with two for mixed quartet. This is an interesting phenomenon, but I would not argue that it implies any sort of cycle.

There are more convincing instances, however. Looking to the part songs of 1839 we would find one such phantom cycle—or perhaps more than one possibility. Composed on 14 and 15 June (i.e. three weeks before Op. 48 No. 1) are three quartet Lieder, undoubtedly the ones sung at the event referred to in Mendelssohn's letter to his mother of 3 July 1839,[7] of which our earliest manuscripts are in Volume 31 of the former *Mendelssohn Nachlaß*,[8] and which were eventually published separately as Op. 100 No. 4, Op. 88 No. 3 (the song 'O Winter, schlimmer Winter' mentioned above), and Op. 48 No. 4. They are preceded by a title page that refers to at least these three songs and perhaps more and reads 'Vierstimmige Lieder / für / Sopran, Alt, Tenor und Bass / im Freien zu singen / Frankfurt a/M Sommer 1839'. Their texts are all based on the experience of nature and the seasons—as mentioned above, a unifying factor that is nevertheless so common in this repertoire that one would not wish to claim that by itself it suggests a cycle. The keys of these three songs are the closely related and forward-directed sequence of tonalities D major, G

---

[6] Richard Kramer, *Distant Cycles: Schubert and the Conceiving of Song* (Chicago: University of Chicago Press, 1994).

[7] See above, n. 5.   [8] D-B, Ms.ms.autogr. F. Mendelssohn Bartholdy 31.

minor/major, and G major, respectively. These three songs are also transmitted
in the same order in another manuscript (N.Mus.ms. 16 in the Staatsbibliothek
zu Berlin — Preußischer Kulturbesitz) that was presumably used for the
performance already mentioned, with a similar unruled cover sheet inscribed
'Drei vierstimmige Lieder im Freien zu singen / zur Erinnerung an den schönen,
frohen Abend im Wald' and dated Frankfurt, 19 June 1839.

The quartets that follow in *Mendelssohn Nachlaß* Volume 31, dating
through the end of the year, include the springtime cycle Op. 48 Nos. 1–3, but
these are interspersed with two other songs which were to join them in Op. 48.
Although this group of five songs, taken as a whole, has the key sequence
E major—C major—A major—E minor/E major—E major, this may not be
a closed group at either end. The first of these five songs begins on the verso
of the page on which the third of the June set concluded, suggesting that
Mendelssohn—having written three other songs on new pages since 15 June[9]
—returned to that page intending to extend the group. That bifolio ends (p. 90)
with the Lenau song 'Die Primel'. The next two songs are on separate units of
paper, and they are bound in reverse chronological order. What happens next
is interesting: Helmine von Chézy's 'Im Grün erwacht der frische Muth',
already composed in 1837, is actually bound next in the volume, and following
on the same bifolio is a revision of 'O Winter, schlimmer Winter'.

We might now review what this evidence reveals about Mendelssohn's
plans in the composition of these songs. First, in mid-June, he composed a set
of three songs. He then wrote them out again in a clean copy, apparently for
a performance, and gave the copy away as a memento. He then began to
add more songs to the set—one in July, a second on 18 November, and a third
shortly thereafter. After two more new songs were composed at the end of
December, bringing the year's output to eight, two already composed songs
were appended to the series. If we assume that 'O Winter, schlimmer Winter'
was to be moved from second position to the end of the group, this produced
a cycle that is now only a phantom, a set of nine nature songs 'im Freien zu singen' with the key plan D major—G major—E major—C major—A major—
E minor/E major—E major—A major—and G minor/G major—the result
of one tonal plan (nos. 3–7) framed by another. Ultimately Mendelssohn
selected just three of these as a closed unit, publishing them as 'Der erste
Frühlingstag', Op. 48 Nos. 1–3, a textually and harmonically tightly unified
cycle.

A very similar process gave rise to another phantom cycle in 1843. As the
Nachlaß Volume 38[2] (today held in the Biblioteca Jagiellońska, Kraków)

---

[9] The autographs for Op. 100 No. 4, Op. 88 No. 3, and Op. 48 No. 4 in D-B, N.Mus.ms. 16.

shows, a set of three songs was composed on consecutive days in the first week of March and another set of five in the third week of June. Again the composer used nature poems for all these songs. The first of the March songs deals with leave-taking from nature, the second expresses the Romantics' universal longing for nature, and the third seems to be asking love to set the now city-bound protagonist free to feel again the joy of nature. All this may easily be interpreted as a brief cycle consisting of a sort of monodrama. The June group opens with a prefatory song greeting spring and a new love. The next three songs, which praise the spring, present the songs of nightingales and other birds as reflections of love. The last of the five—untitled in the manuscript but published (in *Mendelssohns Werke*) as 'Der Glückliche'—rejoices in a love as infinite as nature. From a harmonic point of view, the March songs form the key order E flat major—D major—B minor/B major—no tonal symmetry here, certainly. The June group, however, presents a more symmetrical sequence of keys: G major—A flat major—F major—A major—G major. Common to all these songs are horn-like motifs, again a source of musical unity but perhaps too generic to serve as evidence of deliberate thematic cyclicity (see Ex. 10.1).

As the page numbers given in the left-hand column of the Appendix show, the manuscript presents these songs with the two groups intermingled. It is difficult to conceive a textual or musical explanation for the resulting order; indeed, it seems more an accident than a cycle. That there was some carelessness in the binding of these pages is evident from the fact that the Eichendorff setting 'Durch schwankende Wipfel' is bound with its own pages out of order.

As shown in Table 10.2, Mendelssohn used five of the eight 1843 songs in Op. 59, prefacing that set with 'Im Grün erwacht der frische Muth', already composed in 1837 and previously joined to the 1839 set, as we have seen. Although not explicitly identified as a cycle in the published version (the title page reads 'Sechs / vierstimmige Lieder / für / Sopran, Alt, Tenor und Bass / im Freien zu singen'), Op. 59 may reasonably considered as one. 'Im Grünen' serves as a prefatory song, inviting the city-dweller into the natural world. The second song introduces the new love discovered in the rural setting, and the third suggests a return from nature. The remaining songs then comprise a flashback, a longing to return to nature, and an imagined return. The resulting key plan (if it can be described as such) is A major—G major—E flat major—A flat major—D major—B minor/B major.

Now, I will gladly grant that clever but facile argument can conjure up cycles where none may have existed in a composer's mind. I believe, however, that we cannot entirely set aside the following facts:

Ex. 10.1. 'Horn' motifs in Mendelssohn's part songs: (*a*) Op. 59
No. 2, bars 17–24; (*b*) Op. 59 No. 4, bars 1–5; (*c*) Op. 59 No. 6,
bars 12–16

EX. 10.1. *continued*

(1) Mendelssohn published at least two groups of quartets as brief cycles;

(2) he evidently rearranged and selected quartets in manuscript and published groupings, indicating that textual/musical content and order were important to him;

(3) he apparently constructed narrative designs among the various organizations and reorganizations of the quartets; and

(4) he created at least some groupings that display key unity or an apparent consistency between open-ended tonal design and narrative content.

All these factors certainly suggest that Mendelssohn regarded at least some of his various groupings of songs for mixed quartet as implicit cycles.

TABLE 10.2. Quartet lieder, Op. 59

First line/Poet	Subject	Voice	Key
Im Grün erwacht der frische Muth/Chézy	Invitation to nature	Romantic poet	A
Tage der Wonne, kommt ihr so bald/Goethe	Greeting spring and new love	Romantic poet	G
O Thäler weit, o Höhen/Eichendorff	Regret at leaving nature	Romantic poet	E♭
Die Nachtigall, sie war entfernt/Goethe	Praise of spring (as memory)	Romantic poet	A♭
Wann im letzten Abendstrahl/Uhland	Longing for nature	Romantic poet	D
Durch schwankende Wipfel/Eichendorff	Poet asks love to free him to return to nature	Romantic poet	b/B

III

The history and the sources of the solo songs reveal few such groupings—perhaps surprisingly, since there are so many of them. A few groups that I will not discuss are offered for consideration as Table 10.6.

Small groups of songs concentrating for brief periods on single poets occur several times (see Table 10.3). Such groups, which already appear in the composer's earliest years, include the two songs on texts by Walter Scott (1820) and the group of three songs on poems of Matthison (26 September–1 October 1823).[10] (Like almost all Mendelssohn's juvenile works, none of these saw publication.) In May of 1834 Mendelssohn seems to have become interested in poems from *Des Knaben Wunderhorn*, setting three of them over a period of two weeks. He published only the first of these, 'Leucht heller als die Sonne' (Op. 34 No. 1). The second, 'Ich weiß mir'n Mädchen', though heavily revised and later recopied, was never published. The third, the *Jagdlied* 'Mit Lust thät ich ausreiten', was published in the set for low voices

---

[10] For more on these songs, see Luise Leven, 'Mendelssohn als Lyriker unter besonderen Berücksichtigung seiner Beziehungen zu Ludwig Berger, Bernhard Klein und Adolf Bernhard Marx' (diss., University of Frankfurt am Main, 1926); Luise Leven, 'Mendelssohn's Unpublished Songs', *Monthly Musical Record*, 88 (1958), 206–11; Thomas Stoner, 'Mendelssohn's Lieder not Included in the *Werke*', *Fontes artis musicae*, 26 (1979), 258–66. None of these writings considers the problem of cycles in particular.

TABLE 10.3. Groupings of Mendelssohn's solo songs by single poets, according to sources

Source	Title	Date	Op.	Key
D-B, MN 1	[two songs by Scott]			
	Ave Maria	?/?/1820	—	d
	Raste Kreiger, Krieg ist aus	?/?/1820	—	G
GB-Ob, MDM c. 47	[three songs by Matthison]			
fo. 1ʳ	Am Seegestad	26/9/1823	—	F
fo. 1ᵛ	Durch Fichten	?/?9/1823	—	G
fo. 2ʳ	Ich denke dein	1/10/1823	—	D
D-B, MN 20	[three songs from *Des Knaben Wunderhorn*]			
p. 39	Leucht heller als die Sonne ('Mailied')	11/5/1834	34/1	G
pp. 40–1	Ich weiß mir'n Mädchen ('Andres Mailied')	14/5/1834	—	g
pp. 41–3	Mit Lust thät ich ausreiten ('Jagdlied')	25/5/1834	84/3	E
(p. 44	Warum sind denn die Rosen so blaß; Heine) (inc.)	[n.d.]	—	e
D-DS, Mus. ms. 1444a				
	Leucht heller als die Sonne ('Mailied')	[n.d.]	34/1	G
	Ich weiß mir'n Mädchen ('Mailied', 'Andres Mailied', Hüt du dich')	[n.d.]	—	g
	(Schlummre und träume ['Bei der Wiege', 'Wiegenlied'] Klingemann)	[n.d.]	47/6	B♭
Elberfeld, 1835; *NZfM* suppl., 1838	Two Eichendorff Lieder			
	Wo noch kein Wandrer ging ('Das Waldschloß')	17/8/1835	—	e
	Wenn die Sonne lieblich schiene ('Pagenlied')	25/12/1832	—	a

TABLE 10.3. *continued*

Source	Title	Date	Op.	Key
F-Pc, MS 202; *Album musical auf das Jahr 1837*	Two Byron Romances			
	There Be None of Beauty's Daughters (Keine von der Erde Schönen)	3/8/1833	—	A
	Sun of the Sleepless (Schlafloser Augen Sonne)	31/12/1834	—	e
F-Pc, MS 210	Two songs by Geibel			
	Mein Herz ist wie die dunkle Nacht ('Der Mond')	[n.d.]	86/5	E
	Wenn sich zwei Herzen scheiden ('Fahrwohl')	12/22/45	99/5	e

issued posthumously as Op. 84. In a later manuscript,[11] however, the *Jagdlied* was replaced by Klingemann's lullaby 'Schlummre und träume' (Op. 47 No. 6)—probably in order to create a set of three songs with comparable vocal ranges. One further pairing is formed by two songs on texts of Geibel.[12] Both are love songs, in E major and E minor respectively.

Of course, Mendelssohn also twice paired for publication songs on poems by a single poet, though they were quite separate in composition. The two Eichendorff Lieder published together date from 1835 and 1832 respectively. The pair of Byron romances published in the *Album Musical auf das Jahr 1837* were composed quite separately sixteen months apart in 1833 and 1834.[13] In neither case is there any particular connection between the texts of the songs of the pair, and the close key relationships appear to be coincidental.

IV

One strongly tempting candidate is the possible cycle formed by the four unpublished songs of 1 May 1830 contained in Volume 56 of the former *Mendelssohn Nachlaß* (see Table 10.4). The four songs, on texts by an unknown poet or poets, have certain stylistic features in common, present

---

[11]   D-DS, Mus.ms. 1444a.   [12]   This pair is transmitted as F-Pc, MS 210.

[13]   For an examination of the two Byron settings, see Monika Hennemann, 'Mendelssohn and Byron: Two Songs almost without Words', *Mendelssohn-Studien*, 10 (1997), 131–56.

TABLE 10.4. A possible song cycle (1 May 1830, in D-B, Mus.ms.autogr.
F. Mendelssohn Bartholdy 56)

Title	First line	Subject	Key
Der Tag	'Sanft entschwanden mir'	Loss of childhood's innocence	A
Reiterlied	'Immer fort'	Riding to beloved	C
Abschied	'Leb wohl mein Lieb'	Departure from beloved	B♭
Der Bettler	'Ich danke Gott'	Reunion with beloved	a/A

harmonic and thematic unity as a set, and can be interpreted as the expressions of a single dramatic protagonist.

The texts might be taken as representing moments in the experience of this character. In the first, 'Der Tag', he reflects on his past youth and the discovery of a new experience in the emotional life of adulthood. In the 'Reiterlied' he gallops over the mountains to the castle where his beloved lives. 'Abschied' expresses his consolation to her as he departs to serve his country. Finally, in 'Der Bettler' he seems to have returned in disguise as a beggar (for reasons not clarified in the poem), discovers his beloved still pining for him, and discloses himself to her in a blissful reunion.

The style of these songs is quite unusual. These are not Lieder based on the *volkstümlich* style, like most of Mendelssohn's songs. Instead, they are almost operatically demanding for the singer and often quasi-orchestral in their piano accompaniments. The accompaniment textures change in the course of each song, as the piano responds to the texts far more than in the usual lied (by Mendelssohn or by anyone else; see Ex. 10.2). This makes each one perhaps seem oddly disunified or open, but, by the same token, musical recurrences among the songs tend to connect them to each other, closing the set as a cycle.

The harmonic plan of the group of four songs is quite coherent. The first piece begins and ends in A major, with a middle section in A minor but extending as far afield as C minor. The second song is in C major, but places considerable emphasis on related minor harmonies, including at least passing references to F minor, D minor, G minor, and A minor. The third song, the shortest of the group, is in B flat major but very heavily shaded towards G minor, on which, in fact, it begins. The last piece returns to A major, though it starts in A minor. And at the moment of the return, the melodic line actually quotes the end of the first song, bringing undeniable musical framing to the set as a whole.

Ex. 10.2. 'Der Bettler', bars 1–20

V

Finally, we might scan the sets of lieder as Mendelssohn published them for cycles that resemble those of the part songs, although no such cycles are indicated among the solo sets.

Among the published song *opera* there are two that might invite performance as complete, multi-movement works. The first of these, Op. 9, presents an intriguing layout in the first edition, though this layout was not used in the *Werke*. The twelve songs are grouped into two volumes, the first headed 'Der Jüngling' and the second 'Das Mädchen'. The clear implication is that the

Ex. 10.2. *continued*

songs should be sung by two singers in some sort of alternation, perhaps nos. 1, 7, 2, 8, 3, 9, and so on. Rather than a cycle, such a plan would be better considered a *Liederspiel* for two characters. As it happens, however, the results form a peculiar sort of dialogue, in which the characters seem to be talking at cross-purposes.

The last set of lieder Mendelssohn himself authorized for publication, however, Op. 71, might very well meet the criteria for a cycle. As Table 10.5, part A shows, the situation of the sources is somewhat complicated, though certainly suggestive.

The song that became the fourth of Op. 71, Lenau's 'Auf dem Teich, dem Regungslosen', appears in Volume 20 of the former *Mendelssohn Nachlaß*[14] in close juxtaposition with two songs based on texts in English, the *Venetianisches Gondellied* after Thomas Moore and a solo version of a song by Robert Burns that was published as a duet in Op. 63. Mendelssohn composed these songs about two weeks apart in 1842.

Op. 71 No. 2, 'Der Frühling naht mit Brausen', on a poem by Karl Klingemann, dates from April of 1845. In *Nachlaß* Volume 40 it is shortly followed by two songs dated 22 December 1845: Hoffmann von Fallersleben's 'Werde heiter mein Gemüthe', which became Op. 71 No. 1, and 'Wenn sich zwei Herzen scheiden', on a text by Geibel, posthumously published as Op. 99 No. 5.

At Christmas in 1845 Mendelssohn gave his wife a volume of songs that included four of the songs from Op. 71, but not in direct sequence.[15] A number of the songs in the collection date from earlier in the composer's career, but interestingly, the collection also includes all six of the songs just mentioned from *Nachlaß* volumes 20 and 40. In addition, the volume contains three more songs that seem to date from this time (although, since the source is inaccessible for study, it is not possible to verify that they could not have been composed later and added afterwards to Cécile's collection): Geibel's 'Mein Herz ist wie die dunkle Nacht' (later published as *Der Mond*, Op. 86 No. 5) and two songs that became members of Op. 71, Lenau's 'Ich wandre fort ins ferne Land' (Op. 71 No. 5) and Eichendorff's 'Vergangen ist der lichte Tag' (Op. 71 No. 6).

The four Op. 71 songs—nos. 1, 2, 5, and 6—of (presumably) 1845 all have to do with loss and comfort. This is also true of the Lenau song of 1842, which was brought into the opus as no. 4, and of Lenau's 'Diese Rose pflück' ich

[14] D-B, Ms.mus.autogr. F. Mendelssohn Bartholdy 20.
[15] Sotheby & Co., *Catalogue of the Valuable Holograph, Printed and Engraved Music, Books about Music and Musicians, and Autograph Letters of Composers; 11–12 May 1959*, 52. I am grateful to Richard Macnutt for this reference and for drawing my attention to this valuable source.

TABLE 10.5. 'Songs of loss and comfort' (?), Op. 71

A. AS FOUND IN THE SOURCES

Source	Song	Date	Op.	Key
D-B, MN 20				
pp. 5–6	Wenn durch die Piazzeta ('Rendezvous/Venetianisches Gondellied'); after Moore	17/10/1842	57/5	b
pp. 6–7	O säh ich auf der Haide ('Volkslied'); Burns	17/10/1842	[63/5 duet/B♭]	A
pp. 7–8	Auf dem Teich, dem Regungslosen ('Die Nacht'); Lenau	3/11/1842	71/4	f♯/F♯
PL-Kj, MN 40				
pp. 67–9	Der Frühling naht mit Brausen ('Frühling'); K. Klingemann	3/4/1845	71/2	A
p. 71	Werde heiter, mein Gemüthe ('Tröstung'); Hoffmann von	22/12/1845	71/1	D
p. 72	Fallersleben Wenn sich zwei Herzen scheiden ('Fahrwohl'); Geibel	22/12/1845	99/5	e
Song album for Cécile				
	Wenn sich zwei Herzen scheiden ('Fahrwohl'); Geibel	see MN 40	99/5	e
	. . .			
	Werde heiter, mein Gemüthe ('Tröstung'); Hoffmann von Fallersleben	see MN 40	71/1	D
	. . .			
	Mein Herz ist wie die dunkle Nacht ('Der Mond'); Geibel	by 25/12/1845?[a]	86/5	E
	Ich wandre fort ins ferne Land ('An den Wind'); Lenau	by 25/12/1845?[b]	71/5	b
	Vergangen ist der Lichte Tag ('Nachtlied'); Eichendorff	by 25/12/1845?[c]	71/6	E♭
	Der Frühling naht mit Brausen ('Frühling'); K. Klingemann	see MN 40	71/2	A

TABLE 10.5. *continued*

B. OP. 71 IN PUBLISHED ORDER[d]

First line	Subject	Key
Werde heiter, mein Gemüthe ('Tröstung'); Hoffmann von Fallersleben	God as source of comfort	D
Der Frühling naht mit Brausen ('Frühling'); K. Klingemann	Change of season as model for hope	A
Diese Rose pflück' ich hier ('An die Entfernte'); Lenau	Loved ones should remain close	B♭
Auf dem Teich, dem Regungslosen ('Die Nacht'); Lenau	Loss and memory	f♯/F♯
Ich wandre fort ins ferne Land ('Auf der Wanderschaft'); Lenau	Bitterness at separation	b
Vergangen ist der lichte Tag ('Nachtlied'); Eichendorff	Resolution to praise God with nature, despite sorrow	E♭

[a] Because this source, auctioned by Sotheby's in 1959, is in private hands and its location is unknown, it has not been possible to verify that all the items it contains were part of the original volume and therefore that the compositions must date from before Christmas 1845. If this manuscript does date from 1845, it would be the earliest one known for this song. Another autograph manuscript, together with Op. 71 No. 2, dated 21 Mar. 1846 was also auctioned by Sotheby's in 1959 and also remains in private possession.

[b] See n. 9 regarding the problem of establishing a definitive date for this song. What appears to be a composition score for Op. 71 No. 5 is in PL-Kj 44, pp. 145–6, and bears the date 'Interlaken, d. 27 July 1847'.

[c] See n. 9 regarding the problem of establishing a definitive date for this song. Mendelssohn's biographers have always reported that Op. 71 No. 6 was composed for the birthday of Mendelssohn's Leipzig friend Conrad Schleinitz on 1 Oct. 1847.

[d] Mendelssohn considered including in Op. 71 the 'Altdeutsches Frühlingslied' on a text by F. von Spee, 'Der trübe Winter ist vorbei', composed on 7 Oct. 1847 and eventually published posthumously as Op. 86 No. 6. Its autograph manuscript is GB-Ob, MDM b. 5, fo. 40.

hier', apparently composed on 22 September 1847, which became no. 3. The same sentiments pervade Geibel's 'Wenn sich zwei Herzen scheiden', which, as we have seen, dates from the same time as Op. 71 Nos. 1 and 2 and might form a companion to them in a miniature cycle of three songs. Another song with similar content is the *Altdeutsches Frühlingslied* 'Der trübe Winter ist vorbei' by Spee, composed on 7 October 1847 and reportedly considered by Mendelssohn as a candidate for inclusion in Op. 71.[16]

[16] See Ernst Wolff, *Felix Mendelssohn Bartholdy* (Berlin: 'Harmonie', 1909), 180. For Mendelssohn to have published a set of seven songs would have been highly unusual; it is more likely that the *Altdeutsches Frühlingslied* was considered in place of one of the songs that appear in Op. 71.

Mendelssohn compiled his Op. 71 in October 1847, while still grieving for the death of his sister Fanny.[17] For this set he assembled six songs, of which the earliest dated from 1842, four were apparently from 1845 (if we assume that the Christmas collection for Cécile does indeed form an integral unit), and one was from 1847. These songs might certainly form a coherent set in terms of voice—that of the bereaved poet—and emotional position.

Broadly speaking, then, all six of the Op. 71 songs maintain the same subject position or voice, but they offer subtle differences in their attitude towards the loss with which they all deal. In the first song the poet speaks to himself, appealing to God's goodness as the source of hope in a time of worry and pain. The second song seems to hear an outside voice that calls on the image of spring coming after winter as a model for hope. The third speaks as the poet to his distant 'liebes Mädchen', complaining of their separation and proposing —perhaps now to himself (or to us as listeners) as much as to her—that loved ones should never go farther from each other than the rose bloom can retain its freshness. The fourth, in the same voice as the third and seemingly addressing the same absent one, expresses the sadness of loss experienced in a night-time nature scene, though a sweet memory—mirrored in a shift to the parallel major—appears at the end. The fifth bitterly laments that the loved one departed without a chance for a final word; here the poet refers to the departed in the third person, while he addresses as 'du' only the 'raw, cold breath of the wind'. In the last song the bereaved speaker, having lost his 'Freundes Trost' and 'Liebsten süsser Augenschein', draws on the determination that stems from his spiritual faith and calls on nature to join him in praising God even during the dark period of loss.

It may not be immediately clear from this outline that there is any direction to this group of songs. The keys of the songs, however, might lend some sense of the progression of the singer's spiritual journey (see Table 10.5, part B). The D major and A major of the first two songs open the group with a focus on sources of optimism—the second almost desperately so. The move to B flat that follows in no. 3 represents a darkening of mood as the sentiment turns from comfort to the reflection that such separations should never happen. No. 4 descends by a major third to the mediant of the opening song, another darkening of the mood. The move to major at the end of this song allows it to serve as dominant to the B minor of no. 5. The harmonically decisive move to the relative minor of the opening song provides a sort of closure at this point in the cycle, implying perhaps that the speaker has experienced a descent of the

---

[17] It is interesting to consider that these songs were actually composed before the loss of Fanny, the severest in Felix's experience.

soul from ineffectual suggestions of comfort to simple bitterness. The final
song, in the remote key of E flat, breaks the downward emotional spiral by a
radical new approach—not that there is simple comfort in nature or in God,
but that the true spiritual answer to grief is to join nature in the praise of God
even while one waits through the darkest night of the soul. The tonalities give
no simple symmetry here, but the progression through these keys corresponds to and clarifies the emotional/poetic journey.

VI

In conclusion, one would not want to claim that Mendelssohn's song œuvre is
full of unrecognized cycles. But there are certainly some cycles. As we have
seen, two, at least, unquestionably exist among the published part songs. One
appears to survive unpublished in the set of four songs held in *Nachlaß*
Volume 56. Beyond that there are coherent, cycle-like features in the ways in
which Mendelssohn composed and reordered both his quartet and solo
Lieder. And in the end, it is possible that the last set of songs he published
forms a sort of cycle—following Fanny's death, a musical/poetic apotheosis
of Felix's own deep emotional/spiritual insight into the experience of grief
and one's best response to it.

The Mendelssohn song cycles are phantom-like in their history of disappearing and in their tendency to occur in shifting and changing shapes. The
little cycles of Opp. 41 and 48, solid as they are, have faded from our awareness
as twentieth-century musicians have lost sight of the quartet lied as a genre.
The possible cycle of solo songs in *Mendelssohn Nachlaß* Volume 56 seems to
have disappeared even within the composer's lifetime. The other groupings
discussed here involved songs gathered into varying combinations. In the
end, two groups became fixed, the part songs of Op. 59 and the solo songs of
Op. 71. Yet even these, because the composer did not explicitly name them as
cycles, have remained phantom-like.

TABLE 10.6. Some groupings of Mendelssohn's solo lieder

Source	Item	Date	Op.	Key
GB-Ob, MDM b. 5				
fo. 2$^{\text{r–v}}$	Er ist zerbrochen ('Faunenklag')	8/6/1823	—	e
fo. 3^{r}	Sicheln schallen; Hölty	?/?6/1823	—	D
fo. 3^{v}	Tanzt dem schönen Mai entgegen	?/?6/1823	—	G
[fo. 4$^{\text{r–v}}$ empty]				
fo. 5	Mitleidsworte Trostesgründe ('Glosse'); F. Robert	[n.d.]	—	e
F-Pc, MS 193				
	Wie so gelinde die Fluth bewegt ('Auf der Fahrt'); 'H. Voss'	13/1/1830	9/6	E
	Die linden Lüfte sind erwacht ('Frühlingsglaube'); Uhland	27/1/1830	9/8	E
	Ihr frühlingstrunknen Blumen ('Im Frühling'); Droysen	27/1/1830	9/4	D
GB-Ob, MDM c. 16				
fo. 1^{r}	Bringet des treusten Herzens grüsse ('Reiselied'); Ebert	1/1831	19/6	E
fo. 1^{v}	Ihr frühlingstrunknen Blumen ('Im Frühling'); Droysen	[1/1831]	9/4	D
US-NYpm Lehman				
	Ein Blick von deinen Augen ('Die Liebende schreibt'); Goethe	8/10/1831	86/3	E♭
	Ich reit' ins finstre Land hinein ('Reiselied'); Uhland (inc.)	[n.d.]	—	—
D-B, N.Mus.ms. 98				
fo. 1^{r}	Auf, schicke dich recht feierlich ('Weihnachtslied'); Gellert	19/12/1832	—	E♭
fo. 1^{v}	Wenn die Sonne lieblich schiene ('Der wandernde Musikant'); Eichendorff	25/12/1832	—	a
D-B, MN 28				
pp. 143–4	Ringsum erschallt in Wald und Flur ('Sonntags'); K. Klingemann	29/12/1834	34/5	A
p. 145	Sun of the Sleepless (Schlaflosen Augen Sonne); Byron	31/12/1834	—	e
D-DS, Mus.ms. 1444b				
	Wo noch kein Wandrer ging ('Das Waldschloß'); Eichendorff	[17/8/1835]	—	e
	Ringsum erschallt in Wald und Flur ('Sonntags'); K. Klingemann	[n.d.]	34/5	A
	Sun of the Sleepless (Schlafloser Augen Sonne) ('Erinnerung'); Byron (inc.)	[n.d.]	—	e

TABLE 10.6. *continued*

Source	Item	Date	Op.	Key
GB-Ob, MDM c. 47, fos. 11–12	Wie der Quell so lieblich klinget ('Im Walde'); Tieck	15/8/1838	47/1	A
D-B, MN 31 pp. 234–5	O könnt' ich zu dir fliegen	15/8/1838	—	A♭
D-B, MN 31				
p. 71	Es ist bestimmt in Gottes Rath ('Volkslied'); Feuchtersleben	18/4/1839	47/4	B♭
pp. 72–3	Durch den Wald, den dunklen ('Frühlingslied'); Lenau	17/4/1839	47/3	D
pp. 74–5	O Winter, schlimmer Winter ('Hirtenlied'); Uhland	20/4/1839	57/2	g/G
[p. 76 empty]				
pp. 77–8	Schlummre und Träume ('Wiegenlied'); K. Klingemann	15/8/33	47/6	B♭
p. 79	Was bedeutet die Bewegung? ('Suleika'); Goethe/v. Willemer (inc.)	[n.d.]	57/3	E
PL-Kj, MN 35				
pp. 1–2	Ich hör ein Vöglein ('Im Frühling'); A. Böttger	20/4/1841	—	B♭
pp. 2–3	Laue Luft kommt blau geflossen ('Frische Fahrt'); Eichendorff	29/4/1841	57/6	G
PL-Kj, MN 35				
pp. 10–12	Ein Schifflein ziehet leise ('Das Schifflein'); Uhland	6/6/1841	99/4	E♭
pp. 13–14	Ach, wer bringt die schönen Tage ('Erster Verlust'); Goethe	9/8/1841	99/1	F
US-NH Speck Coll.	Was bedeutet die Bewegung? ('Suleika'); Goethe/v. Willemer	7/6/1841	57/3	E
PL-Kj, MN 38²				
pp. 97–8	Es weiß und rät es doch keiner; Eichendorff	[9/1842]	99/6	g
pp. 99–100	Wenn durch die Piazzeta ('Rendezvous'); after Moore	[n.d.]	57/5	G
D-B, MA Ms. 14 (C/A)				
fos. 1ᵛ–3ʳ	Der Frühling naht mit Brausen ('Frühling'); K. Klingemann	[n.d.]	71/2	A
fo. 3ᵛ	Werde heiter, mein Gemüthe ('Tröstung'); Hoffmann von Fallersleben	[n.d.]	71/1	D

Sources and Dates for Mendelssohn's Quartet Lieder

Manuscript	Item	Date	Op.	Key(s)
D-B, MN 28				
p. 124	Drei Volkslieder; Heine	22/1/1834	41/2–4	E a E
F-Pc, MS 201	('Liebesgeschichte')	22/5/1835	—	—
F-Pc, MS 200				
D-DÜhi (C/A)				
D-B, MN 31				
p. 97	Im Grün erwacht der	23/11/1837	59/1	A
[also see below]	frische Muth ('Im Grünen'); Chézy			
F-Pc, MS 197				
	Der Schnee zerrinnt ('Mailied'); Hölty	23/11/1837	41/5	B♭
	Includes TTBB song 'Im Süden'	24/11/1837	120/3	B♭
	Und frische Nahrung ('Auf dem See'); Goethe (inc.)	[n.d.]	41/6	C
D-B, N.Mus ms. 109				
pts A, C by CMB	Und frische Nahrung ('auf dem See'); Goethe	[1840]	41/6	C
	Im Grün erwacht der frische Muth ('Im Grünen'); Chézy	—	59/1	A
	Includes TTBB song 'Sommerlied'; Goethe	—	50/3	G
US-Wc				
	Und frische Nahrung ('Auf dem See'); Goethe	frag.	41/6	C

Manuscript	Item	Date	Op.	Key(s)
GB-Ob, MDM c. 16				
fo. 2^{r-v}	Der Schnee zerrinnt ('Mailied'); Hölty	—	41/5	B♭
fos. 2^{v}–3^{r}	Ihr Vögel in den Zweigen schank ('Im Walde'); Platen	?/1/38	41/1	A
D-B, N.Mus.ms. 116				
fos. 1^{r}–2^{r}	Und frische Nahrung ('Auf dem See'); Goethe	6/4/1839	41/6	C
fo. 2^{v}	Der Schnee zerrinnt ('Mailied'); Hölty (inc.)	[n.d.]	41/5	B♭
D-B, MN 31				
p. 81 [unruled]	'Vierstimmige Lieder/ für/Sopran, Alt, Tenor und Bass/im Freien zu singen/Frankfurt a/M Sommer 1839'			
pp. 83–4	O Wald, du kühlender Bronnen ('Im Wald')	14/6/1839	100/4	D
pp. 84–5	O Winter, schlimmer Winter; Uhland	14/6/1839	88/3	g/G
pp. 86–7	Wie lieblicher Klang ('Lerchengesang', Canon)	15/6/1839	48/4	G
D-B, N.Mus.ms. 16				
fo. 1^{r}	O Wald, du kühlender Bronnen ('Waldlust')	19/6/1839	100/4	D
fos. 1^{v}–2^{r}	O Winter, schlimmer Winter ('Hirtenlied'); Uhland	19/6/1839	88/3	g/G
fo. 2^{r-v}	Wie lieblicher Klang (Canon)	19/6/1939	48/4	G
D-B, MN 31 (cont.)				
pp. 88–9	O sanfter süßer Hauch ('Am ersten Frühlingstag'); Uhland	5/7/1839	48/1	E

Manuscript	Item	Date	Op.	Key(s)
p. 89	O wunderbares tiefes Schweigen ('Morgengebet'); Eichendorff	18/11/1839	48/5	C
p. 90	Liebliche Blume ('Die Primel'); Lenau	?/?/1839	48/2	A
pp. 93–5	Holder Lenz, du bist dahin ('Herbstklage'); Lenau	26/12/1839	48/6	e/E
[p. 96 empty]				
pp. 91–2	Süßer, goldner Frühlingstag ('No. 3 Frühlingsfeier'); Uhland	28/12/1839	48/3	E
p. 97	Im Grün erwacht der frische Muth—see above	23/11/37	59/1	A
[pp. 97–9 sketches]				
pp. 99–100	O Winter, schlimmer Winter ('Hirtenlied'); Uhland	—	88/3	g/G
GB-Ob, MDM b. 5				
fo. 22ʳ⁻ᵛ	O Wald, du kühlender Bronnen ('Im Wald')	—	100/4	D
PL-Kj, MN 34				
pp. 9–10	Durch Feld und Buchenhallen ('Der wandernde Musikant'); Eichendorff	10/3/1840	88/6	E♭
PL-Kj, MN 38²				
p. 93	O Thäler weit, o Höhen ('Abschied vom Wald'); Eichendorff	3/3/1843	59/3	E♭
pp. 94–5	Wann im letzten Abendstrahl; Uhland	4/3/1843	59/5	D
[p. 96 empty]				
pp. 79–80, 83–4, 81–2]	Durch schwankende Wipfel ('Vorüber'); Eichendorff	5/3/1843	59/6	b/B

Manuscript	Item	Date	Op.	Key(s)
pp. 73–6	Tage der Wonne, kommt ihr so bald ('Frühzeitiger Frühling'); Goethe	17/6/1843	59/2	G
pp. 76–7	Die Nachtigall, sie war entfernt; Goethe	19/6/1843	59/4	A♭
[p. 78 empty]				
pp. 85–6	Kommt, lasst uns geh'n spazieren ('Die Waldvögelein'); Schütz	19/6/1843	88/4	F
pp. 87–8	Saatengrün, Veilchenduft ('Lob des Frühlings'); Uhland	20/6/1843	100/2	A
pp. 88–91	Ich hab' ein Liebchen; Eichendorff	20/6/1843	88/2	G
[p. 92 empty]				
location unknown	Die Nachtigall, sie war entfernt ('Die Nachtigall'); Goethe	12/7/1845	59/4	E♭
location unknown	Berg und Thal will ich durchstreifen ('Frühlingslied')	?1843–4	100/3	D
PL-Kj, MN 39				
p. 16	Mit der Freude zieht der Schmerz ('Neujahrslied'); Hebel	8/8/1844	88/1	E♭
p. 54	Die Bäume grünen überall; Hoffmann von Fallersleben	8/8/1844	100/1	D
D-B N.Mus.ms. 161				
fos. 1ᵛ–2ʳ	Mit der Freude zieht der Schmerz ('Neujahrslied'); Hebel	1/10/1845	88/1	E♭
fo. 2ʳ⁻ᵛ	Die Bäume grünen überall ('Andenken'); Fallersleben	1/10/1845	100/1	D

Manuscript	Item	Date	Op.	Key(s)
PL-Kj, MN 40				
pp. 63–5	Sahst du ihn hernieder-schweben; F. Aulenbach	8/7/1845	116	g
[p. 66 empty]				
pp. 73–5	Wohl perlet im Glase der purpurne Wein ('Der Sänger'); Schiller	30/10/1845, 25/1/1846	—	B♭
[p. 76 empty]				
D-B, MA Ms. 10				
fos. 1ʳ–2ᵛ	Wohl perlet im Glase der purpurne Wein ('Die Frauen und die Sänger); Schiller	—	—	B♭
fo. 2ᵛ	Mit der Freude zieht der Schmerz ('Neujahrslied'); Hebel	—	88/1	E♭
PL-Kj, MN 44				
pp. 54–5	Durch tiefe Nacht ein Brausen zieht ('Deutschland'); Geibel	—	88/5	a

PART IV

Felix and Fanny

11

～～

Similarities and Differences in the Artistic Development of Fanny and Felix Mendelssohn Bartholdy in a Family Context: Observations Based on the Early Berlin Autograph Volumes

HANS-GÜNTER KLEIN

WE know very little about the domestic and musical atmosphere in the Mendelssohn household when Fanny and Felix were children. However, we may assume that this very atmosphere decisively influenced the musical development of the two siblings, apart from their lessons with the house tutors Stenzel and Heyse and from the training in playing musical instruments that Fanny and Felix received. That the stimulation leading to the development of the two artistic personalities had its source in family life can easily be recognized in the area of vocal composition when we know of personal contact with a particular poet or of certain literary works the Mendelssohn children were reading. By investigating the verse Fanny and Felix favoured and parallel settings of verse where these are extant, we arrive at a further level of investigation. For instrumental works, we must limit ourselves to examining when and how the two began to grapple with genres outside of that of the lied. We can pursue the theme of similarities and differences in the music of the children in a cursory way as early as the beginning of the year 1820 in the notebooks of the children.

THE NOTEBOOKS, 1820–1823

According to early accounts, Felix's and Fanny's instruction in the conventional theoretical subjects began with Zelter in 1818. Yet we do not know exactly when these lessons commenced, whether or not brother and sister started at the same time, and how that training was structured. It is certainly a lucky circumstance that one exercise book of Felix's from the years 1819–21 has been preserved. In that book, counterpoint studies up to the complexity of three-part fugues are documented.[1] There is nothing comparable we can point to that has come down to us from Fanny.[2]

Most of the music on loose sheets that represents the first attempts of the two children to compose must be considered lost. Peter Ward Jones has discovered two pieces for two pianos by Felix;[3] for Fanny we can name one composition, which, however, has not been preserved. On 18 August 1819 Fanny wrote to Zelter from the Meierei,[4] where the family used to spend their vacations:

My musical concoction is progressing rather slowly. It is at times pretty difficult for me; especially the songs are giving me a lot of trouble. I have completed the gavottes, that is, twelve of them are down on paper, but you will certainly find fault with much that is there. I am rushing now with the songs in order to finish them before our departure.[5]

This composition, which Fanny herself denigrates as a 'concoction' and which she wants to complete before the family leaves for Dresden to go to Swiss Saxony, has not been preserved. What did it contain? Only songs and gavottes, or perhaps also other old dances? What was the occasion or purpose for which she was composing? In view of the fact that much of what Fanny composed later belonged in the lied category, it is perhaps characteristic that songs form an essential part of her early compositional activity.

---

[1] GB-Ob, MDM c. 43. For a transcription and critical commentary on this notebook see R. Larry Todd (ed.), *Mendelssohn's Musical Education: A Study and Edition of his Exercises in Composition* (Cambridge: Cambridge University Press, 1983), esp. 95–257.

[2] For an evaluation of the counterpoint studies, chorale arrangements, and chorale-based works in her first composition album, see Hans-Günter Klein, *Die Kompositionen Fanny Hensels in Autographen und Abschriften aus dem Besitz der Staatsbibibliothek zu Berlin — Preußischer Kulturbesitz, Katalog* (Musikbibliographische Arbeiten, 13; Tutzing: Hans Schneider, 1995). How these compositions relate to Zelter's lessons has not been clarified. For further information see Gesine Schröder, 'Fannys Studien', in Martina Helmig (ed.), *Fanny Hensel, geb. Mendelssohn Bartholdy: Das Werk* (Munich: edition text + kritik, 1997), 27–32.

[3] See Peter Ward Jones's essay in this volume, Ch. 4.

[4] The reference is to the so-called Bartholdy dairy farm [Meierei] in front of the Silesian Gate in Berlin, which was purchased by Lea's grandfather Daniel Itzig and has gone down in history as the source of the name for Jacob Salomo Bartholdy, and through him also for Abraham Mendelssohn Bartholdy.

[5] 'Mein musikalisches Machwerk rückt ziemlich langsam vor, es wird mir mit unter recht schwer, besonders die Lieder machen mir viel zu schaffen, mit den Gavotten bin ich fertig, das heißt es stehen deren 12 auf dem Papier, woran Sie aber gewiß recht viel werden tadeln müssen. Ich eile nun mit den Liedern, um sie noch vor unsrer Abreise fertig zu machen.' D-B, Manuscript Division, Nachl. Fam. Mendelssohn 4, 1, 3.

In the early compositional attempts of sister and brother, the first parallel action was that each wrote a song on the same text in honour of their father's birthday in 1819.[6] The songs, both entitled 'Ihr Töne, schwingt euch fröhlich durch die Saiten'[7] (Music, rise cheerfully through the strings), were sent to Abraham Mendelssohn in Paris.[8] It is striking that just four months afterwards both children, each for themselves, acquired a music album so that they could write down their own compositions: Fanny started with hers on 4 March 1820, Felix with his on 7 March of the same year.[9] Fanny's book was in the oblong format, whereas Felix had chosen upright format. This difference in format had perhaps a purely practical justification: that one could distinguish the two books at a glance in the household or during composition lessons. In any case, this distinction was maintained for the collections in the years to follow as well. Moreover, the albums differ in the manner in which they are bound. Whereas Fanny's first music composition book is bound in grey paper with a black scaly pattern (type A; see Pl. 11.1), Felix's is bound in medium brown paper with a bright wavy pattern in which the method of manufacture with oil is recognizable (type B; see Pl. 11.2). These volumes, which consist only of blank music paper, could apparently be purchased, but the possibility that they were prepared on special order cannot be ruled out.[10] Because of the expense involved, the parental decision to give both children such volumes acquires special weight: evidently this was a deliberate decision that had far-reaching consequences. Such preparations would show that the parents intended to collect and preserve future compositions of Felix and Fanny.

In the following survey I shall distinguish between 'albums' (for volumes already bound containing blank music paper) and 'convolutes' (for sheets of paper or single scores collected and bound).[11] We shall see that different kinds of binding were not consistently used (see Table 11.1 and Pl. 11.3).

---

[6] According to recent research, 10 Dec. was the father's birthday; but the family celebrated it on 11 Dec. Fanny and Felix composed their songs for the latter date, which is stated in the title.

[7] The autograph for Fanny's composition is in D-B, Mendelssohn-Archiv Depos. Berlin Ms. 3. That for Felix's composition is at GB-Ob, MDM c. 21, fo. 107.

[8] Traces of a fold can be clearly recognized in both autographs.

[9] Both volumes are in D-B. Fanny's album: MA Depos. Lohs 1; Felix's album: Mus. ms. autogr. F. Mendelssohn Bartholdy 1. The shelf marks of the autographs by Felix are: 'Mus. ms. autogr. F. Mendelssohn Bartholdy . . .' and are abbreviated as 'autogr.'. See also Hans-Günter Klein, 'Verzeichnis der im Autograph überlieferten Werke Felix Mendelssohn Bartholdys im Besitz der Staatsbibliothek zu Berlin', *Mendelssohn-Studien*, 10 (1997), 181–213. For the autographs by Fanny, see Klein, *Die Kompositionen Fanny Hensels*.

[10] The identity of the binding of both autographs MA Ms. 32 and 33 supports this thesis. The loose sheet binding MA Ms. 32 was bound *after* the collation of the contents, whereas the album MA Ms. 33 was bound *before* the first entry was made.

[11] For a more exact differentiation between 'album' [Album] and 'convolute' [Konvolut], see Klein, *Die Kompositionen Fanny Hensels*, p. xi.

PL. 11.1. D-B, Mendelssohn-Archiv Depos. Lohs 1, front cover of binding

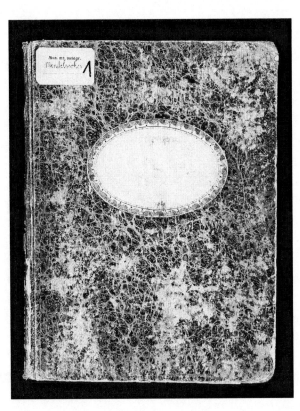

PL. 11.2. D-B, Mus.ms.autogr. F. Mendelssohn Bartholdy 1, front cover of binding

TABLE 11.1. Chronological comparison of Felix's and Fanny's composition notebooks

Felix's Notebooks (all in upright format)	*Fanny's Notebooks* (nos. 1, 3, and 4 in oblong format; no. 2 in upright format)
Mus. ms. autogr. F. Mendelssohn Bartholdy 1 Album 7 Mar. 1820–autumn (?) 1820 Paper binding: type *B* (see Pl. 11.2)	1. Mendelssohn-Archiv, Depos. Lohs 1 Album 4 Mar. 1820–27 June 1821 Paper binding: type *A* (see Pl. 11.1)
Mus. ms. autogr. F. Mendelssohn Bartholdy 2 Album 3 Dec. (28 Nov.) 1820–10 May 1823 Black half-calf binding, covered with violet paper	

Mus. ms. autogr. F. Mendelssohn Bartholdy 3
Bundle of single sheets
1821
Brown half-calf binding, type *A*
	2. Mendelssohn-Archiv, MS 32
	Bundle of single sheets
	29 Jan. 1822–Feb. 1823
	Paper binding type *B*, dark brown
	  with grey wavy lines, partly also
	  in red

Mus. ms. autogr. F. Mendelssohn Bartholdy 4 Bundle of single sheets 6 May 1823–9 June 1824 Paper binding type *A* (title etiquette inscribed by Fanny; see Pl. 11.3)	3. Mendelssohn-Archiv, MS 33 Album 22 Mar. 1823–12 Sept. 1823 Paper binding type *B*, as in no. 2
Mus. ms. autogr. F. Mendelssohn Bartholdy 5 Album Summer 1823 (with entries in 1824 and 1827) Green half-calf binding, covered with green marbled paper	4. Mendelssohn-Archiv, MS 34 Album 15 Sept. 1823–12 Sept. 1824 Paper binding type *B*, as in no. 2
Mus. ms. autogr. F. Mendelssohn Bartholdy 6 Bundle of single sheets 7 Nov. 1822–14 June 1823 Green half-calf binding, covered with green paper	

PL. 11.3.   D–B, Mus.ms.autogr. F. Mendelssohn Bartholdy 4,
label on front cover

VOCAL WORKS

While the acquisition of the composition volumes created only a necessary
prerequisite for writing pieces down, the literary interests in the Mendelssohn
family led more directly to the musical compositions of the children. The
Mendelssohn family, which knew French works in the original, was exceedingly well read. The father was a francophile and had lived for several years in
Paris; the mother had obviously also mastered French. Because of the family
stay in Paris in 1816 and the father's periodic business trips to France, French
culture was always more or less a presence in the family. In fact, during the
Jewish persecution of 1819, the so-called 'Hep-Hep' movement, the family
discussed emigrating and had in the meantime decided to move to Paris for
that purpose. In view of this last circumstance, the country and literature of
France returned forcefully to the foreground. The novels and short fiction of
Jean Pierre Claris de Florian (1755–94), published at the close of the eighteenth century, evidently belonged to the domestic library. Fanny had read at
least five of them,[12] and in the space of only three months could compose
music for eleven poems taken from those volumes.[13] Among these we find

---

[12] *Célestine*; *Claudine*; *Estelle*; *Galatée*; *Gonßalve de Cordoue*.
[13] In Mar. 1821 she set two further texts by Florian. See Annette Maurer, *Thematisches
Verzeichnis der klavierbegleiteten Sololieder Fanny Hensels* (Kassel: Bärenreiter, 1997).

also a short romanzero, 'Pauvre Jeanette', written down on 22 March 1820.[14] This same text was also set by Felix, who noted it down in his exercise book, probably somewhat later.[15] It is characteristic that he did not copy his second song into his composition album; he probably did not consider it important enough. While Fanny had worked herself up into a sort of song frenzy, Felix seems not to be particularly interested in writing songs during this period. Since both songs are in a minor key, feature the same time signature, and are rather similar in expression, we might be able to imagine a specifically family situation as a context for their composition.

The world of poetry also came to the Mendelssohn family in the person of a young doctor who saw the family socially during the winter of 1819–20. Before travelling on to further studies in France, Johann Ludwig Casper (1796–1864) finished his doctoral degree in Halle[16] and then stayed a few months in Berlin, where he introduced the Mendelssohns to his own poems. Fanny opens her composition album with one of them, 'Lied des Schäfers' (Shepherd's Song), on 4 March 1820. Casper's visits also bore fruit for Felix. It was agreed that the doctor would translate the text of a French operetta that Felix would then set to music. In the summer of 1820 Casper did indeed send Felix from Paris the German libretto for 'Soldatenliebschaft' (Soldier Love), which Felix thanked him for on 2 August.[17] Everyone was evidently satisfied with the young doctor's work, since he also prepared texts for the next *Singspiele* of the young composer.[18] Fanny composed one additional poem by Casper, 'Fischers Klage' (A Fisher's Lament), which she copied into her brother's album in March of 1822.[19] Again in 1826 Felix recalled Casper's poems,[20] which he had seemed to ignore during the previous years when Fanny was setting them to music. However, none of Felix's songs on texts by Casper has come down to us.[21]

Another writer whose works Felix, Fanny, and their mother read was Sir Walter Scott (1771–1832). The German first edition of his verse novel

---

[14] D-B, MA Depos. Lohs 1, p. 3.   [15] GB-Ob, MDM c. 43, fo. 21[r].

[16] Casper had begun his studies in Berlin, the city of his birth, and had apparently already at that time been a guest at the Mendelssohns' home, if we can take a remark in Felix's letter of 2 Feb. 1826 literally. See Elvers, *Briefe*, 47.   [17] Ibid. 18.

[18] *Die beiden Pädagogen* (The Two Teachers, 1821); *Die wandernden Komödianten* (The Travelling Actors, 1821–2); *Die beiden Neffen oder Der Onkel aus Boston* (The Two Nephews or The Uncle from Boston, 1822–3).

[19] GB-Ob, MDM d. 8, fos. 47[v]–48.   [20] Letter of 6 Feb. 1826; see Elvers, *Briefe*, 47.

[21] In addition, Fanny Mendelssohn composed music for two poems by Casper's wife: 'Frühlingserinnerung' (A Spring Recollection) on 15 May 1821, at a time when Fanny Robert was not yet married to Casper; and 'Lied der Fee' [Song of the Fairy] on 30 May 1823. Both songs are in D-B, with the shelf marks MA Depos. Lohs 1, p. 90; and MA Ms. 33, p. 23, respectively.

The Lady of the Lake, published in 1819 under the title *Das Fräulein vom See*,[22] apparently caught the fancy of Fanny and Felix around 1820. In that year both set to music the famous 'Hymn to the Virgin' (Ave Maria! Jungfrau mild) from the third song, although they did so in obviously different ways. Felix wrote a somewhat sober song in 3/8 time[23] in which the 'influence of figured bass can be recognized',[24] whereas Fanny composed an expressive prayer in broad melodic lines with broken chords and static harmonies.[25] Probably soon afterwards Felix composed the verses 'Raste Krieger! Krieg ist aus' (Rest, warrior, the war is over)[26] from the first part of Scott's novel in a way very similar to his 'Ave Maria', and Fanny set the sentimental lament 'So mußt ich von dir scheiden' (Then I had to leave you)[27] from the third part of the novel. The difference in expression between the two 'Ave Maria' settings is so pronounced that we must assume that the 11-year-old Felix had not progressed enough in his development to gauge the richness of feeling in this text.

During the spring of 1822 the two siblings probably first became familiar with the poetry of Ludwig Uhland (1787–1862), which held a strong appeal for them both. Felix wrote down the 'Jägerlied' (Hunter's song) (Kein beß're Lust in dieser Zeit) for four-part male a capella choir on 20 April 1822.[28] Just a few days later on, 1 May 1822, Zelter wrote a short choral piece into Fanny's album under the title 'Nimmersatt' (Never satisfied), whose text he attributed to the Swabian poet Uhland.[29] Fanny set Uhland's poem 'Die Nonne' (The Nun) (Im stillen Klostergarten) to music in May of 1822 as a solo song with piano accompaniment.[30] The temporal proximity of these three entries is very telling. Considering that Zelter's small piece was never published, we can infer that he composed it on the spot while visiting the Mendelssohns. Since these poems were new for the children, it appears that on this occasion Uhland must have been a topic of conversation within the family.

[22] Walter Scott, *Das Fräulein vom See*, trans. Adam Storck (Essen: G. D. Bädecker, 1819).

[23] D-B, Autogr. 1, pp. 86–8.

[24] 'Einflüsse der Generalbaßzeit erkennen läßt': Eberhard Rudolph, 'Der junge Felix Mendelssohn: Ein Beitrag zur Musikgeschichte der Stadt Berlin' (diss., Humboldt-Universität Berlin, 1964), 133.

[25] D-B, MA Depos. Lohs 1, pp. 29–31. An edition is also found in *The Harmonicon*, 10 (1832), Part the 2nd, 54–5 (altered, with text in English).   [26] D-B, Autogr. 1, pp. 88–9.

[27] D-B, MA Depos. Lohs 1, pp. 37–9 (13 Dec. 1820). The text is the third stanza of the poem entitled 'Sang', which begins with the line 'Die Nacht bricht bald herein'. For the German edition, see Scott, *Fräulein*, 126.   [28] D-B, Autogr. 2, p. 175.

[29] D-B, MA Ms. 142,1, p. 93; see also Hans-Günter Klein, ' ". . . dieses allerliebste Buch", Fanny Hensels Noten-Album', *Mendelssohn-Studien*, 8 (1993), 141–58 at 146.

[30] D-B, MA Ms. 32, p. 41. The song was published as no. 12 in Felix's Op. 9.

Ex. 11.1. Thematic comparison of (*a*) Mendelssohn, Piano Concerto movement
in D Minor (1820) and (*b*) Hensel, Piano Piece in D Minor (1820)

INSTRUMENTAL WORKS

When we observe the initial notations of the first composition albums of
brother and sister, we see the similar character of the instrumental pieces. The
theme from Fanny's piano piece in D minor from 17 March 1820 is not far
removed in its expressive language from the theme at the beginning of Felix's
piano concerto movement in the same key, which he wrote out on 7 March (see
Ex. 11.1).[31] Such parallels, which surely arose without conscious intent, can be
viewed as characteristic for a household so filled with music as the Mendelssohn
household was. In this setting Fanny began to be concerned with other genres
besides the lied—genres that Felix had already taken up earlier. A comparison
of the siblings' work at this time can highlight the parallels and contrasts in
their artistic development (see Table 11.2).

This table shows that Fanny patterned her works on the corresponding
compositions of her brother; that she may have been stimulated by these works
or felt herself challenged to do things differently. A detailed comparison is not
possible in the present context, but we can observe briefly that Fanny is much
freer in her sense of form than is Felix, who keeps close to traditional forms in
a very clear way, especially with regard to sonata form. The monothematic
principle Felix follows in the first movement of Op. 105 and in the finale of
Op. 1, where the theme of the first area reappears in the secondary area in place
of a thematic contrast, is probably inspired by the works of Joseph Haydn.
Fanny takes over the monothematic principle in her sonata movement in
E major; however, she is very free in her handling of it. If this piece really was
intended to open a sonata,[32] it was composed in an untraditional way, perhaps

[31] Felix: Autogr. 1, pp. 3–4; Fanny: D-B, MA Depos. Lohs 1, p. 2.
[32] In the autograph (D-B, MA Ms. 32, pp. 31–4), the piece has no title. In the table of contents
on the inside cover, Fanny mentions a sonata she has started that can only refer to this piano piece
in E major. We can therefore assume that it should actually have begun a sonata. No one knows
why Fanny did not continue with it.

TABLE 11.2. Chronological comparison of Felix's and Fanny's early
             compositions

Works by Felix	Works by Fanny
PIANO SONATAS	
A minor (May 1820)	
E minor (July 1820)	
F minor (*c.*late autumn 1820)	
G minor, Op. posth. 105	F major (autumn 1821), lost[a]
(16 June–18 Aug. 1821)	
	Sonata movement in E major
	(29 Jan.–19 Feb. 1822)
PIANO QUARTETS	
D minor (*c.*1821)[b]	
C minor, Op. 1 (20 Sept.–18 Oct. 1822)	A♭ major (1 May–23 Nov. 1822)
VIOLIN SONATAS	
F major (autumn 1820)	
F minor, Op. 4 (1823)	Adagio in E major (28 May 1823)

[a] Mentioned as 'Sonata' (but 'piano sonata' was probably intended) in Fanny's letter of
29 Oct. 1821; see Citron, *Letters*, 371. The sonata has disappeared.
[b] On the dating of this work see Friedhelm Krummacher, *Mendelssohn — Der Komponist:
Studien zur Kammermusik für Streicher* (Munich: Wilhelm Fink, 1978), 82.

intentionally as a contrast to the sonata in G minor by Felix. The concertante
style of the first movement of her piano quartet is also uncharacteristic, formally speaking. It is reminiscent more of a concerto movement than of a
chamber music work. It is also markedly different from Felix's piano quartets.
The compositional context of the Adagio for violin and piano is also unclear.
If it was not conceived as a middle movement of a violin sonata, but actually
represents an independent, finished composition, which was not typical for
that era, then it may well have been conditioned by a particular family circumstance—one which, however, remains unknown to us.

Considering the contemporary early compositions of Felix and Fanny
within the family context can help to illuminate the background for particular
works. Conversely, we might ask with respect to specific traits that are conspicuous in the compositions whether these might be explained by certain
family situations, without assuming a primary musical intention. For example,

a special family event has been demonstrated to have shaped the instrumental accompaniment for Felix's 'Frühlingslied' (Spring song), Op. 8 No. 6.[33]

CONCLUSION

If we examine the content of the composition albums of Felix and Fanny from 1820 to 1823 side by side, it becomes clear that Fanny, from her first entry in the first volume, concentrates on the lied and only gradually approaches the one-movement piano piece as an independent, compositionally demanding form. In this regard the pieces written in 1823 that she herself designated as 'practice pieces' (*Übungsstücke*) are only experiments. In her songs to poems by Florian, which she stopped setting to music after 1821, she shows a personal style that we can pinpoint in later songs again and again. While she composed to the lyrics of most poets only for a limited time period, she continued to compose music to Goethe's poems throughout her life.[34]

Felix, conditioned by his own development, remains far removed from the world of the lied in these early years. While practising composing fugues, he concentrates on piano sonatas and chamber music and is busy appropriating the major genres for himself (*Singspiel*, symphony, solo concerto, and sacred choral music). The fact that Fanny did not plan any works in these major genres is not surprising in view of her father's unmistakable message about the different significance music should have in her life as opposed to Felix's.[35] Whether she saw her own works in the piano sonata and chamber music genres as finished or perfected is hard to judge—but some evidence indicates she did not. Perhaps these works, which both in artistic weight and in musical importance lie between the small forms of lied and piano piece on the one hand and the major genres like the symphony and concerto on the other, were not in harmony with the feminine role that she was brought up to fulfil.

—translated by Julie D. Prandi

---

[33] The family event is mentioned by Therese Devrient in her *Jugenderinnerungen* (Stuttgart: C. Crabbe, 1908), 232. See also Klein, *Das verborgene Band*, Cat. No. 116.

[34] Compare the lists in Maurer, *Thematisches Verzeichnis*.

[35] See the letter on her confirmation day, 1820, which is frequently quoted, in Hensel, *Familie* (1880), i. 97.

12

On Stylistic Affinities in the Works of Fanny Hensel and Felix Mendelssohn Bartholdy

R. LARRY TODD

As relatively unusual as prodigies are in Western history, the instances of musical sibling prodigies represent even more rare phenomena. One could argue as the most extraordinary example the children of J. S. Bach, and one would also include, of course, Wolfgang and Nannerl Mozart, celebrated during their English tour of 1764 as infant 'prodigies of nature' ('Wundern der Natur').[1] But the list does not extend much further; indeed, it is conspicuous for its exclusion of such figures as the Haydn brothers, who were certainly celebrated composers, but not child prodigies. Nor does the list include avuncular relationships, such as those of the Gabrielis or the Couperins in the seventeenth century. Nevertheless, there remains one further compelling example: Fanny and Felix Mendelssohn, two musical prodigies reared and educated during the 1820s in the conservative cultural environment of high Berlin society. Like Nannerl Mozart, Fanny was protected by her parents from the travails of a professional career in music; but unlike Nannerl, of whom no compositions survive, Fanny left several hundred works, a substantial testament to her unusual musical gifts and a window into the creative world of her internationally acclaimed brother.[2]

The many parallels between Felix and Fanny are remarkable, to say the least. Like Felix, Fanny inherited from her mother, Lea, Bachian fugal fingers,

---

[1] See Otto Erich Deutsch and J. H. Eibl, *Mozart: Dokumente seines Lebens* (2nd edn., Kassel: Barenreiter, 1981), 25.

[2] For an inventory of Fanny's compositions, see Renate Hellwig-Unruh, 'Werkverzeichnis', in Martina Helmig (ed.), *Fanny Hensel, geb. Mendelssohn Bartholdy: Das Werk* (Munich: edition text + kritik, 1997), 168–77.

so that at age 13, in 1818, she was able to perform from memory twenty-four Preludes from the *Well-Tempered Clavier* (her astonished Aunt Henriette disapproved of this accomplishment, fearing that the exertion was too much for Fanny). The two siblings studied piano with Marie Bigot in Paris and Ludwig Berger in Berlin, and were afforded finishing lessons by Ignaz Moscheles in 1824, who was dutifully impressed. 'This is a family', he reported, 'the like of which I have never known. Felix, a boy of fifteen, is a phenomenon. What are all prodigies as compared with him? Gifted children, but nothing else. This Felix Mendelssohn is already a mature artist, and yet but fifteen years. . . . His elder sister Fanny, also extraordinarily gifted, played by heart, and with admirable precision, Fugues and Passacailles by Bach. I think one may well call her a thorough "Mus. Doc." . . .'[3] Both Felix and Fanny studied theory and composition with Zelter.[4] Both were steeped in the Bachian tradition, and were accomplished contrapuntists at early ages. For Felix, the writing of learned canons and fugues became something of a routine avocation, as it was for Fanny: by the end of 1824, Zelter could boast to Goethe that she had finished her thirty-second fugue.[5] Both Felix and Fanny sang in Zelter's Singakademie, which they joined in October 1820. And finally, both began to compose at an early age (at least as early as December 1819, when Felix, aged 10, and Fanny, aged 14, wrote two lieder in honour of their father's birthday).[6]

   Initially Abraham and Lea Mendelssohn encouraged their children's musical proclivities without discrimination. But this attitude soon changed. In July 1820 Abraham wrote a letter to Fanny explaining that though music might become a profession for Felix, it must remain an ornament for her life.[7] Not surprisingly, around this time we can begin to detect a divide in the siblings' aspirations as composers. While Fanny continued to compose in the smaller, more intimate forms (principally the piano miniature and lied), Felix was encouraged to essay the larger forms. Thus, by October 1820 he was at work on his first full-scale *Singspiel*, *Die Soldatenliebschaft*, which was staged privately at the Mendelssohn home. And in 1821 he began to compose a series of string symphonies, also performed privately, with a continuo realization provided by himself from the piano. By 1824, when Zelter could proclaim his prize pupil a member of the brotherhood of old Bach, Mozart, and Haydn,

[3] *Recent Music and Musicians as Described in the Diaries of Ignatz Moscheles*, ed. Charlotte Moscheles, trans. A. D. Coleridge (New York: H. Holt, 1873; repr. 1970), 65.

[4] See Gesine Schröder, 'Fannys Studien', in Helmig (ed.), *Fanny Hensel*, 23–32.

[5] Letter of 10 Dec. 1824, quoted in *Der Briefwechsel zwischen Goethe und Zelter*, ed. Max Hecker (Leipzig: Insel, 1918), ii. 310.

[6] But see Peter Ward Jones's essay in this volume, Ch. 4.

[7] Sebastian Hensel, *The Mendelssohn Family (1729–1847), from Letters and Journals* (New York: Harper & Brothers, [1881]), i. 84.

Felix had in his portfolio examples of nearly all the principal musical genres of the time (piano, organ, and chamber works, string symphonies, concertos, solo lieder, part songs, cantatas, *Singspiele*, and sacred choral works).

In short, Felix's compositional development was encouraged at the expense of Fanny's. Her musicality found expression chiefly in genres and settings deemed appropriate for ladies of leisure—the smaller forms centred around the piano, for performance in private, domestic settings, a sheltered musical world probably not far removed from those genteel musical settings of an earlier generation so vividly captured in the novels of Jane Austen. Now one might suppose that we need look no further than the patriarchal mores of nineteenth-century Berlin to account for this treatment of Fanny. But there was another factor at work: in addition to being a woman, Fanny was a member of the Berlin upper class; and, as Nancy Reich has pointed out, the bias was as much one of class as it was of gender.[8] Thus, while Fanny performed almost exclusively in private circles (only one public performance is documented, on 27 February 1838, when she played her brother's G minor Piano Concerto in a charity concert).[9] Clara Wieck, a member of the middle class, did pursue a musical career, principally as a pianist, but also to some extent as a composer. In effect, class distinctions enabled Clara, in October 1835 at age 16, to première her Piano Concerto, Op. 7 at a public concert of the Gewandhaus Orchestra, led by its new director, Felix Mendelssohn. A similar event was unthinkable for Fanny.

Fanny's creative world thus remained a private, secluded realm, visited by the members of her immediate family and friends, and, of course, shared intimately with her brother. Felix, in turn, dubbed her his Minerva, his Cantor, and submitted most of his major works to her critical scrutiny. But Felix was duty-bound to observe the strictures of his father and of Berlin society: there could be no question, in his view, of Fanny becoming a professional composer. And so, when six of Fanny's lieder were published in Felix's Opp. 8 and 9 (1827 and 1830), her authorship was carefully suppressed. And when, in 1837, she gave serious consideration to publishing a set of piano pieces, Felix remained firmly opposed[10] (by then, as the eldest son to survive Abraham's death in 1835, he had assumed the patriarchal role of his immediate family). With the exception of a few other songs that appeared in occasional musical albums, Fanny did not venture into print until the last two years of her life, and then she finally won her brother's approval. On 12 August 1846 he sent her his

[8] Nancy B. Reich, 'The Power of Class: Fanny Hensel', in *MHW*, 86–99.

[9] See *AMZ* 40 (28 Mar. 1838), col. 209.

[10] See further the Preface to Camilla Cai's recent edition of Fanny Hensel, *Songs for Pianoforte, 1836–1837* (Madison, Wis.: A-R Editions, 1994).

'professional blessing on becoming a member of the craft': 'may you have much happiness in giving pleasure to others', he wrote; 'may you taste only the sweets and none of the bitternesses of authorship; may the public pelt you with roses, and never with sand; and may the printer's ink never draw black lines upon your soul'.[11] In 1846 her first three publications with opus numbers, the *Sechs Lieder*, *Vier Lieder für das Pianoforte*, and *Sechs Gartenlieder*, were issued; and in 1847 four more collections of piano pieces and lieder followed. A few brief reviews of these works began to appear in the *Neue Zeitschrift für Musik* and *Allgemeine musikalische Zeitung* in 1847,[12] but in May of that year Fanny died, and the critical estimation of her music was left to posterity. Only a few more numbered publications appeared posthumously, in 1848 and 1850, and then, nothing new until the latter half of the twentieth century, when the rediscovery of Fanny Hensel began in earnest, gaining momentum in the 1970s and 1980s, and, of course, continuing to this day.

The many similarities between Fanny's and Felix's music were not lost upon her circle and early critics. In 1843, for example, the young Danish composer Niels Gade, who himself certainly knew how to imitate the Mendelssohnian style, commented on similarities between the siblings' compositions.[13] Not surprisingly, the issue of stylistic commonalty has always loomed large in any consideration of Fanny's music. But until we have a complete edition of her works, we cannot fully and objectively answer the fundamental question of stylistic influences between the siblings. Nevertheless, the presumption has always been that the weight of the evidence argues overwhelmingly for Felix's influence on Fanny, and not the other way. But does this judgement mean that she was only capable of producing slavish copies of Felix's works, that she should be consigned to the epigonal ranks of his imitators? Though her authorship was suppressed, and her professional activities severely restricted, was she unable to find her own individual voice as a composer? To consider this question further, we shall look briefly at some of Fanny's piano compositions that exhibit strong ties to the music of her brother.

The first, *Il Saltarello romano*, was composed in Berlin in 1841, and published in 1847 as Op. 6 No. 4 by Bote & Bock in Berlin. The autograph, dated

---

[11] Letter of 12 Aug. 1846, quoted in Hensel, *Mendelssohn Family*, ii. 326.

[12] See *NZfM* 26 (1847), 14, 38, 89, and 169–70, and the [*Leipzig*] *Allgemeine musikalische Zeitung*, 49 (2 June 1847), cols. 381–3.

[13] See Niels Gade, *Aufzeichnungen und Briefe*, ed. D. Gade (Leipzig: Breitkopf & Härtel, 1894), 42. On Gade's assimilation of the Mendelssohnian style, see R. Larry Todd, 'Mendelssohn's Ossianic Manner, with a New Source—*On Lena's Gloomy Heath*', in Jon W. Finson and R. Larry Todd (eds.), *Mendelssohn and Schumann: Essays on their Music and its Context* (Durham, NC: Duke University Press, 1984), 137–60 at 146–9.

26 March 1841, bears the annotation, 'Das Motiv in Rom aufgeschrieben',[14] from which we may surmise that the piece was inspired by Fanny's experiences during her Roman sojourn (November 1839–May 1840). But a cursory glance at the piece betrays several similarities to the saltarello finale of her brother's 'Italian' Symphony. As we know, the Symphony was inspired by Felix's Italian sojourn of 1830–1, finished in March 1833, performed in London in May 1833, and then revised in 1834, when, as Michael Cooper has shown, Felix reworked the last three movements and made a piano-duet arrangement of the Andante that he sent to Fanny.[15] In August 1834 Fanny wrote to Felix to demur about his alterations of the melodic inflections in the Andante. And she asked him to bring along the original version when he next visited Berlin so that they could discuss the revisions further.[16]

Unfortunately, Fanny's critical reaction to Felix's Saltarello is not documented, but there is little doubt that she knew the movement well. Thus, her *Saltarello romano* is in A minor, begins with a brief introductory flourish before the main motif is established, and uses rhythmic patterns reminiscent of the Symphony (Ex. 12.1(*a*)). As in the 'Italian' Symphony (Ex. 12.1(*b*)), the principal motif is centred around the fifth scale degree, with disjunct motion of a third, the little skip or hop, from which the dance derives its name. Whereas Felix's subject involves the third below ($e''-c''$), and a prominent upper auxiliary note (f''), Fanny's subject is melodically somewhat more complex: the third below is answered by a leap to the third above ($e''-g''$), and the upper auxiliary note f'' is balanced by the raised leading tone $d\sharp''$. Nevertheless, it is difficult to imagine Fanny composing this piano piece without the sound and whirling melodic inflections of her brother's Saltarello in mind.

Quite a different situation obtains in our second example, which, *mutatis mutandis*, documents a compositional response by Felix to one of Fanny's piano pieces, and establishes that the exchange of musical ideas between the siblings *could* work both ways. Fanny's piece in question is the Andante in G Major, composed on 19 July 1836; it survives in an autograph miscellany of eighteen pieces in MS 44 of the Mendelssohn Archive in the Staatsbibliothek zu Berlin — Preußischer Kulturbesitz.[17] As Camilla Cai has recently shown, Fanny numbered ten of these pieces, evidently in an unsuccessful attempt to

---

[14] D-B, MA Ms. 46, 1, pp. 29–33. See further Hans-Günter Klein, *Die Kompositionen Fanny Hensels in Autographen und Abschriften aus dem Besitz der Staatsbibliothek zu Berlin — Preußischer Kulturbesitz, Katalog* (Musikbibliographische Arbeiten, 13; Tutzing: Hans Schneider, 1995), 35.

[15] See John Michael Cooper, ' "Aber eben dieser Zweifel": A New Look at Mendelssohn's "Italian" Symphony', *Nineteenth Century Music*, 15 (1992), 169–87.

[16] Letter of *c*.1 Aug. 1834 from Fanny to Felix, in Citron, *Letters*, 151.

[17] For a description of the manuscript, see Klein, *Die Kompositionen*, 28–9.

EX. 12.1. Comparison of (*a*) Hensel, *Il Saltarello romano*, Op. 6 No. 4,
with (*b*) Mendelssohn, 'Italian' Symphony, Op. 90, Saltarello, bars 1–14

(*a*)

prepare them for publication as a set.[18] Felix was unwilling to encourage her
to publish them, though he nevertheless thought positively of her work,
and in a birthday greeting sent to her on 14 November 1836 selected two for
special praise, including the Andante.[19] When, in 1846, Fanny herself took
the decision to begin publishing her music, Felix's critical praise may have
influenced her to include the Andante as the first of the *Vier Lieder für
das Pianoforte*, Op. 2, with only minor changes (chiefly in dynamics and
articulations).[20]

Ninety-six measures in length, Fanny's Andante is in a ternary ABA form,
with a shortened return of the A section. It is, for all intents and purposes, a
Lied ohne Worte, not at all removed from the stylistic idioms of Felix's piano

[18] See Camilla Cai, 'Fanny Hensel's "Songs for Pianoforte" of 1836–1837: Stylistic
Interaction with Felix Mendelssohn', *Journal of Musicological Research*, 14 (1994), 55–76; and,
for an edition, Hensel, *Songs for Pianoforte, 1836–1837*, 11–15.

[19] Letter of 14 Nov. 1836 (D-B, MA Depositum Berlin, 3, 15). Quoted in Citron, *Letters*, 219.

[20] For a detailed list of the variants, see Hensel, *Songs for Pianoforte*, pp. xvii–xviii.

EX. 12.1. *continued*

(*b*)

lieder, which it reflects, mirror-like. But in this case Fanny's melodic inspiration in turn stimulated the creative energy of Felix, who must have had the opening of the Andante in his ear when, in January 1844, he composed his own Andante in G major,[21] published later that year as the first of the six *Lieder ohne Worte*, Op. 62 (with a dedication, incidentally, to Clara Schumann).

As Exs. 12.2(*a*) and 12.2(*b*) demonstrate, both works begin with a non-tonic opening, in which an anacrusis introduces a dominant seventh on D. Fanny's initial melodic gesture, a sigh-like descent by fifth, is transformed in Felix's lied to a descending fourth. Then, with some rhythmic adjustments,

[21] The autograph, dated 12 Jan. 1844, is in vol. 39 of the *Mendelssohn Nachlaß* in PL-Kj (p. 17).

Ex. 12.2. Comparison of (*a*) Hensel, Andante in G Major, Op. 2 No. 1,
bars 1–38, with (*b*) Mendelssohn, *Lied ohne Worte*, Op. 62 No. 1, bars 1–12,
and (*c*) Mendelssohn, *Lied ohne Worte*, Op. 62 No. 1, bars 34–41

(*a*)

Ex. 12.2. *continued*

Ex. 12.2. *continued*

Felix simply borrows the melodic shape of Fanny's first and second measures, a striking parallel that reveals just how close the sibling musical relationship was. At this point, the two melodies diverge. Whereas Felix is content in bar 2 to relax into the tonic G major, Fanny de-emphasizes the tonic, turning instead to the dominant of the submediant E minor in bar 4. The sigh-like leap is reinvoked, not as a descending fifth but as two expressive diminished fifths that are doubled at the tenth below in the bass. A rising chromatic melodic line, paralleled at the tenth in the bass, then leads to a cadential six-four chord, enabling Fanny to conclude her twelve-bar melodic period with a firm cadence on G major on the downbeat of bar 13.

Felix's opening melody falls into a ten-bar period, in which the sigh figure also plays a prominent role. Thus, the initial fourth is expanded into an expressive seventh ($g''-a'$) in bar 2 and then reinterpreted as a fifth ($e''-a'$ in bar 3—perhaps a subtle allusion to Fanny's fifth, now camouflaged through reharmonization), before resuming its original shape in bar 4, and changing, yet again, into an ascending fourth ($f\sharp'-b'$) as the music moves towards the mediant B minor in bar 8.

Returning to Fanny's Andante, we notice that the arrival on the tonic in bar 13 coincides with an inversion of the melody. Fanny takes advantage of the cadential fifth, D–G, to introduce a statement of the melody on the tonic in the bass. This surprise appearance is imitated a bar later in the soprano, thereby establishing a kind of canonic play between the two voices, and momentarily converting the solo *Lied ohne Worte* into a *Duett ohne Worte*. In bars 21–3 the expressive diminished fifths of bars 4–6 return, and Fanny repeats the material of bars 7–12, with one unexpected twist—a turn to the submediant E minor before the section concludes in the tonic, dovetailing with the middle section in G minor.

Now Felix rarely lost an opportunity to incorporate contrapuntal passages into his music, even in such unexpected contexts as that of the piano miniature.[22] And so it may come as a surprise that in his G major lied he did not follow Fanny's example, for we search in vain for a similar canonic passage. But there is, perhaps, one vestige of Fanny's contrapuntal strategem: in the closing measures of Felix's lied, we do find a brief exchange between the soprano and bass line, in which the falling fourth in the soprano ($d''-a'$) is answered imitatively by a falling fourth in the bass ($G–D$; Ex. 12.2(*c*)). Could this duet-like texture in some way have recalled for Felix Fanny's imitative passage? However the listener should decide this particular question, the weight of the stylistic evidence and the chronology of the sources of the two G major Andantes would seem to document convincingly a musical debt, not one of Fanny, but of Felix.

Our third example concerns Fanny's Allegro moderato in B minor, which was composed on 14 May 1846,[23] one year, to the day, before her death. It appeared posthumously in 1850 as the first of the *Vier Lieder für das Pianoforte*, Op. 8. A detailed analysis of this poignantly beautiful piece must await another occasion, but a cursory reading reveals the depth of Fanny's harmonic imagination, her sophisticated exploration of enharmonic relationships, and her ability to immerse the musical fabric into a kind of chromatic dye that brings us close to the realm of Chopin's late nocturnes. What is also impressive is her melodic inventiveness and richness. In brief, two seemingly different yet related melodic ideas are developed, *alternatim*, in this work. The first (bars 1–8; see Ex. 12.3(*a*)) begins with the fifth scale degree ($f\sharp''$), supported by an expressive upper auxiliary note (g''), and then continues with a stepwise descent to scale degree 2. The second idea (bars 23–6; Ex. 12.3(*b*)) begins on the tonic pitch, b', and then ascends to the fifth scale degree. Rhythmically, the two are related by the use of a trochaic pattern (quarter– eighth), further subdivided in the second idea to accommodate a dotted rhythmic figure on the third beat. There is a second conspicuous change as well: the arpeggiated, slurred triplet figure in the accompaniment to the first idea is reworked, and assigned a staccato articulation. Fanny probably calculated these changes to set off the second idea, and to draw our attention to it. Closer inspection reveals why, for Fanny's second idea is a thinly disguised

---

[22] See e.g. the 'Lied ohne Worte', Op. 30 No. 4, bars 64 ff., where we suddenly find ourselves in the midst of a two-part canon at the octave, with subtle exchanges of the *dux* and *comes* roles between the two parts.

[23] D-B, MA Ms. 49, pp. 34–7; see Klein, *Die Kompositionen Fanny Hensels*, 40.

Ex. 12.3. Hensel, Allegro moderato, Op. 8 No. 1: (*a*) bars 1–14;
(*b*) bars 20–34, compared with (*c*) Mendelssohn, *Die erste Walpurgisnacht*,
Op. 60 (Overture), bars 243–52

(*a*)

reworking of some material from her brother's *Die erste Walpurgisnacht*, which had been composed in 1831 and 1832, premièred in Berlin in 1833, and thoroughly revised in 1842 and 1843, before appearing as his Op. 60 in 1844. The overture to the cantata, which depicts 'Das schlechte Wetter' [the foul weather] and the transition to spring, contains in its recapitulation a passage remarkably similar to Fanny's second idea (Ex. 12.3(*c*)), a rising stepwise line with dotted rhythms on the third beat. There are some differences: Felix's passage ascends from the tonic to the sixth scale degree, whereas Fanny's spans a fifth; nevertheless, the melodic and rhythmic similarities are too conspicuous to pass as mere coincidence. As we know, *Die erste Walpurgisnacht* was a favourite work of Fanny's; indeed, on the day of her death, 14 May 1847, she was in the middle of rehearsing the cantata at the Mendelssohn residence in Berlin when she suffered her fatal stroke. What is impressive in the case of Fanny's Allegro moderato is not so much the allusion to *Die erste Walpurgisnacht*, but the way in which she reworks her brother's idea, thoroughly incorporating it into her piano miniature, and relating it to the material of the piece's opening. The effect here is not unlike what occurs in the eighth of Robert Schumann's *Noveletten*, Op. 21, where Clara Schumann's

EX. 12.3. *continued*

(b)

Notturno, Op. 6 No. 1, appears as a 'Stimme aus der Ferne' that then stimulates Robert's own pianistic reveries.[24]

To return to Fanny and Felix, we might adduce one other similar example in the third movement (titled 'Lied') of her Piano Trio in D Minor, Op. 11, and the tenor aria 'If with all your hearts ye truly seek me' from *Elijah* (No. 4 of Part I). As Exs. 12.4(*a*) and 12.4(*b*) illustrate, the melodic openings of these two works are suspiciously similar, though they subsequently diverge (indeed the similarity is limited to the first two bars of Fanny's lied and four bars of Felix's aria). As we know, *Elijah* was premièred in Birmingham in August

---

[24] See further, R. Larry Todd, 'On Quotation in Schumann's Music', in R. Larry Todd (ed.), *Schumann and his World* (Princeton: Princeton University Press, 1994), 80–112 at 101–2.

EX. 12.3. *continued*

(c)

1846. Almost immediately Felix began to revise the oratorio, and during a trip to Berlin in December 1846 played the work at the piano for Fanny.[25] This occasion evidently marked her first introduction to *Elijah*. According to her son, Sebastian, during the winter of 1846 and 1847 Fanny then composed her Piano Trio for her sister; and it was premièred on 11 April 1847, Rebecca's birthday, at the first of Fanny's 1847 Sunday musicales in Berlin.[26] From this sequence of events we might conclude that in the lied Fanny once again chose to base one of her compositions on some material of her brother; her lied, then, can be interpreted as a response to, almost an improvisation on, the head motif of the aria from *Elijah*, in much the same way that Felix's Op. 62 No. 1 impresses as a response to Fanny's earlier Andante.

What conclusions may we draw from our four examples? Of course, they document in compelling detail the proximity of the siblings' musical styles. Both Fanny and Felix were practitioners of a Mendelssohnian style, and though that style has been inextricably linked to Felix Mendelssohn, who

---

[25] See her letter of 2 Jan. 1847 to Felix and Cécile, quoted in Citron, *Letters*, 361–2.
[26] Hensel, *Family*, ii. 334.

Ex. 12.4. Comparison of (*a*) Hensel, Piano Trio in D Minor, Op. 11,
Lied, bars 1–10, with (*b*) Mendelssohn, *Elijah*, Op. 70, No. 4
('So ihr mich von ganzem Herzen suchet'), bars 1–15

stood at the forefront of German music during the 1830s and 1840s, the more
critical view would justifiably locate the style in the remarkably parallel developments of two sibling musical prodigies who interacted in a reflective way.
Secondly, though Felix's influence on Fanny's music was powerful, and often
dominant, there is evidence of a two-sided compositional exchange between
the two. Thirdly, Fanny was no mere epigone of Felix. An early reviewer of
her piano music stressed this point in the *Allgemeine musikalische Zeitung*
already in June 1847, and the argument bears repeating today: 'One would err
by counting Frau F. Hensel among the imitators of her brother. Whoever
knows that both siblings enjoyed the same musical education and were raised
in the same artistic environment, in short, experienced their entire musical

Ex. 12.4. *continued*

(*b*)

youth together, would find the familial similarity of the two composers natural, indeed, necessary.'[27] Fourthly, despite the obvious similarities, some stylistic differences in Fanny's music do come to the fore, so that arguably she was, at the end of her life, on the verge of finding her own compositional voice. To quote again from the 1847 review:

[27] 'Ueber die Claviercompositionen von *Fanny Hensel* geb. *Mendelssohn-Bartholdy*', in *AMZ* 49 (2 June 1847), col. 382: 'Man würde irren, wenn man Frau *F. Hensel* zu den Nachahmern ihres Bruders zählen wollte. Wer es weiss, dass beide Geschwister dieselbe musikalische Erziehung genossen, in derselben Kunstanschauung aufgewachsen sind, kurz, ihre ganze musikalische Jugend zusammen verlebt haben, wird eine Familienähnlichkeit der Compositionen beider natürlich, ja nothwendig finden.'

The difference [between the two] is nevertheless clear enough for the more percept-ive eye. *Mendelssohn's* manner of expression is highly precise, he would rather say too little than too much, he always builds [his compositions] on one idea and rounds out the whole in a way that is readily apprehended. *Frau Hensel's* lieder are more complicated; here fantasy is permitted a freer reign, the form is applied in broader strokes, and not infrequently a greater variety is achieved by means of a contrasting middle section.[28]

Some time around June 1837 Fanny sent Felix a copy of a piano prelude in B flat major that she had composed on his wedding day, 28 March. At the beginning of that year, Felix too had written a prelude in B flat major, which he published as his Op. 35 No. 6. Struck by the remarkable similarities between the two independently created preludes, he found an occasion to compare them in a letter of 24 June:

So it is here not merely the same figuration, motion, and structure that astonishes me, but in particular certain details that appear not at all to lie in the theme—that is, the notes—but are nevertheless there—that is, in the mood—and which recur so conspicuously in both of us. . . . Moreover, it is lovely that our thoughts remain so closely related to each other.[29]

Perhaps historians can now give Fanny's music the critical attention that it deserves, and finally appreciate fully one precious yet little-examined facet of the Mendelssohns' genius.

[28] 'Claviercompositionen', 382: 'Die Verschiedenheit ist trotzdem für den schärfer Blickenden klar genug. *Mendelssohn's* Ausdrucksweise ist höchst präcis, er sagt lieber zu wenig als zu viel, er baut stets auf einen Gedanken und rundet das Ganze auf leicht verständliche Weise. Die Lieder der Frau *F. Hensel* sind complicirter; der Phantasie ist hier freiere Bewegung gestattet, die Form breiter angelegt, nicht selten auch durch einen antithetischen Mittelsatz grössere Mannichfaltigkeit erzielt.'

[29] Letter of 24 June 1837 (D-B, MA Depositum Berlin 3, 21): 'So ist es hier nicht bloss die gleiche Figur[,] Bewegung und Anlage die mich erstaunt, sondern namentlich gewisse Kleinigkeiten, die gar nicht im Thema zu liegen scheinen, d. h. in den Noten u. doch die ich darin finde sind, d. h. in der Stimmung, u. die sich also auch bei uns beiden so auffallend wiederholen. . . . Nebenbei ist es hübsch, dass unsre Gedanken einander so nahe bleiben.' See also the trans-lation of the letter and commentary in Ward Jones, *Honeymoon*, 168–9. Fanny's Prelude is avail-able in Hensel, *Songs for the Pianoforte*, 3–10.

13

Virtuoso Texture in
Fanny Hensel's Piano Music

CAMILLA CAI

FANNY MENDELSSOHN HENSEL wrote strongly worded paragraphs opposing Franz Liszt and the virtuoso school of performing and composing, but her words seem at odds with the high level of virtuosity that appears in her own piano music.[1] This seeming contradiction will be shown to stem from her formulation of a useless virtuosity, as epitomized in Liszt's music, which stood in opposition to a pure virtuosity that served the music itself.

Hensel's early pieces show that she had a superior technique, and the many visitors to the Mendelssohn home praised her playing ability and specifically her virtuosity. Her early *Übungsstücke* (practice pieces), études, and a few untitled pieces form a group that deals almost exclusively with her advanced technical capabilities.[2] Pieces with the title *Übungsstück* were written between 1822 and 1824, when she was 16 to 18 years old.[3] Their exclusively technical nature suggests that they would not have been performed at family concerts. She may have composed them in order to have exercises specifically to address

I thank the Centre for Advanced Study at the Norwegian Academy of Science and Letters, Oslo, for providing the support and time to complete work on this article. I also thank the American Council of Learned Societies and the National Endowment for the Humanities Summer Stipends for grants to do the research, as well as Hans-Günter Klein and the Mendelssohn-Archiv of the Staatsbibliothek zu Berlin — Preußischer Kulturbesitz, for generously providing access to archival materials.

[1] See e.g. the various references in her letters to Mendelssohn, in Citron, *Letters*.

[2] The earliest pieces that survive, from 1820 and 1821, are in private collections and unavailable for study. See also Hans-Günter Klein's essay in this volume, Ch. 11.

[3] The first *Übungsstück* (D-B, MA Ms. 33, pp. 1–2) is dated 6 Nov. 1822 to 22 Mar. 1823, and the last (D-B, MA Ms. 35, pp. 2–3) is dated 7 Oct. 1824. One is in a private collection and not available for study. The thirteen remaining ones are in D-B, MA Ms. 33 (eight pieces), MA Ms. 34 (four pieces), and MA Ms. 35 (one piece).

Ex. 13.1. Hensel, *Übungsstück* 'Allegro moderato' (6 Nov. 1822)
(D-B, MA Ms. 33, p. 1): (*a*) bars 1–3; (*b*) bars 32–5

weaknesses in her own technique. Nothing indicates that she considered publishing them or that she used them for teaching. Not surprisingly, some of
these pieces resemble Muzio Clementi's (1752–1832) exercises. Her piano
teacher, Ludwig Berger (1777–1839), had studied with Clementi and Johan
Baptist Cramer (1771–1858), and it is likely that she benefited from seeing
model pieces by these composers,[4] as well as learning from Berger himself.[5]

Each of Hensel's *Übungsstücke* explores a single texture, a pianistic figuration used as a repeating figure. These include rapid parallel-sixth chords,
scales of octave passages for both hands, two-part writing for one hand with
a slow melody and a quickly moving inner voice, and arpeggios with wide
spacing, suggesting that she had large, flexible hands. The *Übungsstück* titled
'Larghetto' and dated 5 June 1823[6] is not rapid but still explores a single technical device: the legato use of the thumb and second finger in chromatic
passages.

Just before Hensel's seventeenth birthday she composed another *Übungsstück* (Ex. 13.1(*a*)) that displays a flexibility of pattern and a musicality that is

---

[4] Victoria Ressmeyer Sirota, 'The Life and Works of Fanny Mendelssohn Hensel' (DMA
diss., Boston University, 1981), 7. See also Peter Ward Jones's remarks on Felix's first composition in this volume, Ch. 4.

[5] Hensel was certainly acquainted with Berger's own études. Berger's other student,
Mendelssohn, wrote 'Songs without Words' that were strongly modelled on Berger's études.
See Richard Kershaw and Michael Musgrave, 'Berger, Ludwig', in *New Grove II*, iii. 336.

[6] D-B, MA Ms. 33, pp. 24–5.

lacking in Carl Czerny's (1791–1857) studies of similar type.[7] Hensel opens
with right-hand thirds alternating with first-inversion chords, but this is not
the piece's only challenge; it also includes substantial passages of scalar
chords and octaves. The move to the area of the lowered submediant, A flat
major, at bar 33 is typical of her inventive harmonic style and shows that even
within a piece written mainly for practice she inserted events of harmonic
interest (see Ex. 13.1(*b*)). These early pieces contain the seeds of her virtuosity, and their patterns reappear in her later compositions to give those pieces
a virtuosic flair.

In her youth Hensel met two important virtuosos, Frédéric Kalkbrenner
(1785–1849) and Ignaz Moscheles (1794–1870). At 18 she was much impressed
with Kalkbrenner: 'We hear him often and try to learn from him. He combines
the most varied merits in his playing, precision, clarity, expression, the greatest
execution, the most untiring strength and endurance. He is a capable musician
and possesses an astonishing overview.'[8] Two years later she wrote to Mendelssohn, 'You characterize Kalkbrenner very well, and thereby conjure up a
lively image of the amiable piano wizard, whom I wanted to hear thunder
across the keys one more time.'[9] Kalkbrenner himself returned the compli-
ment by saying that he admired 'her fine talent for composition and playing
the piano'.[10]

Kalkbrenner did, indeed, directly influence Hensel. On a piece headed only
'Andantino' from 1823, she noted in the margin, 'Kalkbrenner played it very
beautifully' ('hat Kalkbrenner sehr schön gespielt').[11] With such encouragement from the famous virtuoso she decided to compose a new piece right
away. Squeezed onto the bottom of the same manuscript page is a new
Übungsstück. She acknowledged in the margin that it was 'alla K[alkbrenner]'.
This very difficult D minor study[12] has a tempo marking 'Allegro molto

[7] D-B, MA Ms. 33, pp. 1–2; the piece bears the date 6 Nov. 1822. Hensel turned 17 a few days
later, on 14 Nov. Some of her pieces from the early 1820s resemble those in Carl Czerny's exercise collections. Because his published works date from later times it is unlikely that these served
as models.

[8] Letter of late Nov. 1823, translated in Sirota, 'The Life and Works of Fanny Mendelssohn
Hensel', 20; in Hensel, *Familie* (1924), i. 158: 'Wir hören ihn oft und suchen von ihm zu lernen.
Er vereinigt die verschiedenartigsten Vorzüge in seinem Spiel, Präzision, Klarheit, Ausdruck,
die größte Fertigkeit, die unermüdlichste Kraft und Ausdauer. Er ist ein tüchtiger Musiker und
besitzt einen erstaunlichen Überblick.'

[9] Letter of 25 Apr. 1825 in Citron, *Letters*, 12 (English), 377 (German): 'Kalkbr. karakterisirst
Du sehr gut, u. rufst mir den liebenswürdigen Claviernagel wieder recht lebhaft ins Gedächtniß
zurück. Ich wollte ihn einmal wieder über die Tasten blitzen hören.'

[10] Letter of 28 Dec. 1831 from Paris, in Mendelssohn, *Reisebriefe 1830–32*, 316, Kalkbrenner
as quoted by Mendelssohn: 'das schöne Talent für Composition und Spielen'.

[11] D-B, MA Ms. 34, pp. 25–6 (piece dated 24 Nov. 1823).

[12] D-B, MA Ms. 34, pp. 26–7 (piece dated 3 Dec. 1823).

agitato'. Continuous octaves in eighth notes move from one hand to the other every few bars while a simple melody or harmonic support continues in the other hand. It is a tour de force of loose-wrist technique, endurance, and accuracy. This study demonstrates directly the influence of Kalkbrenner on Hensel's composition.

Years later, she was to think differently of Kalkbrenner. His difficult Double Concerto led her to throw him out with one deft swipe: 'Herren Arnold and Taubert[13] hacked away at a new Double Concerto by Kalkbrenner whose compositional value was exceeded only by its rendition and whose rendition was exceeded only by its compositional value.'[14]

To return to the early years, Moscheles, a virtuoso of the previous generation, visited Berlin in the last year of his touring career, in November and December 1824. The Mendelssohns' mother, Lea, asked him to teach Felix and Fanny during this visit.[15] Though this teaching alone could not have shown Hensel her compositional direction, it surely encouraged her to compose. After this visit she wrote in quick succession three untitled pieces and a 'Capriccio'.[16] These show varied influence. The G minor piece is in two-part texture with invertible counterpoint as in a Bach invention, and the 'Capriccio' in F sharp major, the most technically difficult, is a light, lively piece in 4/8 with a sixteenth-note triplet texture that gives an 'elfin' sound as found in Mendelssohn's music. These pieces do not suggest any influence of Moscheles's virtuosity.

The contrast of playing styles between the older virtuoso Moscheles and the young, formidable Kalkbrenner highlights the rapidly changing role of the public musician in the early nineteenth century. Audiences were now interested in the personality of the performer, an outgrowth of German literary Romanticism with its emphasis on the individual artist, but also a product of the economic realities of competing in the performing world. With Nicolò Paganini (1782–1840) as the best example of the new and more insistent virtuosity sweeping Europe, composing and performing became unequal partners in music-making. Composing was pressed even more into the service

---

[13] The references are to Carl Arnold (1794–1873) and Carl Gottfried Wilhelm Taubert (1811–91).

[14] Letter of 28 Feb. 1834, quoted in Citron, *Letters*, 130, 458: 'hackten die Herren Arnold u. Taubert ein neues Doppelconcert von Kalkbrenner ab, das nur in der Composition durch den Vortrag u. im Vortrag durch die Composition übertroffen wurde'.

[15] Two letters from Lea Mendelssohn Bartholdy, quoted in Moscheles, *Briefe*, 1–2.

[16] The untitled piece in G minor (D-B, MA Ms. 35, pp. 10–11) bears no tempo marking, and is dated 5 Feb. 1825. The F sharp major piece titled 'Capriccio' (D-B, MA Ms. 35, pp. 36–8) is from 8 Feb. 1825, with the 'presto' tempo marking crossed out. The untitled F minor piece (D-B, MA Ms. 35, pp. 12–13) is from 25 Feb. 1825 and without a tempo marking. The untitled C minor piece (D-B, MA Ms. 35, pp. 13–14) is from 12 Mar. 1825 and with 'andante con moto' as a tempo marking.

of displaying technique. On the one side were those for whom technique and virtuosity became the means to personal fame based on brilliance, and composing was a vehicle for their performance—Liszt in his touring years, Henri Herz (1785–1849), Kalkbrenner, Johann Peter Pixis (1788–1874), and others. On the other side were Felix Mendelssohn and Robert Schumann, who 'for music's sake' wrote what they understood as art music. The increasing separation of performing styles was also furthered by the reception of the audience. In the growing nineteenth-century bourgeois audience, some wanted entertainment, others communication.

Hensel herself, at age 30 (1834), expressed this shift in values most cogently in a letter of 5 November 1834 when she mentioned 'what a drastic change the art of violin playing has undergone through Paganini' ('was die Kunst der Geige durch Paganini für einen Umschwung erlitten hat').[17] More detailed is a letter of 27 December of the same year:

There will be a point (primarily regarding performance interpretation) where the outer world, or the changeability of time, or the *fashion* (get around the word as you wish) will exert its influence. You remember as well as I that there was a time when we were thoroughly charmed by [Ludwig] Spohr's [1784–1859] music. Now we no longer feel that way. . . . [A]long comes Paganini who plays in a wild, fantastic, and powerful way. All young violinists strive to imitate him and tear the G string. Then, after several years, I hear Spohr again and his sweetness is instinctively more noticeable than before because my ears are now exposed to a totally different style. The public at large is chiefly susceptible to this influence, individuals more or less, but no one is immune to it.'[18]

Fanny Hensel's piano compositions and her performing situation lie at the intersection of these two important trends. Her twenty-six active years of composition, from the age of 16 to 42,[19] straddle the growth period for virtuosos. Her death in 1847 coincides closely with the time when virtuoso music came in for strong criticism by German critics and the German elite, widening the gulf between art music and popular music.

[17] Letter of 5 Nov. 1834, quoted in Citron, *Letters*, 155, 476 (translation modified).

[18] Letter of 27 Dec. 1834, quoted ibid. 165, 483: '[S]o wird es da einen Punkt geben (und der trifft glaub ich hauptsächlich die Execution) wo die Außenwelt, oder die Wandelbarkeit der Zeit, oder (schleiche Dich um das Wort herum wie Du willst) die *Mode* ihren Einfluß üben wird. Du erinnerst Du [*sic*], so gut wie ich, daß es eine Zeit gab, wo wir von Spohrs Musik unendlich entzückt waren. Jetzt sind wir es nicht mehr. . . . Nun kommt Paganini, u. spielt wild, phantastisch, stark, u. alle jungen Geiger bemühen sich es ihm nachzuthun, u. reißen die g Seite entsetzlich. Darauf höre ich Spohr nach einer Reihe von Jahren wieder, und unwillkührlich wird mir seine Süßigkeit mehr auffallen, als sonst, wenn sie sich auch an u. für sich nicht vermehrt hätte, weil ich die Ohren von einer entgegen gesetzten Richtung voll habe. Diesem Einfluß unterliegt natürlich zunächst das Publicum in Masse, die einzelnen Menschen mehr oder weniger, aber ganz frei glaube ich, kann sich Niemand davon sprechen.'

[19] She began composing at 16 or possibly even younger.

Although Hensel was active during this period, she did not participate
in the public manifestation of either direction. As a performer she was not in
the public eye and the bourgeois audience did not see or hear her play. She
performed at private gatherings, both large and small, for invited and elite
audiences. Among those who did hear her were exponents of both approaches
to music: Liszt, the virtuoso, and Clara Schumann (née Wieck, 1819–96),
who by the early 1840s was a force behind art music. Other well-known performers came to the Mendelssohn home as well. At these gatherings Hensel
performed, listened, and became part of a musical life she otherwise experienced only vicariously through Mendelssohn's letters and her own attendance
at public concerts. She travelled little until her trip to Italy in 1840, but by
inviting people from the international music scene to her home she became
fully aware of the latest styles.

Hensel's piano compositions were even less widely known than her
playing. Though a few of her piano works were published in the last year of
her life,[20] she did not live long enough to know the public reaction to them. In
any case, public response came only in the form of a few reviews and then
there was silence.[21]

But while the public did not know her, she had strong opinions about contemporary performers. She wrote of Paganini, 'about this truly miraculous,
unbelievable talent, about this person who has the look of an insane murderer
and the movements of a monkey. A supernatural, wild genius. He is extremely
exciting and piquant.'[22] 'Paganini . . . gave a splendid rendition of a Sonata.'[23]
'He played a so-called *Canto appassionato* in [E]-flat minor. . . . It was very
beautiful and seemed as though he was plumbing the depths of his soul and yet
simultaneously ripping the heart out of the poor violin. The *Hexen* Variations,[24]
in which he imitates the chatter of hoarse old women, are disgusting. He
finished in a very ordinary way, which was a shame.'[25]

---

[20] The piano works of Opp. 2, 4, 5, and 6 were published during her lifetime, but Op. 8 was
published by her family posthumously.

[21] See R. Larry Todd's essay in this volume, Ch. 12.

[22] From Hensel's diary, 9 Mar. 1829, quoted in Citron, *Letters*, 31 n. 8: 'über dieses höchst
wunderbare, unbegreifliche Talent, über diesen Menschen, der das Ansehn eines wahnsinnigen
Mörders, u. die Bewegungen eines Affen hat. Ein übernatürliches, wildes Genie. Er ist höchst
aufregend u. pikant.'

[23] Diary entry of 5 May 1829, quoted ibid. 34 n. 6: 'Paganini, der eine Sonata . . . göttlich spielte'.

[24] i.e. 'Witches' Variations', composed in 1813 and better known as *Le Streghe*.

[25] Undated letter, probably 6 May 1829, quoted in Citron, *Letters*, 36, 393: 'Er spielte einen
sogenannten Canto appassionato es moll . . . es war sehr schön, u. wirklich als wolle er sich seine
ganze Seele ausspielen, u. zugleich der armen Violinen das Herz ausreißen. Die Hexen-
variationen sind eklich, da macht der das Gequäck heiserer alter Weiber nach. Er schloß sehr
unbrillant, das war schade.'

She does not speak ill of his playing, enjoying the virtuosity of it, but she described his variations as 'disgusting', showing that her taste for the purely virtuosic in composition had limits. She expressed the same sentiment towards virtuoso violinist Charles Philippe Lafont (1781–1839): 'his compositions, variations with Herz and Kalkbrenner, etc., are such that not even the most extreme adherence to fashion could excuse them'.[26]

In her comments on these violinists Hensel balanced the marvellous virtuoso playing that she respected and enjoyed with the inferior variation form of composition made for the sake of show. In other words, she did not oppose the new virtuoso movement *in toto*, but rather only the compositions that became too showy or banal for her taste.

When she turned to virtuoso pianists her most disliked target was Liszt. His playing did not impress her, and when he played his own arrangements of the Beethoven symphonies she wrote to her brother, '[f]or all their technical apparatus, I don't doubt for one moment that you could play them ten times more beautifully'.[27] Liszt's own compositions had even less to recommend themselves: 'Liszt invented the art of happily confusing and disfiguring musical orthography . . . to such an extent that he's succeeded in making his compositions, which were already nonsensical and formless, even more nonsensical and formless with the help of his notation.'[28]

In 1837 the playing and compositions of the virtuoso Georg Martin Adolph von Henselt (1814–89) received similar treatment. 'Henselt played some of his own variations at the end of the concert. In spite of their difficulties, there was so little that was brilliant, yet so much that was ugly, that I became quite disgusted, as I am with this type of concert in general.'[29] Two years later her words were even stronger: 'Henselt invented the art of making instrumental music vulgar, and he could take out a patent on it.'[30]

---

[26] Letter of 27 Dec. 1834, ibid. 166, 483: 'seine Compositionen, Variat. mit Herz und Kalkbrenner u. so w. sind doch wol von der Art, daß nicht einmal die äußerste Mode sie entschuldigen kann'.

[27] Letter of 11 May 1840, ibid. 291, 570: 'Bei allem dem Apparat zweifle ich keinen Augenblick, daß Du sie zehnmal schöner spielst.'

[28] Letter of 28 Apr. 1839, ibid. 277, 559: 'Liszt hat die Kunst erfunden, die musikalische Ortographie . . . so glücklich zu verwirren u. zu entstellen, daß es ihm gelungen ist, seine ohnehin schon sinn- u. zusammenhanglosen Compositionen mit Hülfe der Schreibart noch sinn- u. zusammenhangloser zu machen.'

[29] Letter of 2 June 1837, ibid. 235, 530 (translation lightly modified): 'Die Variation. eigener Composit. die Henselt am Schluß spielte fand ich bei aller Schwierigkeit so wenig brillant, u. so häßlich, daß sie mich sehr degoutirten, wie überhaupt dies ganze Concertwesen.' Hensel identifies Henselt as a virtuoso in this letter.

[30] Letter of 28 Apr. 1839, ibid. 277, 558: 'Henselt hat die Kunst erfunden, die Instrumentalmusik unanständig zu machen, er könnte ein Patent drauf nehmen.'

Lest we think her hard on virtuoso pianists and violinists, she had kind words too. The playing of Clara Schumann, both a virtuoso and a player of artistic merit, led her to confide to her diary that Clara's playing 'enchanted' her.[31]

Her brother thought highly of virtuoso Sigismond Thalberg (1812–71) and wrote Hensel a long paragraph that concluded: 'one cannot find anything more exquisite in virtuoso music'.[32] But Hensel, not yet having heard Thalberg, was wary: '[I] am convinced that Thalberg plays magnificently, but I just cannot praise this style of playing.'[33] Still, she was willing to learn: 'I'll acquire the things ahead of time that he will play in order to get the most out of them'.[34] Personally she came to dislike him, finding him 'so virtuoso-like, so posh and self-satisfied' ('so virtuosich, so vornehm u. mit sich selbst zufrieden')[35] that she wrote neither about his compositions nor his playing after that.

Hensel was fully aware that she wrote pieces in the virtuoso style herself. She even called one of her works 'one in C minor, *à la* Thalberg'.[36] This piece can be identified with some certainty as No. 6 from her set of pieces numbered and written in 1836–7 (see Ex. 13.2(*a*)). No. 6 was copied in its final form by 5 October 1837. It is an important piece because, in identifying it as '*à la* Thalberg', even if she meant it humorously or self-deprecatingly, she aligns herself with the virtuoso style and admits its influence on her. However, she had not yet heard Thalberg perform; his first big success had been in Paris only the year before (1836), so only his name and reputation were familiar to her.[37] The designation '*à la* Thalberg' was probably a literary device for describing the piece, not a designation that Hensel wanted to use as a title or even to suggest a specific model.[38]

[31] From her diary, Feb. 1843, Engl. trans. ibid. 316 n. 2; Hensel, *Familie*, ii. 228: 'entzückend schön'.

[32] Letter of 29 Dec. 1838; Eng. trans. Citron, *Letters*, 267 n. 3; Hensel, *Familie*, ii. 62: 'von Virtuosenmusik kann man nichts Exquisiteres finden'.

[33] Letter of 6 Jan. 1839, in Citron, *Letters*, 264, 550: 'ich bin überzeugt, daß Thalberg wunderschön spielt, aber dies Wesen kann ich doch nicht loben'.

[34] Letter of 6 Jan. 1839, ibid. 264, 549–50: 'ich werde, um so viel Nutzen als möglich davon zu haben, mir die Sachen die er spielt, vorher geben lassen, um sie zu kennen'.

[35] Letter of 6–7 Jan. 1839, ibid. 266, 551.

[36] Letter of 16 Nov. 1836, ibid. 217, 519. For more information on the form of this piece, see Camilla Cai, 'Fanny Hensel's "Songs for Pianoforte" of 1836–37: Stylistic Interaction with Felix Mendelssohn', *Journal of Musicological Research*, 14 (1994), 55–76. For further information on dating and identifying this piece, see the Preface to Fanny Hensel, *Songs for Pianoforte*, ed. Camilla Cai (Madison, Wis.: A-R Editions, 1994), pp. viii, x.

[37] Hensel first heard Thalberg in 1839. See her letter of 16 Dec. 1836 in Hensel, *Familie*, ii. 43, in which she says that she has 'never heard Thalberg', and Citron, *Letters*, 264, 266, 549–51.

[38] Hensel uses such a literary device for referring to Mendelssohn's piano pieces when in a letter to Karl Klingemann she calls them 'songs without words', apparently before Mendelssohn himself used the term. See Hensel, *Familie*, i. 212.

Ex. 13.2. Comparison of (*a*) Hensel, No. 6 ('Allegro con brio') from a set of ten pieces (finished 5 Oct. 1837) (D-B, MA Ms. 44, p. 41) with (*b*) theme from Sigismond Thalberg, *Impromptu en forme d'étude*, Op. 36 (Paris: M. Schlesinger, 1839), p. 2, and (*c*) p. 4

However, Thalberg's *Impromptu en forme d'étude*, Op. 36, printed in 1839,[39] does suggest itself for comparison. Its theme (Ex. 13.2(*b*)) is not relevant to Hensel, but its first variation (Ex. 13.2(*c*)) has a pattern somewhat similar to Hensel's No. 6: a quick turn built on the starting note, followed by staccato eighth notes. This pattern, repeated bar after bar, does not appear regularly in the piano literature and therefore stands out as unusual in both pieces. In Hensel's piece the staccato eighth notes follow the harmony; in Thalberg's they follow the melody. Hensel uses this pattern as the arpeggiation figure for almost every harmony. Thalberg uses his pattern constantly as the variation figuration of his simple theme. In both cases they use the material as ornamentation. There are some important differences: Hensel's piece is in an ABA form with a developmental mid-section, while Thalberg's is a theme with variations. Their metres are different; Hensel has a separate melody, Thalberg an 'oom-pah-pah' bass; Hensel's eighth notes continue into the downbeat, while Thalberg's turn begins on the downbeat—but for both the figuration is the dominant textural element.

Hensel harshly criticized variation form in its newer virtuoso guise. Of virtuoso Theodor von Döhler (1814–56) she said, 'If this nice young virtuoso would only adopt a more solid taste, he might become something extraordinary. I cannot understand how it is possible with all the constant revolutions in music for variations to hold their own as they do with both composers and pianists.'[40] Nevertheless, the variation genre and its figuration patterns have echoes in Hensel's music. No. 6, whose left-hand pattern resembles the variation figuration of Thalberg's melody, is no more than one example.[41]

---

[39] Thalberg's own edition (Paris: Maurice Schlesinger, 1839; repr., ed. Jeffrey Kallberg (New York: Garland, 1993), 225–33) includes the theme and variations. The version in François-Joseph Fétis and Ignaz Moscheles, *Méthode des méthodes de piano* (Paris: Maurice Schlesinger, 1840; repr. Geneva: Minkoff, 1973), includes only the variations.

[40] 'Wenn diesem sehr jungen und angenehmen Virtuosen nur ein soliderer Geschmack beizubringen wäre, er müßte außerordentlich werden. Aber wie bei aller Umwälzung der Musik immer Variationen und wieder Variationen gemacht und gespielt werden können, das ist mir ein Rätsel.' In Hensel, *Familie*, ii. 43. Eng. trans. lightly modified from Hensel, *Family*, ii. 32.

[41] Possibly there is an actual relationship between Thalberg's *Impromptu* in theme-and-variation form and Hensel's No. 6. The title page of Thalberg's piece, published in 1839, indicates that it was composed expressly for the *Méthode des méthodes* (1840). The Method was in the planning stages already in 1829, and in the early 1830s Thalberg became a Moscheles student: the two facts suggest that Thalberg's piece could have been conceived for the Method as early as the early 1830s. Since Mendelssohn visited Moscheles regularly during the early 1830s, he could well have heard such a new piece by Thalberg (still in manuscript). Through him Thalberg's *Impromptu* could have found its way to the Mendelssohn home in Berlin and inspired Hensel's No. 6 of 1837.

Another outside influence also suggests itself for Hensel's No. 6. Hensel had a fascination with études at this time.[42] She writes on 2 June 1837, 'I've acquired the Chopin Études, and I'm practicing a few of them diligently.'[43] Playing these études—we do not know which ones—during the very four months that led up to the final version of her No. 6 might well have influenced her thinking about virtuoso elements. Her No. 6 bears the mark of an étude in the same sense that Chopin used the term. It even has a passing resemblance to Chopin's Op. 10 No. 12 ('Revolutionary'), in that it uses a fairly slow-moving octave melody in the right hand with a left-hand figuration that is prominent and difficult. In both pieces this figuration is ultimately subservient to the melody.

Études or studies continued to interest her. She asked for and received Moscheles's *Études* from Mendelssohn in the spring of 1838.[44] Soon after this, on 19 July 1838, she finished a piece titled 'Étude', the first she had written since 1826.[45] This second étude is brilliant and difficult, directly within the virtuoso tradition. Flying thirty-second-note arpeggios in the right hand form a texture supported by almost staccato octaves in the left hand, a sixteenth-note, sixteenth-rest pattern. At a tempo of 'allegro con brio', with sections in both fortissimo and pianissimo, the piece is pure technique.

Hensel had looked not only into Thalberg's, Chopin's, and Moscheles's virtuoso works. As early as 1835 she wrote to Mendelssohn of practising Cramer's *Études* and of wanting to learn them all by Christmas to play for him. She had to admit that their father violently disliked the pieces, and 'he said that he would kill me before Christmas if I played all of them'.[46]

Her late compositions continue to use virtuoso patterns derived from variation and technical exercises. Her piano cycle *Das Jahr*, dating from 1841, provides ample opportunity for virtuoso performers; in fact, unless the performer is highly skilled the cycle can lapse into the very thing Hensel disliked: virtuosity devoid of music. In this set of pieces she shows the results of years

---

[42] 1837 and 1838.

[43] Letter of 2 June 1837, in Citron, *Letters*, 235, 530: 'habe ich . . . mir Chopins Etüden angeschafft, von denen ich einige fleißig übe'.

[44] English trans. from Hensel, *Family*, ii. 38: 'hast du die neuen Moscheleschen Etüden und willst sie mir durch Paul schicken und sie Dir dann selbst wieder abholen', in Hensel, *Familie*, ii. 51. Most likely Moscheles's *Charakteristische Studien*, Op. 95 (Leipzig: Kistner, 1836).

[45] This new piece in G minor is D-B, MA Ms. 44, pp. 89–98.

[46] Letter of 18 Nov. 1835, in Citron, *Letters*, 191, 503: 'er mache mich vor Weihnachten todt, wenn ich sie Alle spielte, sagte er.' This light-hearted comment preceded by hours their father's unexpected death. Abraham Mendelssohn became suddenly and desperately ill that night and died in the morning. See Hensel, *Family*, i. 336–7.

of training in virtuoso playing. A given technical feature or figuration is used consistently through a fairly long section, and its texture will be among the most noticeable features of that section.

Since texture was a major element of composition for Hensel,[47] her handling of texture is often bound up with her use of virtuoso figuration. In 'March' from *Das Jahr* (17 June 1841), the opening melody is repeated at bar 15 with a pure variation figuration in the alto line (see Ex. 13.3). Adding this difficult sixteenth-note inner voice in the right- and left-hand parts looks back to a 'Larghetto' *Übungsstück*, which trained legato use of the thumb and the second finger (see above).[48]

Also in 'March', one bar of pure texture (b. 37) joins the end of one theme (a chorale) to its variation (beginning in b. 38). This 'vamp' (for lack of a better term) becomes a supporting texture of arpeggiated chords for the repeat of the chorale in the upper voice. This full repeat of the chorale makes 'March' a special case. It suggests not only that Hensel was influenced by contemporary virtuoso variation techniques, but also by her education in Baroque techniques of chorale variation.[49]

A less virtuoso example but one portraying the same textural phenomenon is found in 'June' (29 Oct. 1841). After a hauntingly lyrical and peculiarly stable introduction (ending in b. 11), the transition (bb. 12–15) is four bars of textural vamping (see Ex. 13.4(a)). These bars, 'imitating the guitar', alert the listener to the new texture that supports the entire next section. The listener is as if bathed in that texture in advance in order to set the coming mood. The inner-voice opening theme (from bb. 15–16 on) appears again in an inner voice (bb. 87–8 on) with the variation made by a virtuoso figuration of triplets added above (see Ex. 13.4(b)).

In 'February' (28 Aug. 1841) Hensel's prominent use of texture as related to virtuoso technique is demonstrated in the virtuoso patterns that create the musical variation. Her opening texture is, as usual, consistent throughout the first section (Ex. 13.5(a)), but on its reappearance as A′ in bar 134 (Ex. 13.5(b)) it becomes a free virtuoso variation because of its textural handling of syncopation and octaves.

---

[47] See Camilla Cai, 'Texture and Gender: New Prisms for Understanding Hensel's and Mendelssohn's Piano Pieces', in David Witten (ed.), *Nineteenth-Century Piano Music: Essays in Performance and Analysis* (New York: Garland, 1997), 53–93.

[48] Written 5 June 1823, in D-B, MA Ms. 33, pp. 24–5.

[49] I thank Friedhelm Krummacher for this observation. Hensel's knowledge of J. S. Bach's music was extensive, and she composed music in Baroque forms. She had learnt Baroque compositional styles—chorale variation, fugues, preludes, and others—through her composition teacher, Carl Friedrich Zelter.

Ex. 13.3. Hensel, *Das Jahr*, 'March': (*a*) bars 1–7; (*b*) bars 15–18

None of the pieces shown above is *in* variation form *per se*. Yet Hensel unabashedly adopts variation-on-a-theme principles by using textural figurations that are hallmarks of the virtuoso school, that is, excluding Liszt and others that she found offensive. Victoria Sirota's statement that '[v]irtuosity without a solid musical foundation was extremely distasteful to Fanny Hensel'[50] should not be read to mean that Hensel disdained the virtuoso style. Rather, it should be expanded to state more precisely that Hensel had a sophisticated understanding of contemporary virtuoso playing and composing, and

---

[50] Sirota, 'The Life and Works of Fanny Mendelssohn Hensel', 145.

Ex. 13.4. Hensel, *Das Jahr*, 'June': (*a*) bars 9–19; (*b*) bars 88–91

Ex. 13.5. Hensel, *Das Jahr*, 'February': (*a*) bars 1–8; (*b*) bars 132–8

it is this full understanding of the music around her that made it possible
for her to include many virtuoso elements from variation form in her own
music without seeming to contradict or violate her basic intellectual dislike of
virtuosity for its own sake.

14

Felix Mendelssohn and Fanny Hensel: The Search for Perfection in Opposing Private and Public Worlds

FRANÇOISE TILLARD

WRITERS have discussed Fanny and Felix as two aspects of the same entity —at first, as complementary twin talents, and then opposed. F in Dur and F in Moll (F major and F minor), wrote Cécile Lowenthal-Hensel,[1] great-granddaughter of Fanny: Felix major, Fanny minor. 'Major' here denotes the dominant mode and 'minor' the dependent one (which might be irrelevant in music, as we know). This opposition and its use are the subject of this chapter. Felix is handsome, Fanny ugly; Felix travelled, Fanny stayed at home; Felix belonged to the light of the public world, and Fanny remained in the shadow of her damp home. They represent the two poles of perfection, one in the masculine world, the other in the feminine world. This difference between treatment of the man and the woman has been so blatant, right from the beginning, that one begins to question it. The way the family talked about it—that is, the father Abraham, Fanny's son Sebastian, and also Felix himself—seems to imply that a law of nature had been beautifully translated into society.

The first question is: why did they feel they had to prove something obvious, and what did they have to prove? Did they have something to defend? (What is meant here by 'they' is Sebastian Hensel, his family, and his readers: in short, bourgeois society.)

Felix and Fanny Mendelssohn lived at a moment in history where the power of a private world was transmitted to the public world. Their mother was brought up in the eighteenth-century tradition of the salon, that powerful

---

[1] Cécile Lowenthal-Hensel, 'F in Dur und F in Moll', in Felix Henseleit (ed.), *Berlin in Dur und Moll* (Berlin: Axel Springer, 1970).

salon in which revolutions could be brewed. She had as models her aunt Fanny von Arnstein in her brilliant Viennese salon; her mother, Babette Salomon; her aunt, Sarah Levy; and of course Rahel Varnhagen and Henriette Herz. One can imagine that she saw herself as offering her daughter (or daughters) this tradition as heritage, and as bringing her (or them) up to play this very important social and intellectual role. But the nineteenth-century German salon had little to do with the Parisian salons of the eighteenth century, or even those of the nineteenth century. After the Congress of Carlsbad in 1819, the censorship imposed by Metternich had a considerable effect on the freedom of interesting conversation. Because talk about politics was no longer *au courant*, the intellectual vitality of a salon necessarily declined. Not until the 1840s was there a revival of politics in conversation.

Since 1820, the Biedermeier salon in Berlin had been essentially a musical salon, as a matter of both taste and necessity. These were no longer con-versational salons, since speech was no longer entirely free and women did not discuss politics. Bucolic poetry replaced conversation as a form of entertain-ment, and music opportunely lent meaning to words that would otherwise have seemed rather vapid. The whole of Berlin society tended to accord an almost religious importance to cultural models; it waxed enthusiastic over music, theatre, and the visual arts, which were capable of uniting opposing tendencies in a world full of tension. The abstract nature of music—an art the government wanted to make accessible to every social class—appealed to the German people, who saw themselves reflected in it.[2]

Accordingly, much music-making took place in Berlin salons between 1815 and 1848 in the homes of Elisabeth von Staegemann, Princess Luise Radziwill, Amalia Beer, and Lea Mendelssohn Bartholdy, among others. The latter two salons were the most brilliant.[3] Mother of both composer Giacomo Meyerbeer and poet Michael Beer, Amalia Beer compelled recognition by virtue of her personality and the tartness of her remarks; she was known as the Queen Mother. In the Staegemann and Radziwill salons the type of entertainment varied, alternating between music, poetry, and parlour games, whereas the Beer salon was almost exclusively musical—which did not prevent theatrical people and political or scientific celebrities from attending. Lea Mendelssohn Bartholdy, however, did not occupy a throne in her salon, which was distin-guished from the Beer salon by its familial character: it was hosted by an entire

---

[2] Through Zelter's work, particularly. See Martin Geck, *Die Wiederentdeckung der Matthäuspassion im 19. Jahrhunderts, die zeitgenössischen Dokumente und ihre ideengeschichtliche Deutung* (Regensburg: Gustav Bosse, 1967).

[3] Petra Wilhelmy, *Der Berliner Salon im 19. Jahrhundert, 1780–1914* (Berlin: Gruyter, 1989), 144–5.

family, and especially by the mother and the two daughters. Thus Fanny had only to pick up and continue with work already begun. From an eighteenth-century point of view, which was probably Lea's own, a woman with exceptional musical talent could not but be the winner in this context: she had a very clear and important role to play—even clearer than a man's role. Lea might have thought at this point that the destiny of Fanny was clear and secure. She may not have been aware that in Berlin the conditions for listening to music were changing with each passing year.

At the time when Abraham Mendelssohn had launched the famous *Sonntagsmusik*, instrumental concert life in Berlin was very impoverished. There were two orchestras (the Berlin Opera orchestra and the Royal Chapel orchestra) but the actual organization of concerts remains hazy and was left to private initiative.[4] For the Beers and Mendelssohns, inviting musicians into their salon was more than a rich man's indulgence; it was a musical and sociological necessity. Musicians needed private performances in order to exist, and Berliners depended on them for instrumental music.

But the profound changes in society that resulted from the advent of the industrial revolution in Germany had unfortunate repercussions for Fanny as composer and performer. As audiences increasingly became accustomed to paying for their concert tickets and going out to concert halls, private musical salons rapidly became a thing of the past. This wholly public musical world left little room for the private musical world that was the centre of Fanny's activities (although good music was of course still made in private venues). And the public world was accessible only to men. Felix thus was granted a dominant role in the public musical world, and Fanny was left without a venue in which to display her creative work.

Fanny felt strongly that instrumental music demanded more than just a few private performances. It is obvious that the bigger the orchestra, the larger the salon must be, until it became a concert hall. Fanny was quite aware of these problems, and of the role she might have played, had she been a man. As early as 1825 she wrote up a plan for organizing concerts:

Berlin, 17 March 1825
Proposal to establish an amateur's club for instrumental music.
    The present state of instrumental music in Berlin requires the efforts of capable, expert men; this declining art needs a strong hand to elevate it, otherwise it will

---

[4] Christoph Helmut Mahling, 'Zum Musikbetrieb Berlins und seinen Institutionen in der ersten Hälfte des 19. Jahrhunderts', in Carl Dahlhaus (ed.), *Studien zur Musikgeschichte Berlins im frühen 19. Jahrhundert* (Studien zur Musikgeschichte des 19. Jahrhunderts, 56; Regensburg: Gustav Bosse, 1980), 27–287.

disappear in the bad taste of the time, the egotism of the organizers, and pandering to the public.

The sole classical instrumental institution in Berlin, the Möser quartets,[5] benefit from a faithful audience even though the organizer is little concerned with captivating listeners with novel and unusual features, and even though the performances often lack the perfection that this genre, which can count only upon its own intrinsic value and dispenses with outside resources, demands.

Berlin possesses many skilful amateurs who are lovers of this art; the lack of a rallying point for so many scattered talents is tangible. When circumstances permit, people do what they can by inviting quartets or other smaller or larger ensembles to perform in their homes. There are innumerable such private gatherings here, but, being isolated events, they have no effect and propagate a dilettantism more harmful than favourable to art. If all these individual rays, feeble in themselves, could unite in a single bright beam, they could then diffuse their light into the world, just as the Singakademie concept has spread out from its birthplace in Berlin and been transplanted throughout Germany, bearing beneficial fruit.

Symphonies constitute the largest form in this vast domain of instrumental music. Our association must therefore set its sights especially on that genre. Fasch's Singakademie could serve as a model for our institute, as far as the overall organization is concerned, but its aims must and will be essentially different. The Singakademie, which is interested only in sacred music and whose members are for the most part women and young girls, must for that reason distance itself as much as possible from all publicity: serious music is indeed appropriate in churches and not in concert halls, and women of private positions shy away from appearing in public.

Our association is something quite different. Here we find only men who have gathered for the same purpose, namely, to perform great instrumental compositions in a worthy manner. Here everything lends itself to publicity. Vibrant and exciting music demands an enthusiastic audience and loud applause; a large orchestra requires a full hall, lest it drown in its own sounds. An audience gathered for a festivity is as suited to secular symphonies that are joyful, lively, and noisy as a small, quiet circle of devout persons is for a religious chorale or a strict fugue.[6]

---

[5] Carl Möser (1774–1851) was artistic director (as we should now say) of the Royal Chapel and professor of the instrumental classes at the Royal Opera, the first level of the Berlin Conservatory. He arranged concerts with the opera orchestra and played chamber music. He had played in a quartet with Friedrich Wilhelm II, who was a cellist. See Rudolf Elvers, 'Über das Berlinische Zwitterwesen', in Rudolf Elvers and Hans-Günter Klein (eds.), *Die Mendelssohns in Berlin: Eine Familie und ihre Stadt* (Berlin: Staatsbibliothek Preußischer Kulturbesitz, 1983), 31–4.

[6] 'Berlin, den 17. März 1825.

Vorschlag zur Errichtung eines Dilettantenvereins für Instrumentalmusik.

Der gegenwärtige Zustand der Instrumentalmusik in Berlin erheischt die Bestrebungen tüchtiger und sachkundiger Männer, die sinkende Kunst muss mit starker Hand gehoben

The change from private to public performances is pointed out in Fanny's own voice. Music, she feels, must leave the realm of the salon, the realm of women, as much for musical as for social reasons. The development of instrumental music is the domain of men. The wonder is that Fanny still managed to transform her private salon into a semi-public concert hall—something quite unique in the musical world of her day. Her talent for organizing concerts and for conducting and coaching musicians, amateur as well as professional, gave her concerts a quality quite removed from the dilettantism she laments as being more harmful than favourable to art.

The opposition between man and woman had thus become decisive. Fanny and Felix are a case in point. It is remarkable to observe Sebastian Hensel's enormous pride at his mother's having given up any hope of a career. He describes her in 1825 as 'endowed at birth with talent equal [to Felix], yet wishing for nothing other than to stay modestly within the limits Nature has assigned

werden, sonst geht sie ueber in der Geschmacklosigkeit der Zeit, in dem Egoismus der Anführer, in der Verwöhnung des Publicums.

Das einzige klassische Instrumentalinstitut Berlins, die Möserschen Quartette, erfreuen sich einer dauernden Theilnahme, obschon der Unternehmer wenig bemüht ist, seine Hörer durch den Reiz der Neuheit und Abwechselung zu fesseln, und obschon man öfters die Vollendung vermisst, welche diese, nur auf innerm Werth beruhende, und aller äussern Mittel entbehrende Gattung erfordert.

Berlin besitzt viel geschickte und kunstliebende Dilettanten, der Mangel eines Vereinigungspunktes für zo viel zestreutes Talent ist fühlbar, ein jeder Einzelne sucht ihm dadurch abzuhelfen, dass er, wenn es seine Umstände erlauben, ein Quartett, oder eine mehr und minderstimmige Musik bei sich aufführen lässt. Dergleichen Privatversammlungen giebt es Unzählige hier, aber vereinzelt, wirken sie nichts, und verbreiten nur einen der Kunst mehr schädlichen als vortheilhaften Dilettantismus. Wann aber alle diese, an und für sich schwache Strahlen in einen Glanzpunkt vereinigt würden, dann könnten sie ihr Licht weit in die Welt verbreiten, wie dann die Singakademie sich von ihrer Vaterstadt Berlin aus mit segensreichen Früchten über ganz Deutschland verpflanzt hat.

Symphonien sind die grösste Form für diesen grossen Gehalt der Instrumentalmusik. Auf diese müsste unser Verein also sein besonderes Augenmerk richten. Faschs Singacademie könnte, was die äussern Form betrifft, unserm Institute zum Vorbild dienen, ihre Tendenz muss und wird wesentlich verschieden seyn. Die Singacademie, welche sich nur mit heiliger Musik beschäftigt, deren Mitglieder zum grössern Theil aus Frauen u. Mädchen bestehen, muss sich schon aus dem Grunde von aller Oeffentlichkeit möglichst fern halten, weil ernste Musik in die Kirche und nicht in den Konzertsaal passt, und weil Frauen aus dem Privatstande jedes Auftreten vor einem Publicum scheuen.

Ein anders ist es mit unserm Verein. Hier sehn wir lauter Männer, welche zu einem Zwecke versammelt sind, nähmlich grosse Instrumentalkompositionen auf eine würdige Weise darzustellen. Hier neigt Alles zu Oeffentlichkeit. Die rauschende, erregende Musik verlangt ein erregtes Publicum u. lauten Beifall, ein starkbesetztes Orchester erfordert einen gefüllten Saal, sonst übertäubt es sich selbst durch sein Geräusch, ein festlich versammeltes Publicum stimmt eben so wohl zu den weltlich frohen, lebhaft rauschenden Symphonien, als ein kleiner, andächtig stiller Kreis dem religiösen Choral, der strengen Fuge ansteht.' Fanny Hensel, *Tagebuch*, *1829–1834*, Mendelssohn Archives, Berlin, Fot. 8835.

to women.'[7] He mentions a letter from Felix of 1837 relating that Fanny is far too self-respecting a woman to wish to publish her compositions.[8] Hensel's reference to nature in an ethical case is very suspect.

Abraham and Lea Mendelssohn Bartholdy were adamant in raising all their children to strive for the highest standards of perfection. One might well say that they pushed their children to achieve perfection, although the whole idea of achieving perfection directly contradicts the idea of using nature as a guide. Still, I cannot help but wonder whether the conversion of the Mendelssohns from Judaism to Protestantism played a role in their striving for perfection. If so, then it would have been incumbent on Fanny and Felix, as the eldest and most gifted of the four siblings, to be more than perfect in order to prove that their parents did not convert out of worldly interests. That this was an important issue is documented in a letter of 1799 in which Lea relates how much she feared the bad opinion Gentile society held about converted Jews: 'If someone of spotless character were to convert, faithful to his intentions and diplomatic in behaviour (for it is unfortunately behaviour that influences most opinions)—someone who would offer an example worthy of respect—then he would dispel much of this all-too-justified assumption.' She continues: 'It would be a blessing if we could dispense with all this hypocrisy.'[9] In other words, the convert is not allowed to go astray in any way. Felix certainly became this person of spotless character and Fanny was also a perfect housewife. Perhaps Fanny did not enter the public world because she knew that as a converted Jew she would have to be even more perfect than a Clara Schumann or a Josephine Lang.

The question of the influence of conversion is interesting to explore but it probably is a dead end, for it confines Fanny and Felix in an overly deterministic way. The Mendelssohns certainly had to submit to the pressure of growing anti-Semitism, and Felix certainly showed in his life that he was as generous and open-minded as any artist can be. That he became a musician rather than a banker demonstrates that the family did not grant worldly concerns precedence over idealistic ones. In addition to being an advocate for the

---

[7] '. . . Fanny ihm ebenbürtig an Talent und Begabung und doch nichts Anderes begehrend, als bescheiden in den Schranken, die die Natur den Frauen gesetzt, zu verbleiben'; Hensel, *Familie* (1879), i. 155.

[8] This letter (dated 24 June 1834) is usually quoted only as an excerpt. For the full text in English, see Ward Jones, *Honeymoon*, 168–71, and Wilson Kimber, ' "For Art" ', 76 [Eds.]

[9] 'Träte jemand auf, der durch untadelhaften Character, durch Ausdauer in seinen Vorsätzen und Weltklugheit im Benehmen (nach welcher die meisten Urteile ja, traurig genug, gefällt werden) ein achtungswertes Muster darstellte, so würde ein großer Teil dieser nur zu begründeten Behauptung verschwinden. Erfreulich wärs, wenn man dieser Heuchelei entbehren könnte . . .'; Hensel, *Familie* (1908), i. 95. This letter was not included in the first edition of Hensel's memoir.

musicians of his orchestra, he chose oratorio rather than opera, cared for the training of young people in opening a conservatory in Leipzig, and earned his money rather than depending on the family fortune. In his mind and his heart he always behaved like the heir of church musicians, Bach and Handel. Last but not least, he laboured so hard that one could reasonably say that he worked himself to death. Similarly, Fanny, a perfect wife and a perfect mother, was the model housewife. The fact that she renounced the public display of her talent makes this perfection and its merit even greater.

But something must be said here to contradict this merit: Fanny was not interested in a virtuoso career, any more than Felix was; like him, she possessed talent not only for piano and composition, but also for organizing concerts and conducting orchestras—and probably also for editing. The piano in itself was enough for neither of them.

The idea that the Mendelssohns' conversion compelled them to strive for a bourgeois perfection is unsatisfactory because it does not take into account the ideology attempting to prove that the opposition between man and woman is a fact of nature. Why should one try to prove something that needs no proof?

One should remember that Abraham Mendelssohn, father of Felix and Fanny, was a great admirer of Kant and firmly believed in universal moral laws, including the universality of public opinion. A truth, he believed, is universal; therefore, what is universally acknowledged must be true. There is here an obvious need for justification. The general opinion is that man and woman are opposites in every respect, so what is a general opinion must be or is true; conversely, what is a law of nature must, should, or will be reflected in society. The general acknowledgement of gender roles divided between a feminine private sphere and a male public one would have reassured him in his stance.

It would not be relevant to talk about Kant, since Kant never said that the difference between man and woman was an *a priori* concept (one that belonged to the realm of pure reason). But what belongs to a bourgeois ideology—which Abraham Mendelssohn typified in keeping his talented daughter inside the limits of her duty—consists in extrapolating the subjective idea of the differences between genders from the realm of experience to a universal idea. The bourgeois citizenry needed the opposition between sexes as the foundation of their social life, as if their system would not have survived without this opposition. And indeed, the married couple and the family were becoming the core of society.

The question remains: is this ideology reflected in music, and particularly in the music of the Mendelssohns?

I have always wondered about the fact that the same musicians who claimed that their musical style was natural also claimed to be the strongest admirers of Bach. I refer to the mannerist school of composers: the sons of Johann Sebastian Bach and the Berlin school, for instance. Zelter in particular, composition teacher of Fanny and Felix, did not hesitate to change passages in Bach's music to make it more accessible to the audience, or perhaps to suit his own taste. There is here, in my opinion, a contradiction owing to the evolution of the functions of music between the eighteenth and nineteenth centuries. Bach, however dependent on a prince or a city, was certainly serving an abstract idea of music. The advent of bourgeois ideology made music serve a more societal purpose. It became important for everyone to be able to sing and remember a tune, which should accordingly be easy. Again, there is here an idea of universality: everyone breathing together to join in the same tune. The founding of the Singakademie was the result of this ideal (though I certainly do not mean to say that the Singakademie performed only easy music). Zelter, with the support of Goethe, saw in vocal music one of the elements that bonded society together. He wrote thousands of lieder for many different occasions or functions: schools, meals in company, incidental music, and so on.[10]

Were Fanny and Felix Mendelssohn standards of bourgeois perfection in that respect? They were certainly at the same time heirs of Bach and of the first Berlin school of lied composition, which emphasized naturalness and a sense of flow in song. Abraham wrote to Fanny about one of her songs in 1820 (when she was 15 years old): 'I like this lied so much that I've sung it to myself many times since yesterday, whereas I recall nothing of the others, and it seems to me one of the first requirements of a lied to be easily remembered. . . . I strongly advise you to retain this naturalness and ease in your future compositions.'[11] As in the notion of opposition between sexes, I see hypocrisy in this evocation of nature in music. Although I am aware that the concept of nature is too broad to be discussed here, the hypocrisy of such an ideology at this point in the evolution of society cannot entirely escape comment.

What did Fanny and Felix do about this contradiction, which was part of their intellectual and musical training? They certainly subscribed to the idea that music and art should be shared. They saw an orchestra as a gathering of

---

[10] Peter Nitsche, 'Die Liedertafel im System der Zelterschen Gründungen', in Dahlhaus (ed.), *Studien zur Musikgeschichte Berlins*, 11–26 at 16–17.

[11] 'Jenes Lied gefällt mir so wohl, da ich mir es seit gestern sehr oft vorgesungen, während ich von den anderen nichts behalten habe, und Faßlichkeit scheint mir eines der wichtigsten Erfordernisse eines Liedes. . . . Ich rathe Dir sehr, Dich möglichst an diese Natürlichkeit und Leichtigkeit in Deinen ferneren Kompositionen zu halten.' Hensel, *Familie* (1st edn.), i. 90.

musicians who shared the same musical ideal. Music played an integral role in their ethics. Felix at the Gewandhaus in Leipzig and Fanny in her Berlin salon strove to make the musical world better by performing good music rather than fashionable tunes. Felix wrote great religious works and even what is called 'light' in his music remains very abstract and not sentimental. Fanny wrote prodigious quantities of lieder, a cappella duets, trios, and quartets, as well as piano pieces and a few cantatas; most of these works display strong contrapuntal influence and are not as fluid as Abraham might have wished.

The future showed that neither of them was accepted as representative of society. They were brought up as members of the elite, a fact which set them apart from most of this society. Even today Felix's music is hardly understood and is often not recognized; Fanny's music, which is only gradually becoming known, does not fare much better. They are no standards in that respect: they belonged to the Romantic period, but their Enlightenment upbringing was antagonistic to the nationalism, historicism, and subjectivism that overtook the central aesthetic tendencies of the Romantic movement soon after their deaths. One does not know where to classify their music—perhaps because they were brought up to be standards of perfection in an ideal society that never came into being. Living at a turning point of civilization, they could imagine that humanity was on an upward climb, that scientific progress would bring happiness to all, and that music would play a quasi-religious role in the unification and brotherhood of humanity. They were not individualists, and that is not forgiven them. In fact, a real bourgeois society does not want musicians; it wants to make money. Therefore, a starving and outcast person is the best representation of an artist in such a society. Fanny and Felix Mendelssohn were not prepared to play that kind of role.

Fanny wanted to see in Gounod the future of religious music in France, as if it were obvious to her that religious music had that much future. The fact is very striking. Fanny and Felix were looking ahead to quite a different society than the one which was to be. Is it one of the causes of Felix's early death? Of the *Revisionskrankheit* Michael Cooper talks about? In any case, their idea of art was more than consensual; it was messianic. To Fanny, it was important that the couple she formed with Wilhelm Hensel serve as a moral example for his students. When she met Ingres in Rome, she was shocked at his lack of concern for his students of the Villa Medici. Ingres was concerned with his individual work and his study of lines, not with people. This was Fanny's perception, even though Ingres was certainly one of the great masters of French painting of the day. In claiming the rights of the artist to be set apart, Ingres was probably more representative of a bourgeois society than Felix Mendelssohn was.

Nor was Fanny the only one who was cheated by these changes in society.
She was cheated in her role in a salon, and Felix was cheated in an even greater
way. When they were young, they worked together on Bach's *St Matthew
Passion*, preparing one of the most important events of pan-Germanism;
meanwhile, in their garden, Alexander von Humboldt was measuring mag-
netic fields. This confluence presents a perfect example of art and science
working hand in hand to bring a better future. But what had become of this
future by the 1840s? There was a growing impoverishment among the poor
due to ruthless industrialization, science being used to make some people
richer while children were being enslaved. Because it was dependent on a
general audience, music was not getting any better, for the general taste was
becoming increasingly commonplace—a trend that compellingly indicated
the failure of public opinion.

Neither Fanny nor Felix belonged to this mercantile society. They had been
pushed into being standards of perfection in an ideal society, a society that did
not exist. Fanny saw the hypocrisy of it at the end of her life, when she started
publishing. Even polarized gender roles were becoming suspect to her. She
suggested that she would not be a *femme libre* (i.e. a prostitute) just because she
published a couple of songs.[12] The last portraits of Felix, and Schumann's
description of his friend,[13] bring out his depression, his exhaustion, and his
total disappointment in the world in which he was living.

It is significant that we are so interested in them. It may mean that we are
still interested in an ideal society, and ready to make the future better.

[12] 'Schande hoffe ich Euch nicht damit zu machen, da ich keine femme libre u. leider gar kein
"junges" Deutschland bin.' Citron, *Letters*, 611.

[13] Schumann's posthumously published memoir ('Erinnerungen an Felix Mendelssohn
Bartholdy') is available in numerous sources, but the first critical edition of the complete
German text was published in Heinz-Klaus Metzger and Rainer Riehn (eds.), *Felix Mendelssohn
Bartholdy* (Musik-Konzepte 14 / 15; Munich: edition text + kritik, 1980), 97–122.

PART V

Reception History

15

Felix Mendelssohn and his Place in the Organ World of his Time

WM. A. LITTLE

MOST biographers of Mendelssohn correctly portray him as one of the greatest organists of his time, yet the achievement of that distinction came neither easily nor quickly. From earliest youth Mendelssohn was drawn magnetically to the organ, and throughout his life he evinced a fascination with every aspect of the instrument, its music, and its players. Comments and observations on organs and organists abound in his correspondence, overshadowing by far any similar preoccupation with either the piano or pianists. For Mendelssohn the piano was the obvious and eminently practical instrument; the organ, however, was his instrument of choice.

Mendelssohn received his earliest keyboard training from his mother, and in 1816, during a family visit to Paris, he studied briefly with Mme Marie Bigot, a native of Vienna, former member of Beethoven's circle, and a renowned Mozart interpreter. On their return to Berlin, or shortly thereafter, both Felix and his elder sister, Fanny, began formal studies with Ludwig Berger, who was then Berlin's most distinguished pianist and teacher. A student of Muzio Clementi and John Field, Berger successfully shaped Mendelssohn's virtuoso technique, and though Mendelssohn was later coached seriously for a short time by Ignaz Moscheles, it was to Berger that he owed his greatest debt as a teacher.

Sometime in 1819 Mendelssohn's parents engaged Carl Friedrich Zelter (1758–1832), Director of the Berlin Singakademie, to give instruction in counterpoint, canon, fugue, etc. to both Felix and Fanny, and these studies laid the cornerstone of Mendelssohn's formidable theoretical skills.

Presumably, it was Zelter who also instilled in his young protégé that same fascination and passion for the organ that he himself had felt since childhood.

As a boy Zelter had constructed his own model organ, on which he pretended to practise daily.[1] The toy instrument was soon replaced, however, by a real organ, when he began his studies with Johann Ernst Roßkämmer (d. *c*.1788), Organist of the Dorotheenstadtkirche in Berlin.[2] Although Zelter never held a position as church organist, he became a competent, though not virtuoso, organist, and he performed publicly on the organ on numerous occasions, primarily as an accompanist.

In 1815 one of Zelter's brightest pupils, August Wilhelm Bach (1796–1869), became an active member of the Singakademie. Bach, who was not related to the Thuringian line to which Johann Sebastian had belonged, was the son of Gottfried Bach, Organist of the Dreifaltigkeitskirche in Berlin—which also happened to be the Mendelssohn family parish. August Wilhelm, who was one of the bright young talents on the Berlin organ scene, had studied with his father and then briefly with Michael Gotthardt Fischer (1773–1829) in Erfurt.[3] At the time he joined the Singakademie he was studying the piano with Ludwig Berger, as well as composition with Zelter. In 1816, at the age of 20, Bach was appointed Organist of the highly prestigious Marienkirche in Berlin, a post he held until his death.

Sometime, probably in mid to late 1820—or about the same time that Mendelssohn joined the Singakademie—Zelter must have felt it was time for young Felix also to begin his organ studies, and who better to be his teacher than August Wilhelm Bach? It was, to all appearances at least, an ideal choice, since Zelter could then influence Mendelssohn both directly and indirectly. Standing thus doubly under the shadow of Zelter, Mendelssohn seems to have been less influenced by A. W. Bach than he might otherwise have been. On the other hand, Bach's own creative gifts were limited, and his musical orientation was academic in nature.

Almost nothing is known about Mendelssohn's work with A. W. Bach. Neither seems to have referred to it or commented on it in later life. The repertoire that Mendelssohn studied with Bach is also entirely a matter of speculation. It is doubtful that Bach would have used Kittel's *Der angehende praktische Organist* (Erfurt, 1801–8); Kittel was too liturgically oriented, and he addressed a level of proficiency that Mendelssohn had long since achieved and passed.

---

[1] *Tonkünstler-Lexicon Berlins von den ältesten Zeiten bis auf die Gegenwart*, ed. C. Fr. Ledebuhr (Berlin: Rauh, 1861; repr., ed. Rudolf Elvers, Tutzing: Hans Schneider, 1965), s.v. 'Zelter, Carl Friedrich'.   [2] Ibid.

[3] M. G. Fischer, a student of Johann Christian Kittel (1732–1809), who was one of Bach's last surviving pupils. A native of Erfurt and long-time Organist of the Predigerkirche, his many compositions for organ, particularly those in which he revealed his skills as a contrapuntist, achieve a level of distinction rarely attained by his contemporaries.

On the other hand, Bach would probably have introduced Mendelssohn to the works of M. G. Fischer, since he had personally studied with Fischer, and Fischer was one of the great organ figures of the day—both as a performer and as a composer. Moreover, one of Mendelssohn's own early organ works—a set of chorale variations on 'Wie groß ist des Allmächt'gen Güte', expressly based on a chorale in Fischer's *Gesangbuch* (Gotha, 1821)[4]—tends to support his familiarity with Fischer at the time. Otherwise, it seems reasonable to assume that Mendelssohn would also have studied one or another work by August Wilhelm Bach, who at this time was also beginning to make a name for himself as an organ composer.[5] Whether Mendelssohn studied any of J. S. Bach's organ works with A. W. Bach cannot be ascertained, but given his attraction to the Leipzig Cantor it would seem natural for him to have explored certain of the works, especially those not requiring great pedal proficiency.

Finally, among the composers whose works Mendelssohn may have studied or probably did study during his time with A. W. Bach was Christian Heinrich Rinck (1770–1846). Rinck's organ tutor, *Der praktische Organist* (Bonn, 1819–21), had only recently appeared, and although Mendelssohn was already far too advanced to benefit from the manual exercises of Part I, the exercises that open the Second Part of Rinck's work include only the sixty-five pedal exercises and the twelve chorales with variations. A comparison of chorale variations by Mendelssohn just mentioned with the chorale variations in Part II of Rinck's *Praktischer Organist* leaves little doubt as to the model Mendelssohn used for his own composition.

There is no record of how long Mendelssohn studied the organ, but presumably the Mendelssohn family's departure for Switzerland in July 1822 served as an effective break for Felix's studies with both Bach and Zelter. The lessons with Berger had also concluded in April of that year, apparently after a serious altercation with Mendelssohn's father, Abraham.

At the point when lessons with Bach ceased, it can be assumed that Mendelssohn had made fairly good progress in learning the art of registration —a letter from Breslau in 1823, describing a performance by F. W. Berner (1770–1829), Organist of the Elisabethkirche,[6] already shows Mendelssohn's

---

[4] See Felix Mendelssohn Bartholdy, *Complete Organ Works in Five Volumes*, ed. Wm. A. Little (London: Novello, 1990), v, pp. ix, 35–52.

[5] A. W. Bach's first volume of organ music (*Fantasien, Vorspiele und Fugen*) was published in Berlin in 1819; two further volumes appeared in the following year.

[6] Berner (1780–1827) was was long considered to be the dean of the Silesian organ school. For the first complete publication of the entire letter, see Felix Mendelssohn Bartholdy, *Kompositionen für Orgel: Erstausgabe*, ed. Wm. A. Little (Leipzig: Deutscher Verlag für Musik, 1974), Vorwort.

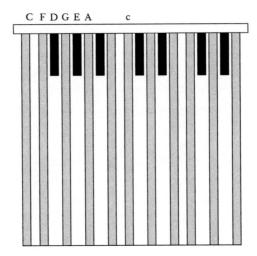

FIG. 15.1. Short pedal board (S. Germany, Austria, Switzerland)

understanding of and sensitivity to registration. It appears, however, that his pedal technique probably had not advanced beyond an elementary or low intermediate level.

The obstacles facing any aspiring young organist—particularly in developing a solid pedal technique—were many, but one of the most serious of these was to be found in the organs themselves—and it was this obstacle that confronted Mendelssohn repeatedly, both at home and abroad. The short pedal board (Fig. 15.1) was a hopeless affair for anyone seriously intent on achieving pedal fluency or on performing the works of J. S. Bach, Buxtehude, Böhm, Tunder, or any of the other North German masters. In England, of course, the G or F pedal board (see Fig. 15.2) had been more or less standard from time immemorial, and only in the 1830s, with the 'Hill-Gauntlett Revolution', were English organ builders successful in any broad sense in introducing the C-compass pedal board (or the 'German system', as it was known; see Fig. 15.3).

Even in Germany, which was Mendelssohn's primary theatre of operations, the C-compass pedal board, which we recognize today as the universal standard, was anything but that until the latter part of the nineteenth century. As Mendelssohn discovered to his dismay over and over again during his travels through southern Germany and Switzerland in the autumn of 1831, almost every organ he encountered was fitted with a short pedal board.

What we recognize today as the standard pedal board could normally be found only in north and north-central Germany—in such cities as Berlin, Leipzig, Dresden, or Hamburg, and their neighbouring areas. It generally

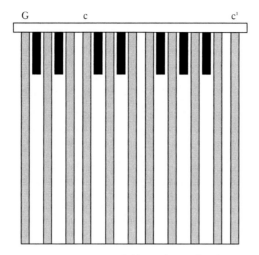

FIG. 15.2. G pedal board (England)

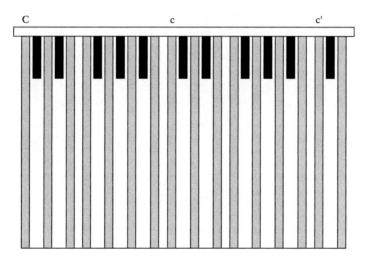

FIG. 15.3. 'German system' pedal board (standard)

consisted of twenty-seven notes and extended from *C* to *d′*. Because of the proportionately greater cost of building the lowest pedal pipes, the low *C♯* was frequently omitted for reasons of economy. (A perusal of J. S. Bach's organ works will reveal not more than three or four instances of a *C♯* in his entire oeuvre for organ.) In southern Germany, Austria, and Switzerland, by contrast, the short pedal board was the rule rather than the exception. It generally consisted of between fourteen and eighteen notes, extending usually, but not always, from *C* to *a* (the actual range could vary significantly from organ to organ).[7]

Given Mendelssohn's perennial resolve to master the organ once and for all—primarily, what he had in mind, of course, was his pedal technique—it is puzzling that he did not pursue this goal by practising on a pedal piano, at least not before the summer of 1837. Such instruments were widely available, as were separate pedal boards that could be attached to a piano. The Schumanns rented one of the latter in the spring of 1845, and both Robert and Clara practised regularly on it. Perhaps in Mendelssohn's mind it was a question of aesthetics: perhaps a pedal piano was simply too pedestrian, or was merely a hapless substitute for the sound and feeling that were to be had from actually playing and hearing an organ. Or perhaps it was really just a matter of finding time to practise—on whatever kind of instrument. In the final analysis, it may well have been a combination of all these factors.

In any case, not until the summer of 1837 did Mendelssohn again address the organ in any serious manner. In the spring of that year he had contracted to participate in the Birmingham Festival in September and had agreed to perform twice on the newly built instrument in Birmingham's Town Hall. Although he had played often in St Paul's Cathedral and elsewhere in London since 1829, and despite the general acclaim that his organ playing had met with, he himself realized all too well that much work still remained to be done before he could feel that he had truly mastered the instrument.

The organ in Birmingham Town Hall, built by William Hill in 1834, was the first major English instrument other than that in St Paul's to be fitted with a full C-compass pedal board, and Mendelssohn may have looked on his commitment to play there as a challenge to finish a task he had long ago begun. In their reviews of his recitals, which included Bach's Prelude and Fugue in E flat, BWV 552, the critics were unanimous in their praise, yet despite these accolades Mendelssohn wrote to Klingemann from Leipzig less than a month later that he had still not achieved on the organ the level of proficiency he aspired to: 'Moreover, this time I have resolved to practise the organ here in earnest; after all, if everyone takes me for an organist, then I am determined to become one.'[8]

---

[7] During the fourteen years that Anton Bruckner was organist of the Cathedral in Linz he had a short pedal board of only eighteen notes, and even when he was able to rebuild and enlarge the organ he retained the old pedal board.

[8] Letter to Karl Klingemann dated 5 Oct. 1837, in Klingemann, *Briefwechsel*, 222: 'Übrigens habe ich mir vorgenommen, diese Zeit hier fleissig Orgel zu studieren, da sie mich doch einmal für einen Orgelspieler halten, damit ich's hintenach auch werde.' Translations here and elsewhere are my own.

In the summer of 1839 Mendelssohn found himself again in Frankfurt, and this time the prospect of an organ recital in the Leipzig Thomaskirche lay before him. Practising several hours each day, either on Friedrich Schlemmer's pedal piano or on the organ in the Catharinenkirche, Mendelssohn finally bridged the gap between excellence and virtuosity. At last, at age 30, Mendelssohn became the organ virtuoso he had always dreamt of becoming.

Mendelssohn's historic recital in the Thomaskirche on 6 August 1840 represents the high point of his career as an organist, and its success was of critical importance to him. As he wrote to his mother afterwards, 'I practised for eight full days before, and in the end I could scarcely stand up straight on my feet any longer, and walked along the street only in pedal passages.'[9]

The programme itself was demanding, but thoroughly conservative, and at the same time it was both expedient and practical (see Pl. 15.1). Given that the recital itself was conceived as a means of raising funds for a monument to Bach, it was entirely appropriate that Mendelssohn chose an all-Bach programme.[10] Nevertheless, in putting it together Mendelssohn exercised considerable caution. Except for the Passacaglia, which he had learnt the previous summer, all the works included had been in his repertoire for many years and lay firmly under his fingers.

The programme also constituted a commendable melding of eighteenth and nineteenth century: by opening and closing with an improvisation, Mendelssohn provided not only a contemporary framework to the programme, but in his thinking these improvisations—especially the latter, which invoked the B-A-C-H motif—may also have represented a conscious personal tribute to Bach.[11]

Altogether, Mendelssohn's active organ repertoire contained between eight and a dozen of Bach's major free organ works and perhaps three or four of the larger chorale preludes. Of the free organ works that Mendelssohn played most frequently, and for which there is ample documentation, are the Prelude and Fugue in E minor, BWV 533; the Pastorale in F, BWV 590; the Toccata and Fugue in D minor, BWV 565; the Prelude and Fugue in A minor, BWV 543; the Fugue in C major, BWV 545; the Fugue and possibly the

---

[9] Letter of 10 Aug. 1840, in *Briefe 1830–47* (1870), 416: 'Ich habe mich aber auch 8 Tage lang vorher geübt, daß ich kaum mehr auf meinen Füßen gerade stehen konnte, und nichts als Orgel-Passagen auf der Straße ging.' Quoted after original in US-NYp.

[10] For a discussion of this programme and especially of Mendelssohn's improvisations in it, see R. Larry Todd, 'New Light on Mendelssohn's *Freie Phantasie* (1840)', in Geoffrey C. Orth (ed.), *Literary and Musical Notes: A Festschrift for Wm. A. Little* (Bern: Peter Lang, 1995), 205–18.

[11] See Robert Schumann's review of the recital in the *NZfM* 13 (1840), repr. in *Gesammelte Schriften über Musik und Musiker von Robert Schumann*, ed. Martin Kreisig (5th edn., Leipzig: Breitkopf & Härtel, 1914), i. 492–3.

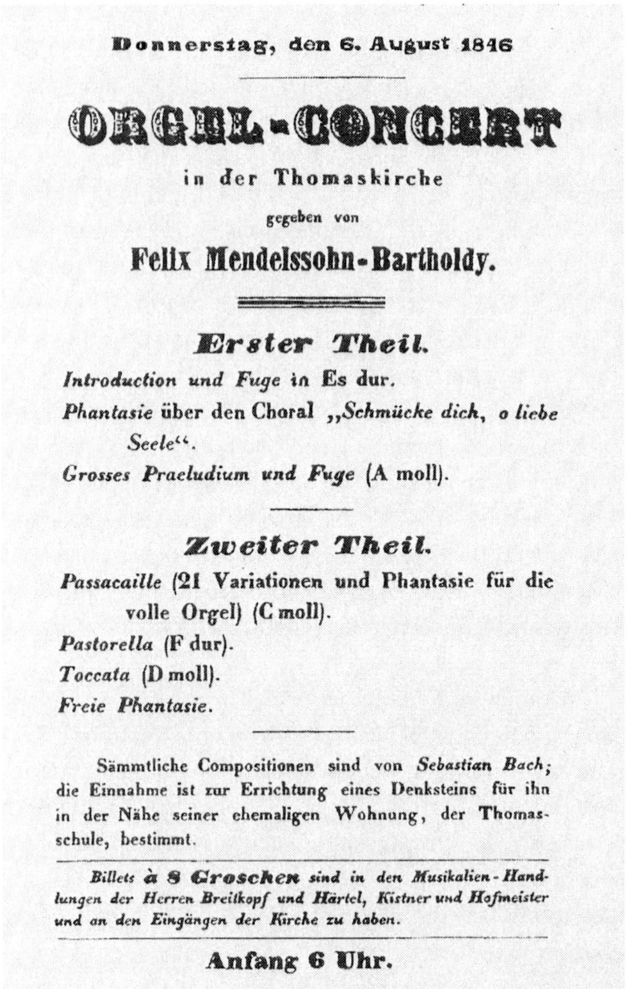

Donnerstag, den 6. August 1846

ORGEL-CONCERT

in der Thomaskirche

gegeben von

Felix Mendelssohn-Bartholdy.

Erster Theil.

Introduction und Fuge in Es dur.

Phantasie über den Choral „Schmücke dich, o liebe Seele".

Grosses Praeludium und Fuge (A moll).

Zweiter Theil.

Passacaille (21 Variationen und Phantasie für die volle Orgel) (C moll).

Pastorella (F dur).

Toccata (D moll).

Freie Phantasie.

Sämmtliche Compositionen sind von *Sebastian Bach;* die Einnahme ist zur Errichtung eines Denksteins für ihn in der Nähe seiner ehemaligen Wohnung, der Thomas- schule, bestimmt.

Billets *à 8 Groschen* sind in den *Musikalien-Hand- lungen der Herren Breitkopf und Härtel, Kistner und Hofmeister und an den Eingängen der Kirche zu haben.*

Anfang 6 Uhr.

PL. 15.1.
Programme for
Mendelssohn's
benefit concert in
the Thomaskirche
(Leipzig), 6
August 1840

Prelude in D major, BWV 532; the Prelude and Fugue in E flat, BWV 552; and the Passacaglia and Fugue in C minor, BWV 582. Writing in 1875, Henry John Gauntlett (1806–76) recalled that 'he brought out a number of pedal-fugues which were not known here. . . . He was the first to play the D-Major [BWV 532], the G-Minor [BWV 542], the E-Major [BWV 566], the C-Minor [per- haps BWV 546], the short E-Minor [BWV 533], etc.'[12] It is impossible to tell from this statement whether Mendelssohn played any or all of the preludes to

---

[12] Quoted from George Grove, 'Mendelssohn', in *Grove's Dictionary of Music and Musicians*, 2nd edn., ed. J. A. Fuller Maitland (New York: Macmillan, 1911), iii. 134.

these works, since it was common practice among English organists of the time to refer to *any* free organ work by Bach as a 'fugue'.

Of the chorale preludes, Mendelssohn had a particular fondness for 'Wir glauben All' an einen Gott, Vater', BWV 740,[13] but his favourite was 'Schmücke dich, o liebe Seele', BWV 654[14]—of which he once remarked to Robert Schumann 'with the most heartfelt expression' that 'if everything in life were taken away from me, this chorale prelude would still comfort me'.[15]

By all accounts Mendelssohn had a prodigious talent for improvisation, yet his attitude about employing that talent was clearly ambivalent. In his view improvisation was a highly demanding exercise, involving both intellect and inspiration, as well as dexterity. It was very much an artistic endeavour, and as such it demanded serious attention. The casual and often mindless improvisations on popular tunes of the day, thrown off at dinner parties and other social gatherings, were anathema to him: 'as a finale I improvised—tried hard to get off, but they made such a tremendous uproar that I was forced to comply, though I had nothing in my head but wine glasses . . . cold roast meat, and ham.'[16] To yield on such occasions and improvise meant not only abusing his art, but prostituting it. At one point he wrote, 'I have seldom felt so like a fool as when I took my place at the piano to present to the public the fruits of my inspiration. . . . My former opinion that it is an absurdity is now confirmed. . . . and I am resolved never again to improvise in public.'[17] History, of course, tells us that on the latter point he changed his mind, but in his thinking about the nature of improvisation he remained firm.

Whether improvising or performing the organ works of Bach, Mendelssohn amazed his audiences by the clarity and brilliance of his playing—even on instruments with the heaviest action. As one reviewer wrote, 'One thing

---

[13] Letter of 14 Nov. 1831 to Fanny Hensel, quoted in Rudolf Elvers (ed.), *Felix Mendelssohn: A Life in Letters*, trans. Craig Tomlinson (New York: International, 1986), 170.

[14] See also Wolfgang Dinglinger's essay in this volume, Ch. 5.

[15] Quoted from Robert Schumann, *Erinnerungen an Felix Mendelssohn Bartholdy: Nachgelassene Aufzeichnungen*, ed. Georg Eismann (Zwickau: Predella, 1947), 39: 'Bei dem Choralvorspiel v. Bach "Schmücke dich o liebe Seele" (in Es dur) sagte er mit d. innigsten Ausdruck: "wenn mir das Leben alles genommen hätte, dies Stück würde mich wieder trösten".'

[16] Letter from Munich, 6 Oct. 1831, in Felix Mendelssohn Bartholdy, *Letters from Italy and Switzerland*, trans. Lady Wallace (Philadelphia: Leypoldt, 1863), 294: '[U]nd zum Schluß . . . mußte ich phantasiren, — wollte nicht, — sie machten aber solch ein furchtbares Gebrüll, daß ich *nolens* heran mußte, obwohl ich nichts im Kopfe hatte, also Weingläser, . . . kalten Braten und Schinken.' *Briefe 1830–2* (1862), 291.

[17] Letter from Munich, 18 Oct. 1831, *Letters from Italy and Switzerland*, 303: 'Ich habe mich recht in meiner Meinung bestärkt, daß es ein Unsinn sei, öffentlich zu phantasiren. Mir ist selten so närrisch zu Muthe gewesen, als wie ich mich da hinsetzte, um meine Phantasie dem Publicum zu produciren. . . . ich werde es öffentlich nicht wieder thun . . .'; *Briefe 1830–2*, 299.

which particularly struck our organists was the contrast between his massive effects and the lightness of his touch in rapid passages. The touch of the Christ Church organ was both deep and heavy, yet he threw off arpeggios as if he were at a piano.'[18] As Grove noted of his physical posture at the keyboard, '[h]is hands were small with tapered fingers. . . . At times, especially at the organ, he leant very much over the keys. . . . He sometimes swayed from side to side, but usually his whole performance was quite quiet and absorbed.'[19]

One of the features of Mendelssohn's playing that his English audiences admired most was his 'wiry, crisp, energetic manner of delivery', which was compared to the late Benjamin Jacob (1778–1829), who 'played in the *legato* manner, and therefore never satisfied us in Bach's organ music'.[20] '[F]reedom of touch is an essential requisite to a tale-telling enunciation of Bach's outline, counterpoints, episodes, and countless modes of diversifying his *motifs*.'[21]

In matters of tempo Mendelssohn held strong opinions, and he had little but contempt for the metronome. In a revealing anecdote Berlioz recalls in his *Memoirs*:

One day, when I spoke of the metronome and its usefulness, Mendelssohn said sharply, 'What on earth is the point of a metronome? It's a futile device. Any musician who cannot guess the tempo of a piece just by looking at it is a duffer. . . . [A few days later he visited me again and] asked to see the score of the *King Lear* overture, which I had just composed in Nice. He read it through slowly and carefully, and was about to begin playing it on the piano (which he did, with incomparable skill), when he stopped and said, 'Give me the right tempo.'[22]

Berlioz thought it all a huge joke, but then, Berlioz always enjoyed needling Mendelssohn and trying to ruffle his aristocratic feathers. Mendelssohn, on the other hand, probably felt his question was simply a tactful gesture.

In his own playing Mendelssohn's tempo of a specific piece tended to vary sharply from one performance to the next. In the words of Wilhelm Wasielewski (1822–96), a pupil and close friend of the composer, 'when playing his *own* works, he was *notoriously* inconsistent regarding tempo'.[23]

So far as I have been able to determine, Mendelssohn did not own a metronome; at least I find no record of his having purchased one, and I have not found one listed among his effects. In preparing his *Six Sonatas for the Organ*, Op. 65 for publication, Mendelssohn had no plan to supply metronome marks; it was only as an afterthought, when his friend E. J. Hopkins

---

[18] Grove, 'Mendelssohn', 134.   [19] Ibid. 156.

[20] *Musical World*, 9 (1838), 210, quoted from Nicholas Thistlethwaite, *The Making of the Victorian Organ* (Cambridge: Cambridge University Press, 1990), 166.   [21] Ibid.

[22] *The Memoirs of Hector Berlioz*, ed. and trans. David Cairns (London: Gollancz, 1977), 292.

[23] David Cairns, 'Tempo and Expression Marks', in *New Grove*, xviii. 675–84.

specifically asked that they be included, that he agreed to add them. But evidently he did so only reluctantly and only at the last minute, scribbling them on the final proofs just before returning them for publication. In a letter written in the spring of 1845 to Charles Coventry, his English publisher, Mendelssohn gave as his reason for not having supplied them earlier the fact that he did not have a metronome at hand.[24]

In his performance of Bach, Mendelssohn surprised his English colleagues by his slow tempos. As Gauntlett recollected, 'he taught us how to play the *slow* fugue for organ'.[25] Elisabeth Mounsey (1819–1905) recalled much the same thing: 'he played Bach *slower* than I expected, but instead of rattling off the semi-quavers he made them flow impressively and seriously'.[26] The extent to which Mendelssohn's own tempos were affected by the heavy action of English organs can only be speculated upon, but it certainly caused him concern. On one occasion in 1846 he refused to play again on the Birmingham Town Hall organ unless something were done to lighten its action.[27]

Regarding manual changes in playing Bach's organ works, there is at least one instance, precisely documented by E. J. Hopkins (1818–1901), where this occurred during one of Mendelssohn's performances. In his playing of the A minor Fugue, BWV 543, Mendelssohn 'took the episode on the Swell, returning to the Great Organ a bar before the entry of the other parts, with very fine effect'.[28] Although this is but a single example, it is of considerable importance in suggesting early nineteenth-century Bach performance practice. It seems unlikely that Mendelssohn would include manual changes in only one of Bach's organ works, but not in any others. Inevitably, the question arises: where did Mendelssohn come by the idea of changing manuals here—and perhaps elsewhere? At the moment we seem to have no answer to this question, but it is not entirely unreasonable to suggest that manual changes in Bach's free organ works were more widespread at the time than many currently believe.

Mendelssohn's reputation and fame in the organ world were grounded not only on his fabled ability as a performer or his published works for the instrument—which until 1845 consisted of but a single opus—but rather on a much broader musical base. Sought after as a conductor, pianist, and composer, Mendelssohn had become by 1840, or even earlier, a household name both in England and on the Continent. Among those who sought his advice and favour were musicians of every caste, including some of the most distinguished

[24] Unpublished letter of 21 July 1845 (GB-Ob, MDM d. 55).

[25] Grove, 'Mendelssohn', 134.   [26] Thistlethwaite, *Victorian Organ*, 520.

[27] Letter of 12 July 1846 in *Felix Mendelssohn Bartholdy's Letters to Ignaz and Charlotte Moscheles*, ed. and trans. Felix Moscheles (London: Trübner, [1888]), 275–6.

[28] Grove, 'Mendelssohn', 134.

organists of the day. For the most part, however, the concerns raised in their letters are but rarely related to the organ. César Franck wrote concerning his first trios (Op. 1);[29] Adolf Friedrich Hesse (1809–63) wrote asking Mendelssohn's opinion of his Third Symphony;[30] and Friedrich Kühmstedt (1809–58), a former student, wrote pleading for a performance of his own Third Symphony.[31] Both Heinrich Sattler (1811–91) and Julius Seidel (1810–56) sent him complimentary copies of their books on organ building,[32] and Robert Schaab (1817–87) and E. F. Richter (1808–79) wrote urging Mendelssohn to write more music for organ.[33] From Munich, Rheinberger's organ teacher, Johann Georg Herzog (1822–1909), sent Mendelssohn the first volume of his tutor, *Der praktische Organist* (Mainz, 1843), with a request for an endorsement.[34] Mendelssohn complied, and Herzog routinely used it in advertising his subsequent organ works. From London the former Rinck student G. French Flowers (1811–72) made the same request,[35] with the same results. Anacker in Freiburg, Sponholtz in Rostock, Granzin in Danzig, and many others sought Mendelssohn's assistance in obtaining or changing positions, and for the most part Mendelssohn did what he could. In much of this correspondence the scent of exploitation can be more than faintly detected, and though Mendelssohn can hardly have been oblivious to it, he invariably responded graciously to even the most importunate requests.

All in all, reading the bulk of this correspondence, almost none of which is published, one comes away with the clear and understandable impression that the organ world regarded Mendelssohn as a kind of Maecenas, whose mere nod could magically open doors and effortlessly secure the very choicest of professional appointments. In reality, of course, this was wishful thinking, but it was not entirely without an element of truth. Mendelssohn's word carried great weight in the corridors of musical power, and in numerous cases the high hopes of his petitioners were neither unfounded nor unrealized. In his role as *Organistenmacher*, but more importantly, as a performing artist on the instrument and (more important still) a composer for it, Mendelssohn, the secular musician, served as a source of inspiration in the liturgical realm. Most importantly, in his contributions to the literature for the instrument he provided clear evidence that the organ was ready to resume its place as King of Instruments.

---

[29] See Léon Vallas, *César Franck*, trans. Hubert Foss (London: Oxford University Press, 1951), 87.

[30] Either GB-Ob, GB V/333.   [31] GB-Ob, GB XVII/52.

[32] Sattler: GB-Ob, GB XI/140; Seidel: XVIII/223.

[33] GB-Ob, GB XVII/221.   [34] GB-Ob, GB XXI/206.

[35] GB-Ob, GB XIX/252.

16

Epigones of an Epigone? Concerning Mendelssohn's String Quartets—and the Consequences

FRIEDHELM KRUMMACHER

THE beginning of Bernard Molique's String Quartet in B flat major could hardly sound more like Mendelssohn. Ludwig Finscher described this work in 1965 as 'at the very least a composition on the same level as its model'.[1] Yet Molique, who died in 1869, was seven years older than Mendelssohn; and after an encounter between the two composers in Stuttgart in 1832 Mendelssohn expressed the same admiration for Molique's violinistic virtuosity that would later be expressed by Schumann.[2] Thus we can hardly speak of a teacher–student relationship, any more than we can speak of personal influences—and in any case Molique's quartet was not published until 1851.

That even an older composer adopted Mendelssohn's manner of expression might well reflect how much Mendelssohn struck the nerve of his times; for it is generally considered an indication of historical significance when a composer exerts this sort of influence. For this reason we are able to speak without embarrassment of the influences exerted by Haydn, Beethoven, or even Schubert, although Schubert's music did not become generally known

---

This chapter is based on parts of a monograph in preparation on the history of the string quartet: *Das Streichquartett*, i: *Von Haydn bis Schubert* (Laaber: Laaber, 2001); ii (in preparation).

[1] Ludwig Finscher, 'Streichquartett', *MGG*, xii. 1584.

[2] Fritz Schröder, *Bernard Molique und seine Instrumentalkompositionen, seine künstlerische und historische Persönlichkeit: Ein Beitrag zur Geschichte des Instrumentalmusik des 19. Jahrhunderts, mit einem Verzeichnis aller nachweisbaren Werke Molique's und einem thematischen Katalog der wichtigsten Instrumentalkompositionen* (Stuttgart: Berthold und Schwerdtner, 1923), 23; *Briefe 1830–47* (1882), i. 338; Robert Schumann, *Gesammelte Schriften über Musik und Musiker*, ed. Martin Kreisig (Leipzig: Breitkopf & Härtel, 1914), i. 315.

until later.[3] But obviously this is not the case with Mendelssohn and the influences attributed to him. On the one hand one might cite—almost sneeringly —Nietzsche's *bon mot* that Mendelssohn represented only 'the nice interlude of German music', suggesting that he was of no historical consequence and therefore second-rate.[4] On the other hand, one might condescendingly point out that his music had been 'imitated too frequently and thus cheapened'.[5] Widespread resonance and inconsequentiality are not opposites, however; they are two aspects of the same disdain. It may be understandable that Mendelssohn's contemporaries found his idiom tiresome as it became increasingly popular, but a different situation obtains when historical consequences also serve as the foundation of historiography. However unavoidable some value judgements may be, their aesthetic dimensions are easily contaminated by historical criteria, which include not least of all the criterion of influence. According to this view, if Mendelssohn is not inconsequential, then we must re-examine the question of his historical influence.

Now we may well be reluctant to assess those epigones who have tarnished Mendelssohn's memory, for some references could probably be detected in the works of Schumann or Brahms as well, and occasionally in those of Bruckner and even Wagner. Yet isolated details divorced from their context say little about historical influences; and these influences should not be considered without regard to genre. In the history of the string quartet between Mendelssohn and Reger, there is a gap of about sixty years that is bridged only by the three quartets of Brahms.[6] Although one might of course point to important individual works by Grieg, Verdi, and Wolf, and to other compositions by Dvořák, Smetana, and Tchaikovsky, if we are to avoid hasty historical constructs we are obliged to consider works of less well-known composers who might otherwise be considered mere epigones of Mendelssohn or Schumann. Before substantive differentiating features of the latter two composers can be defined, however, we must briefly review our historiographic

---

[3] Christian Ahrens, 'Schuberts Kammermusik in der Musikkritik des 19. Jahrhunderts', in *Festschrift für Rudolf Elvers* (Tutzing: Hans Schneider, 1985), 9–27. Joseph Joachim spoke of difficulties in the reception of Schubert's C major Quintet as late as 1860; see *Briefe von und an Joseph Joachim*, ed. Johannes Joachim and Andreas Moser (Berlin: J. Bard, 1912), ii. 108–9.

[4] Friedrich Nietzsche, 'Jenseits von Gut und Böse', in *Friedrich Nietzsche Werke*, ed. Karl Schlechta and Ivo Frenzel (Munich: C. Hanser, 1967), ii. 133; Hans Joachim Moser, *Kleine deutsche Musikgeschichte* (2nd edn., Stuttgart: Cotta, 1949), 244. (The first edition of Moser's study appeared in 1938.)

[5] Alfred Einstein, *Geschichte der Musik von den Anfängen bis zur Gegenwart* (Stuttgart: Pan, 1953), 120.

[6] The two quartets in Reger's Op. 54 were published in 1902; Reger composed these works in the autumn of 1900 and spring of 1901.

models; for only then can we investigate the extent of emulation or influences within a buried tradition.

I

It was with undisguised condescension that Hans Joachim Moser wrote in 1949 that 'much of what later was rejected in Mendelssohn should rather have been blamed on his epigones and their cult of orthodoxy'.[7] These epigones, in Moser's opinion, included Max Bruch and Theodor Kirchner along with Julius Rietz and Carl Reinecke. Yet in his 1924 history of German music Moser wrote: 'The real Mendelssohnians became healthy, rosy-cheeked old men along the lines of Lachner, Spohr, and Gade.' Following the names of Rietz, Reinecke, Bruch, and Robert Franz—who unfortunately did not die as young as their hero did—he lists Albert Dietrich, Woldemar Bargiel, and Joseph Joachim, along with a circle of 'Schumannians' that includes Hermann Goetz and Robert Volkmann along with Kirchner and Adolf Jensen.[8] Reviews in periodicals do begin to speak of influences after about 1840; but pointed differentiations between the 'schools' of Mendelssohn and Schumann were not made until the publication of Franz Brendel's *History of Music* in 1852.[9] Already at that point Brendel raised the question of whether Mendelssohn's influence had always been 'beneficial'; yet he identified first of all Niels W. Gade, Ferdinand Hiller, William Sterndale Bennet, and Johann Verhulst as the 'young artists' who 'relied on Mendelssohn and Schumann, sometime more on one or the other, sometimes equally on both', and then Reinecke and Hermann Hirschbach, even though the latter was a sharp critic of both Mendelssohn and Schumann.

In other words, as soon as the battle lines had been drawn the boundaries and qualifying characteristics became confused. The difficulties created by differentiating so strictly between the two schools are thus complicated by the very postulation of schools. Nevertheless, the existence of these schools soon became a carefully cultivated assumption, one that left a deep impression on the writing of music history. This latter point may be illustrated by a few representative cases.

---

[7] Moser, *Kleine deutsche Musikgeschichte*, 244.

[8] Hans Joachim Moser, *Geschichte der deutschen Musik* (Stuttgart: J. G. Cotta, 1924), ii/2, p. 304.

[9] Franz Brendel, *Geschichte der Musik in Italien, Deutschland und Frankreich* (6th edn., Leipzig: H. Matthes, 1878), 493, 519–21, and 528–31. (Brendel's study was originally published in 1852.)

One such example is Karl Storck, who in 1904 said that 'the concept of academicism' was tellingly associated with Mendelssohn—however 'unjust' it
might be 'to have him pay the penalty for the pettiness and short-sightedness of
those men who may be considered his followers'; Stork then named the usual
persons as belonging to 'the Mendelssohn school'.[10] Even Hugo Riemann
(certainly no disparager of Mendelssohn) distinguished between the 'Leipzig
school', which followed the 'head of the [Leipzig] Conservatory', and the
other composers who followed Schumann; yet Riemann also devoted an entire
separate chapter to the 'epigones' from the 'circle of the Academy in Berlin'
and the 'conservatives outside Berlin', including Reinecke.[11]

Such portrayals reflect an overriding desire to organize the 'battles' of
musical history according to the great masters and their spheres of influence.
It has since become an ineradicable custom to present musical history as con-
frontations not only between Mendelssohnians and Schumannians, but also,
later on, between composers of the 'New German School' and Wagnerians
on the one side, and Brahmsians on the other—all in order to achieve a
redistribution of historical territory by personalizing music history. As a
final example of such differentiations we may cite Ernst Bücken, who in 1929
counted among the 'second-class masters' not only Bruch, Friedrich Kiel,
and Heinrich von Herzogenberg, but also Joseph Joachim and Friedrich
Gemsheim—while at the same time labelling Dietrich and Bargiel as well as
Kirchner and Volkmann as 'posthumous Schumannians'.[12]

There was no place for a buried tradition of chamber music in a concept of
musical history such as that sketched by Carl Dahlhaus;[13] yet that music can be
ignored only in a history of heroes that focuses solely on degrees of progress-
iveness. More recently, art historians have thoroughly rehabilitated not only
historicist architecture, but also the painting of the various academies and
their innumerable followers, with the result that anyone interested is painfully
aware of the drastic price increases commanded for such artworks because
of their efforts.[14] There are, of course, no standardized units of comparative

---

[10]   Karl Storck, *Geschichte der Musik* (Stuttgart: Muth, 1904), 735.
[11]   Hugo Riemann, *Geschichte der Musik seit Beethoven (1800–1900)* (Berlin: W. Spemann,
1901), 264–72, 297–330, 557–74.
[12]   Ernst Bücken, *Die Musik des 19. Jahrhunderts bis zur Moderne* (Wildpark-Potsdam:
Akademische Verlags-Gesellschaft Athenaion, 1929), 235–6.
[13]   Carl Dahlhaus, *Die Musik des 19. Jahrhunderts* (Neues Handbuch der Musikwissenschaft,
6; Wiesbaden: Akademische Verlags-Gesellschaft Athenaion, 1980), 64, 210–12. Nevertheless,
Dahlhaus's assertion that 'the system of aesthetics is the history of aesthetics' led to the conclusion that music must be evaluated according to the criterion of its own time rather than modern
criteria; see Dahlhaus, *Musikaesthetik* (Cologne: H. Gerig, 1967), 10.
[14]   A milestone in this trend was the exhibit devoted to the Düsseldorf school of painting;
see *Ausstellung Düsseldorfer Malerschule: Katalog*, ed. Wend von Kalnein (Düsseldorf: Kunstmuseum, 1979).

market value in music, but if we consider music history as a dialectic of opposing forces that are synthesized to produce historical continuity, even the music of self-styled academics assumes immense importance in the history of musical form; for in such a view even a history that focuses on progressive composition would be dependent on its conservative antagonist for a definition of its standards. By the same token, the greater Mendelssohn's importance became for mere *Kleinmeister*, the paler shone his star, and his superiority almost seemed a fault. For this reason Ludwig Finscher, sketching the history of the string quartet in broad terms, justified the notion that the genre traditions of the string quartet, 'under the strong influence of Mendelssohn', had 'almost of necessity led down the path of academicism'; and because of this, he maintained that Schumann's Op. 41 Quartets should be accorded only a 'clearly subordinate position' relative to those of Mendelssohn, by whom they had been 'strongly influenced'.[15] But what are the facts concerning the leaders of these two compositional schools and their relationship to one another?

Judging from contemporary periodicals, memoirs, and monographs, the string quartets published as Mendelssohn's Op. 13 and Op. 80—works whose conspicuously expressive qualities are particularly prized today—were of only secondary importance in the eyes of the nineteenth century. Mendelssohn's compositional attempts to deal with Beethoven in the difficult Op. 13 quartet made that work relatively inaccessible even in the composer's immediate circle; and the posthumous publication of the Op. 80 F minor quartet made it even less compatible with the image of him that later emerged. Even without statistical documentation we may confidently assert that the central position in the reception of Mendelssohn's quartets was held by the E flat major Quartet, Op. 12, and, along with it, the three quartets published as Op. 44.[16] In fact, these four works do display the style of the mature Mendelssohn especially effectively. In contrast to the experimental Op. 13 quartet, which combines its references to Beethoven with a cyclical transformation of the lied it quotes, the Op. 12 quartet advances such experiments only superficially, by taking up a complete section of the first movement in the finale. Yet what is contained in these lengthy quotations are portions of movements encountered in this form for the first time: a prominent cantabile melody with a steady accompaniment is worked out so that it develops hidden rhythmic affinities. The shapes of the other themes as well as the premises of the quotation-like

[15] Finscher, 'Streichquartett', col. 1584.

[16] For more on Mendelssohn's quartets, see Friedhelm Krummacher, *Mendelssohn — Der Komponist: Studien zur Kammermusik für Streicher* (Munich: Wilhelm Fink, 1978). Interestingly, Mendelssohn's Op. 12 and Op. 44 string quartets figured prominently in the programmes of Paul Hindemith's Amar-Quartet; see Michael Kube, 'Am Quartettpult: Paul Hindemith im Rebner- und Amarquartett, Documentation (Part 3)', in *Hindemith-Jahrbuch*, 22 (1993), 200–37 at 213.

montage itself proceed from these affinities. In comparison to the challenges posed by the outer movements, which are extended in the finale through the step-by-step reduction of the C minor main theme, the inner movements—a Canzonetta that once was especially popular and a short Andante—are even further overshadowed; they might, however, be appealing as episodic character pieces.

Mendelssohn published his Op. 44 string quartets in 1839, after a period of nearly ten years during which he distanced himself from the canon of classical forms and worked instead with the models of historically more remote genres. Therefore, these quartets, including the places where lied-like themes are employed, represent a decisive new beginning that would define the style of the mature Mendelssohn. According to Finscher, these quartets submit to 'classically measured expression . . . at the expense of direct emotional expression', but precisely because of their 'brooding restraint and extremely fine attention to nuance, as well as their enigmatic and subtle simplicity of musical invention, which no longer pours out without reflection but rather is strictly designed', he maintained that they belonged within the classical canon of the genre.[17] The salient feature was not the thoroughly original forms that emerge so prominently in structure and sound—those resulting from the combinatorial working-out of the sonata-form movements, the densely constructed sonata-rondos, the playfulness of the Scherzi, and the distinctively lied-like structures of the slow movements—but the works' pervasive interrelation of themes. In his Op. 44 quartets Mendelssohn achieves a balance between the norms of the classical string-quartet movement and the thoroughly Romantic pervasive integration of melodic and accompanimental materials.

The underlying principles of this new approach to balance permeate Op. 44 and are specifically adapted for each individual movement. The music mediates less between the various themes than between analogous ideas or autonomous sections. When transitional themes do not refer only to the themes themselves and additional material is introduced, this material must then legitimate itself in the course of the work. Integration is achieved by variation and combination, as the possibilities in the thematic material suggest themselves. The work's contrapuntal complexity, which no longer has to be brought ostentatiously into the foreground, further supports this technique. This idiom draws on Mendelssohn's previous works but without any direct imitation; and because it is supported by continuity of movement it is able to appropriate strict procedures in a completely different way than in classical quartets.

---

[17] Finscher, 'Streichquartett', col. 1583.

By relying on this concept, Mendelssohn was able to overcome the limitations of cyclical quotations, and in this fashion the works manage to succeed without any of the formal experimentation that Mendelssohn had tried out, for example, in the earlier Octet for Strings, Op. 20. Of central importance here is the challenge to adhere structurally to the norms of the genre of the string quartet, despite the fundamental change in the nature of the thematic material. If we grant that the concept of 'Classicism' presented a problematical situation hard to escape after Beethoven, then we can appreciate the varied solutions Mendelssohn discovered in his Op. 44 string quartets, completely independently of Schubert.

The norms of the true classical quartet had been established by Haydn, and these norms depended on the relationship between cadential harmonies and metrical periodicity—the so-called 'metrically periodic phrase'—in order to veil this relationship continuously with a lively alternation between the movement's rhythmic impulses and its constant, essentially self-contained structural components.[18] In comparison with the discontinuities that characterize Beethoven's late works, the primacy of continuity was revealed first of all in the late quartets of Schubert, whose melodic and harmonic expressiveness could consequently be interpreted as 'Romantic'. But while there are conceptual parallels between Schubert's late quartets and Mendelssohn's Op. 44 quartets in the techniques employed to legitimate the thematic interrelationships between the sections, Mendelssohn's procedure in the Op. 44 quartets should be regarded as an independently conceived innovation, since Schubert's works became known only later. The contrary approach employed in Robert Schumann's quartets thus stands out as all the more individual, since they make little or no effort to build on melodic and rhythmic continuity in their themes. By relying only secondarily on a mediating elaboration, Schumann, with nothing to fall back on, stakes everything on the moment-to-moment expression of a specific characteristic which has only a precarious relation to the movement as a whole.

Schumann's Op. 41 quartets occupy a special position in his œuvre, since they initiated his 'year of chamber music', 1842. He availed himself of the 'fruit-filled gardens' of chamber music by studying classical-period quartets, despite his proclivity for small forms. Schumann's approach lent itself poorly to development because thematic continuity was endangered if it ventured beyond literal or even varied repetition.

Of course, Schumann's dedication of his quartets to Mendelssohn (who, contrary to a later distortion of the truth, thoroughly admired them) is surely

---

[18] See Stefan Kunze, *Mozarts Opern* (Stuttgart: P. Reclam, 1984); further, Thrasybulos Georgiades, 'Zur Musiksprache der Wiener Klassiker', *Mozart-Jahrbuch* 1951, 50–9.

an indication of a certain collegial respect, but it by no means proves that Schumann was dependent on Mendelssohn.[19] Most obviously, Schumann's A minor Quartet, Op. 41 No. 1 is distinguished by its use of sharply contrasting themes in the transitional passages and in the extended recapitulation: the sharp divisions between structural components remain unmistakable, throwing into relief the respective characters of these components. Almost paradoxically, the Finale is cast as a monothematic sonata form that, while employing the usual structural components, also works against that form by introducing virtually independent episodes. Even the Mendelssohnian Scherzo brings to the foreground the contrasts and phrasing characteristic of an 'intermezzo'. And the lied-like forms of the slow movements also achieve, by means of seemingly formulaic accompaniments, a surprising sense of intensification despite their lack of motivic development. Somewhat less difficult is the graceful Quartet No. 2 in F Major, which compensates for its own modest scope by a series of variations on a theme that is reworked even during its first presentation. But Schumann's procedure in the Quartet in A Major, Op. 44 No. 3 seems most individual of all.

Although Schumann's three string quartets were composed within six weeks, by the last of these quartets his experience is focused with complete mastery—a feat all the more remarkable because of its short distance in time from the first. That the two outer movements both start with a first-inversion subdominant chord has often been pointed out. Although a single chord by itself guarantees neither a certain quality nor a specific function, this chord particularly facilitates more than a thematic realization of harmonic function, leading to different constellations in the slow introduction to the first movement; its characteristic gesture of a falling fifth also opens the main theme of the allegro. But the transition dispenses with this gesture, relying primarily on a consistent harmonic sequence; likewise, the development section avoids thematic working-out by relying instead on changing harmonic progressions. When such sonorous areas flow into one another, as is the case here, motivic stability is relegated to secondary importance.

With its seven refrains comprising a cadence of only two measures, the Finale Op. 41 No. 3 follows the prototype of the rondo. Yet this model lends itself naturally to transposition and abbreviation without jeopardizing its identity, for the movement's rousing élan derives from the syncopated beginning and its successions of chords in dotted rhythms. The potency of these features permits almost mechanical repetitions among which the refrains are interspersed without any mediation. The Scherzo is a variation movement in which the individual sections are delineated by different contrapuntal techniques. But the crowning movement is the Adagio, which, contrary to first appearance, unfolds with almost no motivic development, relying instead on three characteristic gestures, each with its own distinctive harmonic profile. The opening densely voiced chords lead to sections which favour modulations by whole steps or by thirds. Although the rhythmic language contributes to the continuity of the movement, the harmonic gestures are so important that they almost function as themes.

The extraordinary independence Schumann achieves in his Op. 41 quartets can be appreciated only if we understand the history of the genre as a whole; yet this understanding will elude us if we measure these works against his earlier piano music or the classical string quartet. We may of course view the quartets' restrained intimacy as the prize Schumann succeeded in winning after grappling with this challenge, or (following the conventional assessment) as experiments admittedly derived from his piano works. But while the quartets would be unthinkable without the succinctness that characterizes this piano music, precisely this conciseness opens up new possibilities for the string quartet. The interrelationships among the parts are no longer obbligato-like in character; rather, they seem to present timbral regions that may be described either as sections of conventional working-out or as episodic enclaves. In this sense, Schumann's quartets offer new procedures in timbral disposition that would become historically decisive for the genre after Grieg and Smetana. Though the details of these radical procedures may not have contributed much to Mendelssohn's Op. 80 quartet, the basic impulse they represent might have done so. Brahms shied away from such unguarded expressiveness and availed himself instead of the safety offered by concentrated thematic and motivic development.

II

So long as the exponents of a genre remain isolated, we cannot speak of a continuous tradition; but when influences of any given exponent are discerned they should not be simplistically identified as reminiscences or imitations. References to familiar works readily come to mind; yet such 'reminiscences' have long been a major theme in public discussions. Because of this situation, no musician of any consequence would have knowingly exposed himself to accusations of imitation. We shall hardly encounter in the works of other composers exact counterparts of the highly idiosyncratic quartet movements of Mendelssohn and Schumann: there is hardly any other Scherzo whose intricate structure is linked to Mendelssohn's 'elfin music', nor any clear descendant of a character-variation movement such as that in Schumann's F major Quartet. Nevertheless, the principles represented by Mendelssohn's mediating transitions and Schumann's thematic style are valid subjects for examination.

Access to works by Mendelssohn's and Schumann's contemporaries is more difficult today than it is for earlier works, and access to string quartets is particularly complicated because those works (unlike chamber music with piano) were usually printed only in parts, not in score. Even Beethoven was able to have only his last quartets released almost simultaneously in score and parts; Mendelssohn achieved this only with his Op. 44 quartets of 1839, and Schumann's Op. 41 quartets, published in parts in 1843, were not available in score until 1848.[20] In the absence of autograph scores or contemporary copies in score format, one has to reconstruct the score from the extant individual parts. Furthermore, even when there are early studies that can be used, these rarely explain biographical contacts among composers sufficiently. Despite the absence of such direct evidence, however, the image of the 'Leipzig school' was reinforced in the nineteenth century, and the excerpt from the Molique quartet given in Ex. 16.3 demonstrates that such 'distant influences' could exist without direct personal ties among composers. In other words, any preliminary investigation that attempts to adduce even a few significant examples of these influences must remain tentative.

From their earliest meeting in 1822 onwards, Ferdinand Hiller (1811–85) was closer to Mendelssohn than all but a few other musicians; their personal encounters were especially productive during Mendelssohn's stay in Paris in the winter of 1831–2. Hiller's G major quartet, published as his Op. 12 by Hofmeister in Leipzig in 1833, was probably composed after this period (see Ex. 16.1).[21] Since the work is dedicated to Pierre Baillot, we might expect it to belong to the genre of the virtuoso *quatour brillant*—yet that special character is just as absent in this work as Beethoven's influence is in the early works of Mendelssohn; from the outset it is clear that the work looks back to a more traditional phase of the genre's history. Although the two four-bar phrases of the principal theme differ in their cadential structure, they share not only the dotted rhythm with which the theme begins but also a homorhythmic setting

[20] On the publication of Schumann's quartets see Kurt Hofmann, *Die Erstdrucke der Werke von Robert Schumann* (Musikbibliographische Arbeiten, 6; Tutzing: Hans Schneider, 1979), 96–7.

[21] Ferdinand Hiller, *Felix Mendelssohn Bartholdy: Briefe und Erinnerungen* (2nd edn., Cologne: DuMont-Schauberg, 1878), 1–6, 11–27.

Ex. 16.1. Hiller, String Quartet in G Major, first movement, beginning

with constantly doubled voices. After a three-bar extension that serves to vary the dotted opening, a section based on the alternation of paired voices takes over. The even, flowing rhythmic texture reinforces the connections with the preceding material, while the bridge to the second theme barely even begins to suggest motivic links or contrapuntal working-out. The traditional thematic development is replaced by a modulatory passage containing little thematic material, but the work also follows earlier conventions in its structure. The sharply abbreviated reprise, which dispenses entirely with the recapitulation of the principal theme, initially recalls in its own transitional section the non-thematic bridge characteristic of the earlier concept of sonata form. Such a movement explains Mendelssohn's 1837 criticism that he knew his friend's piece to be one that was 'properly developed'.[22]

---

[22] Letter of 24 Jan. 1837, quoted ibid. 73. The same letter is dated one year earlier in *Briefe 1830–47* (ii. 111).

EX. 16.1. *continued*

When Norbert Burgmüller died in 1836 at the age of 26, Schumann lamented his death as a loss almost as severe as the loss of Schubert.[23] During Mendelssohn's Düsseldorf years (1833–5) Burgmüller became sufficiently well acquainted with him that he even hoped to succeed him in the position of Municipal Music Director. Although Burgmüller's D minor Quartet, Op. 7 was written in 1831,[24] it nevertheless represents the work of a composer who was close to Mendelssohn and attracted Schumann's attention (see Ex. 16.2). Already the energetic beginning of the first movement—in which the drop of an octave in the uppermost voice is followed by a figure that rushes up to the

[23] Schumann, *Gesammelte Schriften*, ii. 430–2.
[24] See Heinrich Eckert, *Norbert Burgmüller: Ein Beitrag zur Stil- und Geistesgeschichte der deutschen Romantik* (Veröffentlichungen des Musikwissenschaftlichen Instituts der deutschen Universität in Prag, 3; Augsburg: B. Filser, 1932), 27–8, 31.

Ex. 16.2. Burgmüller, String Quartet in D Minor, Op. 7,
first movement, beginning

EX. 16.2. *continued*

lowered sixth degree, complete with a dotted figure at the cadence—reveals that the aspirations of this work are incomparably higher than those of Hiller's G major Quartet. When the cello frees itself from the pedal point in bar 4 it takes over this same melodic idea, which in turn is picked up by the second violin in the next bar. The next phrase is shortened from the four bars of the first phrase to only three, and after a dramatic measure of silence the theme begins in the Neapolitan, E flat major. Equally concentrated is the bridge to the second theme, in which the melodic idea is presented in inversion and substantially altered metrically. The second theme itself is not so clearly profiled, but is nevertheless linked to the striking gesture of the main theme, permitting it to lead effortlessly back into that theme. The development section, like the exposition, is thematically concentrated, and is also remarkable for the sheer variety of material derived from the themes themselves. The broad harmonic spectrum, extending to G sharp major, contributes to this effect.

This work's proximity to Spohr, with whom Burgmüller studied in Kassel, was observed by Heinrich Eckert in 1932.[25] More pronounced, however, are the quartet's affinities with the works of Beethoven's middle period, especially the F minor Quartet, Op. 95—works that concentrate intensively on a single motivic gesture. This technique is equally evident in the G minor Scherzo of Burgmüller's quartet, in which short, legato unison passages and sporadic chords change into staccato notes, leading to driving waves of increasing chromaticism. A reworked version of this material replaces the conventional trio section, while the two layers are superimposed in the short coda. Neither

---

[25] See Eckert, *Burgmüller*, 18; remarks on Burgmüller's Op. 7 on pp. 65–7. Parts for the Quartet survive in D-B, to which I am indebted for a microfilm copy.

the graceful Andante nor the capricious Finale in D major achieves this level of quality, though both movements are finely wrought. Since, however, influences of Beethoven's late works can be detected no more than those of Mendelssohn's early works, Burgmüller's quartet, like Hiller's, demonstrates that musicians of this circle were able to draw upon fundamentally different traditions without any prior dependency on Mendelssohn.

A different situation obtains in the case of Molique's Op. 42 Quartet (see Ex. 16.3): this work's reminiscences are not limited to the cantabile melodic style of the main theme (which recalls parts of Mendelssohn's quartets Op. 44 Nos. 1 and 2); they also include the syncopated accompaniment typical of Mendelssohn's lieder and *Lieder ohne Worte*. We must also give Molique credit for his grasp of the character of Mendelssohn's themes, and of Mendelssohn's developmental procedures—as, for example, in the bridge to the secondary theme, which combines a triplet figure with the incipit of the theme itself; or especially in the harmonic progression which, like the first movement of Op. 44 No. 3, punctuates the caesurae between the chords of the relative tonic minor and its dominant with rests. These relationships are so obvious that they leave no doubt as to Molique's compositional orientation; yet because of them certain important differences are all the more striking. Molique's quartet does follow Mendelssohn's model in the spinning-out of the main theme, and the expansive development section reveals substantial harmonic affinities as well.

Yet however directly Molique's thematic processes are taken from Mendelssohn, the laborious counterpoint in the second theme remains clumsy. The development section is unable to explore further thematic combinations; and there is no sign of any compositional strategy such as Mendelssohn's revelation of thematic relationships which progress step by step and culminate in the coda. As in Molique's other quartets, which (according to Schröder) are influenced by Spohr, whom Molique had met in Nuremberg in 1815,[26] the following movements of Op. 42 hardly approach Mendelssohn's model. A minuet in G minor that alternates capriciously between 3/4 and 6/8 is followed by a trio in the major mode, in which the whirring figurations of the accompaniment might suggest an allusion to Mendelssohn; this figuration permits a consolidation of the material of the two parts only in the coda. The Andante, by contrast, is overwhelmed with ornamental figurations, while the rondo finale makes no pretence of thematic development. The last movement

---

[26] Schröder, *Molique*, 8; on Molique's quartets, see pp. 53–8, and on Op. 42 in particular see p. 55. A copy of the score in the hand of Otto Scherzer survives in the Württembergische Landesbibliothek, which I thank for the loan of a microfilm.

Ex. 16.3. Molique, String Quartet in B Flat Major, Op. 42,
first movement: (*a*) bars 1–14; (*b*) bars 30–9; (*c*) bars 56–68

(*a*)

Ex. 16.3. *continued*

EX. 16.3. *continued*

(*c*)

is the weakest part of the work, and the quartet as a whole attempts to reach the 'quality of its model' only in the first movement.

The name of Max Bruch, unlike that of Molique, is not forgotten today, though his fame rests primarily on the celebrated Violin Concerto No. 1 in G Minor. Born in Cologne in 1838, Bruch had almost 'outlived himself' by the time of his death in 1920. He achieved widespread recognition at an early age. Although considered a member of the conservative camp, he composed strikingly little chamber music; only his early string quartets, Op. 9 and Op. 10, belong to this genre. As a talent who blossomed early, he studied composition with Heinrich Breidenstein and then, after 1842, with Ferdinand Hiller; he also studied the piano with Carl Reinecke. On Hiller's advice in 1858 he went to Leipzig, where he met Mendelssohn's 'comrades in battle' (Moscheles, Rietz, and Hauptmann). Ferdinand David arranged for the successful performance of his C minor Quartet, Op. 9 in the Gewandhaus on 10 February 1859.[27] Composed around or after 1856, that quartet was followed by the E major Quartet, Op. 10—yet in both works we should consider influences not only of Mendelssohn but also of Schumann, who had become popular in the Rhineland since his Düsseldorf years. Christopher Fifield accepted—clearly with no familiarity with these works—Wilhelm Altmann's largely misguided evaluation of these quartets, and Wilhelm Lauth, in his 1967 dissertation on Bruch's instrumental music, likewise considered them only cursorily.[28]

The slow introduction to Bruch's Op. 10 quartet, with its alternation of widely voiced chords and angular melodic lines, might lead us to expect a potent character similar to that of Schumann's works in the medium. But the obliging tone of the allegro and the melodic spinning-out point in a different direction—without, however, approaching the typical themes of Mendelssohn or their concentrated working-out. The C minor Quartet, Op. 9 is more ambitious (see Ex. 16.4). From the very beginning it refutes Lauth's statement that the lower parts are merely 'filler voices . . . devoid of any thematic or rhythmic life'.[29] The slow introduction is preceded by three bars in the solo first violin that encircle the dominant with leading tones and two dotted rhythms before proceeding up to the dominant in the higher octave. And already here,

[27] Christopher Fifield, *Max Bruch: Biographie eine Komponisten* (Zurich: Schweizer, 1990), 18, 24, 28; further, Johannes Forner, 'Mendelssohns Mitstreiter am Leipziger Konservatorium', *Beiträge zur Musikwissenschaft*, 14 (1972), 185–204. Fifield's study was first published in English as *Max Bruch: His Life and Works* (London: Gollancz, 1988).

[28] Fifield, *Biographie*, 28; Wilhelm Altmann, 'Bruch', in Walter Wilson Cobbett, *Cyclopedic Survey of Chamber Music*, 2nd edn., ed. Colin Mason (London: Oxford University Press, 1963), i. 215; Wilhelm Lauth, *Max Bruchs Instrumentalmusik* (Beiträge zur rheinischen Musikgeschichte, 68; Cologne: Arno Volk, 1967), 25–7.

[29] Lauth, *Instrumentalmusik*, 25.

Ex. 16.4.   Bruch, String Quartet in C Minor, Op. 9,
first movement, beginning

Ex. 16.4. *continued*

the lower voices form motivic variants from which the intensification that leads to the main theme of the Allegro non troppo is derived. The hemiola-like prolongation of the sonority of the first climax (beginning in b. 21) shows considerable skill, as does the transition, with its characteristic rhythmic flexibility. In contrast, the reduction of the voices just before the second theme pairs dotted figures in the outer voices with a prolonged tremolo in the inner ones. This rhythmic impulse recalls Mendelssohn less than it does Schumann, while the second subject is characterized by syncopated inner voices and cantabile outer voices, without being based on a pedal point, as in similar passages in Mendelssohn. The development section, too, is based on the second subject, whose three-note anacrusis is subjected to complementary working-out, leading to a rhythmic intensification that prepares the return of the main theme. Yet the middle of the movement comprises a fugato that begins in B minor and is based on a variant of the main theme. Such a fugal passage in the development, with its thematic transformations and remote tonal position, can hardly be derived from the quartet movements of Beethoven or Mendelssohn; rather, it points to the development section of the first movement of Schumann's A minor Quartet, in which of course the contrapuntal sections derive from the second subject and, to a certain extent, also the cantabile main theme. Thus, in its accomplished technique, expansive harmonic language, and sharply contrasting themes, this movement of Bruch's Op. 9 quartet suggests models in Schumann, while the flowing motion and the transitions in no way belie the approach taken by Mendelssohn. This is also true of the thematic variants in the recapitulation, while the coda represents a compressed net result of all this work.

The A flat major Adagio initially comprises only a filling-out of the alternating lowest notes of the theme by means of continuous eighth-note figurations in the accompaniment. The substantial expansion already achieved in the spinning-out of the melody is deliberately advanced in the E major middle section, and the return of the 'A' section at the end of the movement combines the upper voice with a more compact figuration, in such a fashion that we recognize the model of the lied movement, which was central to Mendelssohn's Op. 44 quartets. The third movement, in triple time, follows the convention of a dance movement with trio and coda; yet its rhythmic alternations, which recall the classical scherzo, stem from thematic material whose dotted quarter notes mark the even metre while a regular pattern of stress appears only in the second strain. The movement derives its appeal from its alternation between stasis and movement, and this appeal remains uncompromised even by lengthy transpositions of the rhythmically calmer trio section. Likewise, the C major finale relies above all on rhythmic impulses. The transition and second subject of this movement constantly stress the 6/8 metre, as often occurs in Mendelssohn's quartets. The thematic mediation when the rhythmic formula of the main theme is added to the cantabile second subject is captivating, as is the unusually dense voicing effected by numerous double-stops. This work's orchestral tendencies might be criticized for leaving so little room for obbligato part-writing. Yet one might also argue that these tendencies parallel Schumann's quartets, which have always been accused of being adaptations of pianistic writing; and such procedures represent explorations of new timbral possibilities that were further developed in the later history of the genre. In other words, Bruch was following a historical trend without relying on Mendelssohn's authority, just as Schumann's procedures also are present only indirectly.

It is certainly not a definitive judgement when one has to concede that a work cannot be considered epigonal. But if Mendelssohn was not an epigone of classicism, then there are certainly rewards to be gained from greater familiarity with the works of a later composer who should be considered not so much an epigone as an intermediary between two generations of master composers.

III

Increasing temporal and geographical distance led to increasing differences between the procedures in the quartets of Mendelssohn and Schumann and those of their generic successors. The only composer who wrote a series of six quartets (as well as an independent quartet movement) during these years was Robert Volkmann—five of whose works in the genre were still in print from the publishers Payne/Eulenberg in London as late as 1892. Born in 1815, Volkmann came from Lommatzsch in Saxony, but except for four years in Vienna, he worked from 1841 onwards primarily in Pest, where he taught at the conservatory under the direction of Liszt from 1875 until his death in 1883. Even if we cannot count Volkmann as part of Mendelssohn's circle, he was nevertheless alleged to be a member of 'the Schumann school'—yet he had no personal ties to either master comparable to those linking him to Brahms from 1874 onwards. Nevertheless, Volkmann studied from 1836 to 1839 with C. F. Becker, who later was involved with the Leipzig Conservatory. Volkmann thus spent his formative years in the city whose musical life centred around Mendelssohn, whom he admired.[30]

---

[30] Hans Volkmann, *Robert Volkmann: Sein Leben und seine Werke* (Leipzig: H. Seemann Nachfolger, 1903), 21.

Volkmann's six quartets were composed over a period of fifteen years, between 1846 and 1861. The first two (Op. 9 in A Minor and Op. 14 in G Minor) were composed, contrary to what their numbers suggest, between 1846 and 1848, while the remaining quartets (No. 3 in G Major, Op. 34, No. 4 in E Minor, Op. 35, No. 5 in F Minor, Op. 37, and No. 6 in E flat major, Op. 43) date from between 1856 and 1861.

Volkmann's quartets, the subject of a recent dissertation by Claudia Krischke, are accessible through scores and, more recently, recordings.[31] Despite some unevenness, Krischke's overview of quartet production and quartet ensembles as they existed in German-speaking countries in the nineteenth century is an important contribution;[32] however, the absence of more detailed examinations of other representative works of the period necessarily creates a gap that can be only partially closed here. For with the exception of the F minor opus, Volkmann's quartets adhere completely to the norms of the character, form, and sequence of movements in the string quartet—yet they cannot be considered direct responses to the quartets of Mendelssohn or Schumann. Rather, we must give them credit not only for their flowing part-writing and learned technical procedures, but also for a thoroughly individual thematic character that they strive to explore within considerable formal constraints. Their themes are not lacking in individual traits, which grant to the melodic language a sharply etched or even striking profile—particularly in the last four works, which surpass their predecessors in quality. Of the pairs of works composed in Vienna (Nos. 3 and 4) and in Pest (Nos. 5 and 6), the quartets in E minor and F minor (Nos. 4 and 5) are especially distinguished, since their departure from the restrictive classicism of their respective counterparts (Nos. 3 and 6) also permits a comparison with Mendelssohn's works in the same keys (G major and E flat major) in the genre.

In Volkmann's quartets, only one of the Scherzi even remotely suggests a Mendelssohnian character; this is the E minor Presto from No. 4, which, however, had been composed already in in 1841 as part of a quartet that was eventually rejected. But in this work the dance movement is in second position, which is usually assigned to the slow movement; like the other scherzi, it retains the traditional simple binary form with trio and coda. In this movement a chordal passage in rapid quarter notes obstructs motivic as well as contrapuntal working-out; groups of eighth notes can break free of the rhythmic lockstep only at structural junctures, and even when the thematic incipit

[31] Claudia Krischke, *Untersuchungen zu den Streichquartetten von Robert Volkmann (1815–1883): Ein Komponist zwischen Schumann und Brahms* (Europäische Hochschulschriften, Reihe 36, Bd. 154; Frankfurt am Main: Peter Lang, 1996). For comments on Volkmann's quartets see also Volkmann, *Robert Volkmann*, 76–7, 89–90.   [32] Krischke, *Untersuchungen*, 175–89.

migrates among the voices the movement proceeds with extremely equal voicing, however innovative it may sound. This procedure changes little in the trio, which is in the parallel major, even though that section is rather more homophonic/chordal and comparatively calm. In Quartet No. 3, the chordal Allegro does begin sharply profiled, with a leap of a sixth and compact melodic paraphrases of the harmony, ending in unison scales. But the lower voices are quickly reduced to the function of accompaniment, and only in the varied reprise do pairs of voices briefly depart from this texture—and the trio, in the parallel major, continues the potent rhythmic language but simplifies the writing still further. Whereas the finale of the three-movement F minor Quartet (No. 5) also assumes characteristics of a scherzo, the distinctive E flat major scherzo from Quartet No. 6 is in 5/4 time—though this is presented in the regular alternation of triple plus duple time, since the measures are virtually analogous rhythmically and are grouped into regular four-bar phrases. The precision of the movement, however, resides less in the metre *per se* than in the increasingly involved complementary rhythmic language, while the second strain of the trio combines an increase in dynamics with chromatic modulations. This movement demonstrates particularly well Volkmann's ability to compose pithy material that is not easily subjected to further manipulation.

The slow movements, except for that in Quartet No. 5, are in triple metres; and since they generally deviate little from strictly homophonic textures they may be considered almost dance-like. The melodic lines predominate in such a fashion that within the ternary structures they permit only an accompanimental role for the other parts. This in no way precludes that within the tripartite structure the closing section turns to paraphrased figuration—as, for example, in No. 3, when the melody is taken up in the bass register, or in No. 6, when it is almost obscured by virtuoso ornamentation. In the ambitious F minor Quartet (No. 5), the duple-metre Adagio in D flat major changes to C sharp minor in its central section, but the constituent parts are linked by a dotted anacrusis figure with striking intervals. The tendency to employ soloistic figurations, which in this work contradict the intended hymnic quality, then wins the upper hand in the closing section, when the characteristic leaps of the melody are filled in by scalar figures. Only the B major Andantino from Quartet No. 4 distances itself from an adversary relationship between chorale-like textures and ornamental figurations. Divided into three analogous sections, this movement comprises just seventy-six bars. It not only retains its hymnic character throughout, but also uses the subordinate voices to reinforce the structural delineation through pronounced nuances in the harmonic language. Precisely because the movement strives for nothing more than what it achieves, within its limitations it is fascinating because of its carefully balanced interrelationships.

Unmistakable rondo-like traits characterize the finales of Volkmann's quartets, and those of Nos. 3 and 4 also assume features reminiscent of sonata form. In the Allegretto sostenuto of No. 3, where the exposition and development are not separated, the alternation of constituent parts recalls more readily the conventions of the rondo. Chordal figures describing a dominant-seventh chord precede the principal thematic idea in 6/8 time, but chordal textures rather than motivic development also characterize the remainder of the movement, which is extensively modified by extended passages of figuration. This part remains ambiguous despite considerable harmonic elaboration, since even the transitions are accomplished more through dynamic and rhythmic means than through motivic mediation. The finale is preceded by a slow introduction only in No. 6, but this Andantino section reveals no motivic relationships to the following rondo, which includes three refrains. The duple metre of the movement is reinterpreted by means of the triplets in the principal voices into 6/8, and there is a touch of humour when the scalar incipit of the refrain (which is characterized by chromatic interpolations) is augmented to quarter notes in the contrasting couplet. But however much the movement's agile character may recall Mendelssohn's compositions, it remains completely devoid of contrapuntal passages, such as those familiar especially from the Finale of Mendelssohn's Octet for Strings (to which the coda of Volkmann's quartet alludes).

As mentioned above, the finale of Volkmann's Quartet No. 5 suggests a rondo in that the energetic dotted figure is repeatedly interrupted by rests of a bar or more (a technique also encountered in rondos in the works of Haydn). In particular the first refrain, with its repetition of entire passages of musical material, resembles the trio section of a dance movement, while the second couplet stands out as an episodic andantino, after which the third refrain immediately states the concluding stretto that smooths the dotted rhythms into repeated notes. The finale of the E minor Quartet (No. 4), cast as a conventional sonata form with repeated exposition, also recalls Mendelssohn. But it is based on repeated articulated eighth notes that also support the second subject as accompaniment and remain present even when the upper voices move in triplets. This movement remains unimposing not only by dispensing with developmental transitions but also by including an unpretentious development section that treats the themes chordally in various transpositions. In the one place where a fugato emerges, the thematic incipit consists simply of a cadential drop of a fourth with an elaboration in triplets; no attempt is made to associate this material with earlier themes. There are thus unmistakable structural differences vis-à-vis Mendelssohn's music, and the allusions to Mendelssohn remain mostly superficial.

The strengths and weaknesses of Volkmann's quartets are most clearly exemplified in the first movements, which especially in Nos. 3 and 6 are cast as sonata forms that owe much to a rather conventional thematic idiom. The resemblance of the main theme of the first movement in Quartet No. 3 to the *Volkslied* from Mendelssohn's *Lorelei* was certainly not intended,[33] but in No. 6 a fanfare-like triadic line is followed by a cantabile melody entrusted only to the uppermost part. In both movements, transitional as well as developmental passages focus solely on the process of modulation; there is no motivic working-out, and the essentially homorhythmic texture changes only slightly.

More significant are the first movements of Quartets Nos. 4 and 5, which unmistakably point to their counterparts in Mendelssohn's quartets Op. 44 No. 2 and Op. 80 not only in their analogous keys. Volkmann's F minor movement, like Mendelssohn's, begins with a tremolo that is initially stated in unison and then expanded chordally. But rather than the smooth timbral surface of Mendelssohn's Op. 80, this movement, with its expressive, irascible gestures and clearly defined cadential structure, cultivates its motivic succinctness. The tremolo thus rapidly becomes a mere accompaniment for the triadic figures of the outer voices. These voices substitute a six-bar solo cadenza for motivic working-out, and the second subject is reduced to a four-bar interpolation accompanied by a continuation of the tremolo. The compact development section also makes do with transposed quotations of material presented earlier rather than thematic working-out, and however emphatic the concluding stretto may seem, the taut overall form of the movement is equally devoid of any intensive thematic development.

The E minor first movement of Quartet No. 4 likewise reveals the dangers of relying too heavily on material that permits only limited development (see Ex. 16.5). The main theme in the uppermost voice may owe something to Mendelssohn's thematic techniques, but the accompaniment consists only of sparsely voiced chords, and the statement of that theme in the viola at the beginning of the bridge (bar 20) marks its last appearance until the retransition. The replacement of deliberate mediation with a mere ordering of groups could hardly be clearer. To be sure, the bridge accomplishes an impressive intensification that culminates in massed chords; the cantabile second subject layers the upper voices over one another quite effectively; and the closing group that immediately follows again reveals the 'elfin character' that Volkmann so

---

[33] See Volkmann's letter commenting on the matter, quoted in Volkmann, *Volkmann*, 91.

Ex. 16.5.   Volkmann, String Quartet in E Minor, first movement, beginning

Ex. 16.5. *continued*

cultivated. But such strongly contrasting themes cancel each other out, and the development section is based exclusively on material from the bridge and the closing group. Only just before the recapitulation does the main theme return, and it also constitutes the end of the coda.

Certainly one might counter that Volkmann downplays the conventions of thematic development in order to rely on the potentials of the themes, as Schumann had done. The predominant melodic voices are already so strongly accented in the themes themselves that the other voices naturally assume the character of accompaniment and even in the development section never function as an obbligato. While the material is hardly transformed or treated contrapuntally, it does create the impression of a certain continuity among the thematic groups. This continuity accounts for the expressive character of the work's themes, but at the same time the thematic material must possess a certain qualitative substance if it is to be treated at such length. The more routine and at the same time expressive the music is, the greater the ambivalence of the relationship between thematic substance and thematic development. Like Bruch, Volkmann seems to be a transitional figure, but the distance from the pithiness of Schumann's themes becomes all the more striking precisely because of Volkmann's reliance on his thematic material. And while the melodic and rhythmic character of Volkmann's themes may be derived from Mendelssohn, they possess none of the subtle construction that characterizes Mendelssohn's melodies. Thus, apart from certain thematic analogies, all that points to a 'Leipzig School' in Volkmann's works is the flowing transitions that are primarily dynamic rather than structural in nature. There is therefore little reason to consider Volkmann one of the 'posthumous Schumannians' even though he did seek to follow the traditions of the genre to a considerable extent.

Despite discernible differences in the quality of individual works, the history of a genre in the nineteenth century does not present itself simply as a composite picture of heroes and epigones. A reasonable judgement must therefore be based on differentiations of compositional techniques if it is to rise above describing apparent stylistic similarities. In this way different levels of achievement become readily evident in cases such as that of Volkmann, who imitates only the tone of Mendelssohn's music. Conversely, an idiom such as Volkmann's need not come to the fore when the discussion focuses on compositional techniques. Thus, Bruch's and Gade's thematic material points primarily to Schumann's influence, even though their themes lack the potential of Schumann's, while their compositional techniques do not distance themselves correspondingly from Mendelssohn's legacy of thematic mediation.

The enduring validity of these techniques may be demonstrated in the quartets by a composer of the 'New German School' such as Joachim Raff as well as in those of 'Leipzig' composers such as Karl Goldmark, Felix Draeseke, and Josef Gabriel Rheinberger. The demise of these techniques did not occur until after the beginning of the new century, with the composition in 1909 of the fifth and final string quartet (G minor, Op. 287) of Carl Reinecke, sovereign ruler of the medium, just a year before his death.[34]

Of course, in the history of musical composition as elsewhere it is the heirs and not the forebears who are responsible for making the most of their heritage. It would thus be misguided to hold Mendelssohn or Schumann responsible for the works of those whom others declared to be their party colleagues. But to the extent that those composers' works deserve careful consideration we may observe in them, just as earlier in the wake of classicism, a desire to achieve a balance and to avoid pure imitation. Only by considering these works along with more familiar ones can we avoid the danger of substituting a selective view of history for viable historiography.

At the same time, such music reveals that the new concept that was signalled by Mendelssohn's quartets and Schumann's reactions to them became a standard far more potent than that of the classical quartet, which was receding into historical distance. Viewed from this perspective, Mendelssohn and Schumann themselves become the classicists of the genre, and the significance of the historic accomplishments that they achieved independently of Schubert in their treatment of classicism becomes fully evident. Only under such conditions could it have been possible for Brahms, after a number of rejected attempts, to develop a completely new process with his Op. 51 quartets. Because of his historical distance, Brahms was able to focus on thematic development with renewed strictness, just as Beethoven had done with far-reaching results earlier in the century. Even when Brahms's thematic complexes are characterized by the sort of continuity that previously had been cultivated by Mendelssohn and Schumann, they are also crucially informed by their motivic usefulness. Such a recourse was possible because of historical caesurae and traditions similar to those that had shaped Mendelssohn's relationship to Bach and to classicism earlier in the century. But the existence of a resonance so extensive that it was able to reverberate so strongly in seemingly

---

[34] *Verzeichniss der bis jetzt im Druck erschienenen Compositionen von Carl Reinecke*, ed. Franz Reinecke (Leipzig: Breitkopf & Härtel, 1889); expanded version by Nikolai Topusov as 'Carl Reinecke: Beiträge zu seinem Leben und seiner Symphonik' (unpublished diss., Berlin, 1943), 445–50. For information on Reinecke's earlier quartets see Wilhelm Josef von Wasielewski, *Carl Reinecke: Sein Leben, Wirken und Schaffen* (Leipzig: J. H. Zimmermann, 1892), 43–4, 49–50.

opposite directions is probably not just an indication of Mendelssohn's historical significance. Ultimately, the historical resonances of Mendelssohn's quartets stem from an aesthetic integrity that functions as a complement to the works' potency as contributions to the history of their genre.

—translated by John Michael Cooper

17

～～

The Composer as Other: Gender and Race in the Biography of Felix Mendelssohn

MARIAN WILSON KIMBER

IN the mid-nineteenth century, Felix Mendelssohn Bartholdy personified the Victorian gentleman; evidence of his 'manliness' was found in his class status, his success, his family relations, and his music.[1] George Grove described the composer as 'one perfectly balanced nature, in whose life, whose letters, and whose music alike, all is at once manly and refined'.[2] Critic Henry Chorley wrote, '[d]emanding as it does, execution without grimace; fancy, cheerful and excursive, but never morbid; and feeling under the control of a serene, not sluggish spirit—Mendelssohn's is manly music; and looses [*sic*] effect beyond that of almost any other of his contemporaries, when attempted by female hands'.[3]

However, by the century's close, both Mendelssohn and his music were criticized as lacking in the very masculine qualities for which they were previously praised. In 1905 Elbert Hubbard, admitting that 'there have been some unsexed, or at least unmanly men, who were great musicians', found that '[t]he character of Mendelssohn was distinctly feminine'.[4] In Aubrey Beardsley's caricature, printed in the *The Savoy* in 1896, Mendelssohn is depicted as effeminate, from the dangling curls of his hair, to the delicate bows on his

---

[1] See Joseph A. Mussulman, *Music in the Cultured Generation: A Social History of Music in America, 1870–1900* (Evanston, Ill.: Northwestern University Press, 1971), 59–63.

[2] Sir George Grove, *Beethoven, Schubert, Mendelssohn* (London: Macmillan, 1951), 391.

[3] Henry Fothergill Chorley, *Modern German Music* (London: Smith, Elder & Co., 1854, repr. New York: Da Capo Press, 1973), 51–2.

[4] Elbert Hubbard, *Little Journeys to the Homes of Great Musicians* (New York: The Knickerbocker Press, 1905), 191, 201.

PL. 17.1. Aubrey Beardsley's caricature of Mendelssohn

shoes (see Pl. 17.1).[5] In 1898 W. S. B. Mathews wrote that Mendelssohn's works are 'more feminine than masculine', and the following year R. Farquharson Sharp suggested, 'in his music this sweetness may sometimes verge on effeminacy'.[6] Even Mendelssohn enthusiast John Sullivan Dwight was forced to admit, 'with all the Jewish masculinity of his Psalms, his male choruses and his part-songs, one feels the feminine, the sentimental minor vein predominate upon the whole'.[7] Daniel Gregory Mason's 1906 treatment

[5] In *The Savoy*, 8 (Dec. 1896), 63, reprinted in Brian Reade, *Beardsley* (London: Studio Vista, 1967), pl. 448. *The Savoy* also published the first article on Nietzsche by Havelock Ellis and 'A Mad Saint' by Cesare Lombroso, two writers whose work figured prominently in discussions of race and gender during this period. See E. Leonore Casford, *The Magazines of the 1890s* (Eugene: University of Oregon, 1929), 21–3.

[6] W. S. B. Mathews, *The Masters and their Music* (Philadelphia: Theodore Presser, 1898; repr. New York: AMS, 1971), 74; R. Farquharson Sharp, *Makers of Music: Biographical Sketches of Great Composers* (New York: Charles Scribner's Sons, 1913), 155. (The first edition of Farquharson Sharp's survey appeared in 1899.)

[7] John Sullivan Dwight, 'Felix Mendelssohn Bartholdy', in John Knowles Paine, Theodore Thomas, and Karl Klauser (eds.), *Famous Composers and their Works*, i (Boston: J. B. Millet, 1891), 416–36 at 435.

best represents the gendered rhetoric used to describe the composer and his music:

His personality is tenuous, over-rarefied; he seems more like a faun than a man. . . . His style . . . lacks the rugged force, the virile energy, the occasional harshness and discordance even, of the natural human voice; its reading of life, in which there is ugliness, crudity, and violence as well as beauty is too fastidiously expurgated. . . . The effeminate element in his work is probably chiefly responsible for the indifference, boredom, or distaste with which it is nowadays so often received.[8]

What did it mean for Victorians to ascribe the quality of 'manliness' to the composer? Why did Mendelssohn's personality and his music become 'feminized' in the late nineteenth century? In this chapter I shall demonstrate how the feminization of Mendelssohn and his music resulted from a larger cultural discourse about masculinity and race that flourished after 1880.[9]

MENDELSSOHN AND VICTORIAN CONSTRUCTIONS OF MASCULINITY

In the past decade, social and cultural historians have begun critical examination of Victorian constructions of masculinity, or 'manliness', and the various changes that took place in masculine ideals late in the nineteenth century.[10] While it would be wrong to suggest that manliness represented a single, easily definable concept restricted to a particular geographical area, in the period

[8] Daniel Gregory Mason, *The Romantic Composers* (New York: Macmillan, 1906), 191–3. Thanks to Jonathan Bellman for pointing out Mason's obviously anti-Semitic attitudes as they are revealed in *Tune in, America: A Study of Our Coming Musical Independence* (New York: Alfred A. Knopf, 1931), 160–2.

[9] This discourse has also affected the reception of Schubert and Chopin. See David Gramit, 'Constructing a Victorian Schubert: Music, Biography, and Cultural Values', *Nineteenth Century Music*, 7 (1993), 65–78; and Jeffery Kallberg, 'Small Fairy Voices: Sex, History, and Meaning in Chopin', in *Chopin at the Boundaries: Sex, History and Musical Genre* (Cambridge, Mass.: Harvard University Press, 1996), 62–86.

[10] See Gail Bederman, *Manliness and Civilization: A Cultural History of Gender and Race in the United Sates, 1880–1917* (Chicago: University of Chicago Press, 1995); Mark Carnes and Clyde Griffen (eds.), *Meanings for Manhood: Constructions of Masculinity in Victorian America* (Chicago: University of Chicago Press, 1990); J. A. Mangan and James Walvin (eds.), *Manliness and Morality: Middle-Class Masculinity in Britain and America, 1800–1940* (New York: St. Martin's Press, 1987); George L. Mosse, *The Image of Man: The Creation of Modern Masculinity* (New York: Oxford University Press, 1996); Michael Roper and John Tosh, *Manful Assertions: Masculinities in Britain since 1800* (London: Routledge, 1991); Anthony Rotundo, *American Manhood: Transformations in Masculinity from the Revolution to the Modern Era* (New York: Basic, 1993). Also useful is Elliot Gorn, *The Manly Art: Bare-Knuckle Prizefighting in America* (Ithaca, NY: Cornell University Press, 1986).

immediately following Mendelssohn's death it became a pervasive feature of middle-class values in Britain and America; George Mosse has suggested that Germany and England shared ideals of masculinity as well.[11] Manliness was derived from the respectability and gentility of the middle class and included the qualities of earnestness, selflessness, and integrity. A man's strong character could be built through exercising his will to control his masculine passions. According to Gail Bederman, manliness consisted of 'the mingled honor, high-mindedness and strength stemming from this powerful self-mastery'.[12] Such control permeated all aspects of a man's life. Thus, this description of the composer from 1869 reflects the ideals of manliness:

Mendelssohn was more than a great musician: he was a great man. . . . [H]is moral qualities balanced the intellectual and aesthetic. He was good as well as great. . . . His domestic relations were tender and pure. His affection for his friends was earnest and enduring. His religious sentiments were throughout his life his master.[13]

Julius Benedict's statement that '[l]ife, to him, was an overflowing cup, of which he drank, fully, indeed, but yet wisely',[14] exemplifies the belief that Mendelssohn exercised manly self-control. Chorley's description of the composer's artistic control, or 'feeling under the control of a . . . serene spirit', was echoed by Mrs A. B. Jameson when she wrote that '[i]n Mendelssohn, the enormous creative power was modified by the intellect and the conscience'.[15]

The numerous descriptions of Mendelssohn in the 1860s and 1870s that stress his moral purity conform to contemporary ideals of manliness. 'Nothing vulgar, affected, or unclean, could approach him' stated a writer for the *Edinburgh Review*.[16] Amanda Gere contrasted Mendelssohn with Chopin, writing, 'There is nothing to forgive, nothing to be sorry for . . . crowned as [Mendelssohn] is with an aureole of purity that is almost saintly.'[17]

While it is easy for modern scholars to dismiss these rhapsodic descriptions as hero-worship in all its Victorian excess, Mendelssohn's reported exemplary behaviour demonstrated that he possessed the necessary personal control

[11] Mangan and Walvin, *Manliness and Morality*, 2; George Mosse, *Nationalism and Sexuality: Respectability and Abnormal Sexuality in Modern Europe* (New York: Howard Fertig, 1985), 21.

[12] Bederman, *Manliness and Civilization*, 12.

[13] Review of Elise Polko, *Reminiscences of Felix Mendelssohn-Bartholdy: A Social and Artistic Biography*, in *Harper's New Monthly Magazine*, 39 (June 1869), 148.

[14] Jules [*sic*] Benedict, *Sketch of the Life and Works of the Late Felix Mendelssohn Bartholdy* (London: John Murray, 1850), 16.

[15] Mrs [Anna B.] Jameson, *A Commonplace Book of Thoughts, Memories, and Fancies* (London: Longman, Brown, Green, & Longmans, 1854), 289.

[16] 'Felix Mendelssohn's Letters', *Edinburgh Review*, 115 (1862), 128.

[17] Amanda R. Gere, 'Frederick Chopin', *Atlantic Monthly*, 31 (Apr. 1873), 420.

for manliness. Indeed, the most important sources of information about the composer published in the nineteenth century, the two collections of his letters and Sebastian Hensel's *Die Familie Mendelssohn*,[18] helped to create the notion of Mendelssohn as a model man. Hensel hoped that his book would be read 'as the chronicle of a good middle-class German family' ('als Chronik einer guten deutschen Bürgerfamilie').[19] Paul Mendelssohn-Bartholdy envisioned his brother's published letters as a potent moral force; in a letter to Karl Klingemann after Felix's death, he wrote that 'alone his work could become, in my opinion, a guiding star for many, many people'.[20] Reviews of the collected letters of 1833–47 suggest that he was not alone in his belief. One English reviewer declared, 'Well would it have been had our young men modeled themselves after his indefatigable industry, his unswerving sense of duty, his upright charity, his resolution to gather knowledge and to recognize what was good in Art, no matter whether it agreed or disagreed with his own individuality!'[21] In America, the *Atlantic Monthly* proclaimed, 'We wish our religious societies would call out a few of the letters of this man and scatter them broadcast over the land. . . . [F]or they are books which our young men, our young women, our pastors, our whole thoughtful and aspiring community ought to read and circulate.'[22]

The reasons both Mendelssohn and his music ceased to be 'manly' by the end of the century are numerous. The most obvious has been suggested by various scholars: the place of Mendelssohn's lieder and small lyrical genres for piano in domestic music-making linked the composer with the women's sphere.[23] In the case of the *Lieder ohne Worte*, the association was further solidified by the composer's dedication of the pieces to women.[24] However,

---

[18] *Briefe 1830–2* (1861); *Briefe 1833–47* (1863); Hensel, *Familie* (1879). These immensely popular volumes also appeared in English translation and went through numerous editions in the following decades. [19] Hensel, *Familie* (1908), i, p. ix.

[20] Letter of 10 Dec. 1847, quoted in Ingeborg Stolzenberg, 'Paul Mendelssohn-Bartholdy nach dem Tode seines Bruders Felix', *Mendelssohn-Studien*, 8 (1993), 179–95 at 184: 'Allein das Werk könnte meiner Meinung nach ein leitender Stern für viele, viele Menschen werden.'

[21] Review of *Letters of Felix Mendelssohn Bartholdy from 1833 to 1847*, from *Athenaeum*, repr. in *Dwight's Journal of Music*, 23 (26 Dec. 1863), 155.

[22] [W. L. Gage], Review of *Letters of Felix Mendelssohn Bartholdy from 1833 to 1847*, in *Atlantic Monthly*, 15 (1865), 127.

[23] See Judith Tick, 'Passed Away is the Piano Girl: Changes in American Musical Life, 1870–1900', in Jane Bowers and Judith Tick (eds.), *Women Making Music: The Western Art Tradition, 1150–1950* (Urbana, Ill.: University of Illinois Press, 1986), 336–8; and Jeffery Kallberg, 'The Harmony of the Tea Table: Gender and Ideology in the Piano Nocturne', in *Chopin at the Boundaries*, 32–8.

[24] Christa Jost has suggested that the women to whom Mendelssohn dedicated the *Lieder ohne Worte* were all accomplished pianists, even if most of them were, by virtue of their gender, amateurs. See her *Mendelssohns Lieder ohne Worte* (Tutzing: Hans Schneider, 1988), 55–63.

Mendelssohn's close relationships with Fanny Hensel and the other women in his family circle, widely reported in contemporary biographical portrayals, also fuelled the association of the composer with the 'feminine'. This notion found a voice early on in Adolf Bernhard Marx's 1865 description of Mendelssohn's youth, in which he asserts that the result of the composer's 'constant company of his sister's young female friends' and his 'dallying in this diminutive and sweetly feminine sphere' was the 'sweet, flirtatious, tender' *Lieder ohne Worte*, a genre that required little talent and less intellect.[25] In an article published in America, Marx's student Hermann Zopff also blamed Mendelssohn's supposed musical failings on the female circles in which he travelled, writing that his artistic vision was

narrowed by that coterie of Berlin ladies, who were in raptures with his every motion, with his every naive or roguish trick or word; who each of them was eager to possess another original little song, with or without words, written by himself and dedicated to herself or the pen with which he wrote or whatever else he used. ... That was the insidious poison that was more and more to strangle the high aspiration for which Nature had endowed him![26]

The gendered characteristics of Mendelssohn's biographical persona were also transformed by larger cultural forces in the period from 1880 to 1910, a period in which the values associated with masculinity underwent tremendous alterations. The new masculine ideal rejected, in part, the values of control and moral purity, and celebrated instead the more 'primitive' aspects of men's natures, such as aggressiveness, physical force, and male heterosexuality. The primal passions, which were to be entirely restrained in an earlier era, were now viewed as part of a man's natural animal energy, and there was a new focus both on athleticism and on men's groups modelled after 'primitive' tribes. The popularity of fraternal organizations, the creation of boys' clubs such as the Boy Scouts, the Young Men's Christian Association and its German counterpart, the Christlicher Verein Jünger Männer, the increasing respectability of working-class entertainments such as pugilism, and the religious movement known as 'muscular Christianity' all reflected the new masculine ideals. The German youth movement of the early twentieth century espoused masculine values of toughness, athleticism, and physical beauty,[27]

---

[25] Adolph Bernhard Marx, *Erinnerungen aus meinem Leben*, i (Berlin: O. Janke, 1865), excerpts translated by Susan Gillespie in *MHW*, 206–20 at 211.

[26] Hermann Zopff, 'Characteristics of Felix Mendelssohn-Bartholdy', *Dwight's Journal of Music*, 11 (15 Aug. 1857), 154.

[27] Mosse, *Nationalism and Sexuality*, 45–6. See also Mosse's *The Crisis of German Ideology: Intellectual Origins of the Third Reich* (New York: Grosset and Dunlap, 1964), 171–89.

and the German Protestant men's morality associations (*Sittlichkeitsvereine*) shaped what John Fout has dubbed 'hypermaleness'.[28]

In the light of these changes, the previous ideal of 'self-possession' was now considered 'effeminate' and 'overcivilized' (the latter term was coined during the 1890s).[29] In a letter to a young protégé, Hans von Bülow called for musicians to adopt a tougher stance: 'The times are now over when artists and those who unfortunately limp after them the most—the musicians, particularly distinguished for their lack of character—were lackeys, milksops, rabbits, molluscs. . . . The religion of Bach, Beethoven, and Wagner demands from its apostles first of all "manliness".'[30] George Trumbull Ladd linked the new masculine ideals to men's compositional abilities: 'it is the coarseness of greed and lust and anger, the more brutal impulse, which moves the male will to its strongest and most determined license of expression'.[31] In this cultural context, Mendelssohn's previous virtues were now seen as vices. 'Has mawkish sentimentality become the shibboleth of the progress, civilization and refinement of this vaunted age?' taunted one defender of pugilism. 'If so, then in Heaven's name leave us a saving touch of honest, old-fashioned barbarism! Then when we come to die, we shall die, leaving men behind us, and not a race of eminently respectable female saints.'[32] Clearly, Mendelssohn now fell in the latter category. That the ideals of self-restraint and morality were no longer considered masculine, but were now feminine, can be seen in C. E. Bourne's 1884 assessment of Mendelssohn:

In the ideal purity of his thoughts and character there is something sacred, that, according to the bent of our nature, we either look up to and reverence afar off, as we do a nobly beautiful and stainless woman, or sneer at and despise as wanting the alloy of brutal roughness or grossness we are inclined to admire in ourselves.[33]

---

[28] John C. Fout, 'The Moral Purity Movement in Wilhelmine Germany and the Attempt to Regulate Male Behavior', *Journal of Men's Studies*, 1 (1992), 3–31; also id., 'Sexual Politics in Wilhelmine Germany: The Male Gender Crisis, Moral Purity, and Homophobia', *Journal of the History of Sexuality*, 2 (1992), 388–421.   [29] Bederman, *Manliness and Civilization*, 17.

[30] Letter of 2 Feb. 1875 from Hans von Bülow to Eduard von Welz, quoted from *Briefe und Schriften von Hans von Bülow*, v: *1872–1880*, ed. Marie von Bülow (2nd edn., Leipzig: Breitkopf & Härtel, 1904), 250–1: 'Die Zeiten des Lakaienthums, des Waschlappenthums, des Kaninchenthums, des Molluskenthums für den Künstler und den leider bisher unter ihnen — den Künstlern — am meisten nachhinkenden, am stärksten durch Charakterlosigkeit hervorragenden Musiker — sind vorüber . . . Die Religion Bach's, Beethoven's und Wagner's verlangt von ihren Aposteln in erster Instanz "Männlichkeit".'

[31] George Trumbull Ladd, 'Why Women Cannot Compose Music', *Yale Review*, 6 (July 1917), 804.

[32] Duffield Osborne, 'A Defense of Pugilism', *North American Review*, 146 (Apr. 1888), 435.

[33] C. E. Bourne, *The Great Composers, or Stories of the Lives of Eminent Musicians* (9th edn., London: Swan, Sonnenschein & Co., 1902), 243–4.

Bourne's 'brutal roughness' and the 'rugged force', 'virile energy', 'crudity', and 'violence' that Mason believed Mendelssohn's music lacked are all part of the rhetoric that described masculinity at the end of the century.[34]

Changes in the understanding of masculinity also affected ideas about the male body. In the 1860s in America, the ideal masculine body was considered 'lean and wiry', but by the end of the century a bulkier, more muscular physique built through 'strenuous exercise' and team sports was desirable.[35] By the end of the century heroes in American magazines were described in terms of their impressive physical size and strength, contrary to the earlier ideal of moral purity.[36] An 1889 article in the *Musical Times* entitled 'Manliness in Music' noted that Apollo, the patron god of musicians, was also a 'considerable athelete', and that many musicians were also 'keen sportsmen'. It assured readers that even though the notation of a composition took place at a desk, the 'actual inspiration' came 'upon composers when in the open air'.[37] Mendelssohn, even with the 'great deal of manliness packed into his little body' recounted by Grove, no longer fit the masculine physical ideal.[38] Stephen S. Stratton's 1901 biography of Mendelssohn exemplifies the attitude that men should be physically and mentally 'tough' when it says that 'if Felix had had to rough it at a public school, his disposition would have been hardened to a certain extent, and he might not have been so easily offended and out of sorts as happened at times'.[39] Spending his childhood in a domestic sphere largely inhabited by women had prevented Mendelssohn from being socialized in a manner that would ensure his masculine nature.

Mendelssohn's upper-class status and cultivated upbringing now seemed to suggest that he lacked the primitive strength necessary for survival.[40] From the 1860s on, medicine had become increasingly concerned with an affliction

[34] On the association of music with the feminine in late 19th- and early 20th-c. American culture, see Judith Tick, 'Charles Ives and Gender Ideology', in Ruth A. Solie (ed.), *Musicology and Difference: Gender and Sexuality in Music Scholarship* (Berkeley: University of California Press, 1993), 90–7; and Catherine Parsons Smith, '"A Distinguishing Virility": Feminism and Modernism in American Art Music', in Susan C. Cook and Judy S. Tsou (eds.), *Cecilia Reclaimed: Feminist Perspectives on Gender and Music* (Urbana, Ill.: University of Illinois Press, 1994), 90–106.

[35] Bederman, *Manliness and Civilization*, 15.   [36] Rotundo, *American Manhood*, 223.

[37] 'Manliness in Music', *Musical Times*, 30 (1 Aug. 1889), 460–1.

[38] Grove, *Beethoven, Schubert, Mendelssohn*, 366.

[39] Stephen S. Stratton, *Mendelssohn* (London: J. M. Dent, 1901), 168. Stratton's source for this idea is Julius Schubring, 'Reminiscences of Felix Mendelssohn-Bartholdy, on his 57th Birthday, February 3rd, 1866', in *Musical World*, 31 (12 and 19 May 1866), reprinted (abr.) in *MHW*, 221–36.

[40] See George Bernard Shaw on how workmen and members of the artisan class hated Mendelssohn's *St Paul* and *Elijah*, in 'Faust at the Albert Hall', *Star* (31 Oct. 1889), reprinted in Dan H. Laurence (ed.), *How to Become a Musical Critic* (New York: Hill & Wang, 1961), 172–3.

called neurasthenia, defined as 'nervelessness—a lack of nerve force'.[41] Those more likely to overtax their limited energies were men with superior intellect; extensive cerebral activity, such as ceaseless composing, for example, would drain the body of its physical power. In his internationally circulated text on neurasthenia, *American Nervousness* (1881), physician George Beard blamed the disease on civilization itself.[42] Neurasthenia was the disease of upper-class overcivilized intellectuals, whose bodies, when stricken, became weak and effeminate. Doubts about Mendelssohn's nerve resources had been expressed as early as 1869 by Eduard Devrient, who wrote that the composer's gifts 'caused me to worry whether the nervous power of the brain could sustain such unreasonable demands through the length of an ordinary life'.[43] R. H. Haweis's *Music and Morals* (1872) described how Mendelssohn's brain was 'overstimulated', how 'premature decay' could not be prevented, and how the composer was 'constantly overtaxed to the limits of endurance by nervous excitement'.[44] The composer's premature death was frequently attributed to exhaustion stemming from the composition of *Elijah*, rather than to any specific medical condition.

The 'self-control' praised by George Grove in Mendelssohn's romantic relationships[45] was transformed into 'passionlessness' in late nineteenth-century and twentieth-century biographical treatments of the composer. His trip to Scheveningen before proposing to Cécile Jeanrenaud, supposedly to test his love for her, was formerly praised as the evidence of his proper self-restraint. In later writings, it is subsequently transformed into proof of his lack of true feeling and is roundly criticized. Hubbard goes so far as to suggest that Mendelssohn should not have married: 'the slight, joyous, girlish youth, should have preserved his Cecilia-like virginity'.[46] The supposed

[41] See Cynthia Eagle Russett, *Sexual Science: The Victorian Construction of Womanhood* (Cambridge, Mass.: Harvard University Press, 1989), 112–14, and Bederman, *Manliness and Civilization*, 84–8.

[42] On the influence of Beard's work on German physicians, see Sander L. Gilman, *Difference and Pathology: Stereotypes of Sexuality, Race and Madness* (Ithaca, NY: Cornell University Press, 1985), 201–4.

[43] Devrient, *Erinnerungen*, 69: 'erregte mir oft die Sorge, ob die Nervenkraft eines Gehirnes solche Zumuthungen eine gewöhnliche Lebensdauer lang ertragen könne?'

[44] R. H. Haweis, *Music and Morals* (New York: Harper & Brothers, [1872]), 286–7.

[45] Grove, *Beethoven, Schubert, Mendelssohn*, 309.

[46] Hubbard, *Little Journeys*, 210–11. Hubbard's description of Mendelssohn as a young man and his relationship with Goethe has noticeable homoerotic overtones. Although Jews were considered more likely to be homosexuals, I have not found any other examples of this kind of treatment in the Mendelssohn literature of this period. The notion has resurfaced in more recent scholarship, however; see Lawrence Kramer, 'The Lied as Cultural Practice: Tutelage, Gender and Desire in Mendelssohn's Goethe Songs', in id., *Classical Music and Postmodern Knowledge* (Berkeley: University of California Press, 1995), 143–73.

'passionlessness' of the composer's otherwise happy marriage became an ongoing theme in his biography and can be found in more recent biographies by George Marek, Heinrich Jacob, and Eric Werner.[47] Mason and others link a lack of passion in Mendelssohn's music with its 'mild, tentative, and restrained application of artistic principles'.[48] Walter Dahms wrote that '[h]is ideal was the classical composers and their striving for architectural effects. What could women be to him?'[49] George Bernard Shaw criticized Mendelssohnian 'culture' for its 'reticence' and its 'chastity'.[50] Many of these writings make at best a nebulous distinction between the supposed lack of musical passion and erotic passion in Mendelssohn's life; the general suggestion is that Mendelssohn lacked both.

While other fin-de-siècle biographies about the composer do not portray Mendelssohn as lacking in masculinity, they often portray him as perpetually child-like. The result is that the prodigy seems to remain a young boy, immature and somewhat asexual, or at least incapable of adult passion. Phrases like 'boyish disposition' and 'childlike simplicity' abound in descriptions of the composer. The continual comparison of Mendelssohn with a child again links him to women, who, according to an 1887 article by psychologist George John Romanes, had a normal emotional state of 'comparative childishness'.[51]

GENDER, JEWISHNESS, AND THE SCIENCE OF RACE

More importantly, Mendelssohn's affiliation with the feminine also stemmed from anti-Semitic racial theories extending well beyond Wagner's *Das Judentum in der Musik* (1851). The influence of Wagner's anti-Semitic assessment

[47] Heinrich Eduard Jacob, *Felix Mendelssohn and his Times*, trans. Richard and Clara Winston (Englewood Cliffs, NJ: Prentice-Hall, 1963), 139–46; George Marek, *Gentle Genius: The Story of Felix Mendelssohn* (New York: Funk & Wagnalls, 1972), 246–59; Werner, *New Image*, 302–8. For a brief survey of how the notion of 'passionlessness' has led biographers to misrepresent Mendelssohn's marriage, see also Marian Wilson [Kimber], 'Mendelssohn's Wife: Love, Art and Romantic Biography', *Nineteenth-Century Studies*, 6 (1992), 1–18.

[48] Mason, *The Romantic Composers*, 193.

[49] Walter Dahms, *Mendelssohn* (9th edn., Berlin: Schuster & Loeffler, 1922; first edn. 1919), 110–11: 'Sein Ideal waren die Klassiker und ihr Streben nach architektonischen Wirkungen. Was konnten ihm die Frauen sein?'

[50] Shaw, review of Wagner's 'On Conducting', *Pall Mall Gazette* (28 May 1887), repr. in *How to Become a Musical Critic*, 132.

[51] George John Romanes, 'Mental Differences Between Men and Women', *Nineteenth Century*, 21 (1887), 659–61, quoted in Russett, *Sexual Science*, 43.

of Jewish musical creativity was far-reaching,[52] and to find anti-Semitic undertones in Mendelssohn literature of the period is not surprising. However, what is more important for our understanding of the change in Mendelssohn biographies at the end of the century is that prevailing scientific and medical ideas gave a new weight to age-old anti-Semitism. The linking of characteristics of gender and race in contemporary scientific thought on human development had as significant an influence on Mendelssohn biography as did the changes in masculine cultural milieux.

The image of the feminized Jew was widespread in the scientific and psychological literature of the late nineteenth century, even in the writings of Jewish scientists. In 1869, the ethnologist Adolf Jellinek wrote, '[i]n the examination of the various races it is clear that some are more masculine, others more feminine. Among the latter, the Jews belong, as one of those tribes that are both more feminine and have come to represent the feminine among other peoples.'[53] Physician Heinrich Singer agreed, writing in 1904 that 'in general it is clear in examining the body of the Jew, that the Jew most approaches the body type of the female'.[54] Viennese author Otto Weininger, whose best-selling *Geschlecht und Charakter* of 1903 summarized many of the ideas of the century, described 'female' and 'Jewish' as states of being which existed on a scale with 'male' and 'Christian' on the opposite end.[55] Carl Jung

---

[52] Of the voluminous literature on Wagner's anti-Semitism, see especially Jacob Katz, *The Darker Side of Genius: Wagner's Anti-Semitism* (Hanover: University Press of New England, 1986); Paul Lawrence Rose, *Wagner: Race and Revolution* (New Haven: Yale University Press, 1992); id., *Revolutionary Anti-Semitism from Kant to Wagner* (Princeton: Princeton University Press, 1990), 358–79; and Marc A. Weiner, *Richard Wagner and the Anti-Semitic Imagination* (Lincoln, Nebr.: University of Nebraska Press, 1995), esp. 176–83. On Wagner and Mendelssohn, see Leon Botstein, 'The Aesthetics of Assimilation and Affirmation: Reconstructing the Career of Felix Mendelssohn', in *MHW*, 5–42; and Donald Mintz, '1848, Anti-Semitism, and the Mendelssohn Reception', in R. Larry Todd (ed.), *Mendelssohn Studies* (Cambridge: Cambridge University Press, 1992), 126–48.

[53] Adolf Jellinek, *Der jüdische Stamm: Ethnographische Studien* (Vienna: Herzfeld & Bauer, 1869), 89, trans. in Sander L. Gilman, *Freud, Race, and Gender* (Princeton: Princeton University Press, 1990), 43: 'In die Reihe der letzteren, der Stämme nämlich, die mehr weibliche Züge in sich tragen und gleichsam die Weiblichkeit unter den Völkern repräsentieren, gehört der jüdische.'

[54] Heinrich Singer, *Allgemeine und spezielle Krankheitslehre der Juden* (Leipzig: Konegen, 1904), 9, quoted in Gilman, *Freud, Race, and Gender*, 42–3.

[55] Otto Weininger, *Geschlecht und Charakter* (Vienna: Wilhelm Braumuller, 1903), translated as *Sex and Character* (London: W. Heineman, 1906; repr. New York: AMS Press, 1975). See also John M. Hoberman, 'Otto Weininger and the Critique of Jewish Masculinity', in Nancy Harrowitz and Barbara Hyams (eds.), *Jews and Gender: Responses to Otto Weininger* (Philadelphia: Temple University Press, 1995), 141–53; and Sander L. Gilman, *The Jew's Body* (New York: Routledge, 1991), 133–7.

also identified Jews with women in that they shared the characteristic of physical weakness.[56]

When the notion of Jews as feminine was taken up by Jewish writers, it was sometimes augmented with the belief that their intelligence was merely compensation for this supposed physical weakness. Thus, physician Martin Engländer wrote that Jews had a greater skull size but smaller chest circumference than non-Jews, and Max Nordau called for 'muscle Jews'.[57] A Prague Zionist journal suggested 'we Jews' must shed 'our overestimation of intellectual factors . . . and our excessive nervousness and physical weakness, which clings to us still from the ghetto. . . . We lecture and debate too much, and play and exercise too little! . . . [W]hat makes a man is not just his mouth, not just his mind, not even just his morals, but discipline . . . what we need is . . . manliness'.[58] The strong physical ideals of manliness appeared to be less possible for members of the Jewish race. Boston eugenist Abraham Myerson, who criticized Jews' rejection of sports, described Jewish children as 'very serious, very earnest, too early devoted to mature efforts, excessively cerebral in their activities, and not sufficiently strenuous physically'.[59] With some modification, Myerson's description could be applied to biographical portrayals of the Mendelssohn children's upbringing.[60]

---

[56] See Sander L. Gilman, 'Psychoanalysis and Anti-Semitism: Tainted Greatness in a Professional Context', in Nancy Harrowitz (ed.), *Tainted Greatness: Anti-Semitism and Cultural Heroes* (Philadelphia: Temple University Press, 1994), 94–5. Although this comment dates from 1933, Jung distinguished between a Jewish and a German psyche as early as 1917. Whether or not Jung actually held anti-Semitic beliefs remains controversial; see Aryeh Maidenbaum and Stephen A. Martin (eds.), *Lingering Shadows: Jungians, Freudians, and Anti-Semitism* (Boston: Shambhala, 1991).

[57] Martin Engländer, *Die auffallend häufigen Krankheitserscheinungen der jüdischen Rasse* (Vienna: J. L. Pollak, 1902), 11–12, quoted in Sander Gilman, *Smart Jews: the Construction of the Image of Jewish Superior Intelligence* (Lincoln, Nebr.: University of Nebraska Press, 1996), 23; Max Nordau, *Zionistische Schriften* (Cologne: Jüdischer Verlag, 1909), 379–81, quoted in Gilman, *Freud, Race, and Gender*, 104–5.

[58] *Selbstwahr* (20 Dec. 1912), quoted in Christoph Stölzl, *Kafkas böses Böhmen* (Munich: text + kritik, 1975), 134: 'wir Juden mit unserer Überschätzung geistiger Faktoren . . . unserer Übergroßen Nervosität und physischen Schwäche . . . die uns noch aus dem Ghetto anhaftet. . . . Nur zuviel wird bei uns referiert und debatiert und zuwenig gespielt und geturnt! . . . daß den Mann nicht nur der Mund macht, auch nicht der Geist, auch nicht nur die Moral: sondern die Zucht . . . wir fordern . . . Mannhaftigkeit.'

[59] Abraham Myerson, 'The Nervousness of the Jew', *Mental Hygiene*, 4 (1920), 96.

[60] Mendelssohn's childhood participation in gymnastics and swimming and his ownership of a horse in Düsseldorf are common features of his biographies, sometimes seeming like a deliberate attempt to make him conform to the model of the athletic male. The gymnastics common in early 19th-c. Europe may have influenced Mendelssohn's upbringing, but in general gymnastics lacked the competitive nature of later team sports. See Mosse, *The Image of Man*, 40–7.

So-called 'nervousness', the first indication of mental illness, was considered a trait of Jews. The French historian Anatole Leroy-Beaulieu's 1893 *Israel among the Nations* linked this nervousness with Jewish musical ability: 'the nervousness which we have already noticed in them predisposes them to the most vibrating of arts, the one which has a sway over the nerves'.[61] Few writers of the period considered such nervousness to be a positive attribute; most believed, like German anthropologist Ludwig Woltmann, that excessive intellectual effort was the main reason for Jewish 'degeneracy of the nervous system' and the resulting physical collapse.[62] Munich psychiatry professor H. Ziemssen suggested that Jews were especially predisposed to neurasthenia: '[t]here is a neurotic quality which runs through the whole race in spite of all abilities and perseverance in their occupations'.[63] Mendelssohn was thus prone to neurasthenia not only because of his class status and the tremendous workload to which he subjected himself, but also because of his alleged racial characteristics.

Darwinian theories of this era seemed to lend scientific validity to anti-Semitic beliefs in the late nineteenth and early twentieth centuries, particularly in literature on inherited genetic characteristics.[64] Even though he determined not to include Jews, Francis Galton lists Mendelssohn in his 1869 inventory; likewise, the composer appears in the writings of Jewish author Joseph Jacobs as a genius of the highest rank.[65] Yet in general the treatment of Mendelssohn's life and career is highly coloured by the scientific dictum that 'ontogeny recapitulates phylogeny'. The phrase, coined by the German scientist Ernst Haeckel to describe the biogenetic law he formulated in 1866, means that 'every individual organism repeats in its own life history the history of its race, passing through the lower forms of its ancestors on its way to maturity'.[66] It was a common judgement of late nineteenth-century science

[61] Anatole Leroy-Beaulieu, *Israel among the Nations: A Study of Jews and Anti-Semitism*, trans. Frances Hellman (New York: G. P. Putnam's Sons, 1895), 236, quoted in Gilman, *Smart Jews*, 46.

[62] Ludwig Woltmann, 'Rassenpsychologie und Kulturgeschichte', *Politisch-Anthropologische Revue*, 3 (1904/5), 355.

[63] Hugo von Ziemssen, *Die Neurasthenie und ihre Behandlung* (Leipzig: Vogel, 1889), 7–8, quoted in Gilman, *Freud, Race, and Gender*, 95–6.

[64] Eric Werner makes this point (but fails to pursue it) in 'Felix Mendelssohn — Gustav Mahler: Two Borderline Cases of German-Jewish Assimilation', *Yuval*, 4 (1982), 240–64 at 247.

[65] Francis Galton, *Hereditary Genius: An Inquiry into its Laws and Consequences* (London: Macmillan, 1869; repr. New York: D. Appleton, 1870), 245; Joseph Jacobs, *Studies in Jewish Statistics* (London: D. Nutt, 1891), p. xlv, cited in Gilman, *Smart Jews*, 70.

[66] Russett, *Sexual Science*, 50. For a modern reassessment of Haeckel's theory and its flawed assumptions, see especially Stephen Jay Gould, *Ontogeny and Phylogeny* (Cambridge, Mass.: Belknap, 1977).

that inferiority was the hereditary predisposition of women and Jews, both considered lower on the evolutionary scale. Suffering from arrested development and unable to reach the full maturity of white men, they were considered developmentally similar to children or savages. As Italian criminologist Cesare Lombroso wrote of the female in 1903, 'she appears equal or superior to men before puberty in strength and size, often in intelligence but then slowly falls behind, leaving in that same momentary superiority a proof of the precocity which is typical of the inferior races.'[67] American evolutionary psychologist G. Stanley Hall noted that adolescent boys typically passed through a 'feminized stage of psychic development'.[68]

Mendelssohn's supposed emotional immaturity and inability to bring his genius to full fruition could thus be explained by his racial inheritance: his development had ceased after the compositions of his adolescence, leaving him in a feminine, under-evolved state. The wonders of Mendelssohn the child prodigy and the seemingly miraculous production of masterpieces such as the *Midsummer Night's Dream Overture* in his youth could be explained by recapitulation theory, which held that the precociousness of women and members of 'lower' races was the peak of their development. Vernon Blackburn's 1904 Mendelssohn biography clearly reflects the tenets of recapitulation theory. Mendelssohn 'was allowed a certain number of years in which to use his genius precisely as his own whimsical fancy led him; then the gates of Israel clanged upon him'. Blackburn concluded bluntly, 'Race prevailed over genius.'[69]

While mid-century writings stress the Mendelssohn family's conversion to Christianity and their assimilation into German society, many of the later feminized treatments of the composer stress his 'Oriental' heritage. In his description of the Mendelssohn family, Percy Colson stated overtly that 'baptism was powerless to change their racial characteristics'.[70] Atavism, the idea that ancestral characteristics could pass through generations undetected, only to turn up in a subsequent generation, meant that Mendelssohn would have been subject to all of the problematic genetic inheritance of his inferior race. Degeneration, which was formulated as a hereditary concept by French

---

[67] Cesare Lombroso and Guglielmo Ferrero, *La donna delinquente, la prostituta e la donna normale* (Turin: Fratelli Bocca Editori, 1903), pp. vi–vii, quoted and translated by Nancy A. Harrowitz, *Anti-Semitism, Misogyny, and the Logic of Cultural Difference: Cesare Lombroso and Matilde Serao* (Lincoln, Nebr.: University of Nebraska Press, 1994), 24.

[68] G. Stanley Hall, *Adolescence* (New York: D. Appleton, 1904), ii. 625.

[69] Vernon Blackburn, *Mendelssohn* (London: George Bell & Sons, 1904), 11.

[70] Percy Colson, 'Mendelssohn: A Fallen Idol', in *Victorian Portraits* (London: Rich & Cowan, 1932, repr. New York: Books for Libraries Press, 1968), 228.

psychiatrist Benedict Morel in 1857,[71] also figures in biographical treatments of Mendelssohn. Morel's notion was a sort of reverse evolution in which each succeeding generation received more destructive genetic material. His examples of problems that occurred in the first generation included many characteristics reported of the Mendelssohn family: nervous temperament, irritability, quick temper, and most notably for a family that suffered numerous strokes, a tendency towards cerebral vascular congestion. Lombroso, whose major study *Genius and Madness* was first published in 1864, specifically linked genius and degeneration; among the symptoms were abnormal sensitivity and a tendency to manic excitement.[72] Both tendencies were stressed in period biographies of Mendelssohn, which typically relied on Devrient's assessment of his 'sensitive' and 'nervous' nature.[73]

The supposedly 'effeminate' nature of Mendelssohn's character and music, his 'nervous' temperament, his failure to 'develop' as a composer after adolescence, and his final exhausted collapse, all commonly emphasized in period biographies, reflected the prevalent racially based scientific dictums. The feminization of Mendelssohn is a product both of the rejection of early Victorian ideals of 'manliness' in the late nineteenth century and of the anti-Semitism of the period. To feminize Mendelssohn is to construct him as 'Other'; as his Jewish genetic characteristics make him different, they also make him less than masculine. For Mendelssohn to have lived a long and productive life, or for him to have composed music that was not inherently flawed, was, according to the cultural discourses of the era, practically a scientific impossibility.

---

[71] Russett, *Sexual Science*, 67.

[72] Eric T. Carlson, 'Medicine and Degeneration: Theory and Practice', in Sander L. Gilman and J. Edward Chamberlin (eds.), *Degeneration: The Dark Side of Progress* (New York: Columbia University Press, 1985), 122–37 at 122, 128, 137. For an overview of the history of the relationship between genius and madness, see Neil Kessel, 'Genius and Mental Disorder: A History of Ideas Concerning Their Conjunction', in Penelope Murray (ed.), *Genius: The History of an Idea* (Oxford: Basil Blackwell, 1989), 196–212.

That Mendelssohn's son Karl Mendelssohn was hospitalized in 1873 for what appears to have been schizophrenia would have granted additional weight to the idea that the Mendelssohn family suffered from degeneration. Most biographies end with the death of Felix or Cécile Mendelssohn, and although one 'Agindos' reported on a sparsely attended lecture by an extremely 'nervous' Professor Mendelssohn in *Dwight's Journal of Music*, 25 (1865), 88, it is unlikely that Karl's mental illness was widely known. See Gisela Gantzel-Kress, 'Karl Mendelssohn-Bartholdy, 1838–1897', *Mendelssohn-Studien*, 8 (1993), 197–225.

[73] That Devrient's *Erinnerungen* can be read as anti-Semitic is suggested by Cosima Wagner's comments in her diary, 28 Jan. 1869: 'this account is like a confirmation of what Richard wrote about Mendelssohn in his essay' (presumably *Das Judentum in der Musik*). *Cosima Wagner's Diaries*, i: *1869–1877*, ed. Martin Gregor-Dellin and Dietrich Mack, trans. Geoffrey Skelton (New York: Harcourt, Brace, Jovanovich, 1976), 57.

THE LASTING CONSEQUENCES
OF ANTI-SEMITISM

Certainly most of the writers cited here whose biographies portray a feminized Mendelssohn are not pivotal figures in Mendelssohn scholarship, and it would be easy to dismiss this sort of writing as merely the product of bad biography permeated with the anti-Semitism of a bygone era. Yet their criticisms, in a somewhat diluted form, continue to pervade the general literature about the composer.[74] This occurs most often in criticisms of the supposedly 'feminine' sentimentality of his music, but also plays a role in assessing his personality, as in the title of Marek's 1972 biography, *Gentle Genius*. Arnold Whittall, in his *Romantic Music* (1987), recalls recapitulation theory in his view of Mendelssohn's development, when he concludes that the composer 'never matured emotionally to a sufficient extent to sustain, still less to consolidate, his adolescent genius'.[75]

Much modern scholarship adopts gendered language in treating Mendelssohn. In spite of his attention to issues surrounding anti-Semitism, Eric Werner sounds surprisingly like earlier writers when he describes the *Lieder ohne Worte* as having a 'respectable attitude' but 'no wild passion or hot eroticism'.[76] Werner also ascribes feminine characteristics to Mendelssohn's music: the solos and duets of the Psalms 'suffer from a certain sentimental softness', and the principal theme of the first movement of the Violin Concerto is 'perhaps a little too effeminate'.[77] In his volume on chamber music, Homer Ulrich writes, predictably, 'Mendelssohn permits no harshness or driving emotion in his works. He is always refined, possibly a bit effeminate, even in his most striking moments.'[78] Donald J. Grout and Claude Palisca, in the 1980 edition of their widely used music history textbook, also echo earlier ideology, writing, 'in general the style is elegant and sensitive, not given to violence or excess bravura', and 'never more than lightly touched with Romantic pathos or passion'.[79] When Charles Rosen writes in his

---

[74] Two scholars who have noted the influence of the stereotype are Michael P. Steinberg, 'Schumann's Homelessness', in R. Larry Todd (ed.), *Schumann and his World* (Princeton: Princeton University Press, 1994), 47–97 at 56, and James Webster, 'Ambivalenzen um Mendelssohn: Zwischen Werk und Rezeption', in Schmidt, *Kongreß-Bericht*, 257–78 at 266–7.

[75] Arnold Whittall, *Romantic Music: A Concise History from Schubert to Sibelius* (London: Thames & Hudson, 1987), 35.

[76] Werner, *New Image*, 221.   [77] Ibid. 414, 420–1.

[78] Homer Ulrich, *Chamber Music* (2nd edn., New York: Columbia University Press, 1966), 287.

[79] Donald J. Grout, with Claude Palisca, *A History of Western Music* (3rd edn., New York: W. W. Norton, 1980), 575. In the fifth edition, published in 1996, the latter phrase is changed to

award-winning collection of lectures, *The Romantic Generation*, that 'Mendelssohn rounds off his phrases, his paragraphs, and eventually his sections with a certain comfortable sweetness' or 'dramatic force now required either a neurotic or even a morbid sense of expression, or else a kind of grit unwelcome or unnatural to Mendelssohn',[80] he unwittingly perpetuates conclusions that originated in nineteenth-century racial rhetoric.

While scholars have attempted to refute the obviously anti-Semitic assessments of Wagner, they have not necessarily recognized that the feminization of Mendelssohn and of his music derives from the same source. Critical reassessment of Mendelssohn's music must take the roots of gendered criticisms of his style into account.

'Mendelssohn's harmony has few of the delightful surprises that one encounters in Schubert, nor do his melodies, rhythms, and forms introduce many unexpected features.' This wording is retained in the most recent (6th) edition, except that the word 'delightful' is deleted.

[80] Charles Rosen, 'Mendelssohn and the Invention of Religious Kitsch', in *The Romantic Generation* (Cambridge, Mass.: Harvard University Press, 1995), 569–98 at 571, 572.

Select Bibliography

ABRAHAM, LARS ULRICH, 'Mendelssohns Chorlieder und ihre musikgeschichtliche Stelling', in Dahlhaus (ed.), *Das Problem Mendelssohn*, 79–87.

AHRENS, CHRISTIAN, 'Schuberts Kammermusik in der Musikkritik des 19. Jahrhunderts', in *Festschrift für Rudolf Elvers* (Tutzing: Hans Schneider, 1985), 9–27.

Ausstellung Düsseldorfer Malerschule: Katalog, ed. Wend von Kalnein (Düsseldorf: Kunstmuseum, 1979).

Autographen, Erstausgaben und Frühdrucke der Werke von Felix Mendelssohn Bartholdy in Leipziger Bibliotheken und Archiven, ed. Peter Krause (Leipzig: Musikbibliothek der Stadt Leipzig, 1972).

BAUER, ELISABETH ELEONORE, *Wie Beethoven auf den Sockel kam: Die Entstehung eines musikalischen Mythos* (Stuttgart: J. B. Metzler, 1992).

BECKER, ROBERT, *Felix Mendelssohn-Bartholdy und Reinerz* (Reinerz: n.pub., 1930).

BENEDICT, JULES, *Sketch of the Life and Works of the Late Felix Mendelssohn Bartholdy* (London: John Murray, 1850).

BERLIOZ, HECTOR, *The Memoirs of Hector Berlioz*, ed. and trans. David Cairns (London: Gollancz, 1977).

BIELSCHOWSKY, ALBERT, *Goethe: Sein Leben und seine Werke* (Munich: Beck, 1920).

BLACKBURN, VERNON, *Mendelssohn* (London: George Bell & Sons, 1904).

BOTSTEIN, LEON, 'The Aesthetics of Assimilation and Affirmation: Reconstructing the Career of Felix Mendelssohn', in Todd (ed.), *Mendelssohn and his World*, 5–42.

—— 'Mendelssohn and the Jews', *Musical Quarterly*, 82 (1998), 210–19.

BOURNE, C. E., *The Great Composers, or Stories of the Lives of Eminent Musicians* (9th edn., London: Swan, Sonnenschein & Co., 1902).

Bref till Adolf Fredrik Lindblad från Mendelssohn, Dohrn, Almqvist, Atterbom, Geijer, Fredrika Bremer, C. W. Böttiger och andra (Stockholm: Bonnier, 1913).

BRENDEL, FRANZ, *Geschichte der Musik in Italien, Deutschland und Frankreich* (6th edn., Leipzig: H. Matthes, 1878).

Briefe an Goethe, ed. Karl R. Mandelkow (Hamburger Ausgabe in 2 Bände, 2nd edn.; Munich: C. H. Beck, 1982).

Der Briefwechsel zwischen Goethe und Zelter, ed. Max Hecker (Leipzig: Insel, 1918).

BRODBECK, DAVID, '*Eine kleine Kirchenmusik*: A New Canon, a Revised Cadence, and an Obscure "Coda" by Mendelssohn', *Journal of Musicology*, 12 (1994), 179–205.

BÜCKEN, ERNST, *Die Musik des 19. Jahrhunderts bis zur Moderne* (Wildpark-Potsdam: Akademische Verlags-Gesellschaft Athenaion, 1929).

BÜLOW, HANS VON, *Briefe und Schriften von Hans von Bülow*, v: *1872–1880*, ed. Marie von Bülow (2nd edn., Leipzig: Breitkopf & Härtel, 1904).

BUSHNELL, HOWARD, *Maria Malibran: A Biography of the Singer* (University Park: Pennsylvania State University Press, 1979).

CAI, CAMILLA, 'Fanny Hensel's "Songs for Pianoforte" of 1836–37: Stylistic Interaction with Felix Mendelssohn', *Journal of Musicological Research*, 14 (1994), 55–76.

—— 'Texture and Gender: New Prisms for Understanding Hensel's and Mendelssohn's Piano Pieces', in David Witten (ed.), *Nineteenth-Century Piano Music: Essays in Performance and Analyis* (New York: Garland, 1997), 53–93.

Catalogue de la Bibliothèque du Conservatoire Royal de Musique, ed. Alfred Wotquenne (Brussels: J.-J. Cossemans, 1898).

CHORLEY, HENRY FOTHERGILL, *Modern German Music* (London: Smith, Elder & Co., 1854, repr. New York: Da Capo Press, 1973).

COBBETT, WALTER WILSON, *Cyclopedic Survey of Chamber Music*, 2nd edn., ed. Colin Mason (London: Oxford University Press, 1963).

COLSON, PERCY, 'Mendelssohn: A Fallen Idol', in *Victorian Portraits* (London: Rich & Cowan, 1932, repr. New York: Books for Libraries Press, 1968).

CONE, EDWARD T., *The Composer's Voice* (Berkeley: University of California Press, 1974).

COOPER, JOHN MICHAEL, ' "Aber eben dieser Zweifel": A New Look at Mendelssohn's "Italian" Symphony', *Nineteenth Century Music*, 15 (1992), 169–87.

—— 'Felix Mendelssohn Bartholdy and the *Italian* Symphony: Historical, Musical, and Extramusical Perspectives' (Ph.D. diss., Duke University, 1994).

—— *Mendelssohn's 'Italian' Symphony* (Oxford: Oxford University Press, 2002).

—— 'Mendelssohn's Works: Prologomenon to a Comprehensive Inventory', in Seaton (ed.), *The Mendelssohn Companion*, 701–87.

CORNET, J., *Die Oper in Deutschland und das Theater der Neuzeit: Aus dem Standpunkte practischer Erfahrungen* (Hamburg: Meißner & Schirges, 1849).

CRUM, MARGARET, *Catalogue of the Mendelssohn Papers in the Bodleian Library, Oxford*, ii: *Music and Papers* (Tutzing: Hans Schneider, 1983).

DADELSON, GEORG VON, 'Die "Fassung letzter Hand" in der Musik', *Acta musicologica*, 33 (1961), 1–14.

DAHLHAUS, CARL, ' "Hoch symbolisch intentioniert": Zu Mendelssohns "Erster Walpurgisnacht" ', *Österreichische Musikzeitschrift*, 36 (1981), 290–7.

—— *Klassische und romantische Musikästhetik* (Laaber: Laaber, 1988).

—— 'Mendelssohn und die musikalische Gattungstradition', in id. (ed.), *Das Problem Mendelssohn*, 55–60.

—— *Die Musik des 19. Jahrhunderts* (Neues Handbuch der Musikwissenschaft, 6; Wiesbaden: Akademische Verlags-Gesellschaft Athenaion, 1980).

—— *Musikästhetik* (Cologne: H. Gerig, 1967).

—— 'Die Symphonie nach Beethoven', in id., *Die Musik des 19. Jahrhunderts*, 125–32.

—— 'Thesen über Programmusik', in id. (ed.), *Beiträge ʒur musikalischen Hermeneutik* (Regensburg: Gustav Bosse, 1975).

—— (ed.), *Das Problem Mendelssohn* (Regensburg: Gustav Bosse, 1974).

DAHMS, WALTER, *Mendelssohn* (9th edn., Berlin: Schuster & Loeffler, 1922; first edn. 1919).

Damen-Conversations-Lexikon, ed. K. B. S. Herloßson (Leipzig: Fr. Volckmar, 1834).

DEUTSCH, OTTO ERICH, and EIBL, J. H., *Moʒart: Dokumente seines Lebens* (2nd edn., Kassel: Bärenreiter, 1981).

DEVRIENT, EDUARD, *Meine Erinnerungen an Felix Mendelssohn-Bartholdy und seine Briefe an mich* (Leipzig: J. J. Weber, 1869).

DEVRIENT, THERESE, *Jugenderinnerungen* (Stuttgart: C. Crabbe, 1908).

DINGLINGER, WOLFGANG, *Studien ʒu den Psalmen mit Orchester von Felix Mendelssohn Bartholdy* (Cologne: Studio, 1993).

DOOLEY, ALLAN C., 'Varieties of Textual Change in the Victorian Era', *Text: Transactions of the Society for Textual Scholarship*, 6 (1994), 225–47.

DÖRFFEL, ALFRED, *Geschichte der Gewandhausconcerte ʒu Leipʒig vom 25. November 1781 bis 25. November 1881* (Leipzig: Breitkopf & Härtel, 1884).

DRAHEIM, JOACHIM, ' "Dies Concert ist auch für Violine transscribirt erschienen": Robert Schumanns Cellokonzert und seine neuentdeckte Fassung für Violine', *Neue Zeitschrift für Musik*, 148 (1987), 4–10.

DROYSEN, GUSTAV, 'Johann Gustav Droysen und Felix Mendelssohn-Bartholdy', *Deutsche Rundschau*, 28 (1902), 107–26, 193–215, 386–408.

DWIGHT, JOHN SULLIVAN, 'Felix Mendelssohn Bartholdy', in John Knowles Paine, Theodore Thomas, and Karl Klauser (eds.), *Famous Composers and their Works*, i (Boston: J. B. Millet, 1891), 417–36.

EBERLE, GOTTFRIED, *200 Jahre Sing-Akademie ʒu Berlin: 'Ein Kunstverein für die heilige Musik'* (Berlin: Nicolai, 1991).

ECKERT, HEINRICH, *Norbert Burgmüller: Ein Beitrag ʒur Stil- und Geistesgeschichte der deutschen Romantik* (Veröffentlichungen des Musikwissenschaftlichen Instituts der deutschen Universität in Prag, 3; Augsburg: B. Filser, 1932).

EDLER, ARNFRIED, *Robert Schumann und seine Zeit* (Laaber: Laaber, 1982).

EHRLE, THOMAS, *Die Instrumentation von Felix Mendelssohn Bartholdy* (Wiesbaden: Breitkopf & Härtel, 1983).

EICHHORN, ANDREAS, *Beethovens Neunte Symphonie: Die Geschichte ihrer Aufführung und Reʒeption* (Kassel: Bärenreiter, 1993).

EINSTEIN, ALFRED, *Geschichte der Musik von den Anfängen bis ʒur Gegenwart* (Stuttgart: Pan, 1953).

ELVERS, RUDOLF, 'Auf den Spuren der Autographen von Felix Mendelssohn Bartholdy', in Günther Brosche (ed.), *Beiträge ʒur Musikdokumentation: Franʒ Grasberger ʒum 60. Geburtstag* (Tutzing: Hans Schneider, 1975), 83–91.

—— 'Felix Mendelssohn Bartholdys Nachlaß', in Dahlhaus (ed.), *Das Problem Mendelssohn*, 35–46.

ELVERS, RUDOLF, 'Ein Jugendbrief von Felix Mendelssohn', in *Festschrift für Friedrich Smend zum 70. Geburtstag* (Berlin: Merseburger, 1963), 93–7.

—— *'Nichts ist so schwer gut zu componiren als in Strophen': Zur Entstehungsgeschichte von Felix Mendelssohns Oper 'Die Hochzeit des Camacho'* (Berlin: Mendelssohn-Gesellschaft, 1976).

—— 'Über das Berlinische Zwitterwesen', in Rudolf Elvers and Hans-Günter Klein (eds.), *Die Mendelssohns in Berlin: Eine Familie und ihre Stadt* (Berlin: Staatsbibliothek Preußischer Kulturbesitz, 1983), 31–4.

—— 'Verlorengegangene Selbstverständlichkeiten: Zum Mendelssohn-Artikel in *The New Grove*', in J. Schläder and R. Quandt (eds.), *Festschrift Heinz Becker zum 60. Geburtstag* (Laaber: Laaber, 1982), 417–21.

—— (ed.), *Felix Mendelssohn: A Life in Letters*, trans. Craig Tomlinson (New York: International, 1986).

—— and Ward Jones, Peter, 'Das Musikalienverzeichnis von Fanny und Felix Mendelssohn Bartholdy', *Mendelssohn-Studien*, 8 (1993), 85–103.

FÉTIS, FRANÇOIS-JOSEPH, and MOSCHELES, IGNAZ, *Méthode des méthodes de piano* (Paris: Maurice Schlesinger, 1840; repr. Geneva: Minkoff, 1973).

FIFIELD, CHRISTOPHER, *Max Bruch: Biographie eines Komponisten* (Zurich: Schweizer, 1990).

FINSCHER, LUDWIG, '"Zwischen absoluter und Programmusik": Zur Interpretation der deutschen romantischen Symphonie', in Christoph-Hellmut Mahling (ed.), *Über Symphonien: Beiträge zu einer musikalischen Gattung. Festschrift Walter Wiora zum 70. Geburtstag* (Tutzing: Hans Schneider, 1979), 103–15.

FISKE, ROGER, *Scotland in Music: A European Enthusiasm* (Cambridge: Cambridge University Press, 1983).

FORNER, JOHANNES, 'Mendelssohns Mitstreiter am Leipziger Konservatorium', *Beiträge zur Musikwissenschaft*, 14 (1972), 185–204.

FOSTER, MYLES BIRKET, *History of the Philharmonic Society of London, 1813–1912* (London: John Lane, 1913).

FRIEDLÄNDER, MAX, 'Ein Brief Felix Mendelssohns', *Vierteljahrsschrift für Musikwissenschaft*, 5 (1889), 483–9.

GADE, NIELS, *Aufzeichnungen und Briefe*, ed. D. Gade (Leipzig: Breitkopf & Härtel, 1894).

GANTZEL-KRESS, GISELA, 'Karl Mendelssohn-Bartholdy, 1838–1897', *Mendelssohn-Studien*, 8 (1993), 197–225.

GARLINGTON, AUBREY S., 'Mega-Text, Mega-Music: A Crucial Dilemma for German Romantic Opera', in Nancy Kovaleff Baker and Barbara Russo Hanning (eds.), *Musical Humanism and its Legacy: Essays in Honor of Claude V. Palisca* (Stuyvesant, NY: Pendragon, 1992), 381–93.

GECK, MARTIN, *Die Wiederentdeckung der Matthäuspassion im 19. Jahrhunderts: Die zeitgenössischen Dokumente und ihre ideengeschichtliche Deutung* (Regensburg: Gustav Bosse, 1967).

GEORGIADES, THRASYBULOS, 'Zur Musiksprache der Wiener Klassiker', *Mozart-Jahrbuch* 1951, 50–9.

GERE, AMANDA R., 'Frederick Chopin', *Atlantic Monthly*, 31 (Apr. 1873), 420.

Gesammelte Schriften über Musik und Musiker von Robert Schumann, ed. Martin Kreisig (5th edn., Leipzig: Breitkopf & Härtel, 1914).

Goethes Briefe, ed. Karl R. Mandelkow and Bodo Morawe (Hamburger Ausgabe in 4 Bände, 2nd edn.; Hamburg: Christian Wegner, 1968–76).

GOLDHAN, WOLFGANG, 'Felix Mendelssohn Bartholdys Lieder für gemischten und Männerchor', *Beiträge zur Musikwissenschaft*, 17 (1975), 181–8.

GOLLMICK, CARL, 'Glossen über Operntexte, Schluß,' *Neue Zeitschrift für Musik*, 42 (24 May 1842), 165–6.

GORRELL, LORRAINE, *The Nineteenth-Century German Lied* (Portland, Ore.: Amadeus Press, 1993).

GOSLICH, SIEGFRIED, *Die deutsche romantische Oper* (Tutzing: Hans Schneider, 1975).

GRAMIT, DAVID, 'Constructing a Victorian Schubert: Music, Biography, and Cultural Values', *Nineteenth Century Music*, 7 (1993), 65–78.

GROUT, DONALD J., with PALISCA, CLAUDE, *A History of Western Music* (3rd edn., New York: W. W. Norton, 1980; 6th edn., 2001).

GROVE, GEORGE, *Beethoven, Schubert, Mendelssohn* (London: Macmillan, 1951).

Grove's Dictionary of Music and Musicians, 4 vols. (London: Macmillan, 1878–89).

GUNDOLF, FRIEDRICH, *Goethe* (Darmstadt: Wissenschaftliche Buchgesellschaft, 1963).

HALLMARK, RUFUS (ed.), *German Lieder in the Nineteenth Century* (New York: Schirmer, 1996).

HAND, FERDINAND, *Aesthetik der Tonkunst*, i (Leipzig: C. Hochhausen & Fournes, 1837).

HANSLICK, EDUARD, *Vom Musikalisch-Schönen* (Leipzig: R. Weigel, 1854; repr. Darmstadt: Wissenschaftliche Buchgesellschaft, 1991).

HAUSER, RICHARD, ' "In rührend feierlichen Tönen": Mendelssohns Kantate *Die erste Walpurgisnacht*', in Metzger and Riehn (eds.), *Felix Mendelssohn Bartholdy*, 75–92.

HAWEIS, R. H., *Music and Morals* (New York: Harper & Brothers, [1872]).

HEINE, HEINRICH, *Werke, Briefwechsel, Lebenszeugnisse*, ed. Lucienne Netter, x (Berlin: Akademie-Verlag, 1979).

HELLMUNDT, CHRISTOPH, 'Anton Christanell und seine Beziehungen zu Felix Mendelssohn Bartholdy', *Mendelssohn-Studien*, 11 (1999), 77–102.

—— 'Mendelssohns Arbeit an seiner Kantate *Die erste Walpurgisnacht*: Zu einer bisher wenig beachteten Quelle', in Schmidt (ed.), *Kongreß-Bericht*, 76–112.

HELLWIG-UNRUH, RENATE, 'Werkverzeichnis', in Helmig (ed.), *Fanny Hensel*, 168–77.

HELMIG, MARTINA (ed.), *Fanny Hensel, geb. Mendelssohn Bartholdy: Das Werk* (Munich: edition text + kritik, 1997).

HENNEMANN, MONIKA, 'Mendelssohn and Byron: Two Songs almost without Words', *Mendelssohn-Studien*, 10 (1997), 131–56.

HENSEL, FANNY, *The Letters of Fanny Hensel to Felix Mendelssohn*, ed. Marcia J. Citron ([Stuyvesant, NY]: Pendragon, 1987).

—— (née Mendelssohn), *Songs for Pianoforte, 1836–1837* (Madison, Wis.: A-R Editions, 1994).

HENSEL, SEBASTIAN, *Die Familie Mendelssohn 1729–1847: Nach Briefen und Tagebüchern* (1st edn., 3 vols.; Berlin: B. Behrs Buchhandlung, 1879; 2nd edn., 1880; 15th edn., 2 vols, 1908; 17th edn., Berlin: Walter de Gruyter, 1921; most recent edition, ed. Konrad Feilchenfeldt, Frankfurt am Main: Insel, 1995).

—— *The Mendelssohn Family* (London: Sampson Low, Marston, Searle, & Rivington, 1881).

—— *The Mendelssohn Family (1729–1847), from Letters and Journals* (New York: Harper & Brothers, [1881]).

HILLER, FERDINAND, *Felix Mendelssohn-Bartholdy: Briefe und Erinnerungen* (Cologne: M. DuMont-Schauberg, 1874; 2nd edn., 1878).

—— *Mendelssohn: Letters and Recollections*, trans. M. E. von Glehn (London: Macmillan, 1874).

HINCK, WALTER, *Die deutsche Ballade von Bürger bis Brecht* (Göttingen: Vandenhoeck & Ruprecht, 1968).

HOFMANN, KURT, *Die Erstdrucke der Werke von Robert Schumann* (Musikbibliographische Arbeiten, 6; Tutzing: Hans Schneider, 1979).

HORSLEY, CHARLES EDWARD, 'Reminiscences of Mendelssohn by his English Pupil', *Dwight's Journal of Music*, 32 (1872), 345–7, 353–5, 361–3; repr. in Todd (ed.), *Mendelssohn and his World*, 237–49.

HUBBARD, ELBERT, *Little Journeys to the Homes of Great Musicians* (New York: The Knickerbocker Press, 1905).

JACOB, HEINRICH EDUARD, *Felix Mendelssohn and his Times*, trans. Richard and Clara Winston (Englewood Cliffs, NJ: Prentice-Hall, 1963).

JOACHIM, JOSEPH, *Briefe von und an Joseph Joachim*, ed. Johannes Joachim and Andreas Moser (Berlin: J. Bard, 1912).

JOST, CHRISTA, *Mendelssohns Lieder ohne Worte* (Tutzing: Hans Schneider, 1988).

KALLBERG, JEFFERY, 'Are Variants a Problem? "Composer's Intentions" in Editing Chopin', *Chopin Studies*, 3 (1990), 257–67; repr. as 'The Chopin "Problem": Simultaneous Variants and Alternate Versions', in Jeffrey Kallberg, *Chopin at the Boundaries: Sex, History, and Musical Genre* (Cambridge, Mass.: Harvard University Press, 1996), 215–28.

—— 'Chopin in the Marketplace', in id., *Chopin at the Boundaries*, 161–214.

—— 'The Harmony of the Tea Table: Gender and Ideology in the Piano Nocturne', in id., *Chopin at the Boundaries*, 32–8.

—— 'Small Fairy Voices: Sex, History, and Meaning in Chopin', in id., *Chopin at the Boundaries*, 62–86.

KAPP, REINHARD, '*Lobgesang*', in Josef Kuckertz, Helga de la Motte-Haber, Christian Martin Schmidt, and Wilhelm Seidel (eds.), *Neue Musik und Tradition: Festschrift Rudolf Stephan* (Laaber: Laaber, 1990), 239–49.

KATZ, JACOB, *The Darker Side of Genius: Wagner's Anti-Semitism* (Hanover: University Press of New England, 1986).

KLEIN, HANS-GÜNTER, ' ". . . dieses allerliebste Buch", Fanny Hensels Noten-Album', *Mendelssohn-Studien*, 8 (1993), 141–58.

—— *Die Kompositionen Fanny Hensels in Autographen und Abschriften aus dem Besitz der Staatsbibiliothek zu Berlin — Preußischer Kulturbesitz, Katalog* (Musikbibliographische Arbeiten, 13; Tutzing: Hans Schneider, 1995).

—— 'Korrekturen im Autograph von Mendelssohns Streichquartett Op. 80: Überlegungen zur Kompositionstechnik und zum Kompositionsvorgang', *Mendelssohn-Studien*, 5 (1992), 113–22.

—— 'Verzeichnis der im Autograph überlieferten Werke Felix Mendelssohn Bartholdys im Besitz der Staatsbibliothek zu Berlin', *Mendelssohn-Studien*, 10 (1997), 181–213.

KOHLHASE, HANS, *Die Kammermusik Robert Schumanns: Stylistische Untersuchungen* (Hamburger Beiträge zur Musikwissenschaft, 19; Hamburg: Musikalienhandlung K. D. Wagner, 1979).

KONOLD, WULF, *Die Symphonien Felix Mendelssohn Bartholdys: Untersuchungen zu Werkgestalt und Formstruktur* (Laaber: Laaber, 1992).

KRAMER, RICHARD, *Distant Cycles: Schubert and the Conceiving of Song* (Chicago: University of Chicago Press, 1994).

KRAMER, LAWRENCE, ' "Felix culpa": Goethe and the Image of Mendelssohn', in R. Larry Todd (ed.), *Mendelssohn Studies* (Cambridge: Cambridge University Press, 1992), 64–79.

—— '*Felix culpa*: Mendelssohn, Goethe, and the Social Force of Musical Expression', in id., *Classical Music and Postmodern Knowledge* (Berkeley: University of California Press, 1995), 122–42.

—— 'The Lied as Cultural Practice: Tutelage, Gender and Desire in Mendelssohn's Goethe Songs', in id., *Classical Music and Postmodern Knowledge*, 143–73.

KRAUSE, PETER, *Autographen, Erstausgaben und Frühdrucke der Werke von Felix Mendelssohn Bartholdy in Leipziger Bibliotheken und Archiven* (Leipzig: Musikbibliothek der Stadt Leipzig, 1972).

KRETSCHMAR, HERMANN, *Führer durch den Konzertsaal, 1. Abtlg.: Sinfonie und Suite*, 6th edn. (Leipzig: Breitkopf & Härtel, 1921).

KRETTENAUER, THOMAS, *Felix Mendelssohn Bartholdys "Heimkehr aus der Fremde": Untersuchungen und Dokumente zum Liederspiel op. 89* (Augsburg: Dr. Bernd Wißner, 1994).

KRISCHKE, CLAUDIA, *Untersuchungen zu den Streichquartetten von Robert Volkmann (1815–1883): Ein Komponist zwischen Schumann und Brahms* (Europäische Hochschulschriften, Reihe 36, Bd. 154; Frankfurt am Main: Peter Lang, 1996).

KRUMMACHER, FRIEDHELM, 'Aussichten im Rückblick: Felix Mendelssohn in der neueren Forschung', in Schmidt (ed.), *Kongreß-Bericht*, 279–96.

—— *Mendelssohn — Der Komponist: Studien zur Kammermusik für Streicher* (Munich: Wilhelm Fink, 1978).

—— 'Mendelssohn's Late Chamber Music: Some Autograph Sources Recovered', in Jon W. Finson and R. Larry Todd (eds.), *Mendelssohn and Schumann: Essays on their Music and its Context* (Durham, NC: Duke University Press, 1984), 77–80.

KUBE, MICHAEL, 'Am Quartettpult: Paul Hindemith im Rebner- und Amarquartett, Documentation (Part 3)', in *Hindemith-Jahrbuch*, 22 (1993), 200–37.

KUNZE, STEFAN, *Mozarts Opern* (Stuttgart: P. Reclam, 1984).

LADD, GEORGE TRUMBULL, 'Why Women Cannot Compose Music', *Yale Review*, 6 (July 1917), 804.

LAMPADIUS, WILHELM AUGUST, *Felix Mendelssohn-Bartholdy: Ein Denkmal für seine Freunde* (Leipzig: Hinrichs, 1848; 2nd edn., Leipzig: F. E. C. Leuckart, 1886).

LAURENCE, DAN H. (ed.), *How to Become a Musical Critic* (New York: Hill & Wang, 1961).

LAUTH, WILHELM, *Max Bruchs Instrumentalmusik* (Beiträge zur rheinischen Musikgeschichte, 68; Cologne: Arno Volk, 1967).

LEVEN, LUISE, 'Mendelssohn als Lyriker unter besonderer Berücksichtigung seiner Beziehungen zu Ludwig Berger, Bernhard Klein und Adolf Bernhard Marx' (diss., University of Frankfurt am Main, 1926).

—— 'Mendelssohn's Unpublished Songs', *Monthly Musical Record*, 88 (1958), 206–11.

LEWIS, NIGEL, *Paperchase: Mozart, Beethoven, Bach—The Search for their Lost Music* (London: Hamish Hamilton, 1981).

The Life of Jenny Lind Briefly Told by her Daughter Mrs. Raymond Maude (London: Cassell, 1926).

LITTLE, WM A., 'Mendelssohn and the Berlin Singakademie: The Composer at the Crossroads', in Todd (ed.), *Mendelssohn and his World*, 65–85.

LOEWENBERG, ALFRED, *Annals of Opera*, i (2nd rev. edn., Geneva: Societas Bibliographica, 1955).

LOWENTHAL-HENSEL, CÉCILE, 'F in Dur und F in Moll', in Felix Henseleit (ed.), *Berlin in Dur und Moll* (Berlin: Axel Springer, 1970).

LYSER, JOHANN PETER, *Zur Biographie Mendelssohn Bartholdys*, repr. in *Ein unbekanntes Mendelssohn-Bildnis von Johann Peter Lyser* (Basle, 1958).

MAHLING, CHRISTOPH HELMUT, 'Zum Musikbetrieb Berlins und seinen Institutionen in der ersten Hälfte des 19. Jahrhunderts,' in Carl Dahlhaus (ed.), *Studien zur Musikgeschichte Berlins im frühen 19. Jahrhundert* (Studien zur Musikgeschichte des 19. Jahrhunderts, 56; Regensburg: Gustav Bosse, 1980), 27–284.

MAREK, GEORGE, *Gentle Genius: The Story of Felix Mendelssohn* (New York: Funk & Wagnalls, 1972).

Martens, Gunter, and Zeller, Hans (eds.), *Texte und Varianten: Probleme ihrer Edition und Interpretation* (Munich: C. H. Beck, 1971).

Marx, Adolph Bernhard, *Erinnerungen aus meinem Leben*, i (Berlin: O. Jahnke, 1865).

—— 'Etwas über die Symphonie und Beethovens Leistungen in diesem Fache', *Berliner Allgemeine musikalische Zeitung*, 1 (1824), 165–7.

—— *Ludwig van Beethoven: Leben und Schaffen* (Leipzig: A. Schumann, 1902; originally published Berlin: O. Jahnke, 1859).

—— 'Symphonie mit Schlußchor über Schillers Ode an die Freude', *Berliner Allgemeine musikalische Zeitung*, 3 (1826), 373–6.

Mason, Daniel Gregory, *The Romantic Composers* (New York: Macmillan, 1906).

—— *Tune in, America: A Study of Our Coming Musical Independence* (New York: Alfred A. Knopf, 1931).

Mathews, W. S. B., *The Masters and their Music* (Philadelphia: Theodore Presser, 1898; repr. New York: AMS, 1971).

Maurer, Annette, *Thematisches Verzeichnis der klavierbegleiteten Sololieder Fanny Hensels* (Kassel: Bärenreiter, 1997).

Mendelssohn Bartholdy, Felix, *Briefe*, ed. Rudolf Elvers (Frankfurt am Main: Fischer, 1984).

—— *Briefe an deutsche Verleger*, ed. Rudolf Elvers (Berlin: de Gruyter, 1968).

—— *Briefe aus den Jahren 1830 bis 1847*, ed. Paul Mendelssohn-Bartholdy and Carl Mendelssohn-Bartholdy (2nd edn., Leipzig: Hermann Mendelssohn, 1870; 3rd edn., 2 vols. in one, 1875; 5th edn., 2 vols. in one, 1882).

—— *Briefe aus den Jahren 1833 bis 1847 von Felix Mendelssohn Bartholdy*, ed. Paul Mendelssohn-Bartholdy and Carl Mendelssohn-Bartholdy (Leipzig: Hermann Mendelssohn, 1863; 2nd edn., 1864; end edn. 1870).

—— *Briefe aus Leipziger Archiven*, ed. Hans-Joachim Rothe and Reinhard Szeskus (Leipzig: Deutscher Verlag für Musik, 1972).

—— *Briefe einer Reise durch Deutschland, Italien und die Schweiz, und Lebensbild*, ed. Peter Sutermeister (Zürich: Max Niehans, 1958).

—— *Briefe von Felix Mendelssohn-Bartholdy an Ignaz und Charlotte Moscheles*, ed. Felix Moscheles (Leipzig: Duncker & Humblot, 1888).

—— *Briefwechsel mit Legationsrat Karl Klingemann in London*, ed. Karl Klingemann [jun.] (Essen: G. D. Baedeker, 1909).

—— *Complete Organ Works in Five Volumes*, ed. Wm. A. Little (London: Novello, 1990).

—— *Kompositionen für Orgel: Erstausgabe*, ed. Wm. A. Little (Leipzig: Deutscher Verlag für Musik, 1974).

—— *Letters from Italy and Switzerland*, trans. Lady Wallace (London: O. Ditson, 1862; Philadelphia: Leypoldt, 1863).

—— *Letters to Ignaz and Charlotte Moscheles*, ed. and trans. Felix Moscheles (London: Trübner, [1888]).

MENDELSSOHN BARTHOLDY, FELIX, *Orgelstücke, nach Autographen, Abschriften und Erstausgaben*, ed. Wolfgang Stockmeier (Munich: Henle, 1988).

—— *Reisebriefe von Felix Mendelssohn Bartholdy aus den Jahren 1830 bis 1832*, ed. Paul Mendelssohn Bartholdy (Leipzig: Hermann Mendelssohn, 1861; 2nd edn., 1862; 9th edn., 1882).

—— *Sonate F-Dur für Violine und Klavier*, ed. Renate Unger (Leipzig: Deutscher Verlag für Musik, 1977).

—— *Sinfonie A-dur op. 90, "Italienische": Alle eigenhändigen Niederschriften in Faksimile*, ed. John M. Cooper and Hans-Günter Klein (Wiesbaden: Dr. Ludwig Reichert, 1997).

—— *Three Preludes and Fugues, Opus 37, Duets, and Preludes and Fugues*, ed. Wm A. Little (Complete Organ Works, 1; London: Novello, 1989).

—— *Zwei Stücke — Sonate D-dur, Sonatensatz g-moll — für zwei Klaviere*, ed. Joachim Draheim (Wiesbaden: Breitkopf & Härtel, 1998).

The Mendelssohns on Honeymoon: The 1837 Diary of Felix and Cécile Mendelssohn Bartholdy, together with Letters to their Families, ed. and trans. Peter Ward Jones (Oxford: Clarendon Press, 1997).

MERCER-TAYLOR, PETER, 'Mendelssohn's "Scottish" Symphony and the Music of German Memory', *Nineteenth Century Music*, 19 (1995/6), 68–82.

METZGER, HEINZ-KLAUS, 'Noch einmal: *Die erste Walpurgisnacht*', in Metzger and Riehn (eds.), *Felix Mendelssohn Bartholdy*, 93–6.

—— and RIEHN, RAINER (eds.), *Felix Mendelssohn Bartholdy* (Musik-Konzepte 14/15; Munich: edition text + kritik, 1980).

MILLER, NORBERT, 'Felix Mendelssohn Bartholdys italienische Reise', in Dahlhaus (ed.), *Das Problem Mendelssohn*, 23–34.

MINTZ, DONALD, '1848, Anti-Semitism, and the Mendelssohn Reception', in R. Larry Todd (ed.), *Mendelssohn Studies* (Cambridge: Cambridge University Press, 1992), 126–48.

MOSER, HANS JOACHIM, *Geschichte der deutschen Musik* (Stuttgart: J. G. Cotta, 1924).

—— *Kleine deutsche Musikgeschichte* (2nd edn., Stuttgart: Cotta, 1949).

MUSSULMAN, JOSEPH A., *Music in the Cultured Generation: A Social History of Music in America, 1870–1900* (Evanston, Ill.: Northwestern University Press, 1971).

NITSCHE, PETER, 'Die Liedertafel im System der Zelterschen Gründungen', in Dahlhaus (ed.), *Studien zur Musikgeschichte Berlins*, 11–26.

NOGGLER, ARSENIUS, 'Das Schicksal einer Komposition Felix Mendelssohn-Bartholdys', in *Programm des öffentlichen Obergymnasiums der Franziskaner zu Bozen: Veröffentlicht am Schlusse des Schuljahres 1907–08* (Bozen: Selbstverlag der Anstalt, 1908), 1–11.

NOHL, LUDWIG, *Musikerbriefe* (2nd edn., Leipzig: Duncker & Humblot, 1873).

Notenbeilage in *Orpheus: musikalisches Taschenbuch für das Jahr 1840*, ed. August Schmidt (Vienna: Riedl, and Leipzig: Liebeskind, [Dec. 1839]).

PEAKE, LUISE EITEL, 'The Song Cycle: A Preliminary Inquiry into the Beginnings of the Romantic Song Cycle and the Nature of an Art Form' (Ph.D. diss., Columbia University, 1968).

PELKER, BÄRBEL, ' "Zwischen absoluter und Programmusik": Bemerkungen zu Mendelssohns Hebriden-Ouvertüre', in Annegrit Laubenthal and Kara Kusan-Windweh (eds.), *Studien zur Musikgeschichte: Eine Festschrift für Ludwig Finscher* (Kassel: Bärenreiter, 1995), 560–71.

PLANCHÉ, JAMES ROBINSON, *The Recollections and Reflections of J. R. Planché* (London: Tinsley Brothers, 1872).

POLKO, ELISE, *Erinnerungen an Felix Mendelssohn-Bartholdy: Ein Künstler- und Menschenleben* (Leipzig: F. A. Brockhaus, 1868).

PRANDI, JULIE, *'Dare To Be Happy': A Study of Goethe's Ethics* (Lanham, Md.: University Press of America, 1993).

RANFT, PETER, *Felix Mendelssohn Bartholdy: Eine Lebenschronik* (Leipzig: Deutscher Verlag für Musik, 1972).

Recent Music and Musicians as Described in the Diaries of Ignatz Moscheles, ed. Charlotte Moscheles, trans. A. D. Coleridge (New York: H. Holt, 1873; repr. 1970).

REICH, NANCY B., 'The Power of Class: Fanny Hensel', in Todd (ed.), *Mendelssohn and his World*, 86–99.

REISSMANN, AUGUST, *Felix Mendelssohn-Bartholdy: Sein Leben und seine Werke* (Berlin: Guttentag, 1867).

RICHTER, ARND, 'Felix Mendelssohn Bartholdy: "Die erste Walpurgisnacht" Op. 60', *Neue Zeitschrift für Musik*, 11 (Nov. 1986), 33–40.

RIEMANN, HUGO, *Geschichte der Musik seit Beethoven (1800–1900)* (Berlin: W. Spemann, 1901).

RIMSKY KORSAKOV, A. N., *Muzykal'nye sokrovishcha Rukopisnogo otdeleniya Gosudarstvennoy Publichnoy Biblioteki imeni M. E. Saltykova Shchedrina: Obzor muzykal'nykh rukopisnykh fondov* (Leningrad: Izdanie Gosudarstvennoy Publichnoy Biblioteki, 1938).

ROSEN, CHARLES, 'Mendelssohn and the Invention of Religious Kitsch', in id., *The Romantic Generation* (Cambridge, Mass.: Harvard University Press, 1995), 569–98.

SCHMIDT, CHRISTIAN MARTIN, 'Konzeption und Stand der Mendelssohn-Gesamtausgabe', in *Felix Mendelssohn — Mitwelt und Nachwelt. 1. Leipziger Mendelssohn-Kolloquium am 8. und 9. Juni 1993* (Wiesbaden: Breitkopf & Härtel, 1996).

—— (ed.), *Felix Mendelssohn Bartholdy: Kongreß-Bericht Berlin 1994* (Wiesbaden: Breitkopf & Härtel, 1997).

SCHMIDT, THOMAS CHRISTIAN, *Die ästhetischen Grundlagen der Instrumentalmusik Felix Mendelssohn Bartholdys* (Stuttgart: M & P Verlag für Wissenschaft und Forschung, 1996).

SCHMIDT-BESTE, THOMAS, ' "Alles von Ihm gelernt?" Die Briefe von Carl Friedrich Zelter an Felix Mendelssohn Bartholdy', *Mendelssohn-Studien*, 10 (1997), 25–56.

SCHRÖDER, FRITZ, *Bernard Molique und seine Instrumentalkompositionen, seine künstlerische und historische Persönlichkeit: Ein Beitrag zur Geschichte der Instrumentalmusik des 19. Jahrhunderts, mit einem Verzeichnis aller nachweisbaren Werke Molique's und einem thematischen Katalog der wichtigsten Instrumentalkompositionen* (Stuttgart: Berthold und Schwerdtner, 1923).

SCHRÖDER, GESINE, 'Fannys Studien', in Helmig (ed.), *Fanny Hensel*, 27–32.

SCHUBRING, JULIUS, 'Reminiscences of Felix Mendelssohn-Bartholdy, on his 57th Birthday, February 3rd, 1866', in *Musical World*, 31 (12 and 19 May 1866), reprinted (abr.) in Todd (ed.), *Mendelssohn and his World*, 221–36.

SCHUMANN, ROBERT, *Erinnerungen an Felix Mendelssohn Bartholdy: Nachgelassene Aufzeichnungen*, ed. Georg Eismann (Zwickau: Predella, 1947).

—— *Gesammelte Schriften über Musik und Musiker*, ed. Martin Kreisig (Leipzig: Breitkopf & Härtel, 1914).

SEATON, DOUGLASS, 'A Draft for the Exposition of the First Movement of Mendelssohn's "Scotch" Symphony', *Journal of the American Musicological Society*, 30 (1977), 129–35.

—— 'The Problem of the Lyric Persona in Mendelssohn's Songs', in Schmidt (ed.), *Kongreß-Bericht*, 167–86.

—— 'The Romantic Mendelssohn: The Composition of *Die erste Walpurgisnacht*', *Musical Quarterly*, 68 (1982), 398–410.

—— 'A Study of a Collection of Mendelssohn's Sketches and other Autograph Material, Deutsche Staatsbibliothek Berlin Mus. ms. autogr. Mendelssohn 19' (Ph.D. diss., Columbia University, 1977).

—— 'Vorwort', *Lobgesang*, op. 52 (Carus, 1990).

—— (ed.), *The Mendelssohn Companion* (Westport, Conn.: Greenwood, 2001).

SEIDEL, WILHELM, '9. Symphonie d-Moll op. 125', in Albrecht Riethmüller, Carl Dahlhaus, and Alexander L. Ringer (eds.), *Beethoven: Interpretationen seiner Werke* (Laaber: Laaber, 1994), ii. 252–71.

SHARP, R. FARQUHARSON, *Makers of Music: Biographical Sketches of Great Composers* (New York: Charles Scribner's Sons, 1913).

SILBER BALLAN, JUDITH, 'Marxian Programmatic Music: A Stage in Mendelssohn's Musical Development', in R. Larry Todd (ed.), *Mendelssohn Studies* (Cambridge: Cambridge University Press, 1992), 149–61.

—— 'Mendelssohn and his "Reformation" Symphony', *Journal of the American Musicological Society*, 40 (1987), 310–36.

—— 'Mendelssohn and the "Reformation" Symphony: A Critical and Historical Study' (Ph.D. diss., Yale University, 1987).

SINGER, HEINRICH, *Allgemeine und spezielle Krankheitslehre der Juden* (Leipzig: Konegen, 1904).

SIROTA, VICTORIA RESSMEYER, 'The Life and Works of Fanny Mendelssohn Hensel' (DMA diss., Boston University, 1981).

SMITH, CATHERINE PARSONS, ' "A Distinguishing Virility": Feminism and Modernism in American Art Music', in Susan C. Cook and Judy S. Tsou (eds.),

Cecilia Reclaimed: Feminist Perspectives on Gender and Music (Urbana, Ill.: University of Illinois Press, 1994), 90–106.

SPEYER, EDWARD, *Wilhelm Speyer, der Liederkomponist* (Munich: Drei Masken, 1925).

SPOSATO, JEFFREY L., 'Creative Writing: The [Self-]Identification of Mendelssohn as Jew', *Musical Quarterly*, 82 (1998), 190–209.

STEINBECK, WOLFRAM, 'Der klärende Wendepunkt in Felix' Leben: Zu Mendelssohns Konzertouvertüren', in Schmidt (ed.), *Kongreß-Bericht*, 232–56.

STEINBERG, MICHAEL P., 'Schumann's Homelessness', in R. Larry Todd (ed.), *Schumann and his World* (Princeton: Princeton University Press, 1994), 47–79.

STOLZENBERG, INGEBORG, 'Paul Mendelssohn-Bartholdy nach dem Tode seines Bruders Felix', *Mendelssohn-Studien*, 8 (1993), 179–96.

STONER, THOMAS, 'Mendelssohn's Lieder not Included in the *Werke*', *Fontes artis musicae*, 26 (1979), 258–66.

STORCK, KARL, *Geschichte der Musik* (Stuttgart: Muth, 1904).

STRATTON, STEPHEN S., *Mendelssohn* (London: J. M. Dent, 1901).

STRESEMANN, WOLFGANG, *Eine Lanze für Felix Mendelssohn* (Berlin: Stapp, 1984).

TANK, ULRICH, *Die Geschwister Schloss: Studien zur Biographie der Kölner Altistin Sophie Schloss (1822–1902) und zur Geschichte des Musikalienverlages ihres Bruders Michael (1823–1891)* (Beiträge zur rheinischen Musikgeschichte, 115; Cologne: Arno Volk, 1976).

Thematisches Verzeichnis der im Druck erschienenen Compositionen von Felix Mendelssohn Bartholdy (Leipzig: Breitkopf & Härtel, [1853]; 3rd enlarged edn., 1882).

THISTLETHWAITE, NICHOLAS, *The Making of the Victorian Organ* (Cambridge: Cambridge University Press, 1990).

TICK, JUDITH, 'Charles Ives and Gender Ideology', in Ruth A. Solie (ed.), *Musicology and Difference: Gender and Sexuality in Music Scholarship* (Berkeley: University of California Press, 1993), 90–7.

—— 'Passed Away is the Piano Girl: Changes in American Musical Life, 1870–1900', in Jane Bowers and Judith Tick (eds.), *Women Making Music: The Western Art Tradition, 1150–1950* (Urbana, Ill.: University of Illinois Press, 1986), 336–8.

TILLARD, FRANÇOISE, *Fanny Mendelssohn*, trans. Camille Nash (Portland, Ore.: Amadeus Press, 1996).

TODD, R. LARRY, *Mendelssohn: The Hebrides and Other Overtures* (Cambridge: Cambridge University Press, 1994).

—— *Mendelssohn's Musical Education: A Study and Edition of his Exercises in Composition* (Cambridge: Cambridge University Press, 1983).

—— 'Mendelssohn's Ossianic Manner, with a New Source—*On Lena's Gloomy Heath*', in Jon W. Finson and R. Larry Todd (eds.), *Mendelssohn and Schumann: Essays on their Music and its Context* (Durham, NC: Duke University Press, 1984), 137–60.

Todd, R. Larry, 'New Light on Mendelssohn's *Freie Phantasie* (1840)', in Geoffrey C. Orth (ed.), *Literary and Musical Notes: A Festschrift for Wm. A. Little* (Bern: Peter Lang, 1995), 205–18.

—— 'On Mendelssohn's Operatic Destiny: *Die Lorelei* Reconsidered', in Schmidt (ed.), *Kongreß-Bericht*, 113–40.

—— 'On Quotation in Schumann's Music', in id. (ed.), *Schumann and his World* (Princeton: Princeton University Press, 1994), 80–112.

—— 'An Unfinished Symphony by Mendelssohn', *Music & Letters*, 61 (1980), 293–309.

—— (ed.), *Mendelssohn and his World* (Princeton: Princeton University Press, 1991).

Tonkünstler-Lexicon Berlins von den ältesten Zeiten bis auf die Gegenwart, ed. C. Fr. Ledebuhr (Berlin: Rauh, 1861; repr., ed. Rudolf Elvers, Tutzing: Hans Schneider, 1965).

Topusov, Nikolai, 'Carl Reinecke: Beiträge zu seinem Leben und seiner Symphonik' (unpublished diss., Berlin, 1943).

Turchin, Barbara, 'Robert Schumann's Song Cycles in the Context of the Early Nineteenth-Century Liederkreis' (Ph.D. diss., Columbia University, 1981).

Turner, J. Rigbie, 'Letters to Eduard Devrient', in R. Larry Todd (ed.), *Mendelssohn Studies* (Cambridge: Cambridge University Press, 1992), 200–39.

Tusa, Michael C., *Euryanthe and Carl Maria von Weber's Dramaturgy of German Opera* (Oxford: Clarendon Press, 1991).

Ulrich, Homer, *Chamber Music* (2nd edn., New York: Columbia University Press, 1966).

Vallas, Léon, *César Franck*, trans. Hubert Foss (London: Oxford University Press, 1951).

Verzeichniss der bis jetzt im Druck erschienenen Compositionen von Carl Reinecke, ed. Franz Reinecke (Leipzig: Breitkopf & Härtel, 1889).

Vitercik, Greg, *The Early Works of Felix Mendelssohn: A Study in the Romantic Sonata Style* (Musicology: A Book Series, 12; Philadelphia: Gordon & Breach, 1992).

Volkmann, Hans, *Robert Volkmann: Sein Leben und seine Werke* (Leipzig: H. Seemann Nachfolger, 1903).

Wagner, Cosima, *Cosima Wagner's Diaries*, i: *1869–1877*, ed. Martin Gregor-Dellin and Dietrich Mack, trans. Geoffrey Skelton (New York: Harcourt, Brace, Jovanovich, 1976).

Ward Jones, Peter, *Catalogue of the Mendelssohn Papers in the Bodleian Library, Oxford*, iii: *Printed Music and Books* (Tutzing: Hans Schneider, 1989).

—— 'Mendelssohn and his English Publishers', in R. Larry Todd (ed.), *Mendelssohn Studies* (Cambridge: Cambridge University Press, 1992), 240–55.

—— 'Mendelssohn Scores in the Library of the Royal Philharmonic Society', in Schmidt (ed.), *Kongreß-Bericht*, 64–75.

WARRACK, JOHN, 'Mendelssohn's Operas', in Nigel Fortune (ed.), *Music and Theatre: Essays in Honour of Winton Dean* (Cambridge: Cambridge University Press, 1987), 263–97.

—— Macdonald, Hugh, and Köhler, Karl-Heinz, *The New Grove Early Romantic Masters, 2: Weber, Berlioz, Mendelssohn* (London: Macmillan, 1980).

WASIELEWSKI, WILHELM JOSEF VON, *Carl Reinecke: Sein Leben, Wirken und Schaffen* (Leipzig: J. H. Zimmermann, 1892).

WEBSTER, JAMES, 'Ambivalenzen um Mendelssohn: Zwischen Werk und Rezeption', in Schmidt (ed.), *Kongreß-Bericht*, 257–78.

WEHNER, RALF, 'Bibliographie des Schrifttums zu Felix Mendelssohn Bartholdy von 1972 bis 1994', in Schmidt (ed.), *Kongreß-Bericht*, 297–351.

—— ' "... ich zeigte Mendelssohns Albumblatt vor und Alles war gut." Zur Bedeutung der Stammbucheintragungen und Albumblätter von Felix Mendelssohn Bartholdy', in Schmidt (ed.), *Kongreß-Bericht*, 37–63.

WEISSWEILER, EVA, *Fanny Mendelssohn: Ein Portrait in Briefen* (Frankfurt: Ullstein. 1985).

WELTER, FRIEDRICH, 'Die Musikbibliothek der Singakademie zu Berlin', in *Singakademie zu Berlin: Festschrift zum 175jährigen Bestehen*, ed. Werner Bollert (Berlin, 1966).

WERNER, ERIK, 'Felix Mendelssohn — Gustav Mahler: Two Borderline Cases of German-Jewish Assimilation', *Yuval*, 4 (1982), 240–64.

—— *Mendelssohn: A New Image of the Composer and his Age* (London: Free Press of Glencoe, 1963).

—— *Mendelssohn: Leben und Werk in neuer Sicht* (Zurich: Atlantis, 1980).

WHITTALL, ARNOLD, *Romantic Music: A Concise History from Schubert to Sibelius* (London: Thames & Hudson, 1987).

WILHELMY, PETRA, *Der Berliner Salon im 19. Jahrhundert, 1780–1914* (Berlin: Gruyter, 1989).

WILSON [KIMBER], MARIAN, 'Felix Mendelssohn's Works for Solo Piano and Orchestra: Sources and Composition' (Ph.D. diss., Florida State University, 1993).

—— ' "For Art Has the Same Place in your Heart as Mine": Family, Friendship, and Community in the Life of Felix Mendelssohn', in Seaton (ed.), *The Mendelssohn Companion*, 29–75.

—— 'Mendelssohn's Wife: Love, Art and Romantic Biography', *Nineteenth Century Studies*, 6 (1992), 1–18.

WITTE, MARTIN, 'Zur Programmgebundenheit der Sinfonien Mendelssohns', in Dahlhaus (ed.), *Das Problem Mendelssohn*, 119–27.

WOLFF, ERNST, *Felix Mendelssohn Bartholdy* (Berlin: 'Harmonie', 1909).

WOLFF, HELLMUTH CHRISTIAN, 'Zum Singspiel "Dichterliebe" von Mendelssohn', *Mendelssohn-Studien*, 6 (1986), 151–62.

WORBS, HANS CHRISTOPH, *Felix Mendelssohn Bartholdy mit Selbstzeugnissen und Bilddokumenten* (Reinbek bei Hamburg: Rohwolt, 1974).

WÜSTER, ULRICH, *Felix Mendelssohn Bartholdys Choralkantaten: Gestalt und Idee — Versuch einer historisch-kritischen Interpretation* (Frankfurt am Main: Peter Lang, 1996).

——— ' "Ein gewisser Geist": Zu Mendelssohns "Reformations-Symphonie" ', *Die Musikforschung*, 44 (1991), 311–30.

ZAPPALÀ, PIETRO, 'I *Preludi* dei "Präludien und Fugen" op. 37 di Felix Mendelssohn Bartholdy', in Maria Caraci Vela (ed.), *La critica del testo musicale: metodi e problemi della filologia musicale* (Studi e testi musicali, Nuova serie, no. 4; Lucca: Libreria Musicale Italiana, 1995), 287–318.

ZOPFF, HERMANN, 'Characteristics of Felix Mendelssohn-Bartholdy', *Dwight's Journal of Music*, 11 (15 Aug. 1857), 154.

General Index

Index of Works by Fanny Hensel and Felix Mendelssohn Bartholdy